*Understanding and Teaching
the Age of Revolutions*

The Harvey Goldberg Series
for Understanding and Teaching History

The Harvey Goldberg Series for Understanding and Teaching History gives college and secondary history instructors a deeper understanding of the past as well as the tools to help them teach it creatively and effectively. Named for Harvey Goldberg, a professor renowned for his history teaching at Oberlin College, Ohio State University, and the University of Wisconsin from the 1960s to the 1980s, the series reflects Goldberg's commitment to helping students think critically about the past with the goal of creating a better future. For more information, please visit www.GoldbergSeries.org.

Series Editors

John Day Tully is a professor of history at Central Connecticut State University and was the founding director of the Harvey Goldberg Center for Excellence in Teaching at Ohio State University. He has coordinated many Teaching American History grants and has received the Connecticut State University System's Board of Trustees Teaching Award.

Matthew Masur is a professor of history at Saint Anselm College, where he has served as codirector of the Father Guerin Center for Teaching Excellence. He has also been a member of the Teaching Committee of the Society for Historians of American Foreign Relations.

Brad Austin is a professor of history at Salem State University. He has served as chair of the American Historical Association's Teaching Prize Committee and has worked with hundreds of secondary school teachers as the academic coordinator of many Teaching American History grants.

Advisory Board

Leslie Alexander   Associate Professor of History, University of Oregon
Kevin Boyle   William Smith Mason Professor of American History, Northwestern University
Ross Dunn   Professor Emeritus, San Diego State University
Leon Fink   UIC Distinguished Professor of History, University of Illinois at Chicago
Kimberly Ibach   Principal, Fort Washakie High School, Wyoming
Alfred W. McCoy   J.R.W. Smail Professor of History, Director, Harvey Goldberg Center for the Study of Contemporary History, University of Wisconsin–Madison
David J. Staley   Associate Professor of History, Director, Harvey Goldberg Center for Excellence in Teaching, Ohio State University
Maggie Tran   Chair of Social Studies, McLean High School, Virginia
Sam Wineburg   Margaret Jacks Professor of Education and (by courtesy) of History, Director, Stanford History Education Group, Stanford University

Understanding and Teaching the Age of Revolutions

Edited by

BEN MARSH

MIKE RAPPORT

The University of Wisconsin Press

The University of Wisconsin Press
1930 Monroe Street, 3rd Floor
Madison, Wisconsin 53711-2059
uwpress.wisc.edu

3 Henrietta Street, Covent Garden
London WCE 8LU, United Kingdom
eurospanbookstore.com

Printed in the United States of America

This book may be available in a digital edition.

Library of Congress Cataloging-in-Publication Data

Names: Marsh, Ben, 1976- editor. | Rapport, Michael, editor.
Title: Understanding and teaching the Age of Revolutions /
    edited by Ben Marsh and Mike Rapport.
Other titles: Harvey Goldberg series for understanding and teaching history.
Description: Madison, Wisconsin: The University of Wisconsin Press, [2017]
    | Series: The Harvey Goldberg series for understanding and teaching history
    | Includes bibliographical references and index.
Identifiers: LCCN 2016050489 | ISBN 9780299311902 (cloth: alk. paper)
Subjects: LCSH: Revolutions—History—18th century—Study and teaching.
    | Revolutions—History—19th century—Study and teaching.
    | History, Modern—18th century—Study and teaching.
    | History, Modern—19th century—Study and teaching.
Classification: LCC D299 .U53 2017 | DDC 909.7071—dc23
LC record available at https://lccn.loc.gov/2016050489

On the cover: Tito Salas, *El terremoto de 1812 con Simón Bolívar en Caracas.* (1929,
    mural, Casa Natal de Bolívar, Caracas; https://www.flickr.com/photos
    /ctam/5636530829/in/photostream/; photograph by Cristóbal Alvarado
    Minic under Creative Commons)

Everything I see is sowing the seeds of a revolution that will inevitably come, though I shall not have the pleasure of witnessing it. Step by step, the light has spread so wide that it will burst out at the first chance, and so there will be a great uproar. Young people are truly fortunate; they will see some great things.

François-Marie Arouet (Voltaire),
letter to Henri-Philippe Chauvelin, 2 April 1764,
in Voltaire, *Oeuvres Complètes de Voltaire,*
avec des Notes et une Notice Historique sur la Vie de Voltaire
(Paris: Chez Furne, 1835–38), 12:461

Contents

Contents

Contents

Acknowledgments

We would thank a number of friends and colleagues for their sage advice, encouragement, critiques, and recommendations during the long journey between this volume's conception and its completion. First, our contributors, whether the authors listed overleaf or those who have made indirect contributions and helped refine the project as it developed—as anonymous reviewers of proposals and manuscripts, commentators, and people generally willing to give of their time and expertise, notably Bill Weber. Second, we owe a significant debt of gratitude to Brad Austin and his fellow series editors (John Tully and Matthew Masur), whose enthusiasm and guidance has been much appreciated and helped move things along at key moments. Gwen Walker and her great team at the University of Wisconsin Press have been a model of patience and efficiency. David Staley and the Harvey Goldberg Center at Ohio State University generously supported a session involving volume contributors at the American Historical Association (AHA) meeting in Atlanta in 2016, and we thank attendees for facilitating invigorating discussion of the Age of Revolutions. Our only regret is that there was not more space or time to integrate the many other ideas, essays, angles, and avenues that might have been explored within this subject, but we hope this book proves to be an appetizing starting point. Our largest debt goes to our students, past, present, and future, who continually refresh our thinking and impel us forward as teachers and scholars.

Last, we thank our families for their indulgence: Lils and Helen, and Alfie, Lily, Thomas, Ella, and Tess. We hope the kids develop the same traits that Harvey Goldberg was most admired for and saluted in his description of Jean Jaurès: "the integrity to be partisan, the courage to be revolutionary, the humanism to be tolerant."

*Understanding and Teaching
the Age of Revolutions*

Introduction

BEN MARSH and MIKE RAPPORT

The "Age of Revolutions" has proved to be an enduring phrase, a way of crudely describing the political, social, economic, and intellectual upheavals that ravaged European and American societies sometime between the late eighteenth and early nineteenth centuries. It stands as an integral component of most courses on European, Atlantic, or world history, marking an era that was peculiarly transformative and whose legacies were profound. Reduced to its most simplistic, the Age of Revolutions heralded the arrival of ideas, systems, and influences that shaped the meaning of modernism. This opaque period witnessed decolonization on a virtually hemispheric scale, the collapse of long-standing social and religious orders, violent wars and uprisings, new polities and political actors, beside which we might throw in a fair bit of industrialization, antislavery, the creation of new liberal and conservative ideologies, and much more. The sense of accelerating momentum and linkage that led John Adams to propose "the age of revolutions and constitutions" as a moniker for 1775–1815 has stuck, despite huge regional disparities and contradictions. Most accept that this watershed period, based on largely military and geopolitical considerations (as viewed by an Anglo-American, Adams), was only part of a bigger picture. Just how big depends on how we choose to define *revolution* (a problem discussed later in this introduction) and adjust the parameters of our courses in time and space; teaching convention now finds the Age of Revolutions often spanning from the mid-eighteenth century through to the 1830s or beyond, by which time Latin America had fully joined the party, when a new sweep of revolutionary activity was happening in Europe, and reverberations were echoing around an increasingly interconnected world. By the middle of the nineteenth century, there had been a step change in the thinkability of social and political transformation. This shift in consciousness was both political and cultural and has crystallized into a language of revolution and accompanying panoply of symbols, models, and assumptions that are still with us today—constantly fitted to new upheavals, umbilically tied to Marxism and its derivatives, and most recently emerging amid the revolutionary dominos of the so-called Arab Spring of the 2010s.

Acknowledging in broad-brush terms the lasting and self-sustaining impact of the Age of Revolutions on subsequent history is one thing, and it is quite another getting to grips with the subject's sheer complexity. In recent decades, historians of all stripes have further mapped out and interrogated its geographic, chronological, and cultural range. Few resources exist to help teachers translate this complexity effectively into the classroom. *Understanding and Teaching the Age of Revolutions* aims to freshen up how university, college, and high school teachers approach the subject, offering important connective insights across revolutions; some bright ideas and resources for how particular themes, places, and events can be addressed in the classroom; and a quick and painless crib sheet for instructors keen to stay up to date with the latest developments in research and pedagogy. It is not intended as a replacement or competition for the many fine textbooks and monographs that teachers and students quite understandably cling to as ballast, as they hastily navigate through a world in motion in the late eighteenth and early nineteenth century, with its rich diversity of revolutionary transformations and accompanying array of facts and figures. Rather, the volume hopes to entice instructors—and through them, new generations of learners—to dwell on some of the places, pictures, sounds, sights, and concepts that preoccupied denizens of the Age of Revolutions, to encourage teachers to plot small diversions to less charted locales, and to fill their sails with some of the latest scholarship and most exciting themes in the continued search for fuller understanding. The volume carries something of the spirit of the age with it: it is eclectic, fast-moving, and polyphonic in tone and style, and contributors bring their own inflections, urging us to think about what revolutions meant in different ways and different places.

The Age of Revolutions we collectively present here absorbed its energy from a host of crises in imperial legitimacy and environmental stability, and then disgorged it in waves that crashed differently on social, racial, and cultural landscapes—tending always to celebrate freedom and yet dispense its fruits unequally. In pondering the reconfigurations that resulted, and the legacies of the Age of Revolutions— whether self-conscious unitary achievements (such as new nations or emancipations) or unthinking multifarious consequences (such as new global economic relationships or mythologies about revolution)— learners of all ages can find salient and resonant lessons. These include learning to challenge what is presented at face value, listening more intently and reading with more nuance, and roaming beyond familiar tropes or terrains. Perhaps the most productive way for instructors to approach reading the volume is to view each essay as an exemplar—an indication of how the big questions in any subfield have been or could be constructively brought into the orbit of students by experts in the profession. Because of the increasing diversity of the backgrounds, ages, and stages of students treating the subject (from high school through graduate courses and across global educational models), instructors will need to modulate their pitch accordingly, helped by the concise suggestions for further reading at the end of each essay. Some chapters may intrude to improve lecture or survey coverage, whereas others may prompt new assignments, group exercises, or forays into comparative readings, but there is a rich transferability in even those discussions limited to one place, period, or discipline.

Models of the Age of Revolutions: Past, Present, and Future

Teaching the Age of Revolutions has changed—sometimes at a glacial pace, sometimes like a torrent—because of transformations in the broader world in which we all live. "Historiography" (which has an increasingly quaint ring as the discipline absorbs an ever broader range of approaches and methods) is one driver of change, and another is the concerns that teachers and students bring into the classroom from outside, as we seek perspectives on modern-day challenges and debate them with reference to the past. Such contextual influences have always ensured that the way we teach and learn history is never "neutral"— and among those who found themselves at the sharp end of this point were Jacques Godechot and Robert R. Palmer, the authors of the now classic and much-critiqued thesis first posited in the 1950s of an age of "democratic" or "Atlantic" revolution.

Dates of Independence in the Americas. (created by Ben Marsh. Map data © 2016 Google. US Dept of State Geographer. Image Landsat. Data SIO, NOAA, US Navy, NGA, GEBCO)

"All of [the] agitations, upheavals, intrigues and conspiracies were part of one great movement," wrote Palmer of the American, French, and European revolutions between 1760 and 1800, arguing that "they reflected conditions that were universal throughout the western world." The interpretative journey that has run since has been bumpy, argumentative, and fiery—and we have by no means reached a final destination or consensus. Initially this was because the "Atlantic" thesis appeared to challenge the existing Marxist orthodoxy of the French Revolution as *the* "world-historical" event—the "bourgeois" revolution of 1789 that eventually sired Russia's proletarian revolution of 1917.

6

The earliest critics of the Palmer-Godechot thesis came from scholars of the Left in the 1960s and 1970s, who (as Peter McPhee relates in his richly reflective chapter in this volume) objected to the French Revolution being tethered to others, including the American, which they claimed did not share the radicalism and far-reaching consequences of the former. The thesis also met with a hostile reception on the Left because of the wider context of the Cold War. A no doubt stunned Palmer and Godechot saw their North Atlantic perspective being labeled as the historiographical equivalent of NATO—a way of waging the Cold War by cultural means. In a more seriously academic vein, in the 1970s and 1980s historians researching in detail on the experience of agitation, revolution, and war in regions like the Rhineland and the Low Countries in Europe found that the overwhelming response of populations confronted by the democratic principles of the eighteenth-century revolutions was usually to reject them.

If the Palmer-Godechot thesis was broken apart by some of these critiques, the transnational framework—if not the content—that it built has over the past twenty-five years been enlarged and filled with more varied and richer material. It has been enlarged because historians doubtful about the essentially North Atlantic, Euro-American scope of the original thesis have put other revolutions into the mainstream (which is why those in Haiti and South America figure prominently in this volume) alongside the American, the French, and other European upheavals. It is "more varied and richer" because historians skeptical about the narrative of triumphant democratization have explored the limits of the emancipation proclaimed by the revolutionaries and focused on the response of groups excluded from the full enjoyment of the freedoms proclaimed by the new order, including the enslaved, women, indigenous peoples, and the impoverished. All this has brought into sharper view the worlds that underpinned and undermined the political claims of the revolutions in the Atlantic world.

These approaches have also been shaped by the everyday concerns of our world, including the politics of gender and race, forms of identity politics, concerns about humanity's interaction with the environment, and anxieties over the impact of globalization. The search for historical perspectives on these issues—in the pages of scholarship and in the classroom—have enriched knowledge of the Age of Revolutions and how we teach it. The epoch is no longer contemplated along the clear-cut lines of nations, chronologies, and founding precepts. Instead our

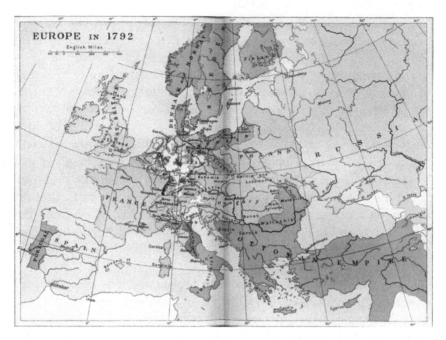

European states in the eighteenth century. (from *The Cambridge Modern History Atlas,* ed. A. W. Ward, G. W. Prothero, S. M. Leathes, and E. A. Benians [London: Cambridge University Press: 1912]. Source: University of Texas Libraries [see others at http://www .lib.utexas.edu/maps/historical/ward_1912.html])

understanding has brought into creative focus peoples, structures, and connections formerly relegated to the background—such as slave revolutionaries, women, the counterrevolutionaries, loyalists, indigenous peoples, and subaltern groups who did not share equally in the benefits of revolution and whose historical position left them vulnerable to long-standing historiographical neglect. The collective processes of rescuing "unknown" revolutions and restoring whitewashed victims across the Age of Revolutions have lately generated a platform from which a bird's-eye view becomes possible—and encourages us to reorient the cultural-political map of the historical Atlantic world in quite radical ways.

In the process, a thickening bed of interpretations has pointed to a more complex series of relationships involving the movement of ideas, symbols, people, and goods. The emphasis has also shifted toward a more multidirectional approach: the story is no longer about the impact of any one revolution on the wider world but on the backlash and, more

Map of the French part of Hispaniola. (from Mathew Carey, "Carte De La Partie Francoise De St. Domingue" [Philadelphia: M. Carey and Son, 1814], which noted that "Places burnt by the Negroes are coloured Yellow"; courtesy of the David Rumsey Map Collection, www.davidrumsey.com, with names appended by Ben Marsh)

complex still, on the whirlpool of connections, impacts, and influences. These connections have flowed far beyond the confines of the Atlantic world and have brought the revolutions into a wider perspective still: a global one. "Western civ" courses have increasingly given way (or been repackaged as segments within) world history courses in the class-room, just as the latest verdicts on the era, offered by the likes of Christopher Bayly and Lynn Hunt, attest to global linkages. These perspectives view it as an "age of imperial revolutions" in which (put crudely) power was rediverted and reoriented not just one-dimensionally (as if vertically within blocks of nation-states) but multidimensionally, spreading new patterns with enormous ideological depth and geographic breadth and interacting with developments in Native America, India, Java, China, and Africa, among others. In this reading, the Age of Revolutions between the 1760s and 1840s was significant not because of its path-clearing tendencies toward democracy or socialism but because it shattered some empires and created new imperial behemoths, because it celebrated freedom yet dispensed its fruits unequally, and because it transformed regional and global balances of power—be they military, economic, or cultural.

At the same time, the very definition of revolution has come under scrutiny, particularly since the Central and Eastern European revolutions of 1989, the crushing of the democratic movement in China that same year, the collapse of the Soviet Union in 1991, and the break-up of Yugoslavia in 1992. With these events came the dissolution of the old political certainties imposed by a bipolar world, accompanied by hope and fear in equal measure: hope for a new democratic, global future, but fear as old ethnic hatreds, long suppressed, boiled violently to the surface. It led scholars to wonder about the meaning of "revolution." For one, the European revolutions of 1989 were uprisings against regimes that had sought legitimacy from a revolutionary heritage (that of 1917) and ideology (Marxist-Leninism and its variants). The dramatically rapid events in the Soviet bloc appeared to uncouple the once presumed historic linkage between the "democratic" French Revolution of 1789 from the "socialist" Russian Revolution 1917. Indeed, "1989" seemed to represent a turn of the wheel—a revolution in the literal sense—back toward the principles of "1789" and away from those of "1917." In the following decades, other upheavals significant enough to be called "revolutions"—Indonesia in 1998; Serbia in 2000; the Rose Revolution in Georgia in 2003; the Orange Revolution in the Ukraine in 2004 (and again in 2014); the Tulip and Cedar Revolutions in Kyrgyzstan and Lebanon, respectively, in 2005; and the Arab Spring of 2011—seemed to suggest that revolution is a common phenomenon in modern politics. The events of 1989 and since prompt the question as to how revolution relates to and shapes modernity. Moreover, the sheer range of forms that recent protests and resistance have taken reflect questions back on the now classic revolutions—such as those in America in 1776 or France in 1789—the models that have shaped our very sense of what revolution is.

Asking students to think about revolution and how its processes and meaning have evolved is a good way of getting them to relate the past to the present, not least because, like our own era, the Age of Revolutions offers a rich variety of models that defy any easy, single definition. One of the best questions to remind classes of this moving target is: When was your secondary source written, and how was the view of revolution changing in that scholar's time? The transnational nature of the origins, course, and impact of our latter-day revolutions—particularly the revolutionary waves or cascades of 1989 in Europe and of 2011 in the Arab states (which also brought to mind the European revolutions of 1848)—offer striking modern parallels with the connections, influences, and currents that were at work in the "Atlantic" or the global revolutions of the eighteenth and nineteenth centuries. This can be overwhelming for teachers, let alone students, so one of the aims of the collective effort in this volume is to suggest ways the fascinating Age of Revolutions can be unpacked, explored in manageable and stimulating ways, and then intellectually reassembled to provide a fuller understanding of this epoch, to instill a deeper knowledge of the globalized sites in which the events unfolded, and to encourage students' critical thinking about the concepts and approaches that may equip us to better interpret that age and our own.

Outline of Volume

All the interpretations and inflections listed here deserve a place in the classroom (where time permits) and warrant coverage in this volume (where space allows). Each essay in its own way exposes some of the strengths and limits of the notion of an Age of Revolutions—asking us to revisit spaces, memories, practices, and traditions; to challenge complacencies; and to open students' minds to new insights, perhaps in unfamiliar areas (be these disciplines or geographies). They are designed as bite-sized overviews, with ideas for classroom deployment and recommendations for where next to go to locate readings and materials. They draw on the expertise of an international set of scholars and are intended to be usable for a range of teachers and specialists interested in diversifying their courses. Although plenty of contributors propose overarching ways of thinking about the Age of Revolutions and approaching its history in the classroom, the volume does not prescribe a coherent or progressive pathway through a singular curriculum. For one thing, the existing distinctive architecture of pedagogy in the field is too erratic to do this effectively, and it would undercut the intention to broaden coverage and encourage variation and creativity in subject selection. The criteria we determined for selection have been on the basis of fresh historical, pedagogical, or historiographical grounds for giving a subject priority. In some cases, such as the Stamp Act riots, the Reign of Terror, and Thomas Paine, it is because the subject matter may be "classic" but there are new inflections or approaches to consider. In others, such as the Haitian Declaration of Independence, gender in the French Revolution, and nature's impact on revolutions, it is because new scholarship has made it possible to integrate new dimensions into the classroom.

The volume is organized, like its sister volumes in the Harvey Goldberg Series for Understanding and Teaching History, in three sections. The first section comprises two reflective essays written by experienced historians, looking back on major changes and influences that have intersected with their teaching on the history of revolutions. They consider developments in the world at large, within teaching and higher education, and in their subjects themselves, and stress how important it is to think about perspective in framing teaching and understanding. They explain from a personal standpoint how they view the main challenges and possibilities inherent in treating the Age of Revolutions—focusing on a European and an American vista, respectively, and inviting readers to open their minds and their courses to the possibility of new configurations in how we approach chronology, geography, and the digital turn.

The second section introduces a selection of methods and sources for engaging with the diverse subject matter of the Age of Revolutions. The contributors offer suggestions as to how teachers can prompt, prod, or enthuse their students into engaging with the rich array of source material (visual, textual, or aural) that has been left us and how to improve students' understanding of cultural and social contexts—such as changing notions of transnational Enlightenment or the "self." Some of these essays explain how best to use familiar or unfamiliar revolutionary documents to teach the subject, and others expand beyond the textual and invite history teachers to consider engaging with different disciplines, concepts, media and resources, including looking at the worlds of art, music, and literature and the linkages across the Atlantic world. The essays address the intellectual sources of revolutionary thinking, the cultural expressions of revolutionary actors, and a range of documentary and visual online primary sources and throw out some tried and tested methods (including classroom exercises and approaches) for involving students more directly with the documents, debates, sounds, cultural artifacts, and languages of revolution.

The essays in the third section ("Specific Themes and Revolutions") provide accessible overviews of important regions, events, or revolutionary forces that show how textured these revolutions are to teach and to study. Some zoom in to offer ways of teaching with individuals (such as Toussant Louverture), groups (such as Boston rioters or French female revolutionaries), or map out regional experiences of revolution (including lesser-known locales) with questions and exercises that encourage students to think comparatively. Others zoom out to highlight salient points where wider phenomena (such as patterns of national identity or environmental change) can be incorporated into teaching. At the very least, the essays illustrate that although we may use "Age of Revolutions" as a convenient catch-all term in our teaching, no two revolutions were alike. There were enough similarities to enable contemporaries and then historians to argue plausibly the case for interconnections, parallels, and comparisons, but there were also significant divergences in origins, processes, participation, and consequences to make the Atlantic world in our long period a particularly fertile space for the study of revolution as a phenomenon.

Collectively, the contributions to this section explore the different ways in which the revolutions unfolded across space—from one society to another—and time, with cases ranging from the 1760s to the 1830s. Instructors will find myriad strategies, questions, and ideas that can be applied in the classroom and cut across some or all of these chapters, but two broad themes emerge. First there is the question of civil rights, equality, emancipation, and liberation: these are threads that run through the rhetoric and aims of all the revolutionary upheavals, but as the chapters in this section show, revolutions rarely if ever deliver these gifts to everyone. Students studying this period can profitably explore the friction between the revolutionary rhetoric of freedom and the reality of how important groups were excluded from the full enjoyment of citizenship. Second, many of the chapters connect with another opportunity, namely, the rich variety of ways students can learn about and understand the complexities of the revolutionary process. Questions such as what a specific revolution constitutes, why it takes place, who the revolutionaries are, how and why revolutions take certain turns and directions, how to explain revolutionary violence and repression, and how their achievements (if any) get consolidated or reemerge in the long run, are variously addressed across this section. So are broad problems such as periodization and geographical scope, both matters that can decisively alter interpretations and perspectives.

Encouraging students to grapple with the nuances and limits of the emancipating vision of the Age of Revolutions, and how excluded groups responded, will provide sparks that can set classrooms alight intellectually. But it also carries import beyond the classroom, for we occupy a world in which questions of human rights, citizenship, identity, and authority are ever more globalized and pressurized, and mythologized history (drawing on the Age of Revolutions one way or another) is contested and invoked as a weapon. Likewise, comparative breadth helps us reflect on "revolution" as an interpretive phenomenon rather than presumptive fact, and by pushing this with our students, we can better make sense of contemporary revolution, protest, state failure, and nation-building across the globe—for it continues to be an important dynamic in the modern world. It is striking, in fact, how many of the volume's contributors encourage their students to reflect on their own worlds and their own experiences and place the past in a dialogue with the present. All of which is to say that, although they make a quirky selection that is to be approached with imagination as well as plundered for specific ideas, together these essays help explain how we can go about understanding more deeply, teaching more creatively, and engaging our students more directly and urgently. If not quite rebuilding the world anew, it is our hope that Voltaire's "fortunate young people" will thereby approach their citizenship with due sensitivity to the seeds and the uproar of history.

KEY RESOURCES

Adelman, Jeremy. "An Age of Imperial Revolutions." *American Historical Review* 113, no. 2 (2003): 319–41.

Armitage, David, and Sanjay Subrahmanyam, eds. *The Age of Revolutions in Global Context, c. 1760–1840*. Basingstoke: Palgrave Macmillan, 2010.

Bayly, Christopher A. *The Birth of the Modern World, 1780–1914: Global Connections and Comparisons*. Oxford: Oxford University Press, 2004.

Forrest, Alan, and Matthias Middell, eds. *The Routledge Companion to the French Revolution in World History*. London: Routledge, 2016.

Hobsbawm, Eric. *The Age of Revolution, 1789–1848*. London: Abacus, 1962.

Jones, Colin, and Dror Wahrman, eds. *The Age of Cultural Revolutions, 1750–1850*. Berkeley: University of California Press, 2002.

Klooster, Wim. *Revolutions in the Atlantic World: A Comparative History*. New York: New York University Press, 2009.

Langley, Lester D. *The Americas in the Age of Revolution, 1750–1850*. New Haven, CT: Yale University Press, 1996.

Palmer, Robert R. *The Age of the Democratic Revolution: A Political History of Europe and America, 1760–1800*, 2 vols. Princeton, NJ: Princeton University Press, 1959–1964.

Polasky, Janet. *Revolutions without Borders: The Call to Liberty in the Atlantic World*. New Haven, CT: Yale University Press, 2015.

Serna, Pierre, Antonino De Francesco, and Judith A. Miller, eds. *Republics at War, 1776–1840: Revolutions, Conflicts, and Geopolitics in Europe and the Atlantic World*. Basingstoke: Palgrave, 2013.

PART ONE

Reflections

Teaching about the Age
of Revolutions,
1971–2016

PETER MCPHEE

I recall first becoming engrossed by the French Revolution when, as an undergraduate at the University
of Melbourne in 1968, I bought a paperback copy of George Rudé's
classic study of *The Crowd in the French Revolution*.[1] In 1968, protest was
in the air: brothers from my residential college had been arrested for
paint-bombing US President Lyndon B. Johnson's car during his visit
to Melbourne in 1966, there were the first very large anti–Vietnam War
demonstrations, and we were hearing heady but dismaying tales from
Paris, Prague, and elsewhere. My ability to read Rudé's quotations from
his sources—all in the original French—excited me that I was listening
to authentic "voices of the people" from an earlier period of radical
change. A decade later, while tutoring for Rudé while he was on a brief
visit to La Trobe University in Melbourne in 1978, I realized how his
great book and his political affiliations had brought an indirect consequence of the French Revolution close to home.

The story began in December 1956, when Oxford scholar and clergy-
man John McManners had taken up the chair of history at the University
of Tasmania. He was then at work on his first book, on the diocese of
Angers in the eighteenth century. McManners arrived in Hobart in the
midst of controversy in that city. Earlier that year, Sydney Sparkes Orr,
a professor of philosophy, had been dismissed for allegedly having
seduced a student. The dismissal became the focus of the most important
case of academic freedom in the history of Australian universities and

was not finally resolved (in Orr's favor) until 1965.[2] Believing that the University of Tasmania had failed to accord Orr "natural justice," university staff associations in Australia urged a boycott of all new posts at the university. McManners was initially dismayed at what the ban would mean for the isolation of his small, beleaguered university, and then was outraged when in 1960 the University Council refused to appoint the young Norwegian English scholar George Rudé on the grounds that he was a communist.[3] McManners resigned and moved to the chair of history at the University of Sydney from 1960, before returning to England in 1965. The book he was writing while in Tasmania, *French Ecclesiastical Society under the Ancien Régime: A Study of Angers in the Eighteenth Century*, was published by Manchester University Press in 1960, the year of his resignation from Tasmania, and became a classic of social history.

Rebuffed by Tasmania, Rudé was quickly offered a position at the University of Adelaide, and his decade there beginning in 1960 was the most productive of his life. He published or completed a major series of books on French, British, and European history, including *Wilkes and Liberty: A Social Study of 1763 to 1774*; *Revolutionary Europe, 1783–1815*; *The Crowd in History: A Study of Popular Disturbances in France and England, 1730–1848*; *Paris and London in the Eighteenth Century: Studies in Popular Protest*; *Hanoverian London, 1714–1808*; and, with Eric Hobsbawm, *Captain Swing*.[4] Rudé was not only a skilled and highly productive historian, he was a charming and brilliant man who had a persuasive impact on most who met or were taught by him. His influence was clear on those with whom I taught as a graduate student, such as my supervisor, Alison Patrick, and Bill Murray, one of those who later resolved to establish the biennial George Rudé Seminar in French History and Civilization in his honor in 1978.[5]

My first teaching position was in 1971–73 at the University of Melbourne as a full-time tutor in a new Age of Revolutions subject, focusing on the American and French Revolutions and the European revolutions of 1830 and 1848. Its coordinator, Alison Patrick, did not like the vague Marxist assumptions of most students in the late 1960s and 1970s and thought they should come to terms with intellectual history. She was no doubt keen to see a new type of survey subject that would break away from a national focus to an international one. For that, the controversies surrounding the concept of an "Atlantic," "Western," or "democratic" revolution, first articulated in the 1950s by Jacques Godechot and R. R. Palmer, were ideal. They had insisted on the direct, fiscal consequences of France's involvement in the American Revolution and on an awareness of how educated contemporaries understood themselves within a transatlantic "republic of letters." In particular, they detailed the intellectual and political similarities and differences between revolutions in France and North America and upheavals in the Low Countries, Latin America, Ireland, Poland, and elsewhere. The Godechot-Palmer thesis gave real substance as an organizing theme for the subject and was bolstered by concentration on Bernard Bailyn's illuminating and elegant exploration of ideological transformation in the republican revolution across the Atlantic.[6]

The Godechot-Palmer thesis was, however, the object of powerful Marxist ripostes by Eric Hobsbawm and Albert Soboul in the 1960s. The transition, they argued, was fundamentally one to capitalism and in the nature of ruling elites rather than to liberal democracy and individual rights. Rudé's masterly surveys of French and European history were in line with their argument. They saw the Godechot-Palmer thesis as reducing the French Revolution to only one (albeit major) episode in a general Western upheaval rather than highlighting its unique radicalism and its place in unleashing other upheavals elsewhere. For example, twenty-two of the twenty-five national constitutions written in these decades were created after French occupation.[7] Most French left-wing historians dismissed or ignored the thesis: the idea that their revolution was the younger brother of the American Revolution was unthinkable. It was, rather, the grandfather of the Russian Revolution of 1917. By the 1970s, however, the debate was increasingly seen as sterile because of its apparent reflection of Cold War politics.

I came to my own research-based teaching on the French Revolution by a circuitous route, having completed a doctoral thesis in 1977 on society and politics in the southern region of Roussillon in the mid-nineteenth century.[8] In that endeavor my intellectual mentors had been historians such as Maurice Agulhon, Alain Corbin, John Merriman, and Ted Margadant, whose knowledge of regional societies and their archives was profound.[9] As for many others of "the Vietnam generation," the "new social history" of the 1980s appealed to me for its attention to geographic and cultural specificities in understanding the origins of mass politics. It resonated with the rural and small-town elements in my personal background. Some of my earliest publications were in journals specializing in peasant studies rather than French history.[10]

At the same time, my research into nineteenth-century rural society highlighted the importance of the French Revolution in creating its socio-economic structures and the collective memories that pervaded it. I was drawn back to research in the revolutionary period: why had the local experience of the revolution been so divergent? What were the lived experiences of the mass of rural and small-town people, and how were these remembered? In answering those questions, my intellectual mentors have again been those most attuned to capturing the fine grain of locality while not losing sight of the interaction between the local and national (even international) contexts: historians such as Michel Vovelle, Albert Soboul, Alain Corbin, Timothy Tackett, Peter Jones, Alan Forrest, and Gwynne Lewis.[11] I found that recounting the story to my students of one small Catalan community, Collioure, the subject of my first book, was the most effective way of raising issues of linguistic and cultural change, the impact of the revolutionary wars and emigration, and the creation of memory.[12]

In the 1970s and 1980s, the challenges of social and feminist historians to the privileging of elite political narratives broadened the range of historical artifacts used as evidence.[13] Since then postmodern and post-colonial historians have reminded us of the power relations implicit in the production of such evidence and the construction of historical narratives.[14] These critics emphasized that "the past" exists only in the forms given to it by those who think and write about it, as representations: in other words, that there is no "objective" reality historians can reconstruct by diligent study of written documents. The brilliant insights of the best of the "new cultural history" have informed my curriculum because they illuminate ways the revolution was made and experienced by people across the spectrum: politicians and peasants, men and women, merchants and slaves. Here I think, among many others, of the work of Daniel Roche, Roger Chartier, Lynn Hunt, Suzanne Desan, and Sarah Maza.[15]

I taught in 1980–1987 at the Victoria University of New Zealand, and on my subsequent return to the University of Melbourne I took responsibility for the old Age of Revolutions subject I had tutored in a decade earlier. Alison Patrick had retired by that point.[16] I made changes to content and approach. With the semesterization of our undergraduate subjects, the comparative dimension of the American and French Revolutions became increasingly difficult to sustain. Finally, I refocused a one-semester course purely on the French Revolution, with a much stronger emphasis than before on its international context.

My undergraduate curriculum on the French Revolution—and the Age of Revolutions more generally—has been characterized by a focus on a narrative informed by insights into the experience and impact of revolution at the local level. This is still the case today, when I ask students to compare the "classic," contrasting conclusions of Soboul, Darnton, and William Doyle about the significance of the revolution and introducing much more recent research, often of a detailed, local type.[17] The great shortcoming in most overviews of the revolution remains their assumption that it was made in Paris and that the amorphous provincial masses were either sullenly passive or violently hostile. My approach argues that the revolution can only be understood if the complexities of the relationship between government and citizenry—and Paris and the provinces—are at the heart of the analysis. That will enable us to explain why the National Convention was able to mobilize the nation's resources successfully in 1792–94, despite resistance, and the magnitude of social change created by the revolution.

So I require students to come to terms with narrative and longstanding debates about the revolution as a first step to considering contrasting new approaches: particularly from social historians (such as Peter Jones and myself), cultural historians (Robert Darnton and Suzanne Desan), and historians of race and sex (Lynn Hunt, Dominique Godineau, and Laurent Dubois). There is a major focus on students working through to their own synthetic understandings.

Students these days find questions of race and sex—much more so than class—particularly interesting, since they confront these topics with perspectives from human rights issues today and with the question of the historicity of these issues. New work on the history of slavery in the Americas, and particular in Saint-Domingue, has served to highlight not only a "Black Atlantic" largely ignored by Palmer and Godechot but also the significance of colonial trade and power in the origins, course, and outcomes of the revolution.[18] Similarly, students find compelling those approaches that investigate diverse groups of women in their lived experience of revolutionary upheaval and which contest dominant discursive and social categories.[19]

The linguistic turn that dominated views of the "invention" of the revolution at the time of the bicentenary in 1989 left me mostly unconvinced, since it put to one side the most difficult and interesting questions about the dynamic interaction of cultural, political, and social history. It seemed largely the work of scholars of the printed word who had not left their university library, the Internet, or—at best—the Bibliothèque Nationale to probe the fascinating interaction of discourse (especially language and symbols) and lived experience. Here, understanding the period dubbed "the Terror" once Robespierrist Jacobins were executed in July 1794 has become an exercise in identifying the discursive roots of paranoia rather than placing these people within the exigencies of war and counterrevolution.[20] The most intractable assumptions students bring to their study of the revolution are that it betrayed its idealistic intentions through the ideology and dictatorship of the Jacobins and that this was epitomized in the violent paranoia of Robespierre.

Happily, the best of the most recent work I have sought to introduce to students has taken the lessons of closer attention to discourse and its dynamics to ask about why particular linguistic and visual images resonated and with what effects.[21] Never before has such a lot of good history been written. In particular, one of the most fertile and exciting areas of study stems from the interaction between the diverse methodologies of cultural and social history, between the close cultural readings offered by micro-history and macro-historical concerns for context and generalization. A doctoral seminar I taught on "new directions in studying the Age of Revolutions" has consequently been able to range across historiography from the debates of the 1960s to some of the most thought-provoking recent work, such as Ian Coller on "The Revolutionary Mediterranean," Sarah Maza on "The Cultural Origins of the French Revolution," and Anne Verjus on "Gender, Sexuality, and Political Culture."[22]

An unfortunate consequence of the rejection of the Godechot-Palmer thesis was a long retreat into an "internalist" view of the French Revolution, which was differentiated sharply from the American Revolution. This approach understood the international context simply as the repercussions from France, especially the rise of counterrevolution. Since the 1990s, however, transnational—rather than international—studies have been revivified by histories of women's cultures and of slavery and slave rebellion, in particular from our perspective of the globalizing world of the twenty-first century. Although I disagree with

Jonathan Israel's recent and repeated insistence that the Age of Revolutions was fundamentally about the international Enlightenment until it was killed off by Robespierre and the other "crypto-fascists," he has surveyed in astonishing breadth the global reach of Enlightenment ideas, not only across the Atlantic but also into and from Latin America, east and south Asia, Eastern Europe, and Java.[23]

One consequence of the renewal of scholarship about the global context of the revolution's origins has been a rediscovery of its economic rather than fiscal origins. Over the past thirty years, there has often been a glib dismissal of the importance of economic change as somehow relegated into the dustbin of history along with Marxist approaches. More recently, a lively, insightful focus on colonialism, commercialism, and a "consumer revolution" has reinvigorated interest in the links between new commercial activity, in part resulting from the long boom in colonial trade, and new or changed behaviors and values, ranging from fashion and luxury goods consumption to debates about social utility and corporate privilege. Scholars have surveyed and synthesized transnational practices of political culture and communication and linked these with changing discourses about everything from privilege and commerce to animals, gardens, and the human body. This research and writing, among the best in recent years, has enlivened the possibilities of teaching about the French Revolution by exploring the range of ways "external" and "internal" tensions and changes may be linked.[24]

In an influential recent collection, David Armitage and Sanjay Subrahmanyam went so far as to conclude that the contrasting theses of Palmer and Hobsbawm were both "strikingly Eurotropic" and that the Age of Revolutions is best understood as "a complex, broad, interconnected, and even global phenomenon."[25] For them, as for Christopher Bayly, Anglo-French rivalry in North America was a spectacular instance of a global competition for commercial empire by European powers—France, Britain, Spain, Portugal—and the mounting costs of the warfare to expand and protect it.[26] From that perspective, "French exceptionalism" is a myth, in Annie Jourdan's formulation, and the French Revolution only the most spectacular and bloody path to change.[27]

Where does that leave the French Revolution? Was the revolutionary crisis one that spread out from the French epicenter, or was France simply the biggest wave generated by a global tide of cultural and economic change? Was the French Revolution one spectacular example of a global crisis of empires or, as in most "internalist" historiography, a unique upheaval with global consequences?[28] These questions require us to examine not only the transnational origins and consequences of the revolution but also the how its internal dynamics after 1789 were powered by a new phase of the global clash of empires.

My own argument is that the "Atlantic" thesis is too constrained geographically and conceptually to explain the origins and repercussions of the French Revolution, but the "global" thesis of Bayly and others is too diffuse to capture what was unique about France. Instead, the revolution is best described as a turning point in world history or "world-historical," its origins and consequences to be understood as global as well as internal, a revolution that unleashed an unprecedented European upheaval and was reactive to a world in change. Of course, French revolutionaries themselves understood their endeavors as "universal" in significance.[29]

The origins and impact of the French Revolution are best understood within an international, even global perspective, not only that of the global clash of empires but also of the long history of the struggles within Europe and its colonies for self-determination, representative government, and individual liberties against entrenched hierarchies of social "orders," corporate privilege, and autocracy. But the French Revolution was also unique. Only in France were the fullest consequences of revolution carried through: popular sovereignty, the full abolition of seigneurialism and corporate privilege, the abolition of slavery, and the introduction of equality of inheritance. Others were enacted and then repudiated: universal manhood suffrage, the separation of church and state, the right to divorce, among others.[30] Only in France was a democratic republic able to mobilize its forces to defeat a European coalition intent on its destruction. That is why this Age of Revolutions was first and foremost the French Revolution in the minds of contemporaries.

The revolution was therefore more than just one spectacular example of a global crisis of empires, but it cannot be reduced, as in most internalist French Revolution historiography, to a unique upheaval with global consequences. The revolution should be inserted into a global narrative of imperial crises of commerce and territory, which in France escalated into an unprecedented political and social revolution for "internal" reasons, itself engendering new international conflicts. Just as there had been revolutionary precedents before 1789—most notably in North America, Corsica, and the United Provinces—the French Revolution encouraged revolutionaries across the continent, most obviously in Ireland in 1798 and in Poland, where after partition in 1793 between Russia, Prussia, and Austria, nationalist rebellion in 1794 temporarily succeeded under the leadership of Tadeusz Kościusko. The collapse of the Holy Roman Empire in 1806 and the consequences for a German Confederation after 1815 had profound effects for European history. The response to news of the French Revolution was also profound but varied around the Mediterranean and in parts of South Asia.

So we are continuing to find fresh and enriching answers to those old questions: what were the causes of the Revolution? Why did it follow a particular course? What were its consequences?

Pedagogy has also changed dramatically. My training as an undergraduate, one that I passed on to my own students, had been based on mastery of political historians' arguments with tutorial discussions characterized by the study of printed "primary" or contemporary sources. Students were taught to ask the key questions of documents— who? what? when? why?—as the most incisive way of reaching historical understanding.[31] It was a strong if traditional education. Lecturers in the early 1970s, myself included, made little if any use of audiovisual material. I prided myself on arriving early to lectures to write point summaries in chalk on a blackboard and used to weave my way across campus with a large rolled-up map to hang up in the theater. Some lecturers used overhead transparencies—often handwritten and smudged—but only later in the 1970s did traditional slides start to become common. Very occasionally we might show a movie: a favorite was Ariane Mnouchkine's marvelous *1789*, filmed from the live production by the Théâtre du Soleil in 1974. A decade later we delighted in Andrzej Wajda's powerful *Danton*, while remaining skeptical as to whether it was more an allegory of contemporary Poland than an accurate portrayal of year II.

Many years of discussion about teaching with postgraduate tutors grappling with enabling lively, rigorous classroom engagement has inevitably changed my teaching, for the better. Electronic information has broadened the range of media through which students learn at all levels. We live in societies where most young people learn history from the Internet, films, and television much more than in the classroom. Electronic media dominate the communication of knowledge in a way that was inconceivable a half-century ago. The digital revolution has led to an inevitable undermining of the authority of the required textbook in both schools and universities. College students are now more likely to be required to purchase a "course pack" compiled by the lecturer and consisting of a selection of types of documents, plus chapters and articles by a range of historians. Little emphasis is placed by most teachers on the mastery of overarching narratives.

I began my teaching career at a time when lectures were seen as the central way of transmitting knowledge, and when teaching aids were basic and occasional. Lectures were not recorded, but their content was often the basis of examinations. The contrast could not be greater with my most recent teaching experience, a MOOC (mass online open course) delivered free across the world to anyone with Internet access and an interest in the French Revolution. This is an intensive six-week course, plus two weeks for final peer group assessment of essays, based on online lectures and readings (available as an e-book), email discussion forums, and social media pages.

The MOOC experience has been fascinating and instructive. Behind the astonishing global enrollment figures—more than 33,000 people from 169 countries in the first cohort—the reality was more modest. Only approximately 20,000 actually "visited" the course; about 16,000 watched at least one lecture, that is, about half of those enrolled actually "tuned up." Of them, about 1,200 submitted the first assessed exercise and 800 the second—5 percent of those who had watched a lecture. More than 8,300 watched the first set of six lectures; this tailed off gradually and by the end of the six weeks of classes about 4,200 had watched all thirty-six lectures, but there were still hundreds joining the course and watching as it closed. In all, about 418,000 lectures were watched, a startling statistic.[32]

These are typical figures for a MOOC, where students are free to "enroll" and "attend" as they please. On the other hand, there have been hundreds of messages sent to me enthusing about the opportunity to study a major historical turning point in an online setting of high quality. The vast majority of the discussion threads are thoughtful, intelligent, and courteous. It is a genuine pleasure to read the interactions of students from radically different societies, although it was obvious that they were dominated by highly educated, Anglophone students (70 percent of those enrolled already have degrees, and 6 percent have doctorates). The discussions are lively, and at times agitated, but there are minimal problems of acerbic or aggressive interactions.

Whatever the potential of such open, online courses reaching huge numbers of interested "students," there are shortcomings of the model as a form of teaching and learning suitable for teaching courses for credit or as part of campus-based programs. One weakness of the MOOC initiative is that the sheer weight of email posts into discussion forums cannot be attended to the same way we would for individual students at universities. Most posts go unanswered, even by other students. But assessment is the greatest weakness, since "objective" short-answer tests and quizzes may be appropriate for online courses such as introductory language instruction but are unsuitable for reflective courses like history. Peer group assessment of short essays is more appropriate and practical. Despite very careful instructions and advice from me about what we were after, however, peer assessed assignments call forth a storm of indignation about comments and grades.

Most important for me, the quality of the production of my mini-lectures has raised fundamental questions about the place of lecture in on-campus undergraduate teaching. Whereas lectures were once the core of teaching, there are now increasing numbers of people who suggest that the lecture is a passive form of learning and is rapidly being made redundant by resources available on the Internet. According to this logic, could students be asked to watch three fifteen-minute lectures online each week rather than come to a face-to-face lecture? This is the logic of the "flipped classroom," in which students watch lectures and other material online and attend small, campus-based tutorials focused on informed problem solving.[33] This approach is rich when well done and there is shared student commitment, but it does sacrifice an important, durable skill: the capacity to listen critically and make discriminating judgments about the key points from a formal lecture.

In contrast, the 2014 US documentary *Ivory Tower*, directed by Andrew Rossi, is a scathing critique of fully online education, seen by him to be intellectually shallow and a stalking horse for making academics redundant. In his lengthy review, David Bromwich used the film's criticism of online learning as the basis of an attack on everything ranging from student evaluations of teaching to attempts to improve facilities and social experiences for students. He contrasts this with his ideal, Deep Springs College in California, where the twenty-six enrolled men (no women yet) spend two years in intense study.[34]

It seems certain that MOOCs will accelerate the trend to fee-based, credit-bearing online courses, particularly at the postgraduate level.

But it would be unfortunate to lose sight of their initial, rather optimistic democratic vision of offering state-of-the-art classes for anyone with access to the Internet. This relates to the importance of historical understanding to the quality of political culture, to a civic education. By far the most agitated online forums in my course occur when students from a range of countries break away from discussing the French Revolution to ask questions about parallels in our own times, particularly the Arab Spring. Some of the posts are silly, even inflammatory, but most are intelligent reflections, for example, about why mass poverty does not automatically cause revolutionary upheaval, and why it proves so difficult to secure revolutionary outcomes that satisfy common longings for civic freedom and social justice. It underscored to me yet again the importance of a democratic but rigorous practice of history.

A key issue of our times is the fracturing of nation-states by the twin pressures of globalization and resurgent ethnic solidarities: will two hundred states inevitably become three thousand micro-nations within a handful of multinational trading blocs? Eastern Europe, to take one example, is on a knife edge of competing claims to identity, torn between the dream of joining a greater Europe and the seduction of far older, primordial claims to ethnic, regional solidarity. What is at stake here is not simply the tragic manifestation of animosities produced by a violent history and smothered for centuries by authoritarian states. It is also a battle over the veracity of competing versions of the past, each of which constructs and legitimizes an ethnic solidarity by exclusion of the hated "other." The social responsibility of historians has never been more pressing than in contemporary debates over reconciliation and what we call identity politics.

The study of history can never return to its nineteenth-century certainties: we are now far more accepting of the notion of multiple meanings, uncertainty, and competing claims. But history can therefore offer ways for the inquiring to write new histories, with new techniques. As Fernand Braudel put it, history is "a song with many voices": we should seek to enrich their range.[35] In part we can do this by making good, scholarly history accessible to a wider public eager for stories which are intelligible and engaging.

There is another, more important responsibility that we share. In their engrossing discussion twenty years ago of the state of the historical discipline in the United States, three eminent historians, Joyce Appleby,

Lynn Hunt, and Margaret Jacob, celebrated the fracturing of the confident nineteenth-century narratives of political history by the practice of feminist, labor, and postcolonial perspectives.[36] At the same time, they insisted on the dangers of a retreat into a resigned relativity: that is, that the erosion of certainty in meta-narratives could mean that historians should examine only isolated texts and fractured moments. Instead, they concluded that they were not prepared to give up claims to what they call a "qualified objectivity," that there can be a correlation between "the past" and the historian's account of it. Like them I celebrate the study of the past for the excitement of encountering difference, for the chance of understanding ourselves better, and above all the skills learned by its practice.

We continue to assert the public function of history as a democratic practice. As students of history, we are committed to the value of a historical education for the skills and sensitivities it teaches in understanding people separate from us in time, place, and culture, and therefore in understanding ourselves. In a multicultural society, we can hardly overestimate the civic importance of a perspective that emphasizes cultural understanding, careful judgment, flexibility of outlook, and respect for difference. Today, no less than in 1971, the challenge—and often the pleasure—of teaching undergraduates about the Age of Revolutions is to keep reexamining the questions we ask and the pedagogies we use to elicit informed responses.

NOTES

1. George Rudé, *The Crowd in the French Revolution* (Oxford: Clarendon Press, 1959).

2. On the Orr case, see Peter McPhee, *"Pansy": A Life of Roy Douglas Wright* (Melbourne: Melbourne University Press, 1999), chap. 5; W. H. C. Eddy, *Orr* (Brisbane: Jacaranda, 1961); Cassandra Pybus, *Gross Moral Turpitude: The Orr Case Reconsidered* (Melbourne: William Heinemann, 1993).

3. The story of Rudé's appointments is recounted in James Friguglietti, "A Scholar 'In Exile': George Rudé as a Historian of Australia," *French History and Civilization: Papers from the George Rudé Seminar* 1 (2005): 3–12; Hugh Stretton, "George Rudé," in *History from Below: Studies in Popular Protest and Popular Ideology in Honor of George Rudé*, ed. Frederick Krantz (Montreal: Concordia University, 1985), 43–54; and work by a former student of Rudé's in Adelaide, Doug Munro, "The Politics of George Rudé's Appointment to the University of

Adelaide," http://espace.library.uq.edu.au/view/UQ:333981/UQ333981_fulltext.pdf.

4. *Wilkes and Liberty: A Social Study of 1763 to 1774* (Oxford: Clarendon Press, 1962); *Revolutionary Europe, 1783-1815* (London: Collins, 1964); *The Crowd in History: A Study of Popular Disturbances in France and England, 1730-1848* (New York: Wiley, 1964); *Paris and London in the Eighteenth Century: Studies in Popular Protest* (London: Collins, 1970); and *Hanoverian London, 1714-1808* (London: Secker & Warburg, 1971); and with Eric Hobsbawm, *Captain Swing* (New York: Pantheon Books, 1968). Discussions of Rudé's work include Frederick Krantz, "'Sans érudition, pas d'histoire': The Work of George Rudé," in *History from Below: Studies in Popular Protest and Popular Ideology in Honor of George Rudé*, ed. Frederick Krantz (Montreal: Concordia University Press, 1985), 3-33; and Harvey J. Kaye, "Introduction: George Rudé, Social Historian," in *The Face of the Crowd: Studies in Revolution, Ideology and Popular Protest—Selected Essays of George Rudé*, ed. Harvey J. Kaye (New York: Harvester/Wheatsheaf, 1988), 1-40.

5. Alison Patrick, *The Men of the First French Republic: Political Alignments in the National Convention of 1792* (Baltimore, MD: Johns Hopkins University Press, 1972); W. J. Murray, *The Right-Wing Press in the French Revolution: 1789-1792* (London: Royal Historical Society, 1986).

6. Bernard Bailyn, *The Ideological Origins of the American Revolution* (Cambridge, MA: Belknap Press of Harvard University Press, 1967).

7. The initial statements of the Godechot-Palmer thesis were in Jacques Godechot, *Histoire de l'Atlantique* (Paris: Bordas, 1947); Robert R. Palmer, "The World Revolution of the West: 1763-1801," *Political Science Quarterly* 69 (1954): 1-14; and their joint article, "Le problème de l'Atlantique du XVIIIième au XXième siècle," *Comitato internazionale di scienze storiche: Congresso internazionale di Scienze storiche, Roma 4-11 Settembre 1955, Relazioni 5 (Storia contemporanea)* (Florence, 1955), 173-239. The classic Marxist rejoinders were Eric Hobsbawm, *The Age of Revolution, 1789-1848* (London: Weidenfeld and Nicolson, 1962), esp. xv-xvi, 17-73; and Albert Soboul, *The French Revolution, 1787-1799: From the Storming of the Bastille to Napoleon*, trans. Alan Forrest and Colin Jones (London: Unwin Hyman, 1989), esp. 3-24.

8. Published as *Les Semailles de la République dans les Pyrénées-Orientales, 1846-1852: Classes sociales, culture et politique* (Perpignan: L'Olivier, 1995).

9. Maurice Agulhon, *The Republic in the Village: The People of the Var from the French Revolution to the Second Republic*, trans. Janet Lloyd (Cambridge: Cambridge University Press, 1982); Alain Corbin, *Archaïsme et modernité en Limousin au XIXe siècle, 1845-1880*, 2 vols. (Paris: PULIM, 1975); John M. Merriman, *The Agony of the Republic: The Repression of the Left in Revolutionary France, 1848-1851* (New Haven, CT: Yale University Press, 1978); and Ted W. Margadant, *French Peasants in Revolt: The Insurrection of 1851* (Princeton, NJ: Princeton University Press, 1979).

10. For example, "Popular Culture, Symbolism and Rural Radicalism in Nineteenth-Century France," *Journal of Peasant Studies* 5 (1978): 238–53; "A Reconsideration of the 'Peasantry' of Nineteenth-Century France," *Peasant Studies* 9 (1981): 5–25.

11. For example, Alain Corbin, *Village Bells: Sound and Meaning in the 19th-Century French Countryside*, trans. Martin Thom (New York: Columbia University Press, 1998); Alan Forrest, *The Revolution in Provincial France: Aquitaine 1789–1799* (Oxford: Oxford University Press, 1996); Peter Jones, *The Peasantry in the French Revolution* (Cambridge: Cambridge University Press, 1988); Gwynne Lewis, *The Advent of Modern Capitalism in France 1770–1840: The Contribution of Pierre-François Tubeuf* (Oxford: Clarendon Press, 1993); Colin Lucas, *The Structure of the Terror: The Example of Javogues and the Loire* (Oxford: Oxford University Press, 1973); Albert Soboul, *Problèmes paysans de la Révolution, 1789–1848* (Paris: François Maspero, 1976); Timothy Tackett, *Religion, Revolution, and Regional Culture in Eighteenth-Century France: The Ecclesiastical Oath of 1791* (Princeton, NJ: Princeton University Press, 1986); Michel Vovelle, *Les métamorphoses de la fête en Provence, de 1750 à 1820* (Paris: Flammarion, 1976) and *Ville et campagne au XVIIIe siècle: Chartres et la Beauce* (Paris: Editions Sociales, 1980).

12. *Collioure et la Révolution Française, 1789–1815* (Perpignan: Le Publicateur, 1989).

13. Dominique Godineau, *The Women of Paris and Their French Revolution*, trans. Katherine Streip (Berkeley: University of California Press, 1998).

14. Hayden White, *Metahistory: The Historical Imagination in Nineteenth-century Europe* (Baltimore, MD: Johns Hopkins University Press, 1973); Dipesh Chakrabarty, *Provincializing Europe: Postcolonial Thought and Historical Difference* (Princeton, NJ: Princeton University Press, 2000).

15. Daniel Roche, *France in the Enlightenment*, trans. Arthur Goldhammer (Cambridge, MA: Harvard University Press, 1998); Roger Chartier, *The Cultural Origins of the French Revolution* (Durham, NC: Duke University Press, 1991); Suzanne Desan, *Reclaiming the Sacred: Lay Religion and Popular Politics in Revolutionary France* (Ithaca, NY: Cornell University Press, 1990) and *The Family on Trial in Revolutionary France* (Berkeley: University of California Press, 2004); Lynn Hunt, *Politics, Culture, and Class in the French Revolution* (Berkeley: University of California Press, 1984) and *The Family Romance of the French Revolution* (London: Routledge, 1992); Sarah Maza, *Private Lives and Public Affairs: The Causes Célèbres of Prevolutionary France* (Berkeley: University of California Press, 1993).

16. See Alison Patrick, *Revolution for Beginners: Reflections on the History of Late Eighteenth-Century France* (Melbourne: University of Melbourne Press, 2006), with an excellent introduction by Timothy Tackett.

17. Soboul, *French Revolution, 1787–1799*; William Doyle, *The Oxford History of the French Revolution*, 2nd ed. (Oxford: Oxford University Press, 2002).

18. Among these contributions are Lester D. Langley, *The Americas in the Age of Revolution, 1750–1850* (New Haven, CT: Yale University Press, 1996); Gad Heuman and Trevor Burnard, eds., *The Routledge History of Slavery* (New York: Routledge, 2010); John Garrigus, *Before Haiti: Race and Citizenship in French Saint-Domingue* (New York: Palgrave Macmillan, 2006); Laurent Dubois, *Avengers of the New World: The Story of the Haitian Revolution* (Cambridge, MA: Belknap Press of Harvard University Press, 2004); Paul Gilroy, *The Black Atlantic: Modernity and Double Consciousness* (London: Verso, 1993); and Jeremy D. Popkin, *You Are All Free: The Haitian Revolution and the Abolition of Slavery* (New York: Cambridge University Press, 2012).

19. Dena Goodman, *The Republic of Letters: A Cultural History of the French Enlightenment* (Ithaca, NY: Cornell University Press, 1994); Harriet Applewhite and Darline Levy, eds., *Women and Politics in the Age of the Democratic Revolution* (Ann Arbor: University of Michigan Press, 1990); Hunt, *The Family Romance of the French Revolution*; Desan, *The Family on Trial in Revolutionary France*.

20. The acute insights of, for example, Dan Edelstein, *The Terror of Natural Right: Republicanism, the Cult of Nature, and the French Revolution* (Chicago: University of Chicago Press, 2009); and Mary Ashburn Miller, *A Natural History of Revolution: Violence and Nature in the French Revolutionary Imagination, 1789–1794* (Ithaca, NY: Cornell University Press, 2011), seem to me to be compromised by selective reading and flawed methodology.

21. For example, David Andress, *Massacre at the Champ de Mars: Popular Dissent and Political Culture in the French Revolution* (Woodbridge, Suffolk: Royal Historical Society, 2000); Antoine de Baecque, *The Body Politic: Corporeal Metaphor in Revolutionary France, 1770–1800*, trans. Charlotte Mandell (Stanford, CA: Stanford University Press, 1997); Michel Biard, *Missionnaires de la République* (Paris: Vendémiaire, 2015); Marisa Linton, *Choosing Terror: Virtue, Friendship, and Authenticity in the French Revolution* (Oxford: Oxford University Press, 2013); Jean-Clément Martin, *Nouvelle histoire de la Révolution française* (Paris: Perrin, 2012); Timothy Tackett, *Becoming a Revolutionary: The Deputies of the French National Assembly and the Emergence of a Revolutionary Culture (1789–1790)* (Princeton, NJ: Princeton University Press, 1996) and *The Coming of the Terror in the French Revolution* (Cambridge, MA: Belknap Press of Harvard University Press, 2015).

22. These are the titles of their contributions to Peter McPhee, ed., *A Companion to the French Revolution* (Oxford: Wiley-Blackwell, 2013).

23. Jonathan I. Israel, *Democratic Enlightenment: Philosophy, Revolution, and Human Rights 1750–1790* (Oxford: Oxford University Press, 2012).

24. See particularly Colin Jones, "The Great Chain of Buying: Medical Advertisement, the Bourgeois Public Sphere, and the Origins of the French Revolution," *American Historical Review* 101 (1996): 13–40; Clare Haru Crowston, *Credit, Fashion, Sex: Economies of Regard in Old Regime France* (Durham, NC:

Duke University Press, 2013); William H. Sewell Jr., "Connecting Capitalism to the French Revolution: The Parisian Promenade and the Origins of Civic Equality in Eighteenth-Century France," *Critical Historical Studies* 1 (2014): 5–46; Rafe Blaufarb, *The Great Demarcation: The French Revolution and the Invention of Modern Property* (New York: Oxford University Press, 2016); and Charles Walton, "The Fall from Eden: The Free-Trade Origins of the French Revolution," in *The French Revolution in Global Perspective*, ed. Lynn Hunt, Suzanne Desan, and William Max Nelson (Ithaca, NY: Cornell University Press, 2013).

25. David Armitage and Sanjay Subrahmanyam, eds., *The Age of Revolutions in Global Context, 1760–1840* (Basingstoke: Palgrave Macmillan, 2010), xviii, xxxii.

26. Christopher A. Bayly, *The Birth of the Modern World, 1780–1914: Global Connections and Comparisons* (Oxford: Oxford University Press, 2004), chap. 3.

27. Annie Jourdan, *La Révolution: une exception française?* (Paris: Flammarion, 2004), part II.

28. Among the best of the rapidly expanding literature on the revolution in global context, see also David Andress, *1789: The Threshold of the Modern Age* (London: Little, Brown, 2008); Ian Coller, *Arab France: Islam and the Making of Modern Europe, 1798–1831* (Berkeley: University of California Press, 2011); Desan, Hunt, and Nelson, eds., *French Revolution in Global Perspective*; Michael Rapport, *Nationality and Citizenship in Revolutionary France: The Treatment of foreigners 1789–1799* (Oxford: Clarendon Press, 2000); Pierre Serna, Antonino De Francesco, and Judith A. Miller, eds., *Republics at War, 1776–1840: Revolutions, Conflicts, and Geopolitics in Europe and the Atlantic World* (Basingstoke: Palgrave Macmillan, 2013); and the contributions of Coller and Rapport to McPhee, ed., *A Companion to the French Revolution*. See, however, the recent reflections by David Bell, "Questioning the Global Turn: The Case of the French Revolution," *French Historical Studies* 37 (2014): 1–24.

29. Bayly, *Birth of the Modern World*, 100; Hunt, "The French Revolution in Global Context," in Armitage and Subrahmanyam, eds., *The Age of Revolutions in Global Context*, 30, 35.

30. For David Bell, the distinctiveness of the revolution lies rather in its "chiliastic fervour": "Questioning the Global Turn," 24.

31. Stuart Macintyre and Peter McPhee, eds., *Max Crawford's School of History: Proceedings of a Symposium Held at the University of Melbourne, 14 December 1998* (Melbourne: University of Melbourne Press, 2000); Fay Anderson and Stuart Macintyre, eds., *The Life of the Past: The Discipline of History at the University of Melbourne, 1855–2005* (Melbourne: University of Melbourne Press, 2006).

32. As with other MOOCs, competition in this teaching "space" has meant that subsequent iterations in 2015 and 2016 have had far fewer but still significant numbers of students.

33. One of the earliest and most influential statements was by Alison King, "From Sage on the Stage to Guide on the Side," *College Teaching*, 41 (1993): 30–35.

There is now a vast literature; among the most recent comments, see "The University Experiment: Campus as Laboratory," *Nature*, October 15, 2014.

34. Review by David Bromwich in *The New York Review of Books*, August 14, 2014, 50–51.

35. Fernand Braudel, *The Mediterranean and the Mediterranean World in the Age of Philip II*, abridged ed., trans. Siân Reynolds (London: Harper Collins, 1992), 657.

36. Joyce Appleby, Lynn Hunt, and Margaret Jacob, eds., *Telling the Truth about History* (New York: Norton, 1994).

Teaching the Age
of Revolutions
in the Americas

LESTER D. LANGLEY

Most of those teaching about the Age of Revolutions in the Americas probably have an abundance of published materials, theories, viewpoints, and approaches to use in class. Unlike my generation, your students may be more nonlinear in their thinking and perhaps more receptive to multidimensional views about revolution and its impact on the making of the modern world. I've been retired since 2000, and although I've continued my writing, I occasionally feel a need to get back into the classroom and talk about the myriad ways the Age of Revolutions in the Americas is still important. If you're still teaching, I envy you for the opportunity.

In another sense, I value my fortune in having been in graduate school in the early 1960s, when many of us specializing in US foreign relations or Latin American and Caribbean history had publishable dissertations and looked forward to a career teaching and writing. President John F. Kennedy had taken a Latin American idea (a hemispheric Marshall Plan) and made it his own; Fidel Castro had insinuated the Cuban Revolution into the hemispheric political and social agenda and thence into the Cold War confrontation with the Soviet Union. Liberals who saw themselves in the middle had adopted modernization theory with a secular leap of faith reminiscent of Southern Baptists' belief in the Book of John. I had dual fields in US diplomatic and Latin American and Caribbean history, and the job market was good.

Revolution—defined both generically and relevant to place and time—figured in all of these. I vaguely recall that one (perhaps the first) question I got on my prelims was, "What is a revolution?" I had recently read Hannah Arendt's *On Revolution* (1963), which to my mind remains the best introduction to the topic (although Eric Hobsbawm's *The Age of Revolution* is my runner-up choice). Arendt's brilliant treatment of revolution reminds us that until the late eighteenth century, the word *revolution* actually meant "restoration." In retrospect, that should have been my response to the question. Instead, I recall saying, "When a wheel goes around once." Fortunately for me, the committee inferred that I understood what Arendt and others were getting at when they used the word *revolution*. Had I tried to be more profound with an observation—a true one, in my estimation—that revolutions are self-defining and conditional on time, place, and circumstance, there probably would have been follow-up questions I could not answer. In any event, teaching as well as writing about revolution, directly or indirectly, proved to be a continuing theme in my career.

For thirty-five years at three different universities—Texas A&M, Central Washington University, and the University of Georgia (1970–2000)—my teaching assignments followed altering courses: US history survey on the lower undergraduate level, Latin American history and US foreign relations on the upper undergraduate level. Teaching about revolution in the Americas became a part of the larger and more complicated content of these courses, especially in a course on US–Latin American relations and in the 1990s when I revived an older course (History of the Americas) that had gone out of fashion after World War II. In the process, I began to think of myself more and more as a "hemispheric historian."

The Americas in the Age of Revolution, 1750–1850 (1996) represented my first attempt at a comparative study of three major revolutions of the Western Hemisphere—the American, the Haitian, and the Latin (principally Spanish) American. The book departed from the northern transatlantic perspective of Robert R. Palmer's massive two-volume study (*The Age of the Democratic Revolution: A Political History of Europe and America, 1760–1800*) and Hobsbawm's *Age of Revolution*. Although more than one commentator has referred to my study as "neo-Palmerian" but never "neo-Hobsbawmian," my *Age of Revolution* is in effect a north–south or dominantly hemispheric account for several reasons. It followed a welcome pattern of greater attention to the revolutions and wars of independence south of the United States, which were largely neglected by Palmer and Hobsbawm. For Palmer, the meaningful revolutions are the French and even more so the American, a choice that irritated several of his contemporary European historians. For Hobsbawm, whose work follows a Marxist approach to the age, the twin revolutions are the Industrial (principally economic and identified with Britain) and the French (principally political).

My account and my approach to the study of the Age of Revolutions in the Americas follow neither pattern. Essentially but not exclusively a political history, *The Americas in the Age of Revolution* relegates Europe to a secondary role. I take the metropole imperial nations (Britain, France, and Spain) and the peripheral entities (the Atlantic seaboard colonies, French Saint-Domingue, and Spanish America) and put the hemisphere at center stage. The book departs methodologically from other studies in its use of the twin theories of chaos and complexity. Chaos theory was developed by a meteorologist, who discovered that even with computer manipulation of data, the slightest variation in circumstance at the onset can have dramatic and often unexpected consequences over time. "Sensitive dependence on initial conditions" is a fundamental principle of chaos theory and, I argue, a necessary factor for understanding revolutionary phenomena and the complexity of revolutionary conditions.

For students and especially for the teachers of revolution and the wars that accompany revolutions, the assessment and measure of revolutions often depends on identifying success and failure—whether the revolution "solved" the "social question" is a familiar and understandable query. Yet this makes it hard to attend sufficiently to revolutions' myriad complexities and dynamics and the ability of leaders to control and contain the forces unleashed by a revolution. I suggest that you can understand rebellion with a linear approach or by projecting backward but not revolution; to further complicate matters, it is difficult to organize and teach a course on revolution without following a linear format.

My hemispheric approach to these three revolutions struck some as a distraction from or even a distortion of contemporary reality. That was neither my point nor my intention. All three episodes in the Americas to some degree owed their origins to conflict and disagreement between European metropole and hemispheric colony (or, as was the Spanish case, "kingdom") and the parallel impact of Enlightenment thought and views about what Europeans called the New World. Nor do I see the hemispheric measure of these revolutions as an alternative perspective to the rapidly growing literature on the Age of Revolutions from a global, local, or "glocal" perspective. On the contrary, an underlying theme of *The Age of Revolution in the Americas* is what happens when we shift our perspective from an east–west (or transatlantic) to a north–south (or hemispheric) angle. I encourage you to try it with your students—either early on in the design and delivery of a course or in a reflective way at the end, once they have a clearer grasp of revolutionary timelines and participants.

Understanding a Hemispheric Age of Revolutions

From a transatlantic view, the dominating issues are European imperial nations attempting to modernize their administration and control of far-flung hemispheric enterprises. These efforts to turn semi-autonomous outposts into colonies brought unexpected consequences in all of them, especially British North America, French Saint-Domingue, and Spanish America. Undeniably, the American Revolution has always been easier to "fit" into and teach from the transatlantic angle for at least three reasons—the strength of the call for independence as opposed to autonomy or equality within transatlantic "nations," the stark and to some degree hypocritical contrast of a revolution begun with declarations of freedom and equality where slavery and racial inequalities were becoming more deeply entrenched, and a revolutionary agenda that underscored the expansionist ambitions of a government and a people on the North American continent. Ultimately, as the years after the Mexican-American War (1846-1848) dramatically illustrated, the price paid for this putative betrayal of the revolutionary promise was the devastating American Civil War. Similarly, albeit for different reasons, the Haitian and Spanish-American revolutions are often found wanting when measured against what we regard as an ideal goal of revolution. Certainly, the Haitian constituted the first successful slave revolt that culminated in an independent country without slavery, although not without a severe labor code and civil war in its early years. Indeed, of the three, it generally qualifies best as the model of a social revolution. In the Spanish-American case, the breakdown of the Spanish "kingdoms" in 1810 in the aftermath of Napoleon usurping the Spanish throne precipitated civil wars, a fierce counterrevolution, and a continental struggle that became an international crisis.

Generations of historians of the American Revolution often assess these other hemispheric revolutions as much costlier in lives and consequences. In actuality, by looking at the American Revolution more from a hemispheric perspective, our judgment of its human costs, its length, and its relationship to the other major upheavals of the Age of Revolutions changes. Although there are significant distinctions in each case, since the mid-1990s (and even earlier for the American Revolution) one can identify in the literature a persuasive argument for viewing the three major revolutions of the Americas as initially movements for autonomy within the British empire, the French empire, and the Spanish empire, respectively, that became wars of independence to achieve equality between motherland and settler colony. The relationship is symbiotic.

Symbiosis is used in biology, psychiatry, and psychoanalysis as an indicator of the nature, benefits, and occasionally harmful effects when organisms or people or groups interact. For the study of the Age of Revolutions in the Americas, I believe, symbiosis is as useful a tool as a traditional comparative study of the similarities or dissimilarities between revolutions or pursuing such questions as the radicalism of a revolution or faulting a revolution for its failure to address the "social question." For example, the American Revolution has a symbiotic relationship with the French Revolution and with the other revolutions in the Americas. The symbiotic relationship between the French and Haitian revolutions is different than that between the Haitian and what I call the "long" American Revolution, even though the topics of focus are race and slavery. Clearly, had there been no French Revolution, there would have been no colored revolt and then no slave revolt that became embroiled in the wars of the French Revolution and ultimately led to Haitian independence in 1804. Similarly, the eruption of revolution and civil war in Spanish America, though differing from place to place, reverberated more from events in Spain and the actions of Napoleon and the British than the example of a presumed successful American Revolution that avoided the human and physical destruction of the Haitian and Spanish-American experiences.

The United States' natural revolutionary bond, Thomas Jefferson believed, lay with the French Revolution, which created two "sister republics" marching to the same revolutionary drumbeat of an inevitably parallel future until the French Revolution turned from its moderate course (in 1792 and early 1793) and then became an enemy in an undeclared war in 1798. That conflict ended one alliance—severing the entangling alliance between American patriots and the French monarchy that as much as any other factor made possible the achievement of independence—but ultimately bequeathed an emotional and human link despite crises between the two governments in the nineteenth century. The intangible and human bonds took various forms—Alexis de Tocqueville's implied validation of American exceptionalism; through migration, especially after the failed European revolutions of 1848; the French gift of the Statue of Liberty, a symbol of the triumph of liberty by ending slavery; and the oft-told remark of General John J. Pershing's aide Charles E. Stanton on landing with the American Expeditionary Force in France during World War I: "Lafayette, we are here."

Framing the American Revolution with its antimonarchical and republican spirit as a New World stepfather of the French is a reminder of transatlantic "ties that bind," an evocative appeal similar to the pre–World War II movement of Atlantic Union with Great Britain. When we view the American Revolution from a hemispheric (rather than transatlantic) perspective and extend its chronological age to the end of World War I (1914–1918), then the relationship of the American with the other revolutions of the hemisphere becomes more apparent and more complicated and the subtle differences between the French and the American become more striking. The ideological impact of the French Revolution in the revolutionary experience of the Americas is undeniable, as is the validity of a Marxist approach, where the issue involves land and labor. But the French Revolution is manifestly a secular affair, and in the revolutionary age of the Americas, race and religion often trumped class and ideology.

The Haitian Revolution, once relegated to a paragraph or so in US history texts (usually in connection with the Louisiana Purchase), had a profound impact on the revolutionary age. It was the first and only successful slave revolt in history, and it sent shock waves in every direction—in France, where the fear and uncertainties of its course prompted two emancipation decrees; in the United States, where Southerners already troubled about slave revolts and the place of people of color in the republic were fearful about the appeal of the slave rebellion among slaves and even free people of color; and in Spanish America, particularly in Venezuela, whose economy and social structure resembled that of the Caribbean plantation societies.

Whether viewed in the narrow framework of the years between 1789 and 1804 or in the context of the long revolutionary era, the legacy of the Haitian Revolution resonates differently when we shift our angle of vision from a transatlantic to a hemispheric perspective. In the United States, it was indirectly linked with the growing fear of slave insurrection and the unmistakable link political leaders made between whiteness and the future of the republic. True, the American Revolutionary legacy in the Eastern states and the states created out of the Old Northwest would follow an abolitionist course, as did federal law in its approval of abolition of the slave trade. But a more unsettling trend in the early years of the nineteenth century was the apprehension about the role of free people of color in the nation and their movement within the country. The issue came up with the admission of Louisiana as a state in 1812 and, after the War of 1812, in the parallel debates over US policy toward the Spanish-American wars of independence and the admission of Missouri into the union. One signal of just how explosive this issue would become was the founding of an organization and an increasingly appealing solution to dealing with it—the American Colonization Society, created in 1816 as the most politically and racially acceptable way of dealing with the growing numbers of manumitted slaves who were deemed unassimilable in the republic. Haiti and the new republic of Liberia would be choices for their destination.

By 1816, the war against the Napoleonic empire in Europe was over and its victors had created at the Congress of Vienna in 1815 an international system to prevent another French Revolution. In the Americas, the hemispheric civil wars had ended in a draw in North America and a reversal of fortune for the patriot cause in Spanish America everywhere except for the revolution in Buenos Aires. With the death of Jean-Jacques Dessalines in 1806, Haiti had split into a northern black kingdom under Henri Christophe and a southern colored republic led by Alexandre Pétion. With the restoration of Fernando VII to the Spanish throne came a repudiation of the liberal Cádiz Constitution of 1812 and the launching of a fierce royalist counterrevolution in Nueva Granada (modern Colombia and Panama) and Venezuela. In 1817, the war entered its second decade as a continental struggle in which the Venezuelan Simón Bolívar emerged as the "George Washington" of the patriot cause, with profound consequences on both sides of the Atlantic. For Europeans, this struggle constituted the "western question," important largely for strategic reasons. For US leaders, the decade after 1816 involved apprehensions of not only French-Spanish collusion in restoring monarchical rule in Spanish America (and the British role in such a venture) but also absorbing the impact of these wars—particularly the savage conflict in the Bolivarian theater—on trade, geopolitics, and debates over slavery and race in US society and politics.

Bolívar renewed the war by making a pact with Pétion, an agreement that included a clause to link his continental war with a commitment to grant freedom to slaves who fought, a practice followed by both sides in the American Revolution. More unsettling to US leaders was Bolívar's pronouncement in 1819 that in the new political entity of Colombia—the union of Venezuela, New Granada, and Quito (modern Ecuador)—there would be unity of people of color with the ruling white classes. Bolívar became widely popular in Britain and with ordinary Americans and with an element in Congress. In the course of the war, US leaders altered their views of the Venezuelan liberator—Colombia was the first new state in Latin American recognized by the United States—although the issue of race cropped up again in debates over sending US emissaries to participate in Bolívar's proposed Panama Congress of 1826, which involved an attempt to create a defensive league of former Spanish colonies. By then, the independence of mainland Latin America, acknowledged by the United States and backed up by British power, seemed irreversible.

Ideas for Teaching a Hemispheric Age of Revolutions

My sense is that most who offer a course on the Age of Revolutions in the Atlantic world use this benchmark date of the mid-1820s (and the effective collapse of Spanish power on the mainland of Latin America) as marking the end of the violent phase and then have a follow-up lecture or discussion about the long-term consequences. Those who take a global perspective on the Age of Revolutions or (like Hobsbawm) whose study of the Age of Revolutions has global implications push on to the mid-nineteenth century. Those who teach the US survey (which usually ends about 1877), or the Latin American and Caribbean survey (both halves), the modern Western civilization course, or the world history course have a different set of problems and emphases in selecting what salient issues, ideas, and theories about revolution are most useful. For the history of the Americas and inter-American (or US–Latin American) relations courses, periodization is less problematic, but even these courses can pose other problems in trying to convey to students what those who experience the chaos of revolution know only too well—what occurs during or in the aftermath of a conflict in which ideas, revolution, civil war, and a struggle for independence are entangled or knotted together can sometimes radically alter the trajectory or course of affairs. In the process, the true believers are confounded about the outcomes.

Regardless of the value you place on these issues and theories, and the wider coverage of your course, I believe that changing the angle of perspective on these three revolutions *and* expanding the chronological benchmark dates from the usual beginning of the mid-eighteenth century or 1775 to the end World War I have particular dividends in explaining revolutionary change. So does a reminder that each revolution was also a civil war. In other words, a hemispheric approach helps us refresh how we think about the first revolutions in the Americas and view them potentially as not just long revolutions but long civil wars. A hemispheric perspective on the revolutionary age can be instructive if not always comforting for those who believe, as Benedict Anderson attests in his widely influential *Imagined Communities*, that the revolutions and wars of independence in the New World offered Europeans afflicted with seemingly unending conflict between rival monarchies a better and more peaceful route to nationhood. One way I like to begin this discussion is to identify the American, Haitian, and Spanish-American revolutions as the first, second, and third American revolutions, which prompts students to think of them more in a hemispheric sense and a reminder that well into the nineteenth century (and technically even today), *America* refers to the Americas. On the eve of my retirement I was planning to offer several courses—history of the Americas and inter-American relations—and collapse them into a new field called hemispheric America, with such courses as "Hemispheric America: A History," "Hemispheric America: An International History," "Hemispheric America: Special Topics," among them, the Age of Revolutions.

The first unsettling characteristic of the Age of Revolutions/prolonged civil wars in the Americas is its length, which I measure from 1775 and the battles of Lexington and Concord to the end of World War I, that is, almost 150 years as compared with the Second Hundred Years' War, which we tend to frame between the benchmark dates of 1689 and 1815. The French recognized US independence in 1778 and the British did so in 1783, but the preservation of the union created by the Articles of Confederation and reaffirmed by the US Constitution remained a contested issue until 1865. Haiti was arguably a nation in 1804, but not until 1825 did the French recognize its independence. Surprisingly stable throughout most of the nineteenth century, its independence became compromised in 1915 with the US occupation, which persisted until 1934. Although the wars of independence in mainland Latin America effectively were over by the mid-1820s, civil conflict and federalist wars involving unsettled issues from the period 1810 to 1825 persisted well beyond that date. From the 1820s to 1867 and the defeat of Maximilian, Mexico reverberated from civil conflict, US invasion in 1847, loss of half of its territory to the United States, and foreign occupation and guerrilla war. The last hemispheric war of independence and revolution within the Spanish empire occurred in Cuba and Puerto Rico, which culminated not in complete independence but as José Martí (who died in the cause) feared, in the exchange of one imperial master for another.

Viewing the American Revolution from a transatlantic or especially a global perspective is a reminder of Thomas Paine's affirmation of its universality in *Common Sense* or Jefferson's belief in a republic unbound from monarchy, tradition, and irrationality that would transform North America into an empire of liberty. This is Jefferson the liberal. His triumph in the sordid election of 1800, he wrote in his first inaugural address, constituted a revolution as compelling as the one crafted in 1776 and reaffirmed (or subverted, as some believe) with the Constitution and the Bill of Rights.

Jefferson's was the revolution of political transformation with powerful social consequences. It was also the revolution that acknowledged the place of slavery—however despicable he found it—as necessary for creating the unified colonies to fight the revolution, a symbiotic union of Massachusetts and Virginia. In the fratricide of the American Civil War, the familiar story goes, the country paid the ultimate sacrifice for that pact. Monarchical Europe and particularly France intervened in the 1770s revolution to ensure US independence; their more ambivalent response in the 1860s to what the victors called the War of the Rebellion helped ensure the union's survival. But the American, Haitian, and Latin American revolutions erupted within the last forty years of the Second Hundred Years' War, and we cannot understand their provenance or legacy by focusing exclusively on their transatlantic connection. We need to bring their hemispheric identity to center stage.

Of the three, the American Revolution was in some respects the most complicated. Certainly, it was the longest. With the War of Independence, it nurtured two entities—imperial America, expansionist and militant, and transnational America, the federation of cultures and ethnicities—that came of age in the early twentieth century. It created three nation-states—the United States, which, I would argue, became a nation not with the end of the Civil War or Reconstruction but with World War I; the Confederacy, born with the counterrevolution of 1861–1865; and Upper Canada (modern Ontario), which with the other provinces and territories became a modern nation in World War II. Calling the war of 1861–1865 a counterrevolution or Lincoln's response a "preemptive" strike (rather than "Civil War") is a reminder of fundamental divisions that came to the fore after the Declaration of Independence and at the Constitutional Convention in 1787. A parallel civil war in North American history was the conflict between republican Americans and monarchist Americans, who fled northward during and after the American Revolution. Despite its nationalistic fervor in politics and verse, the War of 1812 was not really a second war of independence but a civil war (as Alan Taylor eponymously framed it in his 2010 volume), a stage in the long American Revolution.

In the aftermath, these "Canadians" stopped calling themselves Americans. Border clashes persisted, as did the intermittent war between white settlers and Native Americans. American continentalism, which drew its strength from the impact of revolutionary ideology on ordinary people and the strategic calculations of their leaders, directed its energies as much toward Canada as Mexico. Not until the North America Act of 1867 (which created the Canadian confederation) and the Treaty of Washington did those conflicted feelings begin to subside; the British government kept troops in North America until 1871.

Expanding the Age of Revolutions in the Americas, I would argue, fundamentally alters how we look at and teach about the relationship of the hemispheric revolutions and wars of independence to their respective European metropoles and, just as important, to one another. Going further, by factoring in the dynamics of race and slavery into this broader picture, we come away with a different perspective. The customary and often harsh portrayal of the United States as the North American bully confident of its hemispheric mission remains, but there is a sobering reality that contemporaries from George Washington to Theodore Roosevelt and Woodrow Wilson sensed. That reality was the uncertainty about the transatlantic storm accompanying the last forty years of the Second Hundred Years' War and the French Revolution and the survival of the union in the successive political crises of the nineteenth century. That the United States chose the imperial path abroad (particularly in the Americas) and a manifestly racist character within often brings students to question whether this constitutes a denial of its revolutionary heritage.

Answering that question requires going beyond the traditional debates focusing on the growing divisions over slavery and abolition, slave states and free states, and the rise of Jacksonian democracy, among others, to look at the legacy of the American Revolution in a hemispheric perspective. As mentioned, the impact of the French Revolution on the turbulent Federalist era ended in the Quasi-War in 1798, but the parallel effect of the Haitian Revolution on the national US debate over slavery and the dangers of slave rebellion had greater consequences, particularly among increasingly militant Southerners. In the era of not-so-good feelings after the War of 1812, the foreign policy questions related to Latin American wars of independence—particularly the war in the Bolivarian theater and the creation of new republics—intruded into the debates over the role of free people of color in the political and civic life of the United States.

Latin American and Caribbean historians quite rightly point out that slaves and free people of color played a more important role in the wars of independence and were accorded more opportunity and recognition in the new republics than in the American Revolution and in the United States. What must be added to this observation is a recognition that by Lincoln's death there were more than 180,000 freedmen in arms in Union forces and with the Emancipation Proclamation and Thirteenth Amendment, the victor in the war confiscated $3.65 billion of property in human beings. The end of Haitian slavery had been achieved through armed struggle, but recognition of Haitian independence by France came with an indemnity of 150 million francs (later reduced to 90 million), which the Haitians finally paid off after World War II. Abolition in the British West Indies in the early 1830s came with the avoidance of "another Haiti" but with compensation to slaveholders. The United States paid its indemnity not with money (except for compensation to slaveholders in the District of Columbia) but with the Jim Crow legislation that came in the 1890s and its legacy of racial segregation. The decade of the 1890s paralleled the rise of social Darwinism, labor strikes, the increased appeal of socialism, the "whitening" of society (expressed visually at the 1893 World's Columbian Exposition in Chicago), Cuba Libre and the eruption of civil war in Cuba, a ferocious political battle in the 1896 presidential election (in which William Jennings Bryan declared that the question of the gold versus silver standard was "the issue of 1776 over again"), and the dual expressions of the revolutionary age in the Americas, José Martí's "Our America," which invoked the vision of an antiracist, humane purpose to the cause of Cuba Libre as the cause of all Latin America counterpoised against the mighty, industrial imperial America of the north.

Not only students but also their teachers sometimes frame the years from 1880 to 1920 in the Americas as an era of US intrusion and dominance, particularly in the circum-Caribbean and Mexico, a legacy of the expansionist impulses that took root during the French and Indian War, sustained the continentalist mission that even the egalitarian Tom Paine had envisioned, and rejected notions of a common revolutionary heritage. In the course of the nineteenth century, the revolutionary invocation of liberalism opened ever wider the opportunities for collusion between those who held political power and those whose only goal was making money. The creation and realities of US insular empire made a mockery of the professed ideal of self-determination and the meaning of citizenship. As if to validate William Graham Sumner's statement that the United States had taken Spain's place in the Caribbean, Theodore Roosevelt dispatched an "Army of Pacification" to Cuba in 1906, an example of what he had meant in announcing two years before that the United States would exercise a policing role in an unruly hemisphere. (The army commanded by Pablo Morillo in the counterrevolution of 1814–1816 in Nueva Granada and Venezuela was officially an Army of Pacification.) Woodrow Wilson proved to be even more dominating and intrusive in his Caribbean and especially his Mexican policies, explaining to a suspicious European diplomat that the United States had achieved sufficient maturity and stability in its own governance that it had the right to teach smaller and presumably less capable political leaders about the art of good governance. The spirit and even some of the recommendations of the Fourteen Points Wilson offered to a war-torn Europe at Versailles in 1919 echoed the idealism of the revolutionary age.

There is an alternative history of these years that sprang from the revolutionary age. In this forty-year span Europeans who lost their bearing and paid for it with the collapse of the 1814 Congress System in the carnage of World War I. The modern inter-American system grew out of Secretary of State James G. Blaine's plans in the early 1880s for a hemispheric entity that would strengthen economic ties and make an "America for Americans" to counter British influence, echoing Jefferson's idea of America as a hemisphere unto itself. In a time when anti-American sentiments ran high, Latin and North American jurists explored the development of a distinctive hemispheric public law, a legal approach that befuddled some scholars of international law. In what strikes us as the essence of illogic, several Latin American political theorists fashioned out of Monroe's 1823 statement an argument for what some called a hemispheric Monroe Doctrine, which had very little to do with Monroe but spoke to the principle of nonintervention. Four nations—Canada, the United States, Brazil, and Argentina—tried with varying success and with differing outcomes to reshape their identities through large-scale immigration. There was a racial, cultural, and economic motive in this endeavor that had unsettling and disruptive consequences in the twentieth century for the political and social stability of the receiver countries.

It is a provocative and rewarding exercise to invite students to ponder how to some degree most of these changes and issues bore a linkage to the first half-century of the revolutionary age, and the two countries most dramatically altered were Mexico and the United States— places with the longest revolutions and civil wars. From 1910 to 1919, years of political and social strife, Mexico became a nation. The peasant revolt that had failed in 1810 succeeded during the revolutionary and civil war years after 1910, and a generation of revolutionary rivals ultimately succeeded in creating a central state with sufficient strength to deal with urban labor and rural unrest—with laws, with new political organizations, or with force. At the same time Mexico mobilized a latent nationalism and exploited its tenuous German connection to alter its troublesome relationship with its intrusive northern neighbor. Asking the students to reflect on a hemispheric and long-term view of the Age of Revolutions is a fine way of inviting them to draw creatively and laterally on their own senses of place, heritage, and preconception—the more diverse, the better.

For me, the most dramatic achievement in dealing with the lingering and threatening issues of the Age of Revolutions occurred in the United States during the imperial years of the first two decades of the twentieth century. It occurred not so much because of a putative reconciliation between North and South or even the acquiescence in racial segregation.

That scar remained. It came about by reforms and by force—the acceptance of a social mission for government as well as society embodied in the progressive belief in creating a new person. Wilson echoed that commitment in his second inaugural address, when everyone knew the United States was entering the war, that the American people were now "citizens of the world." It was a blatantly hypocritical sentiment, as his critics pointed out, but the attribution reflected a lasting revolutionary ideal. The war itself and the postwar riots and unrest enabled the central government to mobilize public sentiment against naysayers and presumed enemies, from German sympathizers to Wobblies and socialists. But the one group that was brought to bay was the most formidable—more dangerous and more destructive than Natives or revolting slaves—and at the same time, the most useful for sustaining the "muscle" of the long American Revolution and of imperial America—white men.

I concede the universality of the French Revolution for a variety of reasons—its influence in shaping modern politics, the omnipresent state, the modern conception of nation, and its secularity—but the long American Revolution has its own peculiar universality, which often invokes evangelical Christianity, places the individual at center stage, and professes (but historically has often violated) that all are equal in their individual personhood however unequal in wealth, education, or social standing. There is an openness, diversity, and fluidity as well as a strong sense of community and voluntarism in transnational America, which regrettably has sometimes coexisted with racism, meanness, and xenophobia. The roots of imperial America also reach back to the American Revolution. Imperial America got its inspiration from political leaders and the successive generations of land-hungry and ambitious (mostly white) Americans who believed in or tolerated slavery, drew a sharp racial divide, and bought into the notion that their equality and freedom depended on slavery and black inferiority. Transnational and imperial America are knotted together in US history and especially our relationship with the other peoples and nations of the Americas. In the early twenty-first century, both still exist, but through immigration, cultural, economic, and political exchanges as well as the appreciation of diversity, the more inclusive face of transnational America provides a more admirable representation of the exceptional meaning of revolution in a country born without a name yet forgiven for having stolen the name "America," a reminder that it is still a work in progress.

51

PART TWO

Sources and Methods

The Enlightenment

Who, When, and Where?

AMBROGIO CAIANI

> Enlightenment is the point at which the human being departs
> from his self-incurred minority. Minority is the inability to use
> one's own understanding without the guidance of another.
>
> Immanuel Kant, "What Is Enlightenment?"

mmanuel Kant's famous definition of what constitutes
enlightenment remains an excellent starting point for
anybody wishing to delve further into this subject. Even in the twenty-
first century, the ability to think critically and independently remains a
highly prized quality. Many thinkers in the Age of Revolutions were
engaged in a grand struggle against the psychological immobility of the
ancien régime. Such stagnation was captured well by the reactionary
mantra: "the limits of the ancients cannot be moved."[1] Kant defined
such "dogmas and formulas [. . . as] the leg-irons of everlasting immatu-
rity."[2] Until a few decades ago, scholars and historians had the comfort
of knowing that the Enlightenment was the seedbed of modernity and
to a certain extent the incubator of democratic revolutions. Before World
War II, German philosopher Ernst Cassier pronounced confidently:
"The basic idea underlying all the tendencies of enlightenment was
the conviction that human understanding is capable, by its own power
and without recourse to supernatural assistance, of comprehending the

system of the world and that this new way of understanding the world would lead it to a new way of mastering it."[3]

Decades later it was still possible for intellectual historian Peter Gay to argue with little equivocation that "In the course of the eighteenth century the world, at least the world of the literate, was being emptied of mystery. Pseudo-science was giving way to science, credence in the miraculous intervention of divine forces was being corroded by the acid of skepticism and overpowered by scientific cosmology."[4] Secular, rational and modern, the Enlightenment was conceived as a unitary intellectual movement and a catalyst for a surge forward in human progress. In many ways, teaching the Enlightenment during the post-war period must have been paradoxically inspiring and dull. Eager students were taught that the origins of the democratic, liberal, and economically prosperous West they inhabited could be situated in the great intellectual effervescence of the eighteenth century. The contrast with the totalitarian and communist East was none too subtle. Voltaire, Rousseau, Diderot, and their ilk cried, "let there be light . . . and it was so." Unsurprisingly the growing lack of confidence in the Western world's omnipotence and boundless humanitarianism has shattered this old view into countless fragments. In a sense, the Enlightenment has become a victim of its own skepticism.

Very little agreement has survived among historians of eighteenth-century thought about the Enlightenment, except that it was an intel-lectual climate or mood. This disintegration poses a great pedagogical challenge to teachers of history. The concept has acquired a seemingly endless number of adjectives. *Radical, counter, conservative, moderate, democratic, Christian, Jewish, Catholic, Protestant, cosmopolitan*, and *global* are just a few of the terms that have deeply blunted the definitional acuity of "Enlightenment." Many will feel great sympathy for historian Jonathan Israel's monumental project to recover and restate the "Radical Enlightenment's" positive legacy to our modern world.[5] His critics are equally correct (surprisingly so, considering that Israel's argument covers two thousand or so pages) that he has oversimplified the picture by focusing on those thinkers who most resemble today's social liberals in terms of mentality and political outlook.[6]

The great reward in looking for or studying the Enlightenment, for both teachers and students, is that it continues to unsettle assumptions and forces us, as Kant urged so long ago, to think differently. Perhaps the best means of allowing students to taste the complexity of this intellectual effervescence is to use simple questions to uncover its intricacies. The Enlightenment unsettles historians by constantly asking that highly irritating question, "how do you know what you know?" The point is not to seek to reconstruct a "real" Enlightenment. Indeed, such an individual self-contained movement probably never existed. The number of participants, the diversity of ideas, and the transnational (perhaps oceanic) context involved makes this intellectual climate incommensurable. The object of the exercise is to ask better questions to know a little more and, if all goes well, think in more sophisticated ways about the eighteenth century. This chapter shows that seemingly simple questions can help students develop interesting ways of reflecting and learning about the Enlightenment. The following questions will be explored:

1. Who was the Enlightenment?
2. When was the Enlightenment?
3. Where was the Enlightenment?

These queries are by no means exhaustive, and many others could be asked in their stead. But these three serve as accessible points of entry into this challenging subject matter and work well as classroom exercises in their own right, inviting students to search for patterns and orthodoxies.

Who Was the Enlightenment?

The Empress Joséphine, Napoleon's first wife, perhaps provided the clearest answer to this question. In 1812, divorced but receiving a generous pension, she commissioned artist Anicet Charles Gabriel Lemonnier to paint scenes from recent history to decorate her country retreat, the Château de Malmaison.[7] The work he produced (which incidentally adorns the cover of almost every textbook published on the Enlightenment) was titled *An Evening at Mme Geoffrin's Salon* and is accessible online.[8] The scene depicts a gathering of intellectuals eagerly listening to a reading of Voltaire's newest play, *The Orphan of China: A Tragedy*. To all intents and purposes Lemmonier's answer to the question "Who was the Enlightenment?" would seem to be: forty men in silly wigs and five ladies in precarious health. The neatness and stylishness of the image hides from view the messiness of the Enlightenment.

Anicet Charles Gabriel Lemonnier, *An Evening at Mme Geoffrin's Salon*. (1812, oil on canvas, Château du Malmaison, Rueil; https://commons.wikimedia.org/wiki/File:La_Lecture_chez_Madame_Geoffrin.jpg; photograph by Caroline Léna Becker under Creative Commons)

Social membership of the Enlightenment is next to impossible to define in clear terms. The scene of intellectual harmony shown in the painting hides the truth that many of these individuals ranged widely in terms of socioeconomic background and disagreed heartily among themselves; some hated each other, and others barely shared the same cultural vocabulary.[9] Perhaps the artist's great crime is that he makes it all seem so boring! All these men, and a few women, are listening silently and passively to the speaker. The eighteenth century was the great age of conversation. Verbal exchanges were not neat things and indeed produced something of an intellectual cacophony—one that, over time, carried overtones of widening international participation and deepening social sensibilities.

The painting can be a good place to start discussion in the classroom, if framed as an exercise in collective reflection on "what we think the artist is trying to convey or capture about the Enlightenment." Early on, you can expect a range of responses as students typically notice the wigs, stockings, canes, and formality. First-time viewers often draw attention to the elite clothing and ornate accouterments (gold buttons and silks, curtains, and lace), and the high proportion of space in the painting devoted to artwork, culture, and display—some picking out features of neoclassicism in the Georgic scenes and wreathed figures on the walls, seemingly harking back to simpler forms. Close inspection, and sometimes a bit of prompting, brings observations about the different levels of activity in the subjects: many figures are indulging in quiet asides and conversations, some are striking pensive or reflective poses, and the central character seated at the table (a famous Parisian actor named Lekain) gives a more animated performance as he reads the play. Good teachers try their hardest to mute themselves in this kind of open format, perhaps retreating to listing key features on a whiteboard, as respondents in class deliver the usual array of unanticipated interjections (sometimes about who is sleeping or flirting in the painting) that allows the students to drive the discussion. Someone will usually stress the racial uniformity and gender and age imbalances of the audience on display. All of this presents the chance to drive home how the gathering and the occasion of the salon was celebrated, looking back from 1812, and how important the idea of light was: the shimmering silk stockings, blanched wigs, white visages, and the shape of the sunlight coming in from the top left of the frame, drawing us to Madame Geoffrin herself (looking, as it were, to camera). Having exposed something of the false setup, a closing class vote on whether the students feel that the gathering is political, economic, intellectual, social, or cultural is often a good way of winding up the discussion and getting them to think through how these categories overlap.

Arguably the most famous odd couple of the Enlightenment were Voltaire and Rousseau, both depicted in the painting. Attention to their respective careers can provide a useful shorthand and point of entry for students considering *who* championed enlightened thinking.[10] For the greater part of their careers, they were at odds on almost every issue. It would take all the symbolic perversity of the later French revolutionaries to bury these two in facing graves in the Pantheon in Paris. François-Marie Arouet, more commonly known as Voltaire, was probably the quickest wit the Western world has ever spawned—a sparkling correspondent and conversationalist who published epic poems, plays, histories, pop-science books, and satires. He was anticlerical and against established religion to the point that, according to apocrypha, on his deathbed when his confessor asked him, "Do you reject Satan?," he replied, "This is hardly the time to make enemies." Yet for all his anti-establishment talk and public espousal of causes célèbres, Voltaire was quite comfortable in the age in which he lived. He may have defended the victims of miscarriages against obscurantist laws. Famously, he spoke out for the Chevalier de la Barre to counter the charge of blasphemy, defended Admiral Byng from the accusation of cowardice, and defended the Protestant cobbler Jean Calas from the fabricated allegation that he had murdered his son for converting to Catholicism.[11] Despite being a great irritant to the authorities, he was something of a conformist when it came to politics. It should not be forgotten that for part of his career, he was royal historiographer to the Bourbon court and was briefly a chamberlain to Frederick the Great. He admired strong progressive government and never advocated social equality.[12] He wallowed in the manners and refinement of the French aristocracy, which he aped at his country estate of Fernay, near the Swiss border.

Rousseau could not have been more different: slow in his reflections, tortured in his conscience, hypersensitive to criticism, paranoid, and generally very bad company.[13] He started life as a successful composer, who refused a court pension to preserve his artistic independence. His early life was characterized by his close friendship to Denis Diderot, the editor of the French *Encyclopédie*. Rousseau might well have spent the rest of his life as an obscure Swiss friend of a great intellectual, but he experienced literally a Damascene conversion. On the way home from visiting Diderot, who was imprisoned in the fortress of Vincennes for criticizing the government, he read a newspaper. Suddenly his blood ran cold and he felt dizzy with excitement, as if struck by divine inspiration.[14] What had struck his eye was an essay competition on the subject "has the resurgence of the arts and sciences helped to improve mores?" In sharp contrast to the socially polished and smooth Voltaire, Rousseau came to the conclusion that high society's refinement, manners, and culture were not only corrupt but, infinitely worse, corrupting. Man was not born "fallen and mired in original sin" as the Bible would have us believe. It was society, politics, and culture that introduced unhealthy ambitions, egotism, and evil into the hearts of human beings. Rousseau spent the rest of his life writing plays, novels, and most famously a treatise on education called *Emile* (which was probably the greatest publishing success of the century).

These two individuals show the great difficulty in seeking to define who participated in the Enlightenment and whether we can extrapolate a common agenda from their background and writings. The more thinkers one examines, the more tangled the nature of eighteenth-century thought becomes. Once upon a time, Marxist historians argued that the Enlightenment was the intellectual cloak that covered the growing economic power and ambitions of the bourgeoisie.[15] A middle class excluded from office and political influence (due to the meanness of their birth) created an intellectual movement that contested the aristocracy and nobility's right to rule. One of the most intriguing rearticulations of this position came from Princeton historian Robert Darnton.[16] Though not a Marxist himself, Darnton believed that social conflict was at the heart of how the Enlightenment's ideas were disseminated within wider society and ultimately contributed to the outbreak of the French Revolution in 1789. Using an approach called the social history of ideas and drawing heavily from the archives of printing houses, Darnton argued that the "high" Enlightenment was an elite movement. The subversives of the beginning of the century had been tamed by government patronage, pensions, and inducements. The radical philosophes of the 1740s had become the establishment of the 1780s. Many had neither the talent nor the influence to make it in this exclusive world. However, like writers today, the hacks, smut peddlers, and poor devils of the eighteenth century seemed unfazed by failure. They inhabited a demimonde that Darnton has called "Grub Street." Here these failed intellectuals rewrote the "high" Enlightenment into a more popular movement with a radicalized political agenda. Implicit in this model is the idea that the failures of the Enlightenment were the revolutionaries of the future.

Although this theory was presented elegantly and is deeply compelling in its insightfulness, it has not gone unchallenged.[17] It is certainly true that the high Enlightenment was anything but a middle-class phenomenon. As a social sphere, it was infested with the princes, dukes, and other grandees of the ancien régime. Darnton ignored that very many of the early revolutionaries of the 1790s were not the social and intellectual failures of the previous decade.[18] Many thinkers, aristocrats, legal professionals, bureaucrats, and clergy participated as enthusiastically in the French Revolution as they had in the enlightened debates earlier in the century.[19] Therefore, an attempt to identify the essence of the Enlightenment through select individuals or social groups must come with caveats. It was neither made up exclusively of like-minded individuals nor was it a straightforward expression of class interest.

Nonetheless, attempting to locate and narrow the social matrix that surrounded and intersected with the Enlightenment can often be the basis of a productive introductory classroom discussion. It is helpful to direct students toward considering how far the ideas and mental outlook of eighteenth-century writers and thinkers were constrained by their cultural, economic, and social backgrounds.

For example, Voltaire was certainly the great anticlerical celebrity of his age, advocating the destruction of what he saw as the vengeful and irrational God of the Bible. In 1727, François de Pâris, a Jansenist holy man, was buried in the Parisian cemetery of Saint Médard.[20] Over the next few years, pilgrimages to his tomb increased as reports of extraordinary cures and visions were followed by ecstatic convulsions. Such miracles captured the popular imagination, recruiting to the convulsionary movement Voltaire's brother Armand, who was a mystical Jansenist, or Catholic ascetic. The fact that two members of the same family could have such divergent world views is a useful way of reminding us to resist the temptation to treat the Enlightenment as a tight container that can be filled up with the intellectuals and progressive ideas of the Age of Revolutions. Intellectual life and society, then and now, have very wobbly boundaries, which constantly shift. Political, cultural, economic, and social changes may have an impact on such shifts but do not determine them. These processes are dynamic rather than linear. To put it more simply, intellectual thought both shapes and is shaped by society. Too many writing about the Enlightenment try, like Lemonnier did in 1812, to take a snapshot. They make eighteenth-century ideas and society seem static. Nothing could be further from the truth. Each individual, be they like Voltaire or Rousseau, brought something to the Enlightenment. Those who participated in the movement constantly influenced it while simultaneously being altered by it.

Teaching this is not easy, of course, especially in courses that are likely to have large numbers of students and unlikely to have the luxury of time to dwell on individuals. But it is worth making space for, not least because understanding this personal and intellectual dynamism offers a handy framework for students going on to consider the causes, cycles, and cross-influences among the revolutions the Enlightenment may have fomented. One activity that can work well to bring students to appreciate this spectrum of individuals and interests is to combine some independent research and group work with class reportage. The students (perhaps in groups of two to four) are invited to build a

Table 1. List of Enlightenment Figures

Radicals/Free Thinkers	Statesmen/Reformers	Public Intellectuals/ Men of Science
François-Marie Arouet (known as Voltaire)	Cesare Beccaria	Giambattista Vico
Jean-Jacques Rousseau	John Adams	Pietro Giannone
Denis Diderot	Thomas Jefferson	Immanuel Kant
Jean le Rond d'Alembert	Sebastião José de Carvalho e Melo, Marquis of Pombal	Adam Smith
Paul-Henri Thiry, Baron d'Holbach	Frederick II of Prussia	David Hume
Claude Adrien Helvétius	Joseph II Holy Roman Emperor	Benjamin Franklin
Moses Mendelssohn	Catherine II of Russia	Louis Antoine de Bougainville
Julien Offray de La Mettrie	Georges Buffon	Edward Gibbon
Gabriel Bonnot de Mably	Anne-Robert-Jacques Turgot	Charles-Louis de Secondat, Baron de La Brède et de Montesquieu
Baruch Spinoza	Pietro Verri	Étienne Bonnot de Condillac
John Locke	Gaspar Melchor de Jovellanos	Antoine Lavoisier

biographic understanding of a figure from the era and then explain this person's background and significance to the field to the rest of the class. Table 1 has a list of suggestions for people who work as good subjects for this exercise because their varied positions characterize some of the breadth and depth of ideas associated with the Enlightenment, and they collectively convey a sense of the effervescent intellectual prelude to the Age of Revolutions. Alternatively, a more project-oriented activity is to follow the encyclopedists and invite students to track some of the over 140 contributors who were instrumental in advancing this ground-breaking reference work (published from 1751), now available in translation from the University of Michigan. They can do so by either researching the backgrounds and contributions of the approximately three dozen main authors or by tackling the accessible "Preliminary Discourse" written by Jean le Rond d'Alembert in the 1751 as a kind of manifesto, or statement of the philosophy of shared knowledge.[21]

When Was the Enlightenment?

The Musée Carnavalet (museum of the history of Paris), is an exquisite "site of memory" when it comes to the Enlightenment and the French Revolution. The museum's talented curators have organized the permanent exhibition in such a way that the visitor progresses, almost inevitably, from the rooms displaying prize objects from the Enlightenment (the proudest exhibit being Voltaire's armchair) to those celebrating the French Revolution.[22] Most striking perhaps are the decimal calendars and clocks that were manufactured starting in 1793. The revolutionaries of the 1790s believed that to regenerate humanity and sever the umbilical cord with a corrupt past, a new sense of time was essential.[23] The rational number ten was chosen as the basis of a future that was to vanquish superstition and tradition. There would be twelve months, each of three ten-day weeks, and newly designed clocks would record the ten hours of the day (each hour had a hundred decimal minutes, each minute had a hundred decimal seconds). The claim made implicitly through the revolutionary calendar and time was that an enlightened age did not look back to tell the time but gazed forward toward the future.

At first the question "when was the Enlightenment?," may seem absurd. Surely, the answer must be simply "the eighteenth century." This is impossible to deny, but such a facile reply does not specify when this phenomenon began or reached its climax. It could be suggested, with some reason, that there are two ways of considering this issue. First, one can seek, like so many have in the past, the origins of this intellectual explosion. Alternatively, one could discuss how people in the eighteenth century conceived of their relationship with their history and past. The problem of finding start and end dates for historical phenomena (especially political or cultural movements) has always proved problematic. Many historical transformations were imperceptible to contemporaries, or so entangled with other changes that their origins are extremely opaque. This is why historians of philosophical thought have disagreed bitterly about the Enlightenment's periodization. For many decades, it was fashionable to see the Enlightenment as the heir to the scientific revolution of the seventeenth century. According to this narrative, the discoveries of Descartes, Newton, and Leibniz allowed for a seismic shift in mentalities. The belief that divine laws ordering the cosmos could be uncovered by human reason created a form of neoskepticism. Accordingly, these doubts about revealed truth were the midwife for the birth of the Enlightenment.

Following this classic historiographical school, Jonathan Israel has suggested that the work and followers of the Dutch Jewish philosopher Baruch Spinoza influenced the rise of the Enlightenment, especially its radical variety. The great turning point was 1670 when he published his intellectual masterpiece, the highly influential *Tractatus Theologico-Politicus*. As Israel puts it: "While Italian, Jewish, British and what might be termed French indigenous sources played a substantial part around the edges, the central thrust, the main bloc of radical ideas, stems predominantly from the Dutch radical milieu, the world of Spinoza and Spinozism."[24] Perhaps more surprising is Israel's claim that "By the 1750s all major intellectual innovations and accomplishments of the European Enlightenment were well advanced if not largely complete."[25] This highly controversial thesis only works if one bears in mind Israel's rather stiff definition of this movement: "undeniably the Radical Enlightenment was Republican, did reject divine-right monarchy, and did evince anti-aristocratic and democratic tendencies."[26] This stimulating argument has had its detractors, but has certainly reinjected welcome vitality into historiographic debates. Most important, it reminds us that the beginning and end of the Enlightenment is by no means clearly evident. Periodization depends, above all else, on how one defines the phenomenon under scrutiny.

A case in point can be found in the work of scholar John Robertson. Although sympathetic to Israel, he provides a wholly divergent answer to the vexed question of when the Enlightenment was. Unlike its radical variety, the "real" Enlightenment was not a political movement but a vast, trans-European abstract academic discussion about the improvement of humanity. According to Robertson, this immense dialogue focused on three principal lines of enquiry: human nature, political economy, and civilization. This has the implication that "The enlightenment [. . .] remains the movement, which began in the 1740s and ended in the 1790s. There is no need to go so far as to eliminate the use of the terms 'pre,' 'early' or even 'radical' enlightenment to distinguish the period between 1680 and 1740; but by no means do I accept Israel's view that the real business was over by the 1740s."[27] So two contemporary professors who worked in the same university for a time came up with opposite timeframes for when the Enlightenment blossomed! Such disagreements reflect the divisions and sheer variety of intellectual thinking during the eighteenth century. A well-known adage affirms: "what you find depends on what you are looking for." This is valid for much historical work, although good historians will allow the material "found" to alter their interpretations. Israel's starting point was to find a radical pedigree for the modern world. Convincingly, and not by accident, he found it in the Spinozism of late seventeenth-century Europe. In contrast, Robertson defined the Enlightenment in more stylistic and academic terms, which led him to the mid-eighteenth-century debates on political economy. The answer to "when was the Enlightenment?" that seemed so simple at first glance becomes immensely complex when one digs beneath the surface. How to define and circumscribe periods of the past is a fundamental issue. As teachers, we need to help students appreciate that this is not an entirely objective process and that there are important stakes involved. The starting date for the Enlightenment depends on which of the enlightenments one is seeking. One light way to do so is to invite students to think about "formative" periods or moments in their own lives or studies: "at what age was your first happy memory?" soon requires definitional attention to *happy*, and brings varied responses that can be bundled into different criteria such as family, place, taste, and so forth.

Even the literate men and women of the eighteenth century were unsure of how to situate their present in terms of history and the immediate past. Certainly Voltaire and the more radical encyclopedists rejected any inheritances from the credulous medieval era.[28] According to their vision of history, since the fall of Rome Europe had been corrupted by feudal despotism and theocracy. Bizarrely from our perspective, most statesmen and educated elites continued to believe that the population of the world had been in decline since the fifth century.[29] Humanity had not only been kicked out of the Garden of Eden but had also lost the learning and prosperity of late antiquity. As Robert Palmer put it, "classical Greece and Rome focused the student's imagination on a world very different from the world of Louis XV and Louis XVI. It showed him an alternative value system and formed a background for judgement of his own time."[30] While most men of learning who had passed through the eighteenth-century education retained a significant admiration for the classical past, this admiration became increasingly tempered. Some, like Montesquieu and Hume, actually believed that commerce had created a more economically vibrant world than the Romans had ever experienced.[31] The eighteenth century was the last round of one of the greatest intellectual controversies, unleashed during the Middles Ages: the epic battle between the moderns and the ancients. Traditional historiography has stressed that by the 1750s, the proponents of ancient knowledge were fighting and losing the battle against the advance of modern science.[32] Yet as revisionists have shown increasingly, the inspiration and value of antique examples was by no means exhausted.

Older interpretations of the Enlightenment stressed that discarding received historical truths was at the heart of its radicalism. Much research has challenged this simplistic vision that deemed the eighteenth-century mind to be antihistorical. The Enlightenment's scientific methods inspired many moderate and religious men to apply these new approaches to history writing. As John Pocock and David Sorkin have shown, historians, clergy, and religious reformers thought the past and the present could be reconciled, through reasoned debate, to produce a better future.[33] Enlightenment was not just about hard decimal science but also sought a truer understanding of religion, theology, and history. The progress of civilization could not be understood without reference to historical evolution and organic change. For many intellectuals and scholars at this time, the past was not mere jetsam but an object of intense study and reflection. Therefore, although many contemporaries did feel that they lived in an age of light (*lumières* or *lumi*), the later revolutionary caesura with history was by no means inevitable. Even eighteenth-century contemporaries did not have a neat answer to the question of when the Enlightenment was.

Where Was the Enlightenment?

German philosopher Jürgen Habermas has accustomed historians of the eighteenth century to imagine the Enlightenment as an idealized space,[34] in his words, a public sphere (Öffentlichkeit), where private individuals could meet publicly to discuss matters of common interest. As literacy and prosperity grew, so did the opportunities for the enlightened to engage in new forms of sociability away from the gaze of authority. The simple answer to "where was the Enlightenment?" would seem to be in the salons, coffee houses, lending libraries, theaters, and opera houses that sprung up like mushrooms throughout Europe— bustling sites that would drown out the stilted voices emanating from courts and aristocratic circles. Again, this is a deceptively simple answer, for it tells us little about what actually happened in these sites of intellectual sociability. Indeed, the picture becomes even messier when one tries to understand how the Enlightenment grappled with issues of global geography and ideal space.

John Adams, one of the US Founding Fathers, who traveled widely over the course of the American Revolution, had little doubt when it came to this question. In his *Dissertation on the Canon and Feudal Law* he argued that America, especially Massachusetts, was blessed with both providence and geographic distance. The first settlers who had crossed the vast Atlantic discovered a prelapsarian paradise. Unlike continental Europe, North America was uncontaminated by feudalism or popery. Most important for Adams, "The education of all ranks of people was made the care and expense of the public, in a manner that I believe has been unknown to any other people ancient or modern."[35] This had the highly beneficial effect that a "native of America who cannot read and write is as rare an appearance as a Jacobite or a Roman Catholic, that is, as rare as a comet or an earthquake."[36] This was a very pan-English response to overseas expansion. It emphasized the infinite virtues that flowed from the mere fact of being neither French nor Catholic. Concealed in this rhetoric was one of the Enlightenment's many paradoxes. This intellectual movement was global in outlook, but decidedly European in its cultural assumptions.

When reading older histories of the Enlightenment or Marc Fumaroli's *When the World Spoke French*, one could be forgiven for thinking that the answer to "where was the Enlightenment?" is Paris.[37] After all, most of the radical philosophes of the mid-eighteenth century filled the salons of the French capital and bombarded Europe with their books and pamphlets. Students would do well not to underestimate the importance of Paris as a hub for radical intellectual thought. Indeed, events in 1789 make the French capital as good a starting place as any when one searches for the birthplace of "enlightenment."

But overemphasis on the importance of one city can give rise to a distorted understanding of the bigger picture. Indeed, the view still persists that the French encyclopedists and their radical followers established hegemonic control over the Enlightenment. It may be true that many Europeans traveled to Paris to witness this powerful group at work. However, it is often overlooked how some of these foreign visitors heartily disagreed with their French hosts and would go on to foster very different visions or versions of Enlightenment. Thanks to the superb work of Franco Venturi, Roy Porter, and Mikuláš Teich, the

Franco-centrism of past studies has crumbled.[38] New national enlightenments, rich in personality, with their own distinct identity, have emerged. Students, all the more so if of mixed backgrounds, often warm to the challenge of locating these national inflections. Italian thinkers like Giannone, Vico, and Beccaria were at the cutting edge of historic, economic, and legal thought. The Scottish, with Ferguson and Smith, sought to reconcile ethics with economic behavior. As Joachim Whaley puts it: "the German protestant enlightenment was primarily a utilitarian reform movement, deeply committed to the traditional social order."[39] Essentially the Enlightenment, as it extended through the European mainland, became increasingly cacophonous. Although it may have maintained its overarching theme of human betterment, the means of achieving this aim were far from uniform. In Eastern Europe the "State," with its absolute monarchs, came to see itself as the paramount vehicle for humanitarian reform. Frederick the Great of Prussia, Catherine II of Russia, Gustav III of Sweden, Stanislaw August of Poland-Lithuania, and Joseph II of the Austrian Habsburg line (and Holy Roman Emperor) showed immense energy in not just seeking to advance the efficiency of the state's administrative apparatus but also to improve their subjects' lot.[40] In some respects Joseph II was more radical in his social reforms than some of the encyclopedists. His educational, sanitary, health, and religious reforms represented great strides forward in establishing the principle that the welfare of its subjects was a primary duty of the state. As Tim Blanning jokes, "If Joseph had been concerned only with the power of his state he would not have devoted so much time and trouble to its weaker members: not even he could have hoped to transform a deaf, dumb, blind, crippled, lunatic, illegitimate, unmarried mother into an effective fighting unit."[41]

Despite this, the Habsburg monarchy's elites, both intellectual and political, were not wholly appreciative of their radical sovereign. The state's attempts to make inroads into the daily lives of their subjects were resisted bitterly. A frustrated Joseph could only impotently exclaim: "you cannot stop me from doing good" as his empire descended into rebellion and came to the brink of disintegration in 1789. The Enlightenment as an abstract humanitarian project was omnipresent in Europe. Yet no matter how widespread this coverage, it failed to crystallize into a shared system of values, let alone a program for reform.

One useful way to expose these rolling inconsistencies is to encourage students to try to view European-ness from the outside. This reorientation, encouraged by globalization and accompanying scholarly trends,

had a strong basis in the eighteenth century, when there was an expo-
nential increase in trans-European and global encounters.[42] Europeans
came to realize that the world was a much more crowded place, and this
allowed revived forms of moral relativism to seep into the cultural fabric
of the time. The jurist/philosopher Montesquieu set the ball rolling, so
to speak, with his Persian letters in 1721. In this fictitious correspondence,
he eloquently depicted the puzzlement of two Persian travelers writing
home about the wonders, superstitions, and bizarreness of French political and social life. Letter twenty-four, probably the most famous, tells
how:

> The king [of France] is a great magician, for his dominion extends to
> the minds of his subjects; he makes them think what he wishes. If he
> has only a million crowns in his exchequer, and has need of two mil-
> lions, he has only to persuade them that one crown is worth two, and
> they believe it. If he has a costly war on hand, and is short of money, he
> simply suggests to his subjects that a piece of paper is coin of the realm,
> and they are straightway convinced of it. He has even succeeded in per-
> suading them that his touch is a sovereign cure for all sorts of diseases,
> so great is the power and influence he has over their minds.[43]

This created a huge phenomenon in which the innocent "fake"
foreigner or "noble" savage became a privileged commentator on European affairs. Montesquieu inaugurated a genre of satirical and critical
epistolary novels. His work was followed by letters from a Highlander
(1746), Peruvian woman (1747), Chinese (1766), the Ingénu (or travels
of Huron 1767), and an American farmer (1782) to name just a few. The
outsider, a figure of dread, became an insightful critic of European society. The cost of a short exercise in creative writing—asking students to
critique their own community or society (or sports team) in a paragraph,
as if through foreign eyes—can often open the power of this device to
the class. The growing authority of the "fake outsider" critically analyzing European society coincided with a new age for voyages of discovery.
Here Europeans were forced to examine cultures and societies whose
values were quite other to their own. In Voltaire's novella Candide, the
eponymous hero traveled far and wide, beholding great marvels around
the world. This caused him to wonder whether European morality was
superior to that of the indigenous peoples encountered. Anticlimacti-
cally, Candide gives up the quest for "truth" and retires home, where
he tends his own garden. The experience of traveling the world often led
philosophes back home, where they escaped such paradoxes through

deep introspection. Indeed, Bougainville's voyage to Tahiti captured the imagination of audiences—a natural island paradise had fostered a system of morality that was very different, especially in sexual terms, from the rigid and suffocating morality of established Christianity.[44] Perhaps one of the more amusing aspects of how the discovery of the globe captured the European world can be found in Carlo Goldoni's 1750 comedy (later transformed into an opera buffa by Salieri) titled "the world turned upside down."[45] In the antipodes a group of ship-wrecked Europeans land on an island where women rule the roost. They wage war, court men aggressively, and most bizarrely worship large pigeons—obviously the complete opposite of European society. Goldoni meant this play as a farce, screening how disordered society could become when gender relations entered a state of flux. Yet despite itself, it revealed some masculine malaise regarding male "natural preeminence" over femininity. Goldoni's and Voltaire's works lend themselves well to shortened or excerpted considerations, in largish groups, and both can be read aloud. They evince how exploration and cultural discovery unsettled many of the most deeply held convictions of European elites.

Perhaps most important, the Enlightenment's attempt to understand the world allowed it to begin to develop a critique of colonialism and imperialism. The abbé Raynal, with notable contributions by Diderot, wrote one of the most scathing histories of the noxious effects of European expansion overseas. In his multivolume *History of the Two Indies* (1770) he cataloged the misery, exploitation, slavery, and violence that European colonizers had unleashed on the world.[46] For Raynal, "a native of America" was a very different being to what Adams intended. European intellectuals found it extremely difficult to agree on whether the New World was a new Eden or a primitive Hobbesian hell. Perhaps most famously the comte de Buffon in his *Histoire Naturelle* speculated on whether organisms transplanted into the New World would degenerate and devolve.[47] This vision of the Americas as a corrupting climate was roundly countered by Thomas Jefferson, who strongly argued that the North American continent was more salubrious than the Old World, which the Creoles' ancestors had fled. The dark and exploitive side of colonialism was tackled gingerly in such debates. Europe's awakening to its planetary misdeeds culminated, very slowly and reluctantly, with the abolition of the Atlantic slave trade in the nineteenth century. However, the "opening up" did not herald a global equality between the peoples of the Earth.

Looking eastward, the theorist of comparative literature Edward Said famously described the West's attempts to study the other people of the globe as "Orientalism."[48] Knowledge (or better, received wisdom) of the culture, religion, and social organization of the East was not an object process but was a prepackaged argument for the West's supremacy. Put more simply, even the most sympathetic enlightened Europeans still felt that the East needed to benefit from the beneficent intervention of the morally and intellectual superior West. Said certainly takes things too far in his controversial book by stating that the Western "discourse" of the Orientalism was entirely fabricated a priori. Yet he is correct that Montesquieu, Rousseau, and Voltaire, for all their curiosity about the Gold Coast, Persia, and China, limited themselves to caricatures.[49] Their ideal type may have been noble, but he was still savage and in need of taming.

A case in point can be found in the final section of Montesquieu's Persian letters, which descend again to stereotyping.[50] After spending years in Europe, the two intrepid Persians start to feel dissatisfied with the world they left behind, even more so as news arrives that their seraglio (harem) is in disorder. Here visions of female subjugation (culminating in suicide) and the maliciousness of slave eunuchs epitomize what enlightened political commentators described with a flair for the dramatic as "oriental despotism." So while these letters do criticize French society in the early eighteenth century, the author simultaneously stakes out the moral supremacy of the European world with all its faults. The problem for the author was that these flaws, and increasing loss of freedom under its monarchy, brought France closer to the despotism of the East with which these imagined travelers were only too familiar. Within the attempt to understand the other's perspective, there is still an intense sense of cultural supremacy. While viewing the globe, Europeans found it difficult to transcend their context. The Enlightenment may have opened many windows into the outside world, providing views that allowed for colonial self-critique, but the front door remained firmly shut.

Conclusion

Anybody who studies the Enlightenment will undoubtedly feel bewilderment before the immensity of the intellectual ferment and confusion to which it gave rise. An identical sense of disorientation will be experienced when one confronts the large body of historiographical material that has locked horns (with differing degrees of success) with this phenomenon. The eponymous hero of *Candide* expresses well the frustration that all students feel at the twilight of their education. At the end of his travels and misadventures, the hero settles down with his friends simply to cultivate his garden. Although Voltaire's pessimistic view of the world and mockery of optimism may be things teachers should discourage, the novella's rejection of intellectual laziness should be the battle cry of educators. The best way of engaging with the Enlightenment for teachers and students is to start with simple questions and make inroads into its complexities gradually. Some will not like this advice to dive in deeper and come out muddier. Indeed, it goes against the spirit of our age, which demands that education be similar to fast food—that is, easily digested and excreted. To bow to this demand is to do a disservice not just to students but to ourselves. As Dorothy Sayers in the 1940s warned with her cutting and prescient eloquence:

> For we let our young men and women go out unarmed, in a day when armor was never so necessary. By teaching them all to read, we have left them at the mercy of the printed word. By the invention of the film and the radio, we have made certain that no aversion to reading shall secure them from the incessant battery of words, words, words. They do not know what the words mean; they do not know how to ward them off or blunt their edge or fling them back; they are a prey to words in their emotions instead of being the masters of them in their intellects.[51]

By presenting the Enlightenment as a triumphant heritage that makes our present the "best of all possible worlds" is to distort the richness of eighteenth-century thought. We create slaves for new, subtler forms of despotism, rather than nurturing the philosophes of tomorrow. I do not know if there is a perfect way to teach the Enlightenment; indeed, I'm not even sure that there is an Enlightenment to teach. Like Candide, I hope modestly that from these simple interrogations spring more interesting reflections that help us penetrate deeper into eighteenth-century thinking and hopefully better understand some of the inner workings of the historical discipline.

NOTES

1. "Limites quos posuere Veteres non moveto," in Ulrich Im Hof, *Enlightenment* (London: Wiley-Blackwell, 1997), 206.

2. I. Kant, "Beantwortung der Frage: Was ist Aufklärung?" in *Berlinischer Monatsschrift* 12 (1784): 481–94.

3. Quoted in T. C. W. Blanning, *Reform and Revolution in Mainz 1743–1803* (London: Cambridge University Press, 1974), 2.

4. Peter Gay, *The Enlightenment*, 2 vols. (New York: Knopf, 1967), 2:27.

5. Jonathan Israel has published four monumental volumes claiming that the Enlightenment is at the heart of the most progressive ideas in Western society. The first three volumes were all published by Oxford University Press: *Radical Enlightenment* (2001), *Enlightenment Contested* (2006), and *Democratic Enlightenment* (2011). The final volume appears as *Revolutionary Ideas: An Intellectual History of the French Revolution from "The Rights of Man" to Robespierre* (Princeton, NJ: Princeton University Press, 2014).

6. See *H-France Forum* 9, no. 1, http://www.h-france.net/forum/h-france forumvol9.html (accessed January 12, 2015).

7. Christine Le Bozec, *Lemonnier, un Peintre en Révolution* (Rouen: Publications de l'Université de Rouen, 2000).

8. For an enlarged version with commentary in French, see Pierre-Yves Beaurepaire, "Les Salons au XVIIIe Siècle," at http://www.histoire-image.org /pleincadre/index.php?i=1258.

9. See Philipp Blom, *Wicked Company: Freethinkers and Friendship in Pre-Revolutionary Paris* (London: Weidenfeld & Nicholson, 2012).

10. The classic biography for Voltaire is Theodore Besterman, *Voltaire* (New York: Harcourt, Brace & World, 1969); and Peter Gay, *Voltaire's Politics: The Poet as Realist* (Princeton, NJ: Princeton University Press, 1959). For Rousseau, see Robert Wokler, *Rousseau: A Very Short Introduction* (Oxford: Oxford University Press, 2001); or Maurice Cranston's monumental three-volume biography, *Jean-Jacques: The Early Life and Work of Jean-Jacques Rousseau, 1712–1754* (New York: Norton, 1983); *The Noble Savage: Jean-Jacques Rousseau, 1754–1762* (Chicago: Chicago University Press, 1991); and *The Solitary Self: Jean-Jacques Rousseau in Exile and Adversity* (Chicago: Chicago University Press, 1997).

11. David Bien, *The Calas Affair: Persecution, Heresy and Toleration in Eighteenth Century Toulouse* (Princeton, NJ: Princeton University Press, 1960).

12. David William, ed., *Voltaire: Political Writings* (Cambridge: Cambridge University Press, 1994).

13. Robert Zaretsky and John Scott, *Philosophers' Quarrel: Rousseau, Hume, and the Limits of Human Understanding* (New Haven, CT: Yale University Press, 2010).

14. T. C. W. Blanning, *The Romantic Revolution* (New York: Random House, 2011), 11–21.

15. Albert Soboul, Guy Lemarchand, and Michèle Fogel, *Le Siècle des Lumières*, 2 vols. (Paris: Presses universitaires de France, 1977).

16. Robert Darnton, *The Literary Underground of the Old Regime* (Cambridge,

MA: Harvard University Press, 1985), and "The High Enlightenment and the Low-Life of Literature in Pre-Revolutionary France," *Past & Present* 51 (1971): 81–115.

17. Haydn Mason, ed., *The Darnton Debate: Books and Revolution in the Eighteenth Century* (Oxford: Voltaire Foundation, 1998).

18. Robert Darnton, "The Literary Revolution of 1789," *Studies in Eighteenth Century Culture* 21, no. 1 (1992): 3–26.

19. See Daniel Wick, *Conspiracy of Well Intentioned Men: The Society of Thirty and the French Revolution* (New York: Garland, 1987).

20. Dale van Kley, *The Religious Origins of the French Revolution: From Calvin to the Civil Constitution, 1560–1791* (New Haven, CT: Yale University Press, 1996), 89–100.

21. The two relevant sites are: The Encyclopedia of Diderot and d'Alembert, Collaborative Translation Project website, University of Michigan, http://quod.lib.umich.edu/d/did/ (accessed May 30, 2016); ARTFL Encyclopédie Project (containing list of contributors identified by Jacque Proust), ed. Robert Morrissey, University of Chicago, http://encyclopedie.uchicago.edu/node/141 (accessed May 30, 2016).

22. Musée Carnavalet website, http://www.carnavalet.paris.fr/ (accessed January 12, 2015).

23. Matthew Shaw, *Time and the French Revolution: The Republican Calendar, 1789-Year XIV* (London: Royal Historical Society, 2011); Sanja Perovic, *The Calendar in Revolutionary France: Perceptions of Time in Literature, Culture, Politics* (Cambridge: Cambridge University Press, 2012).

24. Israel, *Radical Enlightenment*, 694.

25. Ibid., 20.

26. Ibid., 21.

27. John Robertson, *The Case for Enlightenment: Scotland and Naples 1680–1760* (Cambridge: Cambridge University Press, 2005), 8, 31.

28. Hugh Trevor Roper, *History and the Enlightenment* (New Haven, CT: Yale University Press, 2010).

29. T. C. W. Blanning, *The Pursuit of Glory: Europe 1648–1815* (New York: Penguin, 2008), 40–92.

30. Robert Palmer, *The Improvement of Humanity* (Princeton, NJ: Princeton University Press, 1985), 19.

31. Istvan Hont, *Jealousy of Trade: International Competition and the Nation-State in Historical Perspective* (Cambridge, MA: Belknap Press of Harvard University Press, 2005), 1–39.

32. Joan Dejean, *Ancients against Moderns: Culture Wars and the Making of a Fin de Siecle* (Chicago: University of Chicago Press, 1997).

33. David Sorkin, *The Religious Enlightenment: Protestants, Jews, and Catholics from London to Vienna* (Princeton, NJ: Princeton University Press, 2008); J. G. A.

Pocock, *Barbarism and Religion*, 5 vols. (Cambridge: Cambridge University Press, 2001–11).

34. Jürgen Habermas, *The Structural Transformation of the Public Sphere* (Cambridge: Polity Press, 1992), 1–56; T. C. W. Blanning, *The Culture of Power and the Power of Culture, Old Regime Europe 1660–1789* (Oxford: Oxford University Press, 2002); James Van Horn Melton, *The Rise of the Public in Enlightenment Europe* (Cambridge: Cambridge University Press, 2001).

35. John Adams, "Dissertation on the Canon and Feudal Law," http://teachingamericanhistory.org/library/document/a-dissertation-on-the-canon-and-feudal-law/ (accessed January 12, 2015).

36. Ibid.

37. Marc Fumaroli, *When The World Spoke French* (New York: New York Review Books, 2011).

38. Franco Venturi, *The End of the Old Regime in Europe*, 3 vols. (Princeton, NJ: Princeton University Press, 1989–91); Roy Porter and Mikuláš Teich, eds., *Enlightenment in the National Context* (Cambridge: Cambridge University Press, 1981).

39. Joachim Whaley, "The Protestant Enlightenment in Germany," in *Enlightenment in National Context*, ed. Porter and Teich, 106–17 (117).

40. H. M. Scott, ed., *Enlightened Absolutism: Reform and Reformers in Later Eighteenth-Century Europe* (Ann Arbor: University of Michigan Press, 1990).

41. T. C. W. Blanning, *Joseph II* (London: Longman, 1970), 84.

42. David Armitage and Sanjay Subrahmanyam, eds., *The Age of Revolutions in Global Context, c. 1760–1840* (Basingstoke: Palgrave Macmillan, 2009); David Livingstone, ed., *Geography and Enlightenment* (Chicago: University of Chicago Press, 1999).

43. Charles-Louis de Secondat Baron de de Montesquieu, *Lettres Persanes*, https://archive.org/details/persianletters00montuoft (accessed January 12, 2015).

44. Sankar Muthu, *Enlightenment against Empire* (Princeton, NJ: Princeton University Press, 2003), 11–71.

45. Carlo Goldoni, *Il Mondo alla Roversa, ovvero le donne che comandano* (Amsterdam, 1754).

46. Muthu, *Enlightenment against Empire*, 72–121.

47. James W. Ceaser, *Reconstructing America: The Symbol of America in Modern Thought* (New Haven, CT: Yale University Press, 1997), esp. chaps. 1–3.

48. Edward Said, *Orientalism* (London: Routledge, 1978).

49. George Sebastian Rousseau and Roy Porter, eds., *Exoticism in the Enlightenment* (Manchester: Manchester University Press, 1990).

50. Lisa Lowe, "Rereadings in Orientalism: Oriental Inventions and Inventions of the Orient in Montesquieu's 'Lettres persanes,'" *Cultural Critique* 15 (1990): 115–43.

51. Dorothy Sayers, "The Lost Tools of Learning," http://www.gbt.org /text/sayers.html (accessed January 12, 2015).

KEY RESOURCES

Darnton, Robert. "The High Enlightenment and the Low-Life of Literature in Pre-Revolutionary France." *Past & Present* 51 (1971): 81–115.

Gay, Peter. *The Enlightenment*, 2 vols. New York: Knopf, 1967.

———. *Voltaire's Politics: The Poet as Realist*. Princeton, NJ: Princeton University Press, 1959.

Israel, Jonathan. *Radical Enlightenment*. Oxford: Oxford University Press, 2001.

Livingstone, David, ed. *Geography and Enlightenment*. Chicago: University of Chicago Press, 1999.

Melton, James Van Horn. *The Rise of the Public in Enlightenment Europe*. Cambridge: Cambridge University Press, 2001.

Muthu, Sankar. *Enlightenment against Empire*. Princeton, NJ: Princeton University Press, 2003.

Porter, Roy, and Mikuláš Teich, eds. *Enlightenment in the National Context*. Cambridge: Cambridge University Press, 1981.

Robertson, John. *The Case for Enlightenment: Scotland and Naples 1680–1760*. Cambridge: Cambridge University Press, 2005.

Sorkin, David. *The Religious Enlightenment: Protestants, Jews, and Catholics from London to Vienna*. Princeton, NJ: Princeton University Press, 2008.

Trevor-Roper, Hugh. *History and the Enlightenment*. New Haven, CT: Yale University Press, 2010.

Wokler, Robert. *Rousseau: A Very Short Introduction*. Oxford: Oxford University Press, 2001.

The Haitian Declaration of Independence in the Age of Revolutions

Universal Rights, the Local, and the Global

JULIA GAFFIELD

In recent years, scholars have reframed and reinterpreted the Age of Revolutions by emphasizing the importance of the Haitian Revolution. Previously left at the margins or forgotten altogether in survey textbooks that highlighted the American and French Revolutions, the world's only successful slave revolution is now championed for conceptualizing and realizing the ideals of equality and freedom in unprecedented ways. Although such ideals were eloquently expressed in the United States and France, they were rarely imagined as extending to slaves, women, or native peoples and were certainly never implemented in a universal way. In the new portrayal of the Age of Revolutions, Haiti has become the place where the bonds of slavery were broken and racial hierarchy was overturned for the first time, making its Declaration of Independence a particularly illuminating source for students.

In repositioning the Haitian Revolution as a distinct and significant counterpart to the American and French revolutions, scholars are coming to grips with the complex and contradictory implications of the successful slave revolution that culminated in the Declaration of Independence proclaimed by Governor-General Jean-Jacques Dessalines on January 1, 1804. We now know that this declaration concluded the

Haitian Revolution, but this result was certainly not clear at the time. This fact may help explain why the only extant official copies of the Haitian Declaration of Independence are two printed documents, published by the government printing press in Port-au-Prince. One document is an eight-page pamphlet and the other is a single-page, broadside printing. Both can be found in the National Archives of the United Kingdom, where they are cataloged with the Jamaican colonial and admiralty records.[1] According to a British official at the time, at least one of the documents was printed in the third week of January 1804. No original manuscript copy signed by the founding fathers remains today.

Analyzing the Haitian Declaration of Independence, for so long dwarfed by the better known declarations in North America (1776) and South America (1810–1822), helps students understand several important features of the Age of Revolutions. To make sense of the declaration and its significance, it is necessary to grasp the unique circumstances that inspired the move toward independence, understand Haiti's regional connections within the Caribbean and Atlantic worlds, and appreciate the contested aftermath of the declaration. On one hand, the document relied on imitation and inspiration. On the other hand, Haitian leaders were aware that their situation required a significantly different document from that of the United States. Together, these elements of similarity and difference emphasize the significance of the Haitian experience as a counterpart to the American and French revolutions—and comparing their founding documents is a particularly lively teaching exercise. These similarities and differences reveal Haiti's self-liberation as a generative force in its own right—a force whose ongoing impact critically influenced interpretations of the radical reach and the pragmatic limits of revolutionary ideals in the early nineteenth-century Atlantic world.

The Haitian Revolution

The Haitian Declaration of Independence concluded a long and brutal revolution that involved international and interracial armies composed of both free and enslaved soldiers. The leaders of the revolution issued the Declaration of Independence to preserve the gains they had achieved: freedom and sovereignty. For students, understanding the complexities of the Haitian Revolution and the diverse people who participated is crucial for an analysis of the inspiration for and the implications of the Haitian Declaration of Independence. In the classroom, it is easy to get bogged down in the details of the chronology of events, and in doing so overlook the central themes. It is important to emphasize to students that the Haitian Revolution was not simply a slave rebellion on a large scale. Drawing on David Geggus's work, I find it useful to organize the narrative of the revolution into three tripartite groupings: first, the political goals of the revolution: freedom, equality, and liberty; second, legal-racial groupings: slaves, free people of color, and whites; and finally, international warfare between France, Great Britain, and Spain.[2] The three legal-racial groups sought to secure their own version of freedom, equality, and liberty and the European empires fought to control the Atlantic world's most wealth-producing colony.

The revolution began in 1789 with local rebellions by free people of color who were responding to the French Revolution and demanding equal rights as free citizens. Many historians periodize the Haitian Revolution beginning in 1791, but the resistance (sometimes violent) of the free people of color had a much broader impact for their own legal status and for the actions of the enslaved population. In 1791 enslaved people in the northern plains of Saint-Domingue coordinated a massive uprising and set the sugarcane fields ablaze, destroying the richest area of the colony. The rebels did not articulate their specific goals on paper, but very quickly a division developed between the revolutionary leadership and the population of enslaved people. The leaders sought to secure privileged positions for themselves in a reimagined colonial hierarchy that involved military discipline and plantation labor. The majority of enslaved laborers sought to develop peasant farms on family-owned land.[3] The British and Spanish took advantage of the internal turmoil in Saint-Domingue to try to secure possession of the colony; the Spanish invaded the northeast via Santo Domingo (modern-day Dominican Republic) and the British invaded the south and west via Jamaica. The international conflict helped the rebels secure additional benefits, and they forced the French commissioners to abolish slavery in the colony in 1793. The following year, the French National Convention ratified this decision and expanded its application to the entire French Empire. In the colony, a former slave and slave owner, Toussaint Louverture (fleshed out in more depth by Christopher Hodson in this volume), soon secured control over the colony as the French-appointed governor-general. He invited white plantation owners who had fled the colony to return to their properties and forced former slaves to return to the plantations under the new title of *cultivateurs* (cultivators). Plantation owners were prohibited from whipping as a form of punishment against their laborers, and they were supposed to pay employees a small wage or a share of the crop. Although he implemented these policies with the hope that he could increase colonial production to renew economic productivity, many of the formerly enslaved people criticized them for being far too similar to slavery. Louverture was not the only leader to try to force former slaves back on the plantation, but these policies were only partially successful. For the most part, former slaves refused to return to the sugar plantations, and coffee and cotton became Haiti's primary exports.

In 1801, Louverture issued a colonial constitution that maintained an allegiance to France but also established an autonomous government. Napoléon Bonaparte, newly established as first consul in France, rejected this challenge to his authority and sent forces to disarm Louverture's army and reestablish metropolitan control over the colony. In 1802 a massive army arrived in Saint-Domingue, under the direction of Bonaparte's brother-in-law, Victor Emmanuel Leclerc. The army tricked and captured Louverture and then deported him to France. He died in prison in the Jura Mountains in 1803. The war between Leclerc's forces and the rebel army, then under the leadership of Jean-Jacques Dessalines, was extremely violent. Both sides aimed to completely eradicate the other army. At this point the revolution became a war for independence. Rumors began to spread that Bonaparte aimed to reinstitute slavery in the colony, and Dessalines and his leading generals became convinced that freedom could not be protected under French rule. By the middle of 1803, it was clear that Dessalines's forces were headed toward victory, and he began preparing for independence. He contacted government officials elsewhere in the Caribbean and the United States to notify them of the inevitable move for independence.[4] At the end of November, the French troops evacuated the island but did not concede defeat in the war. They continued to claim ownership of the island until 1825. Between 1804 and 1825, therefore, both the Haitian government and the French government claimed sovereignty over the territory. The Haitian government felt the constant threat of a French reinvasion and the military became a central feature of the state. Warfare never resumed, but until the French recognized Haitian independence in 1825, it was not clear that the revolution was over.

La Liberté ou La Mort (stamp, unidentified 1793–94, Paris). (No. 4821 from Carl de Vinck collection, http://gallica.bnf.fr/ark:/12148/btv1b6948658q; Bibliothèque nationale de France)

Once students have the grounding in the historical events, they can turn to the Haitian Declaration of Independence with an understanding of the context and the motives behind its creation. The signature rallying points of the Saint-Domingue revolutionaries drew on those framed in North America, which students can almost always invoke—a helpful way of shifting the focus to the documents themselves. In 1775, American revolutionary (and wealthy slaveholder) Patrick Henry demanded, "give me liberty, or give me death!" French revolutionaries immediately adopted and adapted the phrase and championed "la liberté ou la mort."[5] The phrase grew in popularity during the Terror, and the meaning transitioned to a threat: give me liberty or I will kill you.[6] The revolutionaries in Saint-Domingue similarly adopted variations on the phrase, and during the war for Haitian independence (1802–1803) Dessalines made the rallying cry "liberté ou la mort" (liberty or death) the official slogan of the Armée Indigène.[7] Their use of the phrase could both be read as a willingness to die for the cause of liberty or as a

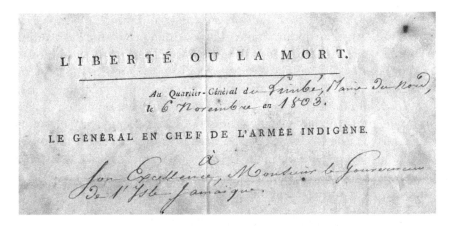

Detail from Jean-Jacques Dessalines to George Nugent, November 6, 1803. (National Library of Jamaica, MS 72 851n; courtesy of National Library of Jamaica)

willingness to kill for the cause. Such continuities illustrate the extent to which the same revolutionary context that produced the American Declaration of Independence also produced the Haitian and later Latin American "acts" of independence.

The founding document of the United States was the first ever declaration of independence and thus served as a precedent for the later initiatives. Indeed, the American Declaration of Independence began a new genre of political writing.[8] "No document in world history before 1776," David Armitage argues, "had made such an announcement of statehood in the language of independence."[9] The document itself does not use the phrase "declaration of independence" or "independence," but Armitage tells us, "for months before July 1776 . . . contemporaries had been speaking of the need for 'an independency,' a 'declaration of independency,' or a 'declaration of independence.'"[10] By 1804, therefore, the phrase would have been incorporated into the vocabulary of the revolutionary Atlantic. Although the content of the Haitian document was different, its publication helped establish the new genre of postcolonial political writing by announcing, like its American predecessor, the independence and sovereignty of a former colony and the people who lived there. This genre centered on a "distinctive assertion of statehood as independence."[11] Two other declarations of independence had been issued after the American one: Vermont's Declaration of Independence in 1777 from the United States and the Manifeste de la

Province de Flandres in 1790 from the Austrian Empire. On the other hand, the American declaration was not written in isolation: as Pauline Maier has demonstrated, many local resolutions bolstered the authority of the Second Continental Congress and provided some of the impetus behind the Declaration of Independence.[12] So if, on one hand, neither the Vermont nor the Belgian declarations created lasting nation-states, they may provide students with examples of the textured way such texts varied according to context across time and the space. On the other hand, the local resolutions in the US colonies, explored by Maier, allow students to see how the American declaration—its language and its support—was buttressed at the grass roots.

The Haitian Declaration

On January 1, 1804, Dessalines assembled his leading generals in the city of Gonaïves. He instructed his secretaries to compose a formal Declaration of Independence.[13] One of the first problems of which students should be aware is that the question of authorship has been a contentious issue with respect to the Haitian declaration. Dessalines did not receive any formal education and he was illiterate, although he could sign his name. Most foreign observers criticized him for being emotional and extremely violent; scholars almost never portray him as a skilled diplomat or a savvy national leader. Nevertheless, it is obvious that Dessalines contributed to the creation of this document and that his authorial voice is clear in all of the proclamations associated with him.[14] Dessalines first tasked his secretary Charéron to write the "acts" that would declare the island independent from France. According to nineteenth-century Haitian historian Beaubrun Ardouin, Charéron composed a document modeled on the American declaration. The text of this first draft no longer exists, but Ardouin claims that it affirmed the rights of "le race noire" (the black race) and articulated the complaints of the population against France.[15] According to Aroudin, Dessalines decided that this document "lacked heat and energy."[16]

Dessalines then instructed his secretary Louis-Félix Boisrond-Tonnerre to rewrite the declaration after hearing Boisrond-Tonnerre state that to write the document someone would need, "the skin of a white to serve as the parchment, his skull for the inkstand, his blood for the ink, and a bayonet for the pen."[17] Although Ardouin did not condone the vengeful sentiments expressed by Boisrond-Tonnerre, he admitted that to understand these emotions, one had to think about the context in which the document was produced—a point on which students should reflect.

When making comparisons with other declarations, students might also ask about the format of the document. The document that we have come to know as the Acte de l'Indépendance or the Declaration of Independence is composed of three parts printed as an eight-page pamphlet and as a single-sheet broadside.[18] The first part, headed "Armée Indigène," recorded the oath sworn and signed by Dessalines and his generals to renounce France forever and die rather than live under its dominion. The second, the longest and most often reproduced section, makes up the proclamation signed by Dessalines and addressed to the people of "Hayti." It explains why they should break their connections with France and concludes with an oath "to live free and independent"; this section is the one closest in substance (if not in form) to other declarations of independence before and after 1804. The third section records another oath by which the generals of the Haitian army affirmed Dessalines as governor-general-for-life, with sovereign powers to make peace, war, and name his successor. The words *indépendance* and *indépendant* appear eleven times in the document, which is dated January 1, 1804 (a new year's day and a traditional holiday on slave plantations), as the first day of Haitian independence (*l'indépendance d'Hayti*). Nowhere does the term *declaration* or its synonyms appear.

The designation as a "declaration" first came from the English-speaking world. When Edward Corbet, a British agent sent to Haiti in early 1804, gave the first copy of the document to the governor of Jamaica in January 1804, he called it "their declaration of independence."[19] This should not be surprising because the American declaration was already familiar. In French documents, it was more often called a *proclamation* or *acte* of independence rather than a declaration, indicating the distinct genres within Anglophone and Francophone legal and political culture. When Haitian foreign minister Jean-Baptiste Symphore Linstant de Pradine collected Haiti's laws in 1851, he began with the "Acte de l'Indépendance" of 1804, the first year of Haiti's independent, postrevolutionary history.[20]

The language of the declaration also offers an opportunity for rewarding analysis for students. One of the first things readers invited to compare the two texts will notice is that most of the Haitian Declaration was written in Dessalines's voice as a proclamation from him personally to the people of Haiti as well as to foreign audiences around the world. In contrast, the American declaration was a group composition that referenced "us" and "our" within an overall claim to be in the name of "our people." Whereas the American document appears to include the population at large, it excludes women, slaves, and natives—it even explicitly bars "the merciless Indian Savages." Also immediately apparent is that in declaring independence, both the Haitian and American governments sought to re-create the country's identity to initiate the nation-building process: both documents renamed the territory over which they were claiming sovereignty. The American declaration was the first to use "the United States of America."[21] In contrast, "Hayti" had been used by the native Taíno before the arrival of Christopher Columbus in 1492, and even in the eighteenth century, the name "Hayti" could be seen on maps. The spelling "Hayti" was used most often in the first decades after 1804, but "Haïti" was also used infrequently. "Hayti" continued to be the official spelling into the mid-nineteenth century when "Haïti" was then adopted. The reason for the transition is unclear.

Why the revolutionary leaders in Saint-Domingue chose the name "Hayti" is not clear, but this was not the only example of native inspiration by these generals. Dessalines's army, for example, was called the Armée Indigène, or Indigenous Army. The army had previously been known as the "Sons of the Inca."[22] In choosing this name, Dessalines and his generals erased the memory of French colonialism and returned to a time of independent rule. The declaration argued that the impact of French colonialism was still too visible on the island. "Everything recalls the memory of the cruelties of those barbarous people," Dessalines argued, "our laws, our manners, our towns, everything still carries the imprint of the French." Renaming the island was one way to erase that memory. He also argued that the job was not over: "the French name still haunts our island."

Revolutionary Goals

The explicit objectives and targets of both revolutionary texts are instructive because "independence" and "freedom" were the goals and justification for the declarations of the United States and Haiti. Students can explore the meanings of these terms with reference to their contexts. Freedom meant freedom from slavery, but for those in the thirteen colonies, freedom was limited to the metaphorical enslavement of colonialism. In the mainland colonies, the primary goal was to end the alleged tyranny of the British Crown. "A Prince whose character is thus marked by every act which may define a Tyrant," the American declaration argued, "is unfit to be the ruler of a free people." "The primary purpose of the American Declaration," David Armitage argues, "like that of most declarations of independence that have been issued since 1776, was to express the international legal sovereignty of the United States."[23]

This language of freedom and independence derived from widely circulated texts of eighteenth-century natural law, most notably the Swiss jurist Emer de Vattel's hugely popular compendium *Le Droit des Gens* (1758). Vattel wrote of the natural condition of humans in the state of nature as "free and independent" (*libre et indépendant*), words that rapidly became integrated into legal and diplomatic vocabularies to describe peoples and states.[24] Vattel's work may have been in the hands of Dessalines's secretaries but his language had long since broken away from its immediate source, as in the refrain of the "Hymne Haytiène" (1803): "Vivons, mourons, ses vrais Enfans, / Libres, indépendans" (Let us live, let us die, his true children / Free, independent).[25] In natural jurisprudence, the connection between individual freedom and collective independence was metaphorical: humans and states were both persons, sharing similar characteristics of autonomy and vulnerability to extinction or unfreedom. In the rhetoric of the Haitian Revolution, the analogy was far more than metaphorical. If the people of Haiti lost their independence, it would mean more than a return to collective subordination within an empire: it could mean their legal reenslavement. While slavery had been abolished in the colony in 1793 and in the French Empire in 1794, this freedom, the Haitians argued, was not secure under French colonialism. French armies arrived in the Caribbean in 1802 to reassert metropolitan control over the colonies, and rumors quickly began to spread that their plan was to reinstitute slavery. Fear in Saint-Domingue magnified when news arrived that slavery had been reinstituted in Guadeloupe and French Guiana.[26] "Swear then to live free and independent" (*vivre libre et indépendant*) "and to prefer death to everything that would lead to replace you under the yoke," urged Dessalines.

Students will observe that the process of targeting guilty parties according to each declaration of independence also produced different goals and justifications. In the case of the United States, the British king was personally responsible for the alleged unlawful impositions on American colonial life. The list of grievances was addressed to the king himself. "Whenever any Form of Government becomes destructive of these ends," they argued, "it is the Right of the People to alter or to abolish it, and to institute new Government." In the early 1790s, white plantation owners in Saint-Domingue similarly—in a comparison that will provide fodder for student thought—argued for greater colonial sovereignty as a way to preserve their slave society because they felt threatened by the egalitarian rhetoric of the French Revolution. "Freedom," in the Haitian Revolution, therefore, had diverse meanings for various participants who sought to advance their own goals.

In contrast to the American, the Haitian declaration held all "Frenchmen" responsible. No French citizen was welcome in Haiti, nor would they ever be. The distinction, of course, makes sense. The Americans targeted government structures and felt enslaved by state economic policies. Haitians, however, felt personally threatened, and each French citizen had the ability to become a slave master. They had experienced their enslavement in a personal and very violent way. The response, as one should expect, matched that violence. These contrasts encourage the students to ground the two declarations in the different contexts and experiences in which they were produced.

Dessalines justified Haiti's independence by focusing on the incompatibility of the two populations. "What do we have in common with these executioners?," he asked. "Their cruelty compared to our patient moderation; their color with ours, the vast expanse of the seas that separate us, our avenging climate, all tell us that they are not our brothers, that they will never be, and that if they find asylum among us, they will again be the instigators of our troubles and our divisions." Dessalines tried to initiate an endless war; he could see no resolution to the conflict between the two countries. In contrast, the American declaration referenced their "British brethren" and specifically targeted the administration. The Americans valued "the ties of our common kindred," and sought to establish normal diplomatic relations with the British Empire; to "hold them, as we hold the rest of mankind, Enemies in War, in Peace Friends."

Students might consider the timing of each document, which also affected its content. The American Declaration was composed and published before most of the war for independence and therefore preceded the bulk of the bloodshed. In contrast, the Haitian Declaration came immediately after the most violent and brutal years of the Haitian Revolution. The memory of the quasi-genocidal policies of the French during the 1802–1803 war for independence shaped the Haitian declaration and the future policies of the Haitian government. The declaration was a call to arms and initiated a series of massacres, ordered by Dessalines, during the first months of 1804.[27] The Haitian army systematically killed white French men, women, and children. Dessalines made a few exceptions, and these people were permitted to join the Haitian nation; this was made official in his 1805 constitution. White citizens of other nations were protected from this violence, but it terrified them nonetheless.[28]

Government and International Profile

Thinking about the suggested framework of governance and sovereignty is another way to encourage students to locate points of similarity and difference across the declarations. In the Haitian Declaration of Independence, Dessalines addressed the "citizens" of Haiti. Thereafter these citizens became passive participants in the new nation. In fact, the continued threat of a French reinvasion led Dessalines to establish a military dictatorship. The eternal war against France required a large army and the war materials to supply that army. To secure these supplies, Dessalines, like Louverture before him, concluded that they had to maintain a strong export economy. To do this, he tried to force former plantation slaves, or cultivateurs, to return to the plantations. He was largely unsuccessful in reviving the sugar economy but Haiti continued to export coffee and other crops throughout the nineteenth century.[29] The Haitian declaration did not reference "rights" and prioritized national independence and universal freedom over individual rights.

Both the American and the Haitian declarations attempted to gain membership in the community of nations and empires in the Atlantic world. "They sought confirmation of their standing alongside other such states," Armitage argues, "by justifying their secession and, in some cases, their recombination with other territories and peoples. In short, they declared their possession of sovereignty both internally, over all their own people, and externally, against all other states and peoples."[30] The American declaration claimed the rights of "Free and Independent states," which gave them "Power to levy War, conclude

Peace, contract Alliances, establish Commerce, and to do all other Acts and Things which Independent States may of right do." Similarly, Dessalines, in his role as governor-general for life, acquired the power "to make peace, war, and to name his successor."

Students will learn much from the declarations by grasping that in order to secure foreign support for their independence projects, the US and Haitian governments composed each document with a public audience in mind and made the text available to foreign readers by printing it for distribution. People around the Atlantic world and beyond could read the text in various newspapers. The US declaration first appeared as a printed document and only later, at the end of July or early August 1776, did the authors sign a handwritten manuscript copy.[31] "After its publication," Armitage reports, "the Declaration rapidly entered national and international circuits of exchange. Copies passed from hand to hand, desk to desk, country to country, often with (to us) remarkable speed, but sometimes with perhaps less surprising inefficiency and mishap."[32]

We do not know which specific document of the Declaration of Independence Boisrond-Tonnerre read aloud to the crowd gathered at Gonaïves on January 1, 1804. As foreign governments reacted to news of the American and Haitian declarations, it became clear that the publication of a document claiming a place "among the powers of the earth" was only the beginning of a protracted period of unprecedented international debate about sovereignty, equality, and freedom. As Eliga Gould's research reveals, it took a contentious debate over almost three decades for the United States to secure equal membership in the community of nations.[33]

The debate about the United States did not expedite or facilitate international consideration of Haiti's Declaration of Independence. Rather, the international community in the Atlantic world reacted inconsistently to Haiti's triumphant and provocative self-liberation, which engendered not only fear and rejection but also opportunism and support.[34] Leaders in Haiti recognized the explicit challenge that their success posed to European and American slave labor systems and quickly reassured foreign governments that Haiti would be a good neighbor to their territories. At the same time, Haitian leaders sought to capitalize on the continuing conflicts among the European powers by making Haiti a new player in the geopolitics of the Atlantic world. Taken together, these ambitions meant that Haitian leaders were prepared to place limits

on their professions of universal freedom so as to protect the achievements of the Haitian Revolution by forming strategic alliances.[35]

Conclusion

The scholarly repositioning of the Haitian Revolution as
a distinct and significant counterpart to the American and French revolutions illustrates the central role of new evidence and perspectives in
inspiring revision of established historical analyses. This makes it an
exciting proposition for students. By systematically comparing the respective historical documents associated with the emergence of the
United States and Haiti, students will be able to understand the ways
ideals such as liberty and equality depended on the context within which
they were articulated and promoted. Clearly, there are pitfalls as well
as benefits in comparing the Haitian declaration to the familiar and celebrated American precedent. It is unrealistic to expect all nations after
1776 to want to mirror the decisions made by the United States in their
effort to establish an independent country. This assumption often begins
with the premise that the United States was the model and all other nations attempted to mimic or measure up. Indeed, discussing the Haitian
Declaration of Independence in classrooms outside Haiti presents specific challenges because the most familiar reference point—not only in
the United States but elsewhere as well—is a document that has come
to symbolize so much of contemporary US identity. Freedom, equality,
and natural rights stand out in popular consciousness as the most important and memorable values articulated in the American Declaration
of Independence. Instructors can certainly anticipate that while most
students would struggle to recall the list of grievances against the British
Crown, they would have some familiarity with the values espoused in
the document. "We hold these truths to be self-evident," reads the American Declaration of Independence, "that all men are created equal, that
they are endowed by their Creator with certain unalienable Rights, that
among these are Life, Liberty and the pursuit of Happiness." The rest of
the text, less familiar today, is equally important in terms of the establishment of an independent and sovereign republic and that is why systematic comparison reveals the significance and meaning of other related
but unique declarations of independence. Although many of the issues
and obstacles were the same, the substantially different contexts of the
thirteen colonies and revolutionary Saint-Domingue meant that how

the respective leaders resolved (or attempted to resolve) each issue not only resulted in distinct documents but also launched the countries on different trajectories.

The case of the Haitian Declaration of Independence illustrates the far more fragmentary historical archive of a country that struggled to gain recognition in an Atlantic world that was largely hostile to the Haitian version of freedom and equality. Close reading of documents such as these declarations deepens students' appreciation of the complex ways specific historical contexts intersect with larger geographic, ideological, and cultural contexts. Concepts such as universal rights have meaning for individuals and groups depending on how they are interpreted and lived. The US declaration targeted state policies, and the Haitian declaration aimed to protect individual freedom. Both targeted enslavement (metaphorical or legal). The result, however, was—at least on the surface—dramatically different. The United States established a democratic republic in contrast to the successive military dictatorships that led the Haitian government for most of the nineteenth century. Students should remember, however, that the proclaimed democracy in the United States excluded enslaved people, women, and Native Americans. During this same period, the population at large was continually excluded from state politics in Haiti.[36] While many historical actors and scholars have referred to Haiti as a "black republic," in 1804, the new country was called "l'État d'Hayti" (the State of Haiti) and was not officially described as a republic. Such complexity further illustrates why new evidence and new perspectives will undoubtedly continue to inspire new ways of interpreting and teaching the local and global, immediate and enduring, consequences of the Age of Revolutions.

NOTES

1. Julia Gaffield, "Haiti's Declaration of Independence: Digging for Lost Documents in the Archives of the Atlantic World," *The Appendix* 2, no. 1 (2014).

2. David Geggus, *The Haitian Revolution: A Documentary History* (Indianapolis: Hackett, 2014), xv.

3. Jeremy Popkin, *A Concise History of the Haitian Revolution* (Malden, MA: Wiley-Blackwell, 2012), 48–52.

4. Julia Gaffield, "Haiti and Jamaica in the Remaking of the Early Nineteenth-Century Atlantic World," *William and Mary Quarterly* 69, no. 3 (2012): 583–614; Philippe R. Girard, "Jean-Jacques Dessalines and the Atlantic System: A Reappraisal," *William and Mary Quarterly* 69, no. 3 (2012): 549–82.

5. Michel Biard, *La Liberté ou la Mort: Mourir en Député, 1792–1795* (Paris: Tallandier, 2015), 9.

6. Many thanks to Jeremy Popkin for his thoughts on this issue.

7. Philippe R. Girard, *The Slaves Who Defeated Napoléon: Toussaint Louverture and the Haitian War of Independence, 1801–1804* (Tuscaloosa: University of Alabama Press, 2011), 262.

8. David Armitage, *The Declaration of Independence: A Global History* (Cambridge, MA: Harvard University Press, 2007), 13.

9. Ibid., 23.

10. Ibid., 17.

11. Ibid., 114.

12. Pauline Maier, *American Scripture: Making the Declaration of Independence* (New York: Knopf, 1997), see esp. the appendixes, 217–34.

13. The document is available for digital download at the National Archives of the United Kingdom's website. Translations are available in Julia Gaffield, *The Haitian Declaration of Independence: Creation, Context, and Legacy* (Charlottesville: University of Virginia Press, 2015), or by Laurent Dubois and John Garrigus at http://today.duke.edu/showcase/haitideclaration/declarationstext.html.

14. Deborah Jenson, "Before Malcolm X, Dessalines: A French Tradition of Black Atlantic Radicalism," *International Journal of Francophone Studies* 10, no. 3 (2007): 329–44.

15. Beaubrun Ardouin, *Études sur l'histoire d'Haïti suivies de la vie du général JM Borgella*, vol. 6 (Paris: Author, 1856), 23.

16. "Manquait de chaleur et d'énergie." Ardouin, *Études*, 23.

17. "Il faut la peau d'un blanc pour servir de parchemin, son crâne pour écritoire, son sang pour encre, et une baïonette pour plume." Ardouin, *Études*, 24.

18. The National Archives of the United Kingdom, CO 137/111, fols. 113–17; for the broadside version see National Archives of the United Kingdom, MFQ 1/184 (removed from the Admiralty records ADM 1/254).

19. Edward Corbet to George Nugent, January 25, 1804, National Archives of the United Kingdom, CO 137/111.

20. Jean-Baptiste Symphore Linstant de Pradine, *Receuil général des lois et actes du Gouvernement d'Haïti depuis la proclamation de son Indépendance jusqu'à nos jours* (Paris: A. Durand, 1851); Parick Tardieu, "The Debate Surrounding the Printing of the Haitian Declaration of Independence," in *The Haitian Declaration of Independence*, ed. Julia Gaffield (Charlottesville: University of Virginia Press, 2015).

21. Armitage, *Declaration of Independence*, 22.

22. David Geggus, "The Naming of Haiti," *New West India Guide* 71 (1997): 43–68.

23. Armitage, *Declaration of Independence*, 21.

24. Armitage, *Foundations of Modern International Thought* (Cambridge: Cambridge University Press, 2012), 223–25.

25. Jeremy Popkin, "Jean-Jacques Dessalines, Norbert Thoret, and the Violent Aftermath of the Haitian Declaration of Independence," in *The Haitian Declaration of Independence*, ed. Gaffield; "Hymne Háytiène" (1803), National Archives of the United Kingdom, CO 137/111.

26. Laurent Dubois, *A Colony of Citizens: Revolution and Slave Emancipation in the French Caribbean, 1787–1804* (Chapel Hill: University of North Carolina Press, 2004); Miranda Frances Spieler, "The Destruction of Liberty in French Guiana: Law, Identity and the Meaning of Legal Space, 1794–1830," *Social History* 36, no. 3 (2011): 260–79. Slavery was not abolished in Martinique since it was occupied by the British Empire between 1794 and 1802.

27. For more on the massacres, see Philippe R. Girard, "Caribbean Genocide: Racial War in Haiti, 1802–4," *Patterns of Prejudice* 39, no. 2 (2005): 138–61; Popkin, "Jean-Jacques Dessalines, Norbert Thoret"; Gaffield, "Haiti and Jamaica."

28. Julia Gaffield, *Haitian Connections in the Atlantic World: Recognition after Revolution* (Chapel Hill: University of North Carolina Press, 2015).

29. Sugar planters in the Spanish colonies of Cuba and Puerto Rico benefited from the collapse of Saint-Domingue sugar and began a new sugar boom in the nineteenth century. For more see Ada Ferrer, *Freedom's Mirror: Cuba and Haiti in the Age of Revolution* (Cambridge: Cambridge University Press, 2014).

30. Armitage, *Declaration of Independence*, 20.

31. Ibid., 12.

32. Ibid., 15.

33. Eliga H. Gould, *Among the Powers of the Earth: The American Revolution and the Making of a New World Empire* (Cambridge, MA: Harvard University Press, 2012).

34. Gaffield, *Haitian Connections*.

35. Julia Gaffield, "'Liberté, Indépendance': Haitian Antislavery and National Independence," in *A Global History of Anti-Slavery Politics in the Nineteenth Century*, ed. William Mulligan and Maurice Bric (Basingstoke: Palgrave Macmillan, 2013).

36. Michel-Rolph Trouillot, *Haiti, State against Nation: The Origins and Legacy of Duvalierism* (New York: Monthly Review Press, 1990).

KEY RESOURCES

Primary Sources

Dubois, Laurent, and John Garrigus, eds. *Slave Revolution in the Caribbean, 1789–1804: A Brief History with Documents*. Boston: Bedford/St. Martin's, 2006.

Geggus, David, ed. *The Haitian Revolution: A Documentary History*. Indianapolis: Hackett, 2014.

"Island Luminous." Digital Library of the Caribbean. http://dloc.com/exhibits/islandluminous.

"Remember Haiti." John Carter Brown Library, http://www.brown.edu/Facilities/John_Carter_Brown_Library/remember_haiti/index.php.

Secondary Sources

Cave, Damien. "Haiti's Founding Document Found in London." *New York Times*, April 1, 2010.

Dubois, Laurent. *Avengers of the New World: The Story of the Haitian Revolution.* Cambridge, MA: Harvard University Press, 2004.

Gaffield, Julia. "Haiti's Declaration of Independence: Digging for Lost Documents in the Archives of the Atlantic World." *The Appendix* 2, no. 1 (2014).

———. *Haitian Connections in the Atlantic World: Recognition after Revolution.* Chapel Hill: University of North Carolina Press, 2015.

———, ed. *The Haitian Declaration of Independence: Creation, Context, and Legacy.* Charlottesville: University of Virginia Press, 2015.

Geggus, David. *Haitian Revolutionary Studies.* Bloomington: Indiana University Press, 2002.

Popkin, Jeremy. *A Concise History of the Haitian Revolution.* Malden, MA: Wiley-Blackwell, 2011.

Deep Revolutions

Inculcating Rousseau's "Unitary Self"—and
an Alternative through Role-Playing Games

MARK C. CARNES

In 1750, an adult French man inhabited a variety of selves. On the Sabbath and other religious occasions, he likely thought of himself as a Catholic, or perhaps a Protestant or Jew. His religious identity was embedded in his name; his formal education, if any, had been supervised by religious officials. At other times his sense of self had been shaped by the distinctive cultural and social traditions of his village or urban neighborhood. His regional identity was imprinted on his speech. The initiatory rites of his craft or business guild conferred yet another identity, which determined how and when he worked and with whom he socialized. When asked "who" he was, he might respond in many different ways: "A Catholic." "A Provencal." "A Lyonnais." "A weaver." Sometimes these selves were mutually supportive, but often not. A murmured prayer to "love they neighbor" in church was often at odds with a promise to abide by the exploitative policies of the guild. A French man was continually obliged to negotiate among his multiple—and often contradictory—selves.[1]

But by the early nineteenth century the hybrid character of the young French man's sense of self had been transformed. If asked about his identity, chances were that he would declare himself to be a Frenchman. The simplest explanation for this shift is that during the previous decades, French society had undergone a structural revolution that more firmly implanted a sense of French national identity on its citizens.

Historians have usually focused on the political implications of this "nationalizing" process. David A. Bell, for example, has concluded that the animating motivation of cultural policies of the 1790s was remaking the French people and imparting to them "new unity and uniformity" that ultimately culminated in the "cult" of the French nation. Thus Robespierre famously insisted on the need to "effect a complete regeneration" and "create a new people." Jacques-Nicolas Billaud-Varenne similarly insisted that the French "dissolve all the ties that bind a degenerate nation." This required reformation of each individual: "It seems that one must, so to speak, strike oneself down."[2] The National Assembly's assault on the guilds, historian Michael Fitzsimmons has observed, constituted "a shift from the paradigm of privileged corporatism to a new ideal of the polity."[3]

The new man who emerged from the revolutionary decades identified more completely with his nation. Many of the Catholic institutions that had imprinted their customs and beliefs on his parents and grandparents had been closed down. Ties to his village had been weakened by service in French armies that had marched across much of Europe. Even his local accent would have become less distinctive. The power of his guild, too, would have been sharply reduced, a casualty of increasingly effective state regulation.

But if historians have been attentive to the political implications of the French man's stronger sense of a national identity, they have often neglected another aspect of this phenomenon. The new man also had fewer components of his self system. His identity had become more unitary and less complicated.

Rousseau: From Natural Man to Citizen

This simpler self can also be understood as fulfillment of the Rousseauian agenda. In *Emile* (1762), Rousseau insisted that everyone (or, perhaps more precisely, every man) was born with a unique individuality. In a state of nature, one's self grew according to its inner necessities, free from social conventions or the demands of others. "Natural man is entirely for himself," Rousseau wrote. "He is numerical unity, the absolute whole which is relatively only to itself or its kind."[4]

Rousseau contended that with the emergence of advanced civilization, and especially with the rise of the bourgeois society during the eighteenth century, people acquired multiple identities. Religious authorities inculcated values and behavioral expectations. Rulers and landlords established systems of authority that perpetuated inequality, status anxiety, and greed. In these and countless other ways, denizens of the modern world had become "double men, always appearing to relate everything to others." Beset by multiple internal contradictions, they lost sight of their own authentic self. "Swept along in contrary routes by nature and by men, forced to divide ourselves between these different impulses, we follow a composite impulse which leads us to neither one goal nor the other. Thus, in conflict and floating during the whole course of our life, we end it without having been able to put ourselves in harmony with [*d'accord*] ourselves."[5]

The antidote to this multiplicity of artificial selves was set forth in subsequent sections of *Emile*, which described how a child—Emile, a fictional construct—could be reared and educated so as to retain the unitary essence of his true self. The principal agent in the boy's education—and acculturation—was a philosopher-tutor whose chief task was to prevent external ideas and conventions from tainting the child's thinking. To implement this "negative" education, the tutor hauled young Emile off to the remote countryside and denied the boy access to all books save one: *Robinson Crusoe*, a primer on survival in a state of nature. If Emile were to read other books, Rousseau warned, the boy might come to believe the words of the author rather than cultivate his own beliefs and opinions. History books were a special danger, because the reader often put himself in the shoes of the subject and if Emile "just once prefers to be someone other than himself—were this other Socrates, were it Cato—everything has failed. He who begins to become alien to himself does not take long to forget himself entirely."[6] But how could such a cosseted person occupy a place in society?[7]

Rousseau's famous answer came in *The Social Contract* (1762), which described a process, infused with religious overtones, by which an individual could refashion his own will so that it conformed to civic necessity. This civilized version of the new man was a citizen who perceived that his own best interests were consonant with those of his polity. The guiding force of the entire system was a unitary will—a General Will—which neatly fused with the wills of those who contracted to join it. Selfless citizens—true to their best unitary selves—were the components of a new type of unitary, General Will.

Whether Rousseau's writings informed the actions of the French revolutionaries and thus gave rise to a unifying sense of French nationalism, or whether other factors during the revolution converged to produce this phenomenon is beyond the scope of this essay.[8] The broader institution-alization of this concept, furthermore, occupied much of the nineteenth century, requiring the establishment and spread of public schooling—in France as well as most other Western nations.[9] But the general ten-dency was toward the Rousseauian ideal, now manifested in a unifying nationalism.

Rousseau's *Emile*, of course, was influential in the diffusion of this idea, but so was Plato's *Republic*, a central influence on Rousseau.[10] Plato's Socrates insisted that if a man took on many roles, he would play none of them well; worse, he could not "remain at unity in him-self."[11] Indeed, the "chief excellence" of the Platonic state was its exclu-sion of poets, orators, and dramatists—those most skilled at evoking alternative selves. While Rousseau's version of Plato was promoting the unitary self in France, the Neoplatonism of Friedrich Schiller and Georg Hegel were having a similar effect on German universities, which later served as models for US institutions of higher learning.

By the late nineteenth century, the concept of a unitary, fundamental self was widely accepted among educational reformers, philosophers, and psychologists. Freud, following Plato, held that while the mind had several components, the self had just one—the ego. Through much of the twentieth century, developmental psychologists have similarly conceived of life as a journey of self-discovery rather than an open-ended exploration. Erik Erikson, whose developmental model influenced generations of educators, insisted that the central danger of adoles-cence was "role-confusion," because teenagers were susceptible to the dangerous allure of different roles.[12] Schizophrenia and even "psychotic episodes" were among the chief dangers. John Dewey, perhaps the most important US educational philosopher of the twentieth century, similarly sought to wean young people from foolish flights of fancy so that they could better perform their proper roles as productive citizens in a progressive society.[13]

This assumption of an essential unitary self is so deeply embedded in our thinking that it pervades our pedagogy. Countless teachers and parents, though perhaps unaware of the writings of Plato, Rousseau, Freud, or Erikson, counsel young people to "buckle down," and "find yourself." Especially by the time a young person gets to college, he or she is expected to "focus."

But modern neurobiology suggests that Plato, Rousseau, Freud, Erikson, and others following in their train are likely wrong. The unitary self may well be the modern equivalent of the medieval soul, a philosophical (or perhaps grammatical) construct with no discernible biological foundation. The brain consists of billions of neural webs; neuroscientists increasingly view the "self" as a neurological habit—a tendency for electrical impulses to flow most readily along familiar neural pathways.[14] This suggests a mutually reinforcing pattern: if our thoughts only resonate within the bubble of our self, as Rousseau proposed for Emile, our sense of our self will likely be stronger and more coherent—but it will also be rigid, opinionated, and ill-informed. The great proponents of pedagogical reform, in preserving a unitary sense of self, succeeded in discouraging creativity and imagination—the flights of fancy, in other words, sometimes foolish and absurd—that cause us to think *differently*.

Therein lies the danger, or so the great educational reformers insisted: if you imagine yourself to be someone else, you may lose hold of your true self. Proof of this danger is perhaps exhibited by college students today, who spend much of their time imagining that they are boozeguzzling fraternity brothers or sorority sisters or that they are car thieves (*Grand Theft Auto*) or blood-drenched warriors (*World of Warcraft*).

But our natural imaginative impulses can also be channeled in other directions. We can be drawn out of ourselves to experience a deeper kind of learning.

Role-Immersion Games: Reacting to the Past

One way is through Reacting to the Past (RTTP), a roleplaying approach to higher education. In RTTP, students play complex games set in the past, their roles informed by classic texts. The games are run by students and usually occupy a month of class time. (These games are played in the classroom; RTTP has no relationship to video gaming.) RTTP has experienced rapid diffusion over the past decade. At present, these games are used by instructors at more then 350 colleges and universities. Fourteen games have been published by Norton, another fifty are in development. Four games, including three that have been published, relate to the Age of Revolutions.[15]

An RTTP game consists of three distinct elements: a gamebook and supplementary texts; a set of roles for students, available only to college instructors; and an instructor's manual, also restricted to faculty (see the website of the Reacting Consortium: www.barnard.edu/reacting

.edu). For example, instructors who wish to teach *Rousseau, Burke, and Revolution in France, 1791* order the gamebook (now available in its 2.0 version) and any of several paperback versions of Rousseau's *Social Contract*. The lengthy gamebook begins with a "you are there" vignette, followed by an explanation of the game and then an essay outlining the historical context of the revolution. The next section explains the game's rules, which are designed to ensure that students adhere to historical plausibility. Another section describes the historical figures and factions in the game and outlines the major intellectual issues. The last section includes primary texts, ranging from Montesquieu's *Spirit of Laws* to edited versions of Rousseau's *First Discourse* and Burke's *Reflections on the Revolution in France*, along with documents such as the Civil Constitution of the Clergy and the Constitution of 1791. Students are also expected to read Rousseau's *Social Contract*.

During three setup sessions, instructors lead students through these materials, often with guided discussions. The goal is not to teach the entire historical and philosophical context—an impossibility—but to provide students with a roadmap through it. Depending on their particular role and the special issues that become crucial in their game, students will write papers and give speeches on a wide variety of subjects in the context of a rapidly shifting game. They must find sources and make sense of them quickly, before the game moves on to another issue.

During the second setup session, students receive their roles, which they find both invigorating and terrifying: now it dawns on them that perhaps within a week, they must write persuasive papers and give controversial speeches—to the entire class!—on issues such as the Civil Constitution of the Clergy or the slave uprising in Saint-Domingue. These anxieties draw students more tightly into their factions, which often meet regularly outside of class. The four main factions are the Jacobins, Feuillants, clerical conservatives, and noble conservatives, nearly all of whom belong to the National Assembly. Students have responsibilities to fulfill the goals of their particular character and their larger faction. The student assigned the role of Henri-Baptiste Grégoire, for example, must not only ensure passage of the Jacobin agenda— approval of the Civil Constitution of the Clergy and defeat of the Royal Sanction (king's veto)—but "he" must also extend the Declaration of the Rights of Man to blacks in Saint-Domingue. Jean-Sylvain Bailly, a leader of the Feuillant faction, must ensure passage of the Constitution of 1791, establishing a constitutional monarchy, and he must preserve order in Paris. Jean-Sifrein Maury, a conservative cleric who has spurned the "obligatory oath," must overturn the Civil Constitution of the Clergy and, failing in that, bring about the collapse of the revolutionary regime. The fourth faction includes the major section leaders of Paris—Danton, Anne-Marie Andall, and Marat, among others. Though they do not belong to the National Assembly, they can devise ways to address that body and decisively influence its deliberations.

Another group of students take on the role of more neutral historical figures in the National Assembly. Players in the partisan factions spend much of the game trying to win over these "indeterminate" players. These figures also bring additional perspectives and ideas into the game. For example, Jean-Baptiste Alquier, a tax lawyer from La Rochelle, seeks to stabilize finances. Thomas Verny, a member of the Academy of Floral Games, provides awards for outstanding essays and speeches. Etta Palm seeks to raise issues of gender.

The three-class setup phase is followed by the six-session game phase, which begins on July 1791 and covers much of the ensuing year. The destabilizing element in the game, as in history, is the sections of Paris, which have the capacity to foment strife. The conservatives—or perhaps Louis XVI acting independently—may secretly try to precipitate foreign intervention; the sections, perhaps backed by the Jacobins, may lash out at presumed enemies of the revolution.

Reacting games are not re-enactments. The outcome of any RTTP game is unknown at the outset. Any faction—through a combination of brilliant strategy, superb research, persuasive argument, and some measure of luck—can win. That was true in history as well (or so the designers of the game believe).

Miguel versus Citizen Miguel

What happens when students assume alternative identities in role-immersion games?[16] For one thing, they often exhibit an astonishing level of engagement. Paul Fessler, chair of the history department at Dordt College, discovered this in 2004, his second year of teaching with RTTP. He had devoted the final month of his Western Civilization course to the French Revolution game. The first three game sessions had proven to be more contentious than he had anticipated.

His class was falling behind. The semester would end before the game had run its course. He told the class he had no choice but to cut the game short, omitting the final debates and sessions. The students howled in protest. Some suggested that they stay after class during the final two weeks, but other students had classes immediately following Western Civ. Fessler told the students that if they could come up with a mutually satisfactory time, he would try to arrange to be there as gamemaster. Several days later the students offered a startling proposition: that they begin their final four classes a half hour early. Fessler was floored. Class normally started at 8:00 am. To his astonishment, every student attended every 7:30 am class.[17]

Over a decade later, I asked Nate Gibson, a student in Fessler's class, why he and his classmates had volunteered to drag themselves out of bed and head for class so early. He explained that the game had nearly taken over their lives. To the consternation of his suitemates, he found that he no longer had time for late-night video games. He and his class-mates worked on the game almost incessantly. "We plowed through the game manual, our history texts, Rousseau, you name it. We spent hours writing articles. I spent several all-nighters editing my faction's newspapers, and the other editors did too." He also developed a deep understanding of Rousseau and, as a section leader of Paris, he found that he understood the plight of the urban poor. "It was like putting on a good pair of glasses," he explained. "I could see *why* people who lived through the revolution did what they did."[18]

Fessler's experience was mirrored by that of Rebecca Ard Boone, a history professor at Lamar University in Texas, who has used the game for over eight years. She recalled a class in 2008 with special clarity. During the first game session, when students were hesitant and unsure of what to do and say, Miguel, from Port Arthur, Texas, delivered a searing speech as Robespierre that galvanized the others. Soon nearly everyone was involved—strategizing, arguing, meeting outside of class.

Six years later, Miguel told me that playing that role influenced him in several ways. First, it had transformed an abstract issue—the French Revolution—into an experience that was tangible and "real." He found that when he read biographies and other historical accounts, Robes-pierre was "just another name in history—separated from anything real." But while playing Robespierre, he wanted to know everything about him. He plunged into biographies and studied Robespierre's speeches. (Miguel's essays in his faction's weekly newspaper—which Professor Boone retained, six years later!—showed a firm understanding of Rousseau and Robespierre.)

Almost immediately, Miguel found that "being Robespierre" provided useful lessons for his own life. He patterned his first speech as Robespierre on Barack Obama's 2004 "We can do better" speech at the Democratic convention, which echoed Robespierre's call for a "new national identity." Miguel was surprised that his speech struck such a responsive chord among classmates, but this merely illustrated something Robespierre had insisted: revolutionary rhetoric could change the world. In 2008 Senator Barack Obama was campaigning against Hillary Clinton for the Texas Democratic primary, and Miguel found that staffers increasingly sent him to give speeches in support of Obama. While playing the game, moreover, Miguel became increasingly involved in political strategy, and these lessons also had resonance in his expanding involvement in the Obama campaign. "The tactics I learned in the game—such as building coalitions—helped me in real life," he added.[19]

But Miguel did not become Robespierre. While absorbing Robespierre's role and example, he began to critique it. He found that rhetoric was at times too powerful, too persuasive: too often listeners applauded the performance and forgot the ideas. Leaders had a responsibility, he learned, to say something of substance rather than just win applause.

By internalizing Robespierre's role and even aspects of his identity, Miguel gained new skills and a different perspective. Yet he retained a capacity to evaluate and criticize the new intruder who had barged into his self system.

A few years ago I happened on another example of what happens when new selves crowd into a student's self-identity. While cleaning out a desk, I found an old video of an RTTP class at Barnard College from 2000. One scene stood out. "Citizen Victoria," leader of a Paris section, was calling on the poor of the city to rise up against the king's troops. "Let us bleed and gag, kill and destroy," she declared, long black hair swaying as she chopped the air. "Tyranny must die. For without the death of tyrants, we cannot live!" She concluded, her voice at fever pitch, "If I must die in order for France to live, I shall die!"

I wondered what had happened to Citizen Victoria in the ensuing decade, so I tracked her down and chatted with her online. Now she was a lawyer in Paris, having been transferred from her firm's New York offices. We joked about her working in Paris 200 years after she had led the city's rabble. I asked if she remembered the speech in which she roused the sections to fight.

"Certainly," she typed instantly. "Die! Die! Die!"

"I completely owned the role," she added. "I didn't feel like I was in a classroom. I didn't feel like a young woman in college. I was in Paris. I felt like I truly was a French revolutionary. I had so completely studied the ideology and the character, I didn't need to think to formulate my answers or find the right words. They just came."

In other words, Victoria had become what Rousseau called a "double person": Victoria now "owned" another identity as Citizen Victoria.

"But if you 'truly' became a French revolutionary," I asked, "what happened to your own real self? Did Citizen Victoria take possession of your thinking?"

"Hardly," she replied. "I believed in nonviolence then. I still do."

For a time we discussed other subjects, than an idea occurred to me.

"If we were in Paris in 1791 and the king's henchmen arrived on the scene, would you call on the crowd to attack them?"

Long pause.

"Perhaps."

During that pause, I suspect that Citizen Victoria and Victoria debated the issue, with Citizen Victoria scoring some points. Victoria had to rethink her pacifism. She had engaged in critical thinking of the deepest kind.

Revolutions in Learning

Professor Boone, who has taught RTTP for nearly a decade, maintained that the games often enlarged her students' sense of self. "Reacting feels to them (I think) more like travel than study," she explained. "It's as though the games give their imagination permission to explore." "The university's mission is to transform the students' lives," she noted, "but many students do not want to be transformed. The beauty of the games is that they take learning out of this adversarial structure by giving students a space in which they can let their imaginations play. The experience of playing an historical figure can be just as transformative as a traditional class based on reading, but the students engage more willingly in the process because they have more agency."[20] Readers should of course be wary of terms such as *transformative* when applied to a particular college class. Nevertheless, the students mentioned here did believe that a single class had influenced their lives. After graduating from Dordt College, Nate Gibson, who was among the students who trooped to class before sunrise, went to Japan to teach school. He remains there now, creating RTTP-type learning experiences for his students. Victoria is still a lawyer—but with great expectations. She asked that her real name not be included here, lest future political foes cite her fictive penchant for violence. After graduating from Lamar, Miguel went to Harvard, where he earned a master's degree in education. He returned to Texas and, again using skills he had acquired in RTTP, campaigned for the school board. Within two years, he was elected president of the sixteenth largest school district in the nation.

The reports of a handful of students and teachers do not constitute proof of the pedagogical power of role-immersion games.[21] The purpose of this short essay has been to outline, with a very wide brush, two pedagogical concepts: the rise of Rousseau's unitary self in the late eighteenth century and afterward and the emergence of a more complex, alternative self through role-immersion games. Though these pedagogical systems are antithetical in concept and structure, they are not incompatible. Indeed, students may benefit most from experiencing both types of learning. They may acquire one type of knowledge by identifying with unfamiliar ideas and peoples and another by stepping back and evaluating those ideas and people in light of their own beliefs. Higher education need not embrace role-immersion games to the exclusion of conventional pedagogies.

A structural revolution in education was nevertheless central to the nationalizing project of the Age of Revolutions. An essential element of that process was the profound transformation of the self. Our own age, however, leans in a different direction. We emphasize diversity, global citizenship, and a respect for the other. We call on students to understand and accept those who are different from themselves. Just how, we don't say.

As instructors ponder next semester's class, we may wish to rethink the customary revision of the syllabus and tweaking of our lectures. One alternative is to embrace a deep revolution in the learning structure of their classroom.

NOTES

1. This was true of women as well. But because this essay advances a broad theoretical issue with special reference to Rousseau, whose gendered language was intentional, the third-person pronoun throughout is masculine.

2. David A. Bell, *The Cult of the Nation in France: Inventing Nationalism, 1680–1800* (Cambridge, MA: Harvard University Press, 2001), 160–61; Robespierre cited on 156, Billaud-Varenne on 140.

3. Michael P. Fitzsimmons, "The National Assembly and the Abolition of Guilds in France," *Historical Journal* 39, no. 1 (1996): 133–54 (140).

4. Jean-Jacques Rousseau, *Emile, or On Education*, trans. Allan Bloom (New York: Basic Books, 1979), 39.

5. Ibid., 41.

6. Ibid., 243.

7. Rousseau concedes that Emile approaches adulthood with "little knowledge": "He does not know even the name of history, or what metaphysics and morals are. He knows the essential relations of man to things but nothing of the moral relations of man to man. He hardly knows how to generalize ideas and hardly how to make abstractions," in ibid., 207.

8. "Instead of Rousseau making the Revolution," Gordon McNeil famously observed, "the Revolution made Rousseau." In Gordon H. McNeil, "The Cult of Rousseau and the French Revolution," *Journal of the History of Ideas* 6, no. 2 (1945): 197–12 (201). This debate was revitalized in recent decades by Francois Furet, Keith Baker, and others.

9. See, for example, James Livesey, *Making Democracy in the French Revolution* (Cambridge, MA: Harvard University Press, 2001), 167–81. Writing of the 1790s, T. C. W. Blanning concluded: "Never was there a time when the Rousseauist dream of a united general will looked feasible," cited in T. C. W. Blanning, ed., *The Rise and Fall of the French Revolution* (Chicago: University of Chicago Press, 1996), 22.

10. "Do you want to get an idea of public education? Read Plato's *Republic* . . . the most beautiful educational treatise ever written." In Rousseau, *Emile*, 40. *Emile* was a reply to and extension of Plato's ideas.

11. Plato, *The Republic*, trans. Desmond Lee (New York: Penguin, 1974), 94, 371.

12. Erik Erikson, *Childhood and Society* (New York: Norton, 1950), 261–63.

13. See Alan Ryan, *John Dewey and the High Tide of American Liberalism* (New York: Norton, 1995), 140–49.

14. See Todd E. Feinberg, *From Axons to Identity: Neurological Explorations of the Nature of the Self* (New York: Norton, 2009); Antonio Damasio, *Self Comes to Mind: Constructing the Conscious Brain* (New York: Vintage, 2010).

15. These include *Patriots, Loyalists and Revolution in New York City, 1775–1776*, by Bill Offutt (New York: Norton, 2014); *Rousseau, Burke and Revolution in France, 1791*, by Jennifer Popiel, Mark Carnes, and Gary Kates (New York: Norton, 2015); *America's Founding: The Constitutional Convention*, by J. Patrick Coby (New York: Norton, forthcoming). Another game, still in development, is *The Crisis of Diderot's Encyclopedia, 1759*, by David Eick and Gretchen Galbraith. This game is set in Mme Geoffrin's weekly salon, when the first volume of the *Encyclopédie* was published, and the game extends through 1759. Students take on roles as *philosophes*, religious authorities, entrepreneurs, and government officials. They accumulate "credit" (social and material) by writing articles for the *Encyclopédie* or criticisms of those articles, and through their clever participation in the discourse on literary and philosophical matters in the salon. For instructor's materials on the published games, consult Norton's website. Faculty interested in playing Eick and Galbraith's game, which is still in development, can do so by contacting the main Reacting website: www.barnard.edu/reacting.

16. Many social scientists—political scientists, especially—use role-playing scenarios or simulations in college-level or graduate-level instruction: "You are President Kennedy in 1962 and you have just learned that nuclear-tipped Soviet missiles have been installed in Cuba . . ." But these simulations usually occupy a single class; often they suffer from what I call the "Connecticut Yankee syndrome," where players, having learned contemporary skills of mediation or problem solving, go back to the past in order to fix it. Reacting employs an entirely difficult psychological process: by being immersed in a game for a whole month, students identify with the roles they play.

17. This story is related in more detail in Mark C. Carnes, *Minds on Fire: How Role-Immersion Games Transform College* (Cambridge, MA: Harvard University Press, 2014), 1–3.

18. Ibid., 3, 74.

19. Phone interview with author, April 27, 2015.

20. Email to the author, May 2, 2015.

21. The most sophisticated study of the psychological and educational impact of Reacting is Steven J. Stroessner, Laurie Susser Beckerman, and Alexis Whittaker, "All the World's a Stage? Consequences of a Role-Playing Pedagogy on Psychological Factors and Writing and Rhetorical Skill in College Graduates," *Journal of Educational Psychology* 101, no. 3 (2009): 605–20.

KEY RESOURCES

Bell, David A. *The Cult of the Nation in France: Inventing Nationalism, 1680–1800.* Cambridge, MA: Harvard University Press, 2001.

Carnes, Mark C. *Minds on Fire: How Role-Immersion Games Transform College.* Cambridge, MA: Harvard University Press, 2014.

Erikson, Erik. *Childhood and Society*. New York: Norton, 1950.

Feinberg, Todd E. *From Axons to Identity: Neurological Explorations of the Nature of the Self*. New York: Norton, 2009.

Reacting to the Past Gamebooks, https://reacting.barnard.edu/.

Rousseau, Jean-Jacques. *Emile, or On Education*. Translated by Allan Bloom. New York: Basic Books, 1979.

Art Matters

Teaching the Visual Arts
in the French Revolution

MARK LEDBURY

W hy should we care about the art produced during the Age of Revolutions, and what is the place of art and visual culture within the profound and often violent social and political upheavals that punctuated the French Revolution? These are the questions historians ask me frequently and students in my art history classes also pose—and when we unpack this kind of question, we usually boil it down to an even more thorny one: is art a symptom, at best a manifestation (in an elite stratum of the social body) of an underlying social or economic state of health or distress, or does art in any way have agency or make anything happen? Whereas there is no question in an art history class that we might find the spare, complex brilliance of Jacques-Louis David's *Marat at His Last Breath* (1793) compelling, the question of its relation to and impact on on the course of events, of its agency, even of its relevance to our understanding of a historical moment, remains in dispute. Did the fact of it in any way change the speeches and actions of the convention in which it hung for a time?

These are questions that challenge teachers and students right at the start. By looking at art, students can engage with the problems of distance between the image and the events themselves. They can learn to discern how paintings—no less than texts—were constructed by artists using rhetorical strategies that attempted to shape the way people and events were represented. They will enjoy exploring how everyday

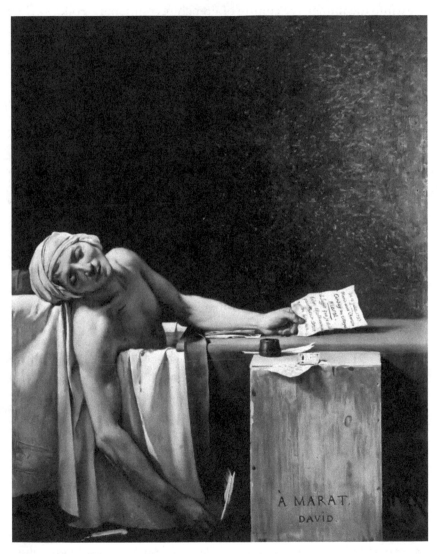

Jacques-Louis David, *Marat at His Last Breath, or The Death of Marat*. (1793, oil on Canvas, Brussels: Musées Royaux; https://www.flickr.com/photos/paukrus/4118748840/in /gallery-87157886@N04-72157631796545106/; photograph by Ruslan under Creative Commons)

culture in the streets—choices of clothing and hairstyles, of symbols and colors—was also embedded with the visual language of political identity. They may find the choreography of the revolutionary festival both ominously prescient of modern political theater and a useful doorway into the immersive culture of French revolutionary politics. They can also explore the double-edged nature of the revolutionary process by scrutinizing images of revolutionary iconoclasm. Students can also learn much from the wider context in which all this activity sprang: the development of the eighteenth-century civic culture in the public sphere and the ways art—we should remind ourselves—was a commodity. Moreover, it is instructive to have students to look at artists—or individual works—that did not enter the canon of the "greats": they tell us much about the vicissitudes of taste, politics, and aesthetics.

To begin with the distance between art and events, one thing is certain: David's *Marat*, beatific and Christ-like, bears little resemblance to any image of Marat that the archival and written sources assemble (links are provided at the end of this chapter to almost all the images cited here). Indeed, historians and students will be disappointed if they seek documentary traces and visual leads in the art of the Age of Revolutions to supplement a textual archive. It is in fact remarkable how little eyewitness art we have to the political events of the French Revolution. A few pencil sketches survive, and we have several engaging prison portraits, ably studied in recent literature, which record the likenesses of those imprisoned at various moments of the revolutionary process, and a scattering of sketches that were perhaps made in the heat of the moment(s) of the revolution, but compared with the rich textual archive, there are slim pickings. If we examine the representations by artists of any significant event or series of events (whether military, social, or political) during the revolutionary moment, we may be struck by the lack of immediacy and spontaneity of the material we have and just how much of the apparatus of art is superimposed on the visual telling of events. In looking at images of the fall of the Bastille, for example, we come across a number of prints produced almost contemporaneously with the event, like that published by Jacques-Louis Bance the elder in 1789, *Prise de la Bastille par les bourgeois et les braves gardes françaises de la bonne ville de Paris, le 14 juillet 1789* but they resolutely refuse to yield witness. This print, like many of its contemporaries, has radically reconfigured the event, ordered it compositionally and rhetorically, as well as socially, giving us perfectly measured and deliberate collaborations between soldiers and revolutionary crowd, attacking a fortress as one might have in the golden years of siege warfare under Louis XIV. It also portrays an almost consensual scene of the arrest of De Launay rather than any sense of a tense, fraught, contingent, and fast-paced improvisation and the social violence of the event, most clearly exemplified by the actual fate of De Launay, lynched before he could be brought to "justice" at the Hôtel de Ville. Print culture here is anything but a documentary witness, and its very nature—regular rectangles, framed by text—as well as its traditional exclusions, stylizations, and generic framing all mediate against any reading of such material as reflecting "what actually happened."

When we teach students who have been so thoroughly immersed in eyewitness news, we do well to make this obvious but fundamental point again and again. Even when we might recognize, at the level of individual portraits, some accuracy of resemblance to actual people, buildings, or other features of revolutionary landscapes or actions, we cannot scale this up to the macro level of the whole composition. We cannot explore David's large-scale sketch from 1791 of the *The Tennis Court Oath* in all its complex brilliance for strictly journalistic purposes— there is just too much of a gap between the event and the image. Time was not the only thing that created this gap, the sketch being presented in public two years after the event, after exhaustive portrait sessions and much artistic labor, toward a grand painting that was never made. By art's very nature, the artist invested his compositional, rhetorical, and affective strategies into the depiction. The work's desperate hyperbole of togetherness is feverishly at odds with the compromise and factionalism that was dominant in 1791 and was beginning to be evident even in the Jeu de Paume in June 1789. It is, then, far from straightforward or historically reliable—even as an "evocation" of the momentous events that gathered the third estate in that Versailles real tennis court—let alone as a verbatim reconstruction of the actual course of events of that day, however much David may have fussed over the accuracy of faces, poses, and clothing.

However, from David's grand and ultimately doomed project (the existing drawing was preparatory "proof of concept" for what was going to be a vast painting and a lucrative subscription print enterprise), we can learn a lot about aesthetics, about David's career and ambitions, and about neoclassical learning, rhetoric, and ideals that shaped the muscular masculinity of the actors in the drawing. This is the heart of the drawing's continuing fascination and usefulness to teachers and students. Like the later *10 August 1792* by David's pupil François Gérard, this is a near ecstatic celebration of revolutionary togetherness under duress, and its attempt to conjure up the power and spectacle of an estate coming into being through an unexpectedly defiant act of solidarity deploys intense scenographic and compositional energy to persuade its viewers of the vital importance of the collective will.

Those rhetorical strategies and compositional energies, of course, are a perfectly legitimate subject of research and teaching; exploring David's methods in the preparation of *The Tennis Court Oath*, his grafting the heads of his real participants onto the heroic nude figures he had learned to draw so deftly after years of academic training, and his enthusiasm for classical statuary tells us much about the way that the neoclassical generation engaged with contemporary events. I often show this drawing alongside the famous drawing of the *Prise de la Bastille* (Storming of the Bastille) by his contemporary, François-André Vincent, to make these points succinctly. Vincent refashions the crowd as heroic groupings of muscular neoclassical athletes, grouped in sculpturally informed affective poses, and renders the scene as ancient as it is contemporary. Through these works, students can learn, among other things, how the imaginations of the revolutionary generation filtered the specificities and contingencies of their contemporary struggle through sensibilities marinated in the Greco-Roman past. David's or Vincent's drawings will never satisfy a historian's desire for the accurate reconstruction of events, but they may help students more clearly and instantaneously grasp the way different rhetorics (verbal or visual) shaped the consciousness of the revolutionary generation. In fact, it is instructive and often effective to teach David's drawing in relation to and alongside excerpts of the great oratory of Danton or Robespierre, or the vast learning and persuasive urging that characterizes the pamphlets of the Abbé Sieyès.

To generalize further from these examples, it helps me in my teaching (and to an extent in my research) to figure art and visual cultures of the revolution not as transparent lenses through which to view events but more as thermometers of social heat and ideological zeal. Even better I think is to see art as a precipitate in both senses of the word: both the outcome of a complex series of causes, and the rich experimental sediment we might explore to help us explain the many components of the volatile comings together and splittings apart that are at the heart of much of what we understand to be the Age of Revolutions. Art is dense, multiplicitous, and opaque but resonant, and it rewards informed, patient, and close examination rather than cursory and utilitarian glance.

The Politics of Appearances and Immersive Culture

I have taken examples principally from the realms of "high art" so far, but one very effective teaching strategy, which has proved beneficial in many classrooms and in much literature, is to move away from Art with a capital A, what we sometimes call high art (the productions of the academicians bought by the elites and often seen by few), to a vaster pool of visual and symbolic culture. What many historians have chosen to emphasize lately in their search for the visual stuff of revolution is not the grand set pieces of history painting but the larger, more diverse, more contingent field of visual culture, a wide range of phenomena including dress and costume, print culture, popular symbolic languages, and bodily markers of identity. The argument of much persuasive literature is that revolution plays out in symbols as well as words and deeds, that the liberty cap, the fleur-de-lys, the cut of one's hose, are part of a rich symbolic and semiotic field of revolutionary struggle. In this combat, identification with one faction or another, or even grander scale national and cultural coherence of identity, was achieved as much through codes of dress, appearance, and behavior as through speech, action, or law. This is what Richard Wrigley has called "the politics of appearances" and gets us in many senses to the fabric of the revolution as culture and event. To help students think about this topic, I have conducted class experiments that involve imagining a divided land in the midst of civil conflict, then splitting groups up into role-playing factions and asking them to come up with symbols that they could carry or wear that they think will pithily encapsulate their ideology and partisanship. They routinely come up with the solutions the revolutionary factions chose—color (using the existing symbolism of color to express political sympathy), natural imagery (trees and plants, and more rarely animals), objects that imply force or strength, and "superheroes." All these symbolic markers turn out to map fairly precisely on to the Cockades, Liberty Trees, scales of justice, and ubiquitous Hercules of the revolutionary era. Such activities, if conducted with historical sensitivity, have the potential, as I have found, to lead into rich conversations about the visual languages of belonging, conversations that certainly resonate with a generation brought up with the subtle distinctions of subcultures and whose own loyalties and senses of belonging are frequently manifest in clothing and body adornment.

This focus on the language of apparel and appearance is a way of expanding our discussion from grand art to the everyday and to the rhythms and concerns of the street in a way that resonates with students. Another phenomenon of revolutionary visual culture that has the capacity to grip students and enliven discussion is the larger multimedia phenomenon, in which visual art plays an important role, which we call the "revolutionary festival." The civic and military events known as "fêtes" or festivals that called for elaborate programs, mass participation, and a combination of music, decor, speech, and dance offer fertile ground for explanation of ideologies and mentalities in the French Revolution, thanks to classic texts by historians Mona Ozouf and others. However, teaching festivals sets challenges to teachers because often the remaining testimony of drawings and prints, and the written descriptions of organizers and participants, tend to appear improbable, risible, or lackluster to students. Perhaps only the virtual reality age will be able to do justice to the importance of the spectacles that punctuated some of the most intense days of the French Revolution with complex combinations of costume drama, symbolism, music, ephemeral architecture, and choreography. Given the almost constant financial and military crises of the years 1789–1794, it remains remarkable that such efforts were made all around France and at all levels from the revolutionary government to local authorities, as they curated mass-participation celebrations of concepts as nebulous and new as "the Supreme Being" or events as charged as "Federation." However, in teaching them, it helps to reach back to a longue durée history of festivity in Europe.

If we see the festival as a uniquely revolutionary form, responding to the urgency of political pressures in the revolution's most heated years, we miss the fact that those involved in creating and directing them had often had significant experience of spectacle in various ancien régime contexts. Architects built elaborate stage decors and contraptions, officials had organized and directed triumphal entries, and musicians had gained experience of large-scale military musical events long before the revolution. Of course, Jacques-Louis David, felicitously designated by David Dowd in his historical biography as the "Pageant Master

Pierre-Antoine De Machy, *The Festival of the Cult of the Supreme Being*. (1794, oil on canvas; Paris, Musée Carnavalet; Photo © RMN-Grand Palais / Agence Bulloz)

of the Republic" because he was placed in charge of the decor and proceedings of various festivals under the Revolutionary Committee of Public Safety with which he was intimately involved, was steeped not only in visual art but also in music-theater (his surrogate father in his formative years, Michel-Jean Sedaine, was one of the most successful librettists of his era, and David was a fanatical theatergoer). He brought his knowledge of both realms to the festivals' creation. Furthermore, from triumphal entries and religious processions of previous epochs, the revolutionaries learned the power of crowd choreography and rolling spectacle—and from the commercial entrepreneurs of burgeoning theater and pleasure gardens they learned how seductive the creation of spaces of festive enjoyment could be in the heart of the city. We must add to this genealogy, of course, the long history of rural festivals, rough music, and celebration of natural cycles, all of which contributed to the festival becoming a very special site of revolutionary affect and belonging. I tend to enter this topic through specific traces—one of them being Pierre De Machy's painting in the Musée Carnavalet of the *Festival of the Cult of the Supreme Being*, which shows vast crowds making their way to and up the artificial mountain, topped by a liberty tree whose apex dwarfs the statue of Hercules on a column. This allows a

117

partial way in to the scale and complexity (and effort) of the festival as well as its coercive and of course, to our modern sensibilities, slightly sinister choreography. I await the day when we can conjure in class the sounds, noises, movement, and spectacle of these events through new technological means—I imagine a future, not too far away, when a thoroughly immersive virtual environment will eventually come to be as standard a teaching tool as a slide show and the projector is in our own day. In such circumstances, the festival might gain an even more prominent place in teaching and understanding the French Revolution.

Breaking and Remaking

Another highly productive approach to giving students a sense of the importance of symbolic visual material and the visual fabric of the revolutionary age is to discuss vandalism and iconoclasm—phenomena of long-standing interest to historians of politics and religion, but which have particular power and valence in the teaching of the ways in which an entire image-rhetoric of kingship was undermined first by acts of derision and satire, then more literally destroyed in the heat of revolutionary processes by violent desecration. I like to teach a long and wide history of revolutionary iconoclasm, one that has roots at least as far back as the satirical graffiti and scurrilous songs that deflated the hyperbolic ambitions of Louis XIV's Place de Nos Conquêtes as wonderfully discussed by art historian Rochelle Ziskin, and which runs through the eighteenth century, taking in the anticlerical pornography of the mid-eighteenth century, with its crude images of monks, nuns, and other authority figures in unlikely and degrading sexual acts, which in turn fed the astonishing "demolition" of Marie Antoinette in her own lifetime through scandalous illustrated tales of incest and bestiality, and which then took physical life in the attacks on royal statues, representations, and tombs in the heat of the revolution.

Now that we are at a golden moment of scholarship in this area (one thinks of diverse recent work by Richard Clay and Dario Gamboni) and in an era when the destruction of images is again front-page news, this is a very rich seam for exploring the motivations and the stakes of one form or another of obliteration and desecration. Art historians are wont to bemoan destruction, of course, and iconoclasts never enjoy the laurels of posterity, but there is no doubt that acts of destruction can be as useful to analyze as acts of creation in our quest to give a rich and deep

Hubert Robert, *The Violation of the Royal Catacombs in the Basilica of Saint-Denis, in October 1793.* (1793, oil on canvas; Paris, Musée Carnavalet; Photo © RMN-Grand Palais / Agence Bulloz)

account of the processes that defined the Age of Revolutions. I some-times set the specific (and mediated) image of one aspect of revolution-ary iconoclasm, Hubert Robert's *La Violation des caveaux des rois dans la basilique Saint-Denis, en Octobre 1793*, which depicts the digging up, de-struction, and dispersal of the bodies of the French kings from their crypt in Saint-Denis cathedral not as a frenzied act but as a planned, coordinated, and methodical process, more akin to building, carried out by self-assured laborers rather than fanatics, who are building as they destroy, so to speak. The artist, Hubert Robert (who was himself imprisoned for a time during the Terror and was lucky to survive, and later was deeply involved in the administration of the great revolution-ary museum project, the Louvre) foregrounds the vast Gothic structure that encloses the whole as if to say that something nasty had to be dug out of the basement to aid the preservation of a grander whole. Yet the image is, perhaps despite itself, pervaded with "night thoughts" melancholy as one laborer is in the act of contemplation of the empty coffin, and the grouping of the three foregrounded workers reminds us of nothing less than Poussin's Arcadian shepherds, as if Robert knew how complex and double-edged was the act being carried out.

Highs and Lows

Does this mean, then, that meaningful study of visual culture and the French Revolution can only or best happen through focus on its most "democratized" forms, in popular civic culture or through the way it relates to social action and political practice? Some would make this case, but my own view and one that has sustained my research and my teaching of the Age of Revolutions is that the entire spectrum of visual art, from the highest of high forms (history painting, sculpture), to the most ephemeral of visual graffiti, is enmeshed in a great human knot of action and representation, and consequently much can be learned from careful study of all kinds of visual art and how it was observed, circulated, and used (and destroyed) during the Age of Revolutions. I have long argued that to exclude grand history painting or sculpture as "elite" and incapable of resonance in the social process of revolution is to miss an important opportunity, and for the rest of this essay I explore how and why this might be the case and my strategies to make it relevant.

First, I find it very helpful and stimulating to remind students that the Age of Revolutions is the moment of the birth of art in the public sphere. This means specifically that art has a prominent place in the narrative of the birth of public space, public debate and circulation, of Jürgen Habermas's notion of Öffentlichkeit (the public sphere). The best way to address this is to plunge students into the heady and intense spaces of the world's first regular, free, mass-participation contemporary art biennials, the salons of the French Royal Academy of Painting and Sculpture, which after a stuttering start, became after the mid-1740s a regular and eagerly anticipated opportunity for Parisian publics to engage with contemporary art in the exhibitions held every two years in the Salon Carré of the Louvre. We know that by the 1780s, tens of thousands of people attended these exhibitions in the six weeks or so they ran—and we know that they fostered a semi-clandestine discourse of criticism and review. Indeed, it is not an exaggeration to say that the kind of comparative occasional discourse of judgment we've come to know as art criticism was born as a result of the encounter with art in these exhibitions: open not only to the elite philosophes but to a lively and informed "Grub Street" generation keen to impress and amuse visitors with pithy, gossipy, elaborate, burlesque, often prescient accounts of the paintings on display. The salons were a marvelous and novel spectacle (perhaps this is best captured in the feverish oil painting on paper by the artist Gabriel de Saint Aubin of the Salon of 1779, which gives the impression of a crowded and overwhelming space and the sense of something unreal and almost ecstatic, a privileged space of engagement and encounter). They were also a political space, one in which the sharpest of critics deliberately displaced their political commentaries into the aesthetic sphere—as when Diderot, one of the most famous and brilliant of the early salon critics and a central figure of the European Enlightenment accused François Boucher of consorting with "prostitutes of the basest sort" in his account of the 1765 exhibition. He was not referring (as far as we can tell) to Boucher as night crawler but to the fact that he had worked so long for the Marquise de Pompadour, long associated by some factions with the sexual corruption and abuses of power of Louis XV's court. As Thomas Crow has shown, in the heated decade of the 1780s, with the buzzwords *vertu* and *patrie* dominating the political discourse of those agitating for renewal of regimes, the fact that artists delved into the repertoire of ancient and modern virtue and foregrounded the dilemmas of ethical and political decision making so often in painting, and the fact that among them, one particular artist seemed to delight in spectacularly breaking the rules of pictorial decorum, allowed a space and a pretext for a new kind of engaged criticism that deployed formal and aesthetic judgment as a substitute or a veil for clearly political sentiment. If I called the art of the revolution a precipitate, the "result" of a reaction, perhaps then the art of the pre-revolutionary decades on display at the salons can be seen rather as a trigger, an agent of reaction, or perhaps a catalyst that stimulated the reactions and emboldened the elements of the political spectrum who would go on to articulate their opposition more forcefully and more directly once the revolutionary process was under way. The history of these exhibitions, of the public seeing art of all genres in many media, is for me a vital part of teaching art's place in the Age of Revolutions.

Art as Commodity

In some senses, the history of art in the public sphere that I have been outlining is associated with a rather heroic and sometimes quasi-teleological history of revolutionary forces gathering pace, first seen in culture and then diffused into politics and social action—and it has sometimes been objected that in fact this mischaracterizes art's true role in eighteenth-century life, which was still predominantly as a private commodity, a luxury good for the delectation of elites. We forget that even as David became the darling of a radical public, he was patronized and supported by a clique of elite patrons and buyers, and one of his great 1780s canvases, *Paris and Helen*, was commissioned by the king's brother, the Comte D'Artois, notorious for his sexual license in the 1780s and even more notorious as a counterrevolutionary émigré and then as a restored king. For art historians and historians, then, the temptation to see artists as vanguard figures of an unstoppable liberal force must be resisted. One way to do this is to explore and teach how art was bought and sold, collected and enjoyed by private buyers and patrons in the later eighteenth century. Colin Bailey's breakthrough book *Patriotic Taste* gave a sense of a practice of enlightened patronage happening in the upper echelons of the administrative and financial bureaucracy of the ancien régime and rightly pointed to the collector as a significant cultural figure in the Enlightenment. This perspective allows us to explore elite networks and understand how art built cultural capital for its owners and how patrons and purchasers fueled the growth of new genres and styles. In my teaching, I like to emphasize these elite practices as part of a broader and very significant practice of visual adornment that was widespread in many (if not all) social classes, as the evidence of postdeath inventories of artisans and bourgeois citizens of Paris and the provinces demonstrates. Many people bought one form or other of artistic reproduction to hang in their homes. Picture factories producing oil paintings on an industrial scale for the bottom end of the market seem to have proliferated—it is said that Watteau and Greuze started their careers churning out images for this kind of enterprise. The work of Hans van Miegroet and others has shown us how art markets can be explored as part of wider economic understandings of the circulation of wealth in the prerevolutionary years, and how particular kinds of manipulation helped keep them afloat at certain times. I try to inject into my teaching that art might legitimately be studied as part of the explosion of the circulation of goods that helped define a hyper-refined consumer society whose thirst for novelty and need for distinction by something other than birth or sheer mass of wealth is worthy of study. We can study engravings and (in the British example, at least) print satires for their political content, and we can fruitfully explore them as part of the story of the circulation of images and the expansion of a verbal-visual literacy, profoundly intertwined with the more general explosion in the circulation of books and pamphlets. To bring students to an understanding of this aspect of art and visual culture is perhaps to dilute a more heroic political or social narrative, but it has the merit of reflecting accurately the wider circulation and consumption of pictures outside the relatively exclusive realm of the Academy and its exhibitions. Of course, this leads to wider discussions of the growth of consumerism, cultural capital, the public consumption of culture, and other concepts that remain resolutely relevant in the lives of my students, who almost without exception have lived the majority of their lives inside hyper-sophisticated consumer societies and who are constantly working on their own strategies for personal and cultural distinction.

Teaching Failure

Another strategy I have adopted to give resonance and relevance to art in the Age of Revolutions is to examine artistic failure. I find this generally useful as a counterweight to a tendency in art history toward lionizing its canonical subjects, but it has special helpfulness in my teaching of this era because it can help students contemplate the part of accident, unpredictability, and misjudgment as part of historical processes. In the Age of Revolutions, grand artistic projects and grand ambitions continued to flounder, and art gambled and often lost. Some of those losses are instructive in general ways, some more specifically, and some are more obviously resonant with "high politics"; others tell a fascinating aesthetic story. Two examples of this are particularly instructive. First, Adolf-Erich Wertmüller's *Queen Marie Antoinette of France and Two of Her Children Walking in the Park of Trianon* (1785), which reflected various grand propagandistic and personal ambitions. It was the artist's keen ambition to make his reputation in his adopted country with a remarkable full-length portrait of grand proportions almost in the English style, and it was the sitter's great hope that a shaky negative public opinion could be convinced by this display of genteel but sincere

Jean-Baptiste Greuze, *Septimius Severus and Caracalla*. (1769, oil on canvas; Paris, Musée du Louvre; Photo © RMN-Grand Palais (musée du Louvre) / Michel Urtado)

motherhood. Both hopes were dashed by an overwhelmingly negative response by that very art critical mass whose growth I discussed earlier in this essay; Wertmüller's quest for artistic success, patronage, and income later carried him to Philadelphia, where George Washington posed for him in Independence Hall in 1794. Working with students to examine the *Marie Antoinette* painting is a stimulating exercise in what I call instructive failure, and I lead them through the contemporary criticisms (alas, not many are translated, so I have to do some translating in advance), show them its physical location in the salon as recorded in engravings, and we think through how it might have struck audiences and why it is inadequate to its various tasks.

Another painting that I often focus on as a locus of instructive failure is Jean-Baptiste Greuze's *Septimius Severus and Caracalla* (1769, Paris, Louvre). Greuze had been the darling of the public exhibitions in the previous decade, showing complex multifigure works celebrating the joys of patriarchy and the well-ordered household, to the delight of Diderot and the advocates of the radical idea of "family values." But Greuze had ambitions as an artist inside the world of artists, aspiring to be seen as a truly great painter and gain access to the full privileges of the Academy by presenting a work showing a historical subject as his "reception piece" (the work that would earn him full membership in the French Royal Academy). After years of deliberation, he presented a painting that was as radical and challenging as it was mystifying and laughable. His friends turned against him, the critics lambasted him, and the academy, in an instructive fudge to anyone tuned to the complex anthropology of elite artistic sociability, decided to admit Greuze but only as a genre painter (a painter of everyday life scenes) and not as a history painter (a painter of complex historical and mythological narratives, the most privileged and noble kind of painter according to the academy's rankings). This moment in 1769 is instructive in many ways for students: I endeavor to help them see just how odd and confronting Greuze's painting was—and at first this is difficult because the painting has none of the compelling immediacy of Fragonard or David—yet it really is an avant-garde work, a radical neo-Poussinian alternative to the Baroque-derived suavity currently in vogue and on display elsewhere in the salon. Its story was both original (never before taken as a subject of history painting) and disconcerting—plucked from the dark days of the end of the Roman Empire, set in the bleak northern wastes of Britain, and involving two of the nastier emperors of the dying days of Roman glory (Septimius Severus and his son Caracalla, both murderers and tyrants, now caught up in a weird tale of failed parricide). Trying to see the almost impossible pressures this tale of grim murderous desire and obstinate authority placed on Greuze involves us reading the accounts he read (and one of the wonders of the digital age is that I can read extracts from his sources without having to be in a rare book room) and then thinking about the sheer oddness of the composition, all extended arms and vast improbable legs, and cowering man-child in the corner. This leads us to discussion of what "correctness" looked like to the age, and what drew painters to try to tell stories in condensed, compacted, and visually arresting ways. We go on to talk of the vital importance to old regime culture of the rite of passage and the rules and regulations that classified human endeavor and rank, socially and culturally. After all, the hierarchy of the genres, a ranking of the value of a painter by the subject matter he or she painted, is itself a telling example of mentalities in many respects—from the obsession with rank as part of French culture (so brilliantly explored by Emmanuel Le Roi Ladurie and others) to wider philosophical frameworks that placed man at the center of a universe ordained by God. Furthermore, the idea of Greuze being treated with patronizing cunning by a body of artists who, although they recognized his talent, despised his arrogance and ambition is also instructive for students grappling the complexities of intellectual and artisan culture in the Age of Revolutions. I find it immensely helpful to tell stories of artists' fates and fortunes to enliven teaching, and with such extraordinary and colorful characters as Greuze, David, and Hubert Robert, let alone the minor figures like Gabriel de Saint Aubin, the "lives of the artists" (to use Vasari's term), help us understand the human dilemmas, passions, and decisions that give the whole revolutionary era its continuing interest and relevance for a generation who otherwise might feel remote from the structures of ancien régime society.

Posterity

All of the strategies and topics I adopt in teaching this era are fueled by new research insights and emphases, and because the era of revolutions is so fundamental to the identities of many nation-states across the world, the pipeline of research flows constantly. My teaching of the complexities of life for artists inside the Académie Royale, for example, is constantly nourished by new studies of community and networks; my teaching of art as a commodity relies on the remarkable new data-crunching powers of large-scale digital humanities initiatives; my emphasis on iconoclasm owes much to the newest research on the complexities of image and monument destruction and preservation in the revolutionary period inspired by new archaeological and historical perspectives. Perhaps that's the final point I would like to make: that teaching the Age of Revolutions never stands still and must be alert to new data and new interests among experts and students. As I've hinted in this essay, I feel that the rapid transformation of teaching and visualizing technologies and the spread of ideas from the worlds of gaming and virtual reality into the space of teaching will lead to significant enhancements in our ability to communicate spatial, visual, and human complexity to students—something that holds enormous promise for all art historians and cultural historians, and I look forward to the day I can use a digital tool to plunge my students into the bewildering floor-to-ceiling experience of an eighteenth-century public exhibition, or drop them into the rolling and ever-changing spectacle of a revolutionary festival, or help virtually reconstruct lost monuments and destroyed statues from plans and texts. None of this will be a substitute for or a deviation from grounded historical and art historical reflection and research, but in the particular case of revolutionary visual culture there is an enormous amount of potential for new technologies to transform teaching and understanding of the Age of Revolutions.

KEY RESOURCES

Artworks Cited in this Essay

Jacques-Louis David, *Marat at His Last Breath* or, *The Death of Marat* (1793, oil on canvas, Brussels, Musées Royaux): available at https://en.wikipedia.org/wiki/The_Death_of_Marat#/media/File:Jacques-Louis_David_-_Marat_assassinated_-_Google_Art_Project_2.jpg.

Anonymous engraver, *Prise de la Bastille par les bourgeois et les braves gardes françaises de la bonne ville de Paris, le 14 juillet 1789* (Seizure of the Bastille by the bourgeous and the brave French Guards of the good city of Paris, July 14, 1789) (1789; etching and aquatint, published by Jacques-Louis Bance, British Museum): available at http://gallica.bnf.fr/ark:/12148/btv1b6942810q.

Jacques-Louis David, *Le serment du Jeu de paume* or *The Tennis Court Oath* (1791, pen and sepia wash, Versailles, Musées Nationaux de Versailles et de Trianon): available at https://en.wikipedia.org/wiki/The_Tennis_Court_Oath_(David)#/media/File:Jacques_Louis_David_-_Le_serment_du_Jeu_de_Paume_-_Google_Art_Project.jpg.

François-André Vincent, *The Taking of the Bastille* (1789, pen and sepia wash, Dijon, Musée des Beaux-Arts).

Pierre De Machy, *The Festival of the Cult of the Supreme Being* (1794, oil on canvas, Paris, Musée Carnavalet): available at https://en.wikipedia.org/wiki/Cult_of_the_Supreme_Being#/media/File:F%C3%AAte_de_l%27Etre_supr%C3%AAme_2.jpg.

Hubert Robert, *La Violation des caveaux des rois dans la basilique Saint-Denis, en Octobre 1793* or *The Violation of the Royal Catacombs in the Basilica of Saint-Denis, in October 1793* (1793, oil on canvas, Paris, Musée Carnavalet): available at http://www.carnavalet.paris.fr/en/collections/la-violation-des-caveaux-des-rois-dans-la-basilique-de-saint-denis-en-octobre-1793.

Gabriel de Saint-Aubin, *A View of the Salon of 1779* (1779, oil on canvas-backed

paper, Paris, Musée du Louvre): available at https://commons.wikimedia
.org/wiki/File:Gabriel_Jacques_de_Saint-Aubin_-_The_Salon_of_1779_-_
WGA20656.jpg.

Adolf-Erich Wertmuller, *Queen Marie-Antoinette of France and Two of Her Children
Walking in the Park of Trianon* (1785, oil on canvas, Nationalmuseum, Stock-
holm): available at https://en.wikipedia.org/wiki/Marie_Antoinette#
/media/File:Adolf_Ulrik_Wertm%C3%BCller_-_Queen_Marie_
Antoinette_of_France_and_two_of_her_Children_Walking_in_The_Park_
of_Trianon_-_Google_Art_Project.jpg.

Jean-Baptiste Greuze, *Septimius Severus and Caracalla* (1769, oil on canvas, Paris,
Louvre): available at https://upload.wikimedia.org/wikipedia/commons
/8/86/Jean-Baptiste_Greuze_-_Septimius_Severus_and_Caracalla_-_
WGA10673.jpg.

Online Resources for the Visual Arts and
Age of Revolutions

www.artstor.org: The Mellon-backed Digital Image Library is a subscription
service but a very important first stop with useful teaching and presentation
tools.

http://frda.stanford.edu/en/images: The French Revolution Digital Archive,
Stanford's collaboration with the Bibliothèque Nationale de France, has
produced an exceptionally useful and rich archive of images and texts related to the French Revolution—a very good starting point for research and
teaching in this area.

https://chnm.gmu.edu/revolution/: Liberty, Equality, Fraternity, a thought-
fully put together site containing 250 images and other multimedia content,
and its sister site, "Imaging the French Revolution," a section of which is
dedicated to images of the revolutionary crowd.

http://www.britishmuseum.org/research/collection_online/search.aspx:
The British Museum is an astonishingly rich repository of visual material
relating to the French Revolution, particularly caricature and print culture
but also objects and ephemera.

http://gallica.bnf.fr: Gallica, the Bibliothèque nationale de France's very rich
and always expanding digital archive gives access to, among other treasures,
the early salon criticism gathered in the Deloynes collection—an archive of
inestimable value to scholars of the Age of Revolutions.

https://chnm.gmu.edu/revolution/imaging/home.html: "Imaging the French
Revolution," a collection of forty images of French revolutionary crowds
and political violence, accompanied by essays written by leading historians
on the subject of crowds, violence, gender, imagery, and more.

http://www.louvre.fr/en/moteur-de-recherche-oeuvres: Given the Louvre's
privileged position as guardian of many of the large-format paintings in the

French revolutionary canon, their database of works is a good place to explore some major and decisive works.

Secondary Sources

Agulhon, Maurice. *Marianne into Battle: Republican Imagery and Symbolism in France, 1789–1880*. Cambridge: Cambridge University Press, 1981.

Arizzoli-Clémentel, Pierre, Philippe Bordes, and Régis Michel. *Aux Armes et Aux Arts! Les Arts de La Révolution, 1789–1799*. Paris: A. Biro, 1988.

Bailey, Colin. *Patriotic Taste: Collecting Modern Art in Pre-Revolutionary Paris*. New Haven, CT: Yale University Press, 2002.

Blanning, T. C. W. *The Culture of Power and the Power of Culture: Old Regime Europe, 1660–1789*. Oxford: Oxford University Press, 2002.

Bordes, Philippe. "Jacques-Louis David's 'Serment Du Jeu de Paume': Propaganda without a Cause?" *Oxford Art Journal* 3, no. 2 (October 1, 1980): 19–25.

Chartier, Roger. *The Cultural Origins of the French Revolution*. Durham, NC: Duke University Press, 1991.

Clay, Richard. *Iconoclasm in Revolutionary Paris: The Transformation of Signs*. Oxford: Voltaire Foundation, 2012.

Crow, Thomas E. *Emulation: David, Drouais, and Girodet in the Art of Revolutionary France*. New Haven, CT: Yale University Press, 2006.

———. *Painters and Public Life in Eighteenth-Century Paris*. New Haven, CT: Yale University Press, 1985.

Darnton, Robert. *The Forbidden Best-Sellers of Pre-Revolutionary France*. New York: Norton, 1995.

Diderot, Denis. *Diderot on Art*, 2 vols. Translated and edited by John Goodman. New Haven, CT: Yale University Press, 1995.

Dowd, David Lloyd. *Pageant-Master of the Republic, Jacques-Louis David and the French Revolution*. Freeport, NY: Books for Libraries Press, 1948.

Gamboni, Dario. *The Destruction of Art: Iconoclasm and Vandalism since the French Revolution*. New Haven, CT: Yale University Press, 2007.

Goodman, Dena. *The Republic of Letters: A Cultural History of the French Enlightenment*. Ithaca, NY: Cornell University Press, 1994.

Herbert, Robert L. *David, Voltaire, Brutus, and the French Revolution: An Essay in Art and Politics*. London: A. Lane, Penguin Press, 1972.

Hunt, Lynn. *Politics, Culture, and Class in the French Revolution*. Berkeley: University of California Press, 1984.

Kennedy, Emmet. *A Cultural History of the French Revolution*. New Haven, CT: Yale University Press, 1989.

Mansfield, Elizabeth C. *The Perfect Foil: François-Andre Vincent and the Revolution in French Painting*. Minneapolis: University of Minnesota Press, 2011.

McClellan, Andrew. *Inventing the Louvre: Art, Politics, and the Origins of the Modern*

Museum in Eighteenth-Century Paris. Cambridge: Cambridge University Press, 1994.

Ozouf, Mona. *Festivals and the French Revolution.* Cambridge, MA: Harvard University Press, 1988.

Roberts, Warren. *Jacques-Louis David, Revolutionary Artist: Art, Politics, and the French Revolution.* Chapel Hill: University of North Carolina Press, 1989.

Taws, Richard. *The Politics of the Provisional: Art and Ephemera in Revolutionary France.* University Park: Pennsylvania State University Press, 2013.

Wrigley, Richard. *The Origins of French Art Criticism: From the Ancien Régime to the Restoration.* Oxford: Clarendon Press, 1993.

———. *The Politics of Appearances: Representations of Dress in Revolutionary France.* Oxford: Berg, 2002.

Ziskin, Rochelle. "The Place de Nos Conquêtes and the Unraveling of the Myth of Louis XIV." *Art Bulletin* 76, no. 1 (March 1994): 147–62.

Music in the Age
of Revolutions

American Anthems

JAMES JACKSON ASHTON

W hy should someone teaching the Age of Revolutions care about music? One reason is that music is a symbol. People use music, and other products of culture, to express ideology and emotion and represent their meaning. But turn this around and you see a second, more fundamental reason: music generates social, economic, and political practices. That is, a musical performance does not just express some underlying meaning, habit, or idea; it builds a world that leads to that idea in the first place. Music in the Age of Revolutions was particularly significant in this respect. By writing, distributing, and performing music, citizens of societies in the midst of revolutionary upheaval engaged in making and making sense of the ideology of revolution, even as they constructed the lattice of cultural practices that constituted the musical world.

For teachers, music as a pedagogical tool can be intimidating. Too often, historians and classroom instructors assume that teaching music requires a level of specialized knowledge that they do not have: an understanding of musicology and music theory—the ability to parse music's formal properties—that they think disqualifies them from engaging music in the classroom. This essay outlines some themes and ideas that will allow the instructor to begin to think about the social, cultural, economic, and political significance of music and thereby illuminate for their students the whirlwind of revolution that swept through the early modern world. At a bare minimum, music serves as an invaluable illustrative tool, but encouraging students to engage with it can open further doors to comprehension and appreciation. As the phenomenon of *Hamilton: An American Musical* shows, music can reach and reinterpret in ways that surprise, challenge, and invigorate history.

To demonstrate the potential uses of music in the classroom, I elaborate three musical case studies spanning the Age of Revolutions in North America: William Billings's "Chester" during the revolution; the political uses of French revolutionary anthems during the young nation's venomous party struggles in the 1790s; and the writing and distribution of the "Star-Spangled Banner" during the United States's second war against Great Britain from 1812 to 1815.[1] In each of these cases, citizens of the new United States used music to narrate to their fellows the ideologies of revolution, republicanism, democracy, and virtuous struggle. Through performing, reading, writing, and distributing music, they began to elaborate a cultural network that was at first tenuous and ad hoc but also a critical ingredient of US political culture, enabling citizens to begin to craft distinctive social and cultural identities. The bottom line is that the Age of Revolutions saw the dawn of a musical world that, in its proud and often bellicose sentiment, set the course for two centuries of distinctive cultural production.

Revolutionary Hymns

William Billings, a Boston native, made his living as a tanner and singing-school master. He was also a prolific composer. Billings, along with the other hymnbook compilers and composers known collectively as the First New England School, developed a style largely removed from European precedents and self-consciously American. His "Chester," a patriotic hymn to New England and to virtuous triumph over oppression, demonstrates how religious songs and symbols could stimulate patriotic sentiment among a group of colonists engaged in constructing a political identity in the face of what they perceived as base tyranny.

Billings's *The New England Psalm-Singer* (1770) and *The Singing Master's Assistant* (1778) included patriotic anthems for performance by church congregations. "Chester" was printed in both hymnbooks and frequently reprinted in tunebooks that compiled songs from different sources. These multiple printings reflected the song's broad appeal in

New England—not surprising, given its tunefulness and rhythmic snap.[2] With "Chester," Billings desired a "strong, powerful, majestic impression," and from the evidence of its popularity, he achieved his goal.[3] In one of his hymnbooks the Rev. Mather Byles wrote approvingly of the "sublimest Sphere" of Billings's music: "Then rolls the Rapture thro' the Air around / In the full Magic Melody of Sound."[4] Harriet Beecher Stowe later recalled the powerful impressions of "Chester" and similar songs of her childhood when she wrote that "there was a grand, wild freedom, an energy of motion . . . that well expressed the heart of the people courageous in combat."[5] In memory, Billings's music was associated with the heroism of the revolutionary generation. It's a revealing exercise to begin simply by playing the song and inviting students to contemplate its intent and effect—perhaps initially without the lyrics.[6]

"Chester" contains a confluence of patriotism with religious feeling that Francis Scott Key later echoed in "The Star-Spangled Banner." Billings's first stanza relates the divine election of the patriot cause. God "inspir'd us for the fight" in the second stanza, and in the final stanza he attributes triumph to divine sanction: "What grateful Off'ring shall we bring? / What shall we render to the Lord?" The cause of God's elect and the cause of the revolution were one and the same. Nathaniel Gould, Boston native, bandleader, and hymn compiler, noted decades later the "mixed character" of "Chester," which "combin[ed] religion and patriotism" and was "a powerful instrument, for the time, in exciting the spirit of liberty."[7] People who sang "Chester" experienced it as both sacral faith and patriotism: invariably printed alongside hymns and thus often sung in churches, "Chester" was a stirring patriotic song in a religious setting.

Billings also wrote revolutionary ideology into "Chester." The "iron rod" of the tyrant and the "galling chains" of slavery suffuse the first two phrases with an ideologically tinged fearfulness and fervor that is resolved in the soaring melody, which seems to point toward God's triumph in the stanza's closing words. Billings was likely familiar with the politics of the revolution: he was a member of the New South Church and acquainted with Samuel Adams. Adams loved music, especially religious music, and made political use of it: a Tory rival remembered that Adams "had a good Voice, & was a Master in vocal Musick. This Genius he improved, by instituting singing Societys of Mechanicks, where he presided; & embraced such Opportunities to ye inculcating

Sedition, 'till it had ripened into Rebellion."[8] With "Chester," Billings inserted sacral patriotism into the venue where ordinary Americans were most accustomed to singing: the church. Some of them, like Adams, took vocal music honed in church to other civic spaces.

"Chester" maintained its popularity into the 1780s, appearing in at least a dozen tunebooks in Massachusetts and Connecticut. Beginning in the 1790s, Billings's music, and the distinctive US style it represented, was eclipsed by what musical tastemakers started to call "ancient music." This reform of sacred music privileged older Protestant psalmody over the new sacred music written by Americans like Billings. Critics like Andrew Law, who had written music similar to Billings's in the 1790s before switching to support the older style, attacked the work of the First New England School as musically incorrect. That is, people like Law began to apply their own aesthetic criteria to religious and patriotic music. "Ancient music" became a matter of proper taste.

Such judgments represented something relatively new in US culture: the beginnings of a separation of cultural production into "proper"—elite—forms, and music that tastemakers like Law deemed vulgar and in poor taste. Law and those who followed him believed they were assessing music's aesthetic value; in their minds, the tastefulness of the right kind of music was contained in its very notes. But in the rough and tumble of cultural practices like the performance of music, their supposedly aesthetic judgments were accompanied by and often came to be ascribed to social separation. Later generations of Americans would mold the association of certain kinds of music with social elites into a distinctive "high-brow" culture, a narrative of cultural bifurcation that had roots in the Age of Revolutions.[9]

In the classroom, "Chester" thus points to elements of popular culture still important today. For example, why do people so often combine religious and patriotic sentiment and use music to express this complex series of nationalistic meanings? During the revolutionary generation, Americans expressed their new national identity as a kind of sacred election, and this affective mode of expression took root, continuing to the present day in songs like Irving Berlin's "God Bless America." At the same time, the history of "Chester" was an early example of what Americans later defined as the tension between popular and elite culture. Teachers can use this history to show how aesthetic judgments had real social consequences. Americans continued to wield music to determine who properly belonged as the country experienced the upheavals of class and racial strife during the long nineteenth century. "Chester" is an entrance to this important discussion in the classroom.

American "Marseillaises"

During the revolution, British colonists forming a new identity used patriotic music to express their often bellicose sense of grievance in a sacral mode. In the two decades after these new Americans signed their constitution, they appropriated music from another revolution to signal political legitimacy to each other. Ironically, in an age that argued so vociferously against the evils of faction, during the 1790s patriotic music tended to exacerbate factional differences instead of unifying the polity. People played and sung patriotic songs to signal their support for Federalism or for the Jeffersonian party. In an uncertain, suspicious environment that rejected the legitimacy of political parties, partisanship was deeply personal, and Americans, wedded to ideals of republican virtue, used patriotic music as an indication of their own virtuous reputations in allegiance to faction. What historians have labeled the culture of sensibility—that is, refined cultural performance to demonstrate one's social position as a member of an elite—dictated political allegiance and required republican men and women to, as they saw it, cultivate sensibility in the polity broadly. Americans sang French revolutionary songs in something of a cultural war of musical performance. In their minds, they were both signifying their own social standing and demonstrating the perfidy of their political opponents.

Jeffersonian Republicans thought that the French Revolution sanctioned the outcome of the North American colonists' own revolt against the British: after all, republican France espoused an ideology similar to that of the new United States.[10] The French had likewise been quick to mobilize collective music as an instrument of protest, revolution, and consolidation, emphasizing the importance of the choral as a cultural expression of the people.[11] Americans, still insecure in their new polity and lacking the sort of deep, mythologized national past that might otherwise have provided grist for the patriotic mill, reacted passionately in support and opposition to the ideological ferment in France. Their particular interpretations of the political and philosophic ideals of revolutionary France could by extension demonstrate their own party's rectitude as the true republican inheritors of their revolution. In due course, their eyes cast anxiously toward Europe, Americans expressed their own patriotism with reference to the Napoleonic wars their government was so anxious to avoid.

Americans appropriated several French patriotic anthems, including most prominently the "Marseillaise," for their own partisan purposes. The lyrics of these patriotic songs were couched largely in ideological terms familiar to the revolutionary generation. During the sojourn of the French ambassador "Citizen" Genêt in Philadelphia, for example, toasts during dinners in his honor overflowed with virtuous republican sentiment. A typical series of toasts was punctuated by "the Marseillaise hymn," which at one dinner was requested after the toasts and sung "with great taste and spirit, the whole company joining in the chorus."[12] It included two new stanzas, "replete with truly patriotic and republican sentiments," composed by Genêt himself in honor of the French navy.[13] At a similar dinner the following week, artillery salutes, a ubiquitous accompaniment to martial and patriotic music, accompanied several toasts. These were also interspersed with four new patriotic songs; at least two newspapers subsequently published their lyrics. A typical stanza, like Genêt's rendition of "La Marseillaise" replete with common republican sentiments, read "Let us with France agree, / And bid the world be free / While tyrants fall / Let the rude savage host / In their vast numbers boast / Freedom's almighty truth / Laughs at them all." "La Marseillaise" was again a highlight, sung in both French and English.[14]

The songs sung at dinners honoring Genêt and more generally the American appropriation of "La Marseillaise" and other French revolutionary songs, demonstrate patriotic sentiment aimed specifically at ideological enemies, both external and internal. Evidently newspaper editors were interested mostly in the ideological content of the lyrics sung at the June dinner: none of the four listed indicated a tune, and the songs do not seem to have long survived the event. These editors wanted to express a pro-French (and therefore anti-British, anti-Federalist) position at that particular moment. The lyrics of "La Marseillaise," contrasting the glorious French with the tyranny and savagery of the foe, suited the purpose well. During the height of American–French amity in the early to mid-1790s, Jeffersonian Republicans employed French revolutionary anthems to express their patriotism and color their opponents as British sympathizers.

Although French patriotic music might receive full-throated support from Jeffersonians, to their opponents it was suspect at best, traitorous at worst, and was met with contentious, sometimes violent disapproval. By the spring of 1798 the nationalist music of the French Revolution was as liable to be vilified as resoundingly as it had been cheered five years earlier. No longer simply representing the triumph of the true republican spirit, it had instead become for many the music of the enemy, whose emulation of the Americans' shining example had run to unchecked democracy and finally tyranny. Yet the oppositional character of patriotic music and its performance remained in place. For example, in Baltimore in 1798, during the so-called quasi war with France, Federalists met a performance of the "Marseillaise" with "violent hissing and hooting" that drowned out the musicians and halted the performance. Calls rang out in the hall for the "President's March" (soon to be the tune for "Hail, Columbia") and "Yankee Doodle."[15] Especially as diplomatic relations between the United States and the new French Republic soured, Federalists responded to the continuing Jeffersonian use of French national songs with their own music. Dueling patriotic songs stood in for ideological arguments aimed at domestic foes that were identified with the French or British. A universally popular body of patriotic music that referenced the national past while reflecting a supposedly consensual patriotism was still to come.

Citizens of the fledgling United States in the 1790s were still searching out the forms that patriotic performance would take. In this environment, with memories of revolution and oppression still fresh, the political uses of music loomed large, no less than across the pond, where Napoleon shortly repudiated and later banned the "Marseillaise" and its insurrectionary overtones (it remained banned under the Second Restoration from 1815). In the classroom, teachers can emphasize the importance of culture in politics by linking songs like the "Marseillaise" to primary evidence from the period like playbills and newspaper reports describing fraught musical performances in public forums. Indeed, teachers can easily link the political culture of music in the Early Republic to the culture of patriotism in today's United States, where performances of songs like "Proud to Be an American" can provoke political division as much as they are used to signal unity. The divisiveness of patriotic culture at the end of the eighteenth century in the United States, with its distinctive appropriation of music, may seem unfamiliar to students, but it is a chance to demonstrate the importance of popular culture to politics. Today, Americans are accustomed to thinking of patriotic sentiment as a unifying cultural force, but during the early

American republic it remained for a member of the Maryland gentry to pen the song that came to symbolize political consensus at military victory at the end of the Age of Revolutions, after twenty years of faction.

Star-Spangled Banners, Broadsides, and Newspapers

The story of Francis Scott Key writing the "The Star-Spangled Banner" as he watched the bombardment of Baltimore's Fort McHenry from the deck of a British warship is so familiar it is almost cliché.[16] But there is more to the story than the tropes of the dawn's early light revealing the triumphant flag floating over the battlements. Key's song, and especially its early uses, illuminate several ways music and its performance began to suffuse the early American republic and play a key role in its burgeoning imperial power. The rapid dissemination of "The Star-Spangled Banner" in print and performance reflected the elaboration of a cultural network that only grew stronger and more intricate throughout the nineteenth century. It also came to symbolize a civil society that throughout the first half of the nineteenth century, viewed the lessons of republicanism learned during the Age of Revolutions through a lens of martial virtues. "The Star-Spangled Banner" and songs like it were symbols of what many saw as the most sublime patriotism: proud sentiments that reflected victory in battle.

Key's anthem, like many songs patriotic and otherwise in antebellum America, used an existing popular tune. English composer John Stafford Smith probably wrote the tune sometime before the revolution. It was not, however, a patriotic song. Titled "To Anacreon in Heaven," it was instead associated with the Anacreontic Society in London, a genteel social club.[17] American elites emulated the practices of refined British society, using genteel music to signal social difference. "To Anacreon in Heaven," like many songs before and after it in an era before copyright laws, was set indiscriminately to a variety of lyrics. In its original form, the song quickly crossed the Atlantic and, after its first US publication in 1778, made its way into a variety of media, including sheet music and books of songs. The tune recirculated in a variety of contexts. For example, a 1799 song book in Philadelphia set the lyrics of two different patriotic songs to it, while the 1804 *Baltimore Musical Miscellany* contained both the lyrics of "To Anacreon in Heaven" and another song "for a literary society" set to the former's tune.[18] Most famously, the Federalist party song "Adams and Liberty" was set to the tune of "Anacreon in

Heaven" in 1798. Its genteel origins were obscured in its broad use, but the sentiments of Key's lyric reflected the cultural project of the American elite, as they saw it.

The burgeoning print culture of the United States provided genteel men of letters with their most effective mechanism for attempting to spread what they considered proper nationalist sentiment to a broad audience. Elites had a complex relationship toward the popular print media of the early Republic, including the newspapers, almanacs, broadsides, and books that an increasingly broad readership used to make sense of their community and the world. Although there was always a tension between the desire to appeal to an exclusive group of one's peers and the wish to have one's writing circulated widely, in the early Republic genteel men of letters increasingly wanted the products of what was originally their private associational life to influence the wider society. Performing and publishing songs demonstrating republican sensibilities was an important way to cultivate nationalism.[19] The tune of "To Anacreon in Heaven" was used for just such a purpose.

Key himself was the child of an elite Federalist planter family, but he reluctantly supported "President Madison's war." He disapproved of political partisanship, especially what he saw as the treasonous dissension of New England Federalists during the War of 1812, and his lyrics capture his preference for patriotic sentiment in the face of dissenting opinion, rather than propagating the earlier model of two factions locked in ideological struggle. For Key, patriotism was a sacred duty, an emotional element of nationalist sentiment pointing back to the religious patriotism of Billings. Key's thoughts on the war were suffused with the sense—a sense he shared with many Jeffersonian Republicans— that the conflict was God's trial, a fire that while painful, might refine the new nation in the end. "The Star-Spangled Banner" reflected this sense of trial and unity: it invited its readers, listeners, and performers to experience vicariously the passionate emotions encompassing a sublime and martial patriotism. Students are often surprised at the numerous references to a military enemy in the second and third stanzas: "the foe's haughty host," "that band" who brought "havoc of war"; as well as "the hireling and slave" contraposed in the fourth stanza with the "heav'n rescued land" of America and its courageous "freemen," its just cause, and its trust in God.[20]

Unifiers like Key could thank the elaboration of musical culture throughout the first half of the century for the increasing dominance of the martial mode of patriotism: performance spaces were in the process of being built, genres normalized, and musical discourse extended. The dissemination of "The Star-Spangled Banner" was an example of this burgeoning musical culture. The first broadside printing of his song appeared the day after it was written, intended for local performance in Baltimore's taverns and in Fort McHenry. It reflected the importance Americans of the Age of Revolutions placed on martial music: as one observer noted, no one could deny "the power of the ear-piercing fife and spirit-stirring drum" which would "do more to excite martial ardor than the most elaborate essay."[21] The first printing of "The Star-Spangled Banner" was an answer to this clarion call, and furthermore its supporters took advantage of the rapidly developing print networks of the young nation to spread Key's effusion throughout the country in newspapers. In less than a month it had reached as far south as Savannah, Georgia, and as far west as Louisville, Kentucky. This was about as fast as it was possible for news—or a song—to travel in 1814.

The transmission of "The Star-Spangled Banner" reflected the strengthening culture and networks of musical performance in the United States overall. We can see this by tracing the travels of one performing family, the Durangs. Charles and Ferdinand Durang, who sang "The Star-Spangled Banner" along with a group of fellow militiamen in front of a tavern next to Baltimore's Holliday Street Theatre just days after it was written, were performers who had joined the defense of Baltimore. The family patriarch, John Durang, was a dancer, singer, musician, propmaster, set designer, and salesman—a jack-of-all-trades in the musical world. His career, and those of his sons, typified that of the peripatetic performers whose multiple talents filled nearly every role a musician could in antebellum America. The Durang family and others like them created and traveled along the ligaments of a performative network that knit together disparate spaces into a musical culture, disseminating patriotic music across the nation and consolidating the unifying valence of nationalist sentiment hinted at in "The Star-Spangled Banner."

During this era, as Americans began to construct musical institutions, spaces, and routes, performers and audiences together elaborated a symbolically rich musical culture that was initially characterized by a broad variety of multipurpose venues and temporarily repurposed spaces. The development of musical culture in secondary urban centers such as Cincinnati and Baltimore was propagated throughout the country by performers who could adapt quickly and readily to local needs and were willing to find or even build temporary performance spaces as needed. As they elaborated this cultural network, Americans increasingly desired permanent spaces for their music, a process that accelerated later in the century. This led to more spaces that were coded as appropriate for specific genres of music: an opera house, for example, or a public garden for dance music. At the same time, many venues retained the flexibility to be considered both commercial and civic space: theaters could be rented for a melodrama or a genteel concert, while that same public garden could host a Fourth of July celebration.

During the early Republic, performers like John Durang used patriotic music and symbolism as a point of reference as they built up local and regional performance networks from a grab bag of temporary venues. These venues were not defined by individual genres or well-codified standards of comportment, as modern venues often are. Performers instead used what was locally available, improvising spaces as needed. This elaboration of performance spaces occurred alongside the growth of print networks, and performers used the combination to their advantage. For example, John Durang's journal records the result in Harrisburg, Pennsylvania, where on the Fourth of July 1815 "the 'Star Spangled Banner' was sung in many companies."[22] A year after the composition and initial print dissemination of Key's song, it was a familiar part of performance across the nation. The spatial network, integrated with local print media, framed patriotic music as a popular and broadly shared national form.

I have focused on "The Star-Spangled Banner" and several other patriotic songs to illustrate how music directly influenced the elaboration of politics and society: music, motivation, and mobilization became inextricably intertwined during the Age of Revolutions. A song like "Chester" linked the revolutionary generation to sacral celebrations of the past even as it spelled out the hopes of colonists to overthrow what they considered tyranny. Less than two decades after the revolution, citizens of the new and as-yet-uncertain American polity used music on the front lines of bitter partisan battles as they fought to define the republican virtues supposedly gained so recently. Finally, during the War of 1812, which many citizens thought of as a second revolution to confirm the country's ideals, Key's "Star-Spangled Banner" laid out a new way of thinking about those ideals: as a means to a fervently martial nationalism, and even—as it later became—an imperialism ("conquer we must, when our cause it is just"). Key's anthem also traced the paths of a burgeoning musical culture as it traveled from street corner to tavern to theater, from broadside to newspaper. Only belatedly in March 1931, like the French "Marseillaise" before it in 1879, was it formally recognized as a national anthem.

For the classroom teacher and students tackling the Age of Revolutions, small forays that combine listening to and analyzing these songs (and others) can yield rich rewards, for they do more than just evoke some of the sound and spirit of the era. By treating music as more than the sum of its formal properties, and considering the spaces, publications, and social patterns it illuminates, teachers can help their students understand how groups of people in the midst of revolution could craft and give meaning to new political entities. The collision of music, modernism, and revolution left indelible imprints on all three in the late eighteenth and early nineteenth centuries, and we remain exposed to the consequences, as when "The Star-Spangled Banner" was performed for the first time by the Coldstream Guards outside Buckingham Palace after 9/11, or "La Marseillaise" echoed around Union Square in New York in response to the terrorist attacks on Paris in November 2015.

NOTES

1. These case studies are adapted from the first chapter of my "Patriotic Sublime: Music and the Nation in America, 1790–1848" (PhD dissertation, Johns Hopkins University, 2015).

2. Richard Crawford and David McKay, *William Billings of Boston: Eighteenth Century Composer* (Princeton, NJ: Princeton University Press, 1975), 30; Richard Crawford, *America's Musical Life: A History* (New York: Norton, 2005), 42–43.

3. Gilbert Chase, *America's Music: From the Pilgrims to the Present* (New York: McGraw-Hill, 1955), 142. See also Crawford, *William Billings of Boston*, passim.

4. Both quoted in Chase, *America's Music*, 142.

5. James A. Keene, *A History of Music Education in the United States* (Hanover, NH: University Press of New England, 1982), 33.

6. The sheet music and lyrics of the 1778 version are available at https://en.wikipedia.org/wiki/Chester_(song), while a range of evocative performances can be found on YouTube, such as the Fairfax High District Chorus (2012): https://www.youtube.com/watch?v=E_St8bsx31A.

7. Nathaniel Duren Gould, *Church Music in America* (Boston: A. N. Johnson, 1853), 43.

8. Crawford and McKay, *William Billings*, 66–67.

9. See, for example, Lawrence W. Levine, *High-Brow, Low-Brow: The Emergence of Cultural Hierarchy in America* (Cambridge, MA: Harvard University Press, 1988); Pierre Bourdieu, *Distinction: A Social Critique of the Judgment of Taste* (New York: Routledge, 1984, 2010); Richard Butsch, *The Making of American Audiences: From Stage to Television, 1750–1990* (New York: Cambridge University Press, 2000).

10. Stanley Elkins and Eric McKittrick, *The Age of Federalism* (Oxford: Oxford University Press, 1993), 308–9.

11. Leora Auslander, *Cultural Revolutions: The Politics of Everyday Life in Britain, North America and France* (Oxford: Berg, 2009), 141–42.

12. *Federal Gazette*, Philadelphia, May 22, 1793.

13. Ibid. See also W. A. Newman Dorland, "The Second Troop Philadelphia City Cavalry," *Pennsylvania Magazine of History and Biography* 46, no. 182 (1922): 169.

14. *Dunlap's American Daily Advertiser*, Philadelphia, June 4, 1793; *Federal Gazette*, Philadelphia, June 5, 1793.

15. *Federal Gazette*, Baltimore, April 17, 1798; Philadelphia *Gazette*, April 19, 1798; John Thomas Scharf, *History of Baltimore City and County* (Philadelphia: L. H. Everts, 1881), 681, 689.

16. The best history of "The Star-Spangled Banner" remains Oscar Sonneck, *Report on "The Star Spangled Banner," "Hail Columbia," "America," and "Yankee Doodle"* (Washington, DC: Library of Congress, 1909).

17. Sonneck, *The Star Spangled Banner*, 36. See ibid., 9–63, for a detailed discussion of the history of the song's authorship. For a typical description of "To Anacreon in Heaven" as a "drinking song," see for example Walter Lord, *The Dawn's Early Light* (New York: Norton, 1972), 296.

18. *A Collection of Songs, selected from the works of Mr. Dibdin* ... (Philadelphia, 1799); P. W. Filby, Edward G. Howard, *Star Spangled Books: Books, Sheet Music, Newspapers, Manuscripts, and Persons Associated with the Star Spangled Banner* (Baltimore: Maryland Historical Society, 1972), 85.

19. Catherine O'Donnell Kaplan, *Men of Letters in the Early Republic: Cultivating Forums of Citizenship* (Chapel Hill: University of North Carolina Press, 2008), 69–70; David Waldstreicher, *In the Midst of Perpetual Fetes: The Making of American Nationalism, 1776–1820* (Chapel Hill: University of North Carolina Press, 1997), 110–11; Richard D. Brown, *Knowledge Is Power: The Diffusion of Information in Early America, 1700–1865* (Oxford: Oxford University Press, 1989), 198–99.

20. The earliest known manuscript of Key's song and printed copies, as well as an audio performance of the piece as played in 1854 can be found at the

Smithsonian website: http://amhistory.si.edu/starspangledbanner/the-lyrics
.aspx.

21. "National Music," *Chronicle or Harrisburgh Visitor*, Harrisburg, PA,
September 5, 1814. Reprinted from the *Baltimore American*.

22. A. S. Downer, ed., *The Memoir of John Durang, American Actor* (Pittsburgh:
University of Pittsburgh Press, 1966), 135.

KEY RESOURCES

Ahlquist, Karen. *Democracy at the Opera: Music, Theater and Culture in New York
City, 1815–60*. Champaign: University of Illinois Press, 1997.

Chase, Gilbert. *America's Music: From the Pilgrims to the Present*, 3rd ed. Champaign: University of Illinois Press, 1992.

Darlow, Mark. *Staging the French Revolution: Cultural Politics and the Paris Opéra,
1789–1794*. New York: Oxford University Press, 2012.

Gramit, David. *Cultivating Music: The Aspirations, Interests, and Limits of German
Musical Culture, 1770–1848*. Berkeley: University of California Press, 2002.

Johnson, Victoria, Jane F. Fulcher, and Thomas Ertman, eds. *Opera and Society in
Italy and France from Monteverdi to Bourdieu*. Cambridge: Cambridge University Press, 2007.

Mason, Laura. *Singing the French Revolution: Popular Culture and Politics, 1787–
1799*. Ithaca, NY: Cornell University Press, 1996.

Weber, William. *The Great Transformation of Musical Taste: Concert Programming
from Haydn to Brahms*. Cambridge: Cambridge University Press, 2008.

Thomas Paine and the *Common Sense* of Revolutions

EDWARD LARKIN

For many of our students, *revolution* is a received term that signifies in somewhat flat, albeit loaded ways. In the United States they identify the idea with the American Revolution, and with the kind of popular technological changes that television and print advertisements play on. As a result of this sloganeering, the term has been emptied of its danger and subversion. Students tend to think of revolution and the revolutionary as unambiguously positive terms and have emptied them of the kind of fundamental challenge to the status quo that Thomas Paine and his contemporaries felt quite palpably. By asking students to think about the difference between a revolution and a rebellion, we can begin to reintroduce some of that subversive quality to the term. This often enables a conversation about the violence of the American Revolution (conceptual as well as literal). Paine's influential *Common Sense*, of course, insists that the Americans are already at war with the British. He reminds his readers of the events of April 19, 1775, in Lexington and Concord, Massachusetts. More vividly, as I elaborate later, he underscores the violence perpetrated against Americans in the destruction of property and the deaths of citizens. Of course, he doesn't address the fact that much of that civil violence was perpetrated by patriots against loyalists—but that's a topic for another day (or that can be unpacked using the American revolutionary Reacting to the Past game titled *Patriots, Loyalists, & Revolution in New York City*). Early Americans experienced the violence of revolution not only in the battlefield but in the civil disturbances and conflicts that simmered to a boil in most of the colonial urban centers.

A second goal that accompanies my interest in impressing on students a sense of the danger and violence that revolution engenders is reminding them of the uncertainty of the outcome. Most of my students are flabbergasted when they learn that around a third of American colonials in the thirteen colonies opposed the revolution. Just as surprising for them is the idea that, at least in John Adams's estimation, another third were neutral and a final third were for independence. They, like so many denizens, have no sense of how very controversial the American Revolution was. Instead, they think of it as a historical inevitability and assume that it wasn't really a question for the colonists. Paine's pamphlet is an excellent antidote for this perception. His tone, his sense of urgency, and the emotional pleas that emerge in the latter half of the pamphlet speak to this sense of uncertainty and division among the colonists. I often present students with examples of loyalist arguments against the revolution: William Smith's "Cato's Letters" are a fine example, and so are the wonderful loyalist poems in Milcah Martha Moore's "Common-place Book." Poems about the disruption and human loss caused by the revolution help humanize the loyalist perspective and add texture and complexity to the story of the revolution. They also offset Paine's vicious and caricatured accounts of loyalists in *Common Sense*. Paine wanted early Americans to feel the threat to their liberty, and I want the students to at least glimpse some of the sense of danger and uncertainty that those early Americans felt. Students, I hope, can begin to see the local human face of the revolution in addition to its broad literary and historical significance.

Paine's text is thus a perfect vehicle to humanize the revolution and recover its literary and historical contingencies. It opens up both conceptual and local literary and historical questions. From the very nature of revolution as a form of social and historical change to the specific political and aesthetic debates that preoccupied early Americans, *Common Sense* vividly brings to life fundamental questions that are still relevant. The challenge of transforming the world for the better, imagining a new social and political order, taking risks and rethinking fundamental assumptions about how the world works—these are also questions that resonate with our students who are preparing themselves to go out into a world that they often find alien and mysterious. At his core, Paine's thought is about demystification. His goal is to render the world and its systems, social, political, economic, religious, and so on comprehensible and available. He understood that those in power strategically used opacity and mystification to maintain their grip on the social and political order. This is why above all Paine was interested in inventing a new language of politics. Language held the key because it was both the vehicle of mystification and the means to its undoing. To understand Paine is to understand that language, style, and form matter, perhaps more than anything else. Another way to say this would be that I use Paine's text to re-mediate their understanding of the revolution.

Most often I teach Thomas Paine and the American Revolution within the context of courses on early American literature, which poses some particular challenges. To begin with, students don't think of political writing as literature. English majors choose the field because they love reading (and sometimes writing) novels, poems, plays, and short stories. They think of those kinds of texts as creative works of the imagination with themes, characters, and plots, that provide emotional as well as intellectual stimulation. These are not qualities they associate with the kinds of political and social theoretical texts Paine wrote. In a way, we could say that most students, whether they are English, history, or political science majors, don't really know *how* to read the genres Paine practiced. But, of course, his political and social theory texts are also imaginative works with characters, themes, and plots that are often infused with a significant emotional charge. In *Common Sense*, and his other major works, Paine's goal is to reimagine and reinvent the world. He hopes to convince his readers to take risks and pursue revolutionary action in their political, social, and religious lives. To accomplish this end, he has to tell a story, or more accurately, a series of complementary stories, that will appeal to readers' imaginations and emotions as much as their reason. This is the version of Paine and political writing that I want my students to grasp, and when they do, it can change how they think about the categories of literature and writing and how they think about political theory, revolution broadly defined, and the American Revolution in particular.

This means that I teach the American Revolution as a literary event. What I mean by this is that my focus is on how the kinds of questions that motivate literary analysis played an essential role in the revolution, and specifically in texts like *Common Sense*, *The Federalist*, and the Declaration of Independence. I want to show students that questions about language and form are as important to those political texts as they are to the novels, plays, and poems of the time. We focus on how language, rhetoric, imagery, symbolism, tropes, and other literary strategies and devices played a crucial role in shaping the arguments for independence and the young republic that emerged out of the split with the British Empire. The American Revolution, my students learn, took place in writing and language as much as on the battlefield. Paine's *Common Sense* presents a perfect venue to illustrate this point. It is a painstakingly crafted work of literature in which the attention to language and the way it can be manipulated, revised, and reinvented takes center stage. In this respect, the pamphlet is as well-crafted a piece of writing as any work of literature published in the late eighteenth century. To understand its power, we need to come to grips with its remarkable and inventive approach to language and form—what we might call its literariness.

As numerous critics, especially ones averse to Paine's politics, have pointed out, the ideas in *Common Sense* weren't especially novel or groundbreaking. What was groundbreaking, and this is one of the fundamental ideas informing the pamphlet and its strategy, was the idea that these theories of politics and government could be made accessible to a broader public. Heretofore, most thinkers and politicians believed, as John Adams shows so vividly in his response to *Common Sense* titled "Thoughts on Government," that theories of government were only comprehensible to an elite class who were free from the encumbrances of daily life. The general public supposedly did not possess the education or the inclination to understand how government worked. Moreover, the stresses of everyday life meant that they would be too self-interested to seek the public good. The idea, which we now readily recognize as ideological, was that the wealthy were free from the constraints of self-interest (at its crassest, thus virtue was equated with an absence of financial obligations) and able to pursue the common weal. Paine was not only skeptical of such elitism, he was also able to formulate a counterargument in a language that was widely accessible, first in *Common Sense* and later, more ambitiously, in *Rights of Man* and *The Age of Reason*.

When I teach Paine's works, then, my goal is for students to come to recognize the radicalism of this democratization of politics that is dramatized in his language as much as in his ideas. From a the point of view of teaching literature, this is essentially a lesson in the relationship between form and content: how does the form of the text complement its content? The key here is not to see the form or the content as primary, but to understand them to work in tandem to produce particular effects in the text. In the case of *Common Sense*, that end is revolution. The endpoint to my lesson on the pamphlet focuses on the way it dramatizes, through its language and structure, the process of revolution. In other words, this is a story about the language and forms that made the revolution possible and were renewed and infused with new power by it.

Typically I begin at the beginning. The first paragraph of *Common Sense* is truly a tour de force of language and illustrates how focused the pamphlet is on language and its operations as a fundamental structure for making sense of the world. It opens with a challenge to the reader's basic assumptions about language and meaning: "Perhaps the sentiments contained in the following pages, are not yet sufficiently fashionable to procure them general favor; a long habit of not thinking a thing *wrong*, gives it a superficial appearance of being *right*, and raises at first a formidable outcry in defence of custom. But the tumult soon subsides. Time makes more converts than reason" (45). The pamphlet thus begins with a fundamental epistemological question: how do we know what we think we know? What makes us confident that what we believe to be true is actually true? Paine has phrased it in the negative such that he emphasizes the way error can root itself in our consciousness. One of the first questions I ask students about this passage is precisely what it means and how it works. Why is it phrased this way? It works by implication as much as direct statement. That is, Paine subtly implies that what we think we know is probably wrong, but we have yet to recognize our error. Custom or habit thus becomes the enemy of true knowledge. This process works on multiple levels: psychological, historical, and temporal. That is, we resist new ideas because they are new and therefore we aren't accustomed to them (psychological), because the old ideas have become ingrained in the culture (historical). The last simple declarative sentence is key, though, because it introduces a temporal element: in time these new ideas will become the customary ones. Change, it suggests, is inevitable.

The narrative embedded in this paragraph plays on the reader to suggest that they might want to be ahead of history rather than behind it. Rhetorically, the passage serves a crucial function in the text: it prepares the reader for what's to come and invites us to join in the future rather than letting it pass us by—a theme Paine returns to throughout *Common Sense*. At the same time, the passage doesn't reveal the specific choices facing the colonists. Instead, Paine establishes a tone or expectancy that over the course of the pamphlet shifts into a sense of urgency. Crucially, though, he keeps the reader in suspense. The brief introduction is designed to invite readers to consider a question and open their minds. Therefore, it speaks more to a disposition than to a specific political position. Paine's strategy is to prepare the reader for what he knows will be a challenging argument, and his opening lines hint at that dynamic, but he also seeks to limit potential resistance to his text by postponing its most concrete claims and call to action.

At this point in the lesson, I often like to show the students the table of contents from an early edition of *Common Sense*. It allows me to introduce them to a basic print culture strategy (look at the book as a material object!), and reinforces the logic of form that is so central to this discussion. When we look at the contents, we see that nothing there tells us what the argument or political conclusions of the pamphlet will be:

I. Of the Origin and Design of Government in general; with concise Remarks on the English Constitution
II. Of Monarchy and Hereditary Succession
III. Thoughts on the present State of American Affairs
IV. Of the present Ability of America, with some miscellaneous Reflections

These chapter headings read like vague political theory or even contemporary newspaper or magazine article titles. They reveal very little about the political purpose of the pamphlet. I want students to see how meticulously Paine has crafted his text to create a sense of possibility and open inquiry. He doesn't want to scare off readers by advertising his argument up front. Instead, the pamphlet is designed to invite readers to open their minds and consider possibilities they may not have thought of yet. He wants to lead readers to a conclusion by first establishing a set of basic premises or a common understanding that will undergird the pamphlet's major claims, rather than ask them to subscribe to a proposition without preparing them for it. Paine knows this is a huge leap he will be asking colonial Americans to take, so he first asks readers to accept a series of more modest claims that lead, seemingly inevitably, to the conclusion that independence is the only reasonable choice. His conclusions, which are dangerous and transformative, are thus set up as the logical extension of an earlier set of much less threatening propositions.

At the same time, it's important to acknowledge that most early American readers would have known the central point of the pamphlet before reading it, but conceptually I think it's quite significant that Paine wants the reader to experience the argument as it unfolds, inductively rather than deductively. As you will have already surmised, this leads to a useful discussion of the difference between deductive and inductive logic. I ask my students to write papers during the semester, and here is one of the great advantages of teaching Paine in a literature course: he can serve as a model for a certain style of argumentative prose. I don't want my students to adopt his style, but I do want them to see how he assembles an inductive argument with evidence, persuasion, analysis, and, most important, by drawing inferences from data. These are the most challenging aspects of analytical writing for my students. They struggle particularly with the concept of inferences because they have been trained to describe and summarize rather than to analyze and argue. They often equate arguing with expressing an opinion rather than with developing an interpretation on the basis of evidence and analysis. Over and over, in *Common Sense* Paine presents his readers with evidence (or at least what passes for evidence) and then draws inferences from it. His reading of the Bible and its account of the origin of monarchy is a classic example of textual interpretation and analysis. I often use that section of the text to illustrate how to draw inferences from close readings of passages. Paine doesn't simply summarize what the Bible says about kings; instead, he assembles the data strategically and offers analyses of key passages to pursue an argument about its implications for political theoretical arguments justifying monarchical authority.

But that discussion of Paine's account of the origins of monarchy in the Bible often takes place on the second day of our class conversation. I first want to keep their attention on the opening pages of the pamphlet to emphasize the value of close reading. In particular I focus on the author's persona and voice in these early pages, where he works so hard to craft a soothing voice that counteracts any potential for shrillness. He writes aphoristically (formulating pithy phrases that sound as if they reflect a widely shared understanding) to reduce any anxiety that might begin to infect the reader's mind. The entire text of *Common Sense* is infused with this aphoristic language, but it's especially remarkable in these early pages where Paine stacks one aphorism on top of another. We see this vividly in the last sentence of the first paragraph, "Time makes more converts than reason," but even the opening statement regarding the fashionableness of the ideas advocated in it is structured as an aphorism (albeit a long, convoluted one). He begins the next paragraph with another aphoristic statement and wraps up the introduction with one of the most famous aphorisms in the pamphlet: "The cause of America is in a great measure the cause of all mankind" (45). Paine understands that the best way to lead his readers to dramatic change is to wrap that change in an aura of security to make it seem as unthreatening as possible.

By adopting this aphoristic tone, he inflects his prose not only with a sense of self-evident truth but, more important, with the idea that what he is asking of his readers is merely that they follow their common sense. This is a key moment in teaching the pamphlet. What exactly do we mean by common sense? How would it have been understood in the late eighteenth century? For undergraduates the idea that language and ideas can be historically contingent and specific is often a novel concept that requires explanation. What exactly did Paine mean by "common sense?" How did that phrase signify in the late eighteenth century? Frequently, I begin this part of the conversation by asking the students what they understand the term to mean. This enables a productive conversation about language and how words make meaning, which is an important underlying theme in Paine's pamphlet. The idea is to play with both terms, *common* and *sense*, and how they interact: how did the words *common* and *sense* signify, separately and together, in the eighteenth century. This in turn allows for a discussion of the historical contingencies of language. I can introduce them, briefly, to Scottish Common Sense philosophy (which rebutted skepticism and stressed people's shared intuition), and John Locke's influential epistemology. Then I can invite them to think about how the term *common sense* has evolved to our current usage. The idea is to bring questions about language as a complex code of meaning making to life for them.

My hope is that the students will come to understand the radical implications of Paine's particular application of the idea of common sense for a discussion of politics. As with his use of an aphoristic tone, Paine disguises what is a radical political innovation in a language that makes it seem like it poses no threat to the current order. To clinch this idea, I turn to the beginning of the third section of the pamphlet, "Thoughts on the present State of American Affairs," where Paine first uses the term *common sense*: "In the following pages I offer nothing more than simple facts, plain arguments, and common sense" (61).

Focusing on this series of terms allows me to reinforce the lesson of the discussion of the meanings of "common sense." How students treat this second series of terms provides a useful index into what they have learned from our initial discussion. The first question to explore here is the difference between simple facts, plain arguments, and common sense. Does Paine offer them as synonyms? Or do they function as complementary terms? In what ways do they supplement one another? One approach to exploring this question is to think about the adjectives: *simple, plain,* and *common.* How do the differences between them matter? *Plain* also invites a discussion of the plain style, which could occupy a good portion of the conversation or could be glossed quickly depending on your aims in the rest of the syllabus. A discussion of the plain style can be particularly useful since it too reflects a broader set of ideas about form and content in its specific application (as a way to equate simplicity of expression with honesty and transparency) and in its currency as a national narrative (the United States' plainness and simplicity contrasts with Europe's sophistication and corruption).

With this passage, though, I really want the students to think about the conceptual relationship between these three terms. In my most recent course, the students (a smart bunch), quickly wanted to move on to think about the nouns, facts, arguments, and sense, to explore the subtle play between them. What makes something a fact instead of an argument? What is the relationship between an argument and a fact? When does a fact become sense? What role do the senses play in establishing facts or arguments, and so on. Fun! My last move here is to suggest that these three terms, *simple facts, plain arguments,* and *common sense,* operate on a narrative level at this pivotal moment in the pamphlet when Paine turns to address the specifics of the American political situation. They describe a sequence as the thinker and reader move from simple facts, to plain arguments, and from there to the common sense, or shared understanding, that Paine hopes will be the effect of his pamphlet on the reader.

If my first day on the pamphlet has focused more intensively on form, I shift that focus on the second day to its arguments. As I suggested already, I often lead off the second day with a discussion of the section on the biblical narrative of the origins of monarchy to effect this transition. The discussion of the biblical passages and Paine's approaches to them often leads to a conversation about the nature of evidence in *Common Sense.* What kinds of evidence does Paine employ in his pamphlet?

Why does he choose these types of evidence? I love to point in particular to his bogus charts and numbers to invite students to think about the rhetorical impact of statistics and even the visual power of a chart to make something appear to be true, even when the content of the chart is a complete fabrication. I want them to appreciate the sheer variety of arguments Paine presents in favor or independence. Among his examples he cites the Bible, nature, geography, astronomy, economics, Milton, pedagogical theory, household advice, and political philosophy to advocate for his views. He mobilizes a wide range of branches of knowledge to imply the breadth of his arguments and to convey a sense of the modern and traditional coming together, which reflects his participation in the "long" Enlightenment.

We move quickly to a discussion of the third section of the pamphlet where Paine explicitly calls for American independence. I ask students to think about how the authorial voice shifts here now that the pamphlet's central argument is presented. I want them to identify some of the continuities, especially the continued reliance on aphoristic statements, but I also direct them to the eruption of a more emotional tone and set of arguments. In particular I want them to think about the three paragraphs where Paine asks readers to consider the fate of those who have been directly harmed by the outbreak of hostilities: "Hath your house been burnt? Hath your property been destroyed before your face? Are your wife and children destitute of a bed to lie on or bread to live on? Have you lost a parent or a child by their hands, and yourself the ruined and wretched survivor?" (67). I want students to think about the dramatic shift in tone at this moment of direct address. How does it change the dynamic of the pamphlet? Why might Paine want to interrupt his more reasoned prose with such a personal and emotional appeal? How does a passage like this suggest a rethinking of what he might mean by *common sense*? How does the relationship between theory and practice, which has been a key theme of the text from its opening lines, come to a head in a passage like this one?

Paine thus moves from a set of general theories about human nature, social relations, and government to the specifics of the local situation in the colonies. The theoretical and the practical are never far apart, as his narrative of the origins of government in the first few pages of the pamphlet illustrates. Paine tells this story beginning with the third paragraph of the first chapter of *Common Sense*. It is presented as a historical speculation, but the story he tells resembles nothing so much as the settlement of the British colonies in North America. Perhaps the most telling detail is the account of the town gatherings under a large tree ("Some convenient tree will afford them a State-House" [48]). Along a similar vein, Paine's examples and analogies are often taken from daily life such that the theory remains grounded in an experiential reality that was common to a wide range of Americans and not exclusive to the upper classes.

That discussion of theory and practice, which is meant to echo the question of form and content, sets up the key point I generally like to conclude with in my discussions of *Common Sense*. The central problem that *Common Sense* seeks to tackle and really shapes all of Paine's major writings is the question of mediation. The major conceptual problem that he wrestles with as a thinker throughout his career is that of mediation: how can we build more direct and transparent relationships between the people and their government, between humans and the divinity, but perhaps most important, between humans. This question becomes much more explicitly manifest in *The Age of Reason*, but it is also what drives Paine's aphoristic style in *Common Sense* and what underwrites his objection to British rule in America. What Paine is seeking as a writer is a more direct relationship with his readers, hence his emphasis on terms like plain truth and common sense. He insists repeatedly that he is not privy to any special knowledge or education. As the introduction to the pamphlet emphasizes, he is not really telling his readers anything they don't already know. The problem is not that they don't know it, but that they have not yet been able to accept it.

The moment in the text that I think best illustrates Paine's anxieties about mediation in the political realm is his plan for a government. I ask students to read that passage and consider how different Paine's proposal is from the kind of government that the United States ultimately adopted (although I also point out that Pennsylvania's first constitution was not terribly different from this plan). I ask them to consider the implications of Paine's plan with its single-house structure and annual elections. Why would he prefer that approach? I want them to see that at a local level it would make sense as a reaction to British imperial rule and to understand that such a structure is designed to reduce the distance between the government and the governed. Partly, I am setting up a later discussion of *The Federalist* and the US Constitution, where that distance is justified as a way of ensuring deliberation. More urgently, though, I want them to understand that this is also about narrowing the gap between representative and represented or, in the terms of literary theory, between signifier and signified. In other words, the central questions of American representative democracy are also fundamentally questions about aesthetics and language, as much as they are about political theory.

Common Sense thus reflects Paine's concern with problems of mediation from beginning to end. He begins his pamphlet with an attempt to overcome the way language mediates between the author and the reader. He attacks the monarchy by suggesting that in the biblical account none other than God rejects monarchy because it introduces an intermediary between the divinity and the people. In the American context, he emphasizes the way the distance between the colonies and the metropole has created an emotional and a political gap between the ruler and his people. Paine emphasizes proximity, directness, and transparency, in his prose and in his political theories, because he sees them as the best antidote to the dangers of mediation, which, by introducing distance between the government and its people, creates the conditions for corruption and misrule. For Paine this is as much about an emotional or affective gap as it is about a theory of representation. Over and over in *Common Sense* the problem is that distance removes rulers from the emotional impact of their policies. To drive this point home at a pivotal moment in the pamphlet when the author asks of early Americans: "Hath your house been burned down?" Just as he does with his aphorisms, Paine is trying to create a greater sense of immediacy. The idea of sympathy in the eighteenth century was built on this very principle. To put yourself in the shoes of another is simply a metaphor for closing the distance between yourself and the other person to gain a more direct understanding of what they feel and think. The genius of the question of whether one's house has been burned down, therefore, is that it speaks simultaneously to the ties binding one colonist to another and to the distance between the colonists and the Crown.

Those are the usual key points that I want to discuss with my students when I teach *Common Sense*. But as teachers will infer, many of the techniques and perspectives associated with the hunt for "literariness" in *Common Sense* lend themselves equally well to other revolutionary texts and contexts. Students gain much from rummaging through contemporary publications and then discussing them in class, with the challenge of placing their literary facets in the foreground.

Paine's work straddled revolutions, but to broaden the authorial and geographic base, teachers could invite students to pick over Jean Paul Marat's *L'Ami du Peuple* (France's most influential paper in 1789–1793, with short, sharp editions consisting overwhelmingly of the author's critique of unfolding events and urging of action), or to analyze the Abbé Sieyès's seminal rallying cry, *What Is the Third Estate?* ("Qu'est-ce que le tiers-état?" of January 1789), or to dissect Ecuadorian Vicente Rocafuerte's comparative *Ideas Necesarias a Todo Pueblo Americano Independiente: Que Quiera Ser Libre* (an 1821 work proposing a kind of hemispheric Americanism that imitated US constitutional precepts and sought to localize some of their possibilities and exclusions). The trick is to help students not just to absorb the ideas but also identify how ideas are interwoven with new language and form. Even in the process of thinking more critically about language and historicized argumentation, students can be encouraged to think about how they do the same in their own papers and essays (playing with how and where to deploy evidence, opinion, analysis, and inference).

Most recently, however, I had a rare chance to construct an entire course around Paine, for which I experimented with a new approach that was made possible by the singular focus of the course. The course was meant to fulfill our department's "Texts in Time" rubric, which introduces students to what we generally think of as historical contextualized readings. The goal is to teach students how to analyze literary texts in relation to the contexts in which they are produced. In my course's case, I wanted to focus on the conversations that Paine's texts participated in, often directly, in the late eighteenth century. I divided the course into three segments around each of Paine's major texts. For the section on *Common Sense*, we read Paine's pamphlet alongside the major responses to it by John Adams, William Smith, and other loyalist commentators, and Paine's rebuttal to his critics in his Forester's Letters. My sense has been that too often students encounter literary texts, philosophical ideas, and historical events or concepts in isolation. I want them to begin to discern ideas in motion and thereby gain more of a sense of an ongoing historical conversation within which these major arguments and ideas about liberty, democracy, representation, freedom, and so on were evolving. Not only does Paine's text not emerge out of nothing, his ideas don't just remain static or become reified. Instead, they enter into the culture where they are discussed, debated, misrepresented, reinvented, and deployed strategically in new forms.

To accomplish this goal, I wanted students to see how Paine was borrowing from others. For their first writing assignment, I asked them to write an essay about Paine's brief but telling quotation from Milton's *Paradise Lost*. Here's how I phrased the assignment:

> On p. 68 of Common Sense Paine cites a passage from Milton's influential epic poem Paradise Lost. The passage comes from a speech Satan makes early in Book 4 of the poem. Find the speech and use it as a context for exploring Paine's ideas about revolution. Some questions you might consider could include: How might Lucifer's speech and its place in Milton's poem shape a reading of Paine's text? How does Lucifer position himself in the speech? What arguments does he make against God's authority? What does it mean to invoke Lucifer, even this poetic version, to bolster your argument? Why might it be significant that Paine cites Milton as the author of the line, but does not attribute it to Lucifer?

The purpose of this assignment is for the students to think about how Paine's ideas emerge in dialogue with other thinkers and to show them how those conversations can take place across large historical gaps. Even a century after his death, Milton remains relevant for Paine. This gives me an opportunity to talk with the class about the importance of poetry in the eighteenth century, more specifically about Milton's heroic statue to radical dissenters and their descendants in the colonies. At the same time, it complements the discussions about the commonality of Paine's style and his desire for a wide audience because of Milton's popularity with readers. This is why he would have cited *Paradise Lost*, which was one of the most widely read texts in the colonies. Paine knew his readers would know Lucifer's speech well and would be able to fill in the context.

My students responded to the challenge of this essay in a variety of interesting ways. Some focused on the problem of aligning the colonies with Lucifer's rebellion against God. The best of these essays recognized the way Paine's invocation of Lucifer here echoes his attacks on authority elsewhere in the pamphlet. They also identified with the emotional power of Lucifer's appeal and understood its relevance to Paine's effort to mobilize the colonists. Other students, perhaps ones who had read *Paradise Lost* in another class, focused intently on the parts of Lucifer's speech that Paine does not cite. They used Lucifer's words to think about Paine's approach to fomenting revolution and, in one especially effective instance, considered the difference between rebellion and revolution, where I began. In the successful essays the common thread was that the students were able to put the two texts into conversation. They were able to see how by setting the two side by side they could open up questions about both texts' representations that enabled them to gain greater insights into the nature of revolution in the eighteenth century.

Ultimately the assignment and the course are designed to invite students to think about the forms revolution takes. When we think about revolution, that is, we are thinking as much about a form (an architecture of rhetoric, affect, ideas, peoples, etc.) as we are a historical event or phenomenon. This is where the literary becomes so useful in our effort to explore and think about the contingency and danger inherent in any revolution. We can trace how those qualities of the revolutionary moment manifest in the forms writers adopt to promote and oppose the proposed changes to the social or political fabric. Like so many of his contemporaries, Paine employed the pamphlet, a hybrid form that was part broadside, part occasional print, and part book, but not entirely any of those. His prose mixes poetic, historical, and philosophical modes of thinking and writing with anecdotes, household advice, and casual observation. The tenor can be sympathetic but also violent, logical and calculating but also passionate and emotional, witty and funny but also sad and tragic. These are all characteristic of revolution, qualities we can often lose sight of if we only engage the event from an ideological, constitutional, or intellectual perspective. By engaging with the forms of any single revolution we can thus gain a greater understanding of its urgency and its contingency for those who experienced it. For students, in turn, this makes the American Revolution and the people who participated in it more real. They begin to perceive not only its relevance but the nature of its challenge.

KEY RESOURCES

Political Documents

Declaration of Independence
US Constitution
Articles of Confederation
Constitution of Pennsylvania (1776)

Primary Sources

Adams, John. *Thoughts on Government: Applicable to the Present State of the American Colonies: In a Letter from a Gentleman to His Friend*. Philadelphia: Dunlap, 1776.

———. Letters to James Lloyd (January 1815) and Benjamin Waterhouse (October 29, 1805). "Founders Online." http://founders.archives.gov/ (accessed October 9, 2015).

Hamilton, Alexander, James Madison, and John Jay. *The Federalist.* Edited by J. R. Pole. Indianapolis: Hackett, 2005.

Moore, Milcah Martha. *Milcah Martha Moore's Book: A Commonplace Book from Revolutionary America.* Edited by Catherine LaCourreye Blecki and Karin Wulf. College Park: Pennsylvania State University Press, 1997.

Paine, Thomas. *Common Sense.* Edited by Edward Larkin. Peterborough, ON: Broadview, 2004.

Secondary Sources

Ferguson, Robert. "The Commonalities of Common Sense." *William and Mary Quarterly,* 3rd ser., 57, no. 3 (July 2000): 465–504.

Foner, Eric. *Tom Paine and Revolutionary America.* New York: Oxford University Press, 1976.

Keane, John. *Thomas Paine: A Political Life.* Boston: Little, Brown, 1995.

Larkin, Edward. *Thomas Paine and the Literature of Revolution.* New York: Cambridge University Press, 2005.

Solinger, Jason. "Thomas Paine's Continental Mind." *Early American Literature* 45, no. 3 (2010): 593–617.

PART THREE

Specific Themes and Revolutions

Women's Rights and the Limits of Revolutions

LINDSAY A. H. PARKER

Teaching Challenges

The women of revolutionary France fascinate us. Marie Antoinette, Charlotte Corday, and the blood-thirsty Madame Defarge types are female villains whose legends extend well beyond their mortal inspirations into the realms of myth and art.[1] These larger-than-life characters are one facet of women's history of the revolution. They stand out from the vast majority of female revolutionaries and counter-revolutionaries whose lives were less operatic. Those ordinary women merit even more of our time as we study the process of making a revolution and founding a republic. The importance of understanding the history of women's experiences of the French Revolution lies in the fact that this history is integral to the history of democracy. If we consider the question of revolution as a struggle for citizenship and human rights, then women are not just incidental to the Age of Revolutions: they are central to it. One way to bring women into the mainstream of this history is to approach the whole revolution through the problems of gender. Yet teaching that history poses three challenges.

The first challenge is the largest and the most critical to address: resisting the temptation to segregate women's history into its own unit. This approach is common in textbooks and surveys. In part, the division is a result of the fact that women were a group apart from the active revolutionaries, the men who could vote, fight, and lead the government. As legally defined "passive citizens" who experienced the double sub-ordination of second-class citizenship and a long-standing ideology of gender hierarchy, women and their revolutionary activity existed, we tend to explain, on the periphery of official politics. When they do come in from the margins, their actions seem exceptional rather than part of the total experience of the revolution. In the women's history unit, the story often begins in October 1789 during the October Days; it ends in autumn 1793 when the Jacobin government thwarted the influence of militant women by forbidding women's political clubs or public assembly. This narrative tells a succinct story of women's public activity, expressed first in a grandiose and exceptional event, then waning to the point of extinction.

Ideally, during discussion, the women's history unit would be connected with political history, leading to a differentiated understanding of how events affected particular groups. Even when that goal is maintained, problems with this approach remain. This arc of women's influence on politics is too neat, eclipsing complexities and contradictions; it leaves the false impression that female political will was only briefly relevant. More important, separating women's experience of the revolution from the traditional narrative reinforces the notion that women exist outside the march of history. The idea that their participation was peripheral (even if that was sometimes true) leads us too easily to classify it as inconsequential. Relying on this simple arc to chart women's place in the revolution misses an opportunity to teach students how to think critically about liberty, the complexity of the past, and the multiplicity of factors that led individuals to embrace particular political ideologies. The other two challenges that accompany teaching women's history pertain to critical thinking.

The second challenge is to teach contradictions and synthesize them to encourage thoughtfulness. We must avoid the intellectual surrender of concluding that the revolution was good for some and bad for others. It is not sufficient to teach students that women represent an exception to the history of democracy. We need to help them wrestle with that exception, synthesize men's gains and women's losses (and the reverse), and improve their ability to think critically about any historical or present moment. Questions that can guide this critical thinking include: how did the historical actors think critically about equality, and where did their reason fail? How did they change their thinking about gender throughout the course of the revolution? How can we define citizenship to include the way disenfranchised people expressed their political will? How do we enter that participation into the "master" narrative of citizenship and democracy? How should we examine democracy today to avoid excluding groups from rights that are declared universal? What got in the way of that then, and what gets in the way now?

As my last question indicates, the third challenge is to make this history (complicated as it is) and the conclusions we draw from it (nuanced though they might be) relevant to students in the twenty-first century. Invariably, when my students discuss women's rights from earlier times, they say confidently that those struggles exist only in the past. They cite their working mothers and women in high posts of government. Very often when a student offers a different perspective, she begins by assuring the class that she is "not a feminist, but . . ." Reluctance to question the state of equality today, or perhaps the inability to do so objectively, is problematic. The solution is to develop critical thinking skills that help students decipher not just gender inequality but all problems related to social justice.

Overcoming these teaching challenges by incorporating a rigorous women's history component into teaching about revolutions is necessary, because by understanding the relationship between women and revolution, we understand the process of democracy: not the indefatigable and inevitable march toward a modern world but the struggle to overcome prejudices that inhibit the complete realization of noble goals. In this chapter, I concentrate on the French Revolution, explaining both content objectives and critical thinking opportunities as we integrate women more fully into its history. The same logic and opportunities exist for better synthesizing gender history across other revolutions of the era.[2]

Historical Debates

I begin by offering the following primer on scholarship on women and the revolution and how each area of study can affect our teaching. Because of their sex, women experienced a different revolution than men did. But women were not always disadvantaged in these parallel histories. The complexity of historical thinking on this topic has increased in recent years.

Initial research explored how and why women did not experience the same explosion of liberty and equality that men did. Early in the course of events, women were placed into the category of "passive" citizens who had fewer civic rights than "active" male citizens, and this categorization was never seriously reconsidered by government leaders. Women's opportunities further diminished when convents were closed, eliminating girls' convent education and nuns' autonomous space.[3] Historians uncovered the fact that the concept of *woman* failed to make gains. As the individual man became a citizen and joined others in equal fraternity, *woman* continued to be spoken of in very similar ways as in prerevolutionary France: fragile, unreasonable, and dependent. During the revolution, women's patriotism was to be expressed by staying at home and becoming a Republican Mother, a title that perhaps gained some additional respect but did not change women's lives at all.[4] On the other side of a long-lived dichotomy of appropriate and inappropriate femininity, women who failed to perform acceptable roles were vilified as out-of-control zealots, unruly mobs, or gender transgressors.

This lack of progress was not present to the same degree in other subordinate groups. Eventually, the vote extended to all men regardless of their property holdings, and the pursuit of equality led to the brief emancipation of the slaves. The first point students should understand, then, is:

1. Women's rights were not equal to men's rights. But citizenship spread gradually to many previously subordinate people, which means that gender difference was something more influential in leaders' thinking than were other differences.

Research that probed deeply into the reasons behind this gender divide pointed to the very old discourses of gender difference that continued throughout the eighteenth century. Although the Enlightenment marked a shift in the way gender difference was thought about, science, law, and religion all continued to affirm in one way or another that men and women were significantly different in body and mind. To assume the attributes of the opposite sex would result in a monstrosity, especially if women took on masculine characteristics. Bodily and mental differences placed men and women in a hierarchical relationship in both public and private life.

In 1989, Geneviève Fraisse took a prolonged look into this persistent separation of the sexes. She suggested that during "any period of political upheaval, in reformulating the social bond as a whole," relations between the sexes are questioned.[5] Because the revolution unsettled so much of the structure of French society, even progressive thinkers stopped short of leveling gender relations. Extending equality to that relationship threatened stability because stark divisions between male and female, including the roles played in public and private life, prevented the chaos of gender confusion. The revolutionaries clung to the separation of the sexes to preserve some familiar order. Fraisse writes, "The fear had been that men and women would become too similar. To avoid competition and 'brotherhood' between man and woman, one had only to separate them, to oppose them to each other, as good and evil."[6]

In 1992, Lynn Hunt fleshed out the psychological underpinnings of this fear of gender equality. She explained that the idea of fraternity was critical for understanding revolutionary psychology. The male revolutionaries, she suggested, wanted to be equal brothers, emancipated from the rule of the father (the king). This fraternity led to concern over women: when the father was killed (when Louis XVI was executed), would the sisters also be liberated? Like Fraisse, Hunt argued that the revolution's destructive impact on "patriarchy, custom, and tradition" forced revolutionaries to articulate what would be "the justification for women's separate, different, and unequal roles in both the family and the state."[7] While the revolutionaries struggled with this question, ultimately fear over the corruption of femininity, represented by powerful royal mistresses and Queen Marie Antoinette (slandered by accusations of incest), led to women's confinement in the domestic sphere.

For many years, the prevailing historical argument asserted that the affirmation of gender difference was written into the fabric of liberalism. The belief that men and women held different social roles was a fundamental truth on which the rest of the revolution was built. Joan Landes's argument that "the bourgeois republic was constituted in and through a discourse on gender relations"—discourses that propagated a hierarchical relationship putting women in the domestic sphere—helped shape the way we understood the relationship between women and liberalism.[8] Joan W. Scott added more depth to this argument by demonstrating how the individual of the revolution was coded male, making it difficult for feminists to argue for equality because calls for universal rights were already, paradoxically, exclusionary.[9] The next point for students to think about is:

2. The limits placed on women's rights were partly a result of the persistence of very old ideologies of gender difference and hierarchy. The "man" who was declared equal was not a universal person without gender. In practice, this liberated individual could only be an independent man.

Meanwhile, many scholars reminded us that there is diversity within the group *woman*, and many women had different goals. A particularly gendered problem was the revolutionaries' attack on the Church. Historians explained that pious laywomen and nuns openly opposed the revolution because it threatened their religion and their way of life. These women's active protests formed a major feminine political movement. As the de-Christianization campaign increased its attack on men and women religious throughout 1790-1794, many of France's fifty-five thousand nuns proved more than willing to defend themselves and the refractory priests—those who opposed the Civil Constitution of the Clergy. In some instances they did so by using the language of the revolution to argue that their pastoral services were useful to the nation and a form of patriotism; on the other hand, revolutionaries who imposed their will on the nuns were likened to tyrants. Such an appropriation of political discourse offers in intriguing example of women behaving politically in order to fight against the revolution. In other instances, nuns harbored refractory priests and suffered violence at the hands of mobs as a result.

The fact that some women mobilized against the revolution reinforced the idea that women were too irrational to participate in civil society, too religious to participate in the modern state, and too out of control to be permitted the level of freedom that men enjoyed. Mita Choudhury thus concluded that "the eradication of women religious by 1794 symbolized the triumph of masculine reason over feminine fanaticism."[10] In spite of their elimination, religious women left a deep impression on memories of the revolution. Olwen Hufton argued that after the First Republic fell, the image of the religious, counterrevolutionary woman was the most lasting representation of femininity. More important than the militant women of the early 1790s, whose success was so significant that leaders banned women's speech as a way of controlling crowds, the counterrevolutionary women were the "beasts" who came to symbolize revolutionary men's dashed hopes. Irrational and untrustworthy women "kept [men] from earthly paradise."[11] Counterrevolutionary women teach us:

3. The fact that some of the most outspoken Counterrevolutionaries were women reminds us that not all women viewed the revolution as something that could benefit them. The existence of counter-revolutionary women played a role in one way femininity was constructed during and after the revolution: a potentially corrupting force threatening masculine progress in secular, rational, democratic government.

Like the population at large, women were divided on the debate catalyzed by the Civil Constitution of the Clergy. Although many ordinary women supported nuns and refractory priests, others supported and protected the constitutional clergy who swore the oath to the new law. In 1791, women's political clubs were already engaged in charity work that was similar to nuns' social roles—teaching and caring for the sick and poor—and publicly defended the constitutional clergy. Thus many women who opposed and supported the anticlerical measures came from women's organizations, convents, and political clubs that performed feminine, caring functions. They saw themselves as relevant actors in public, by virtue of their charity work, as well as in politics, as they mobilized to support the opposing groups of priests. While the de-Christianization campaign was not as much a "women's issue" as it was an issue of political philosophy to nuns and republican women, it was a galvanizing subject for both groups.

The history of women's political clubs is further illuminating for two more reasons: it represents a method for women to engage in politics, and it highlights the friction between female activists and male leaders. While some political clubs were open to both sexes, it was more common for women to join women's clubs. These clubs existed throughout France, including about sixty of them in the provinces, and they were often encouraged by government representatives to perform philanthropic services. The leaders were typically bourgeois wives of men who were active in men's clubs. Through their support for the constitutional clergy, charity work, and complementary efforts to organize festivals along with men's clubs, these middle-class and artisan women operated within comfortable boundaries of women's public outreach.[12]

However, women's clubs also generated feminist agendas. Women in several towns "reproached the Convention in scarcely veiled terms for excluding them from the 'right to express their suffrage,'" demanded the right to vote, and wrote that "the Rights of Man 'are also *their rights.*'"[13] It was therefore not a great leap between sanctioned, auxiliary female political participation and uncomfortable demands for greater equality. Thus Suzanne Desan found three essential anxieties that these clubs produced for the male leadership: that clubs were unnecessarily political, that women would politicize their private lives and challenge male authority within the home, and that this activity would change the interior nature of women. Even revolutionary activity could easily cross the threshold between women as helpers and women as out-of-control gender transgressors. The forced closing of women's clubs in the fall of 1793 conveniently shelved these worries.

Women's groups who opposed and supported political causes were not usually doing so *for* women, but they did act collectively *as* women, sometimes developing consciousness as a group of counterrevolutionaries or patriots. Women's awakening as a political force eventually led to a backlash from the government. Students should be aware that:

4. Supportive revolutionary activity on the part of women was valued initially, though concerns about blurring gender distinctions eventually overpowered recognition that women were beneficial political participants.

Emphasis on the blowback against female activists should not obscure the real work women performed to advance their political agendas and their well-being as women in a society under revision. Historians have emphasized that although women's citizenship status was less than that of men's, their prorevolutionary activity should be recorded as an integral part of all revolutionary activity. Dominique Godineau's study of working-class Parisian women detailed their active support of the revolution. She noted a range of political activity, including attending the sessions of the legislature, protesting economic hardships and counterrevolutionary groups, mobilizing the crowds, informing themselves of current events, knitting for the soldiers, wearing revolutionary colors, and joining insurrections. Women "acted as citizens" and claimed "a natural right to which they were entitled," and male revolutionaries approved because women, as half the nation, were necessary to the success of the revolution.[14] Male leaders seemed to agree that women formed an important part of the nation. Until the radical phase of the revolution, it was generally accepted that women should take part in public life, as indeed working-class women had always done by virtue of their economic roles.

The issue of women's work, in fact, was one topic that naturally became a political issue that galvanized women's sense of political identity. Women of Les Halles, small retailers, had to negotiate and protest laws and ordinances that had negative effects on their livelihoods. In particular, they resisted restrictions on moving merchandise early in the morning, complained about hoarders who withheld their wares, and protested the price maximums that left them no room for profit between wholesale and retail prices. In other trades, women suffered when demand for their products, especially silk and lace, declined. In response to their plight, the government created workshops, which employed women and indigent and elderly men in the task of sewing for soldiers. These workshops became seedbeds of activism among the working class. Women sought fair wages and treatment, and although they did not fight for equal pay with men, they were conscious of fair pay for their labor.[15] Like the topics discussed already, fair remuneration was not a feminist issue for women workers, but it was an avenue that led them to political consciousness. As Godineau expresses it, "They were not just women but citizens who worked."[16] Again, like so many other issues, the workers' protests were eventually suppressed in the interest of restoring stability and halting the tide of populist politics.

5. The division between male "active" and female "passive" citizens in law should not lead us to believe that women were inactive. In fact, many men and women expected women to participate in revolutionary events. Working women's complaints, riots, and protests had an effect on governing the economy. Although not part of the voting public, women affected policy.

Subtler investigations into women's revolutionary experiences looked to the private sphere. Historians argued that there, too, women developed political ideologies and helped shape revolutionary society. Suzanne Desan explained that by examining the family, we see that women's status was indeed revolutionized, and in many ways improved, during the revolution. Like the cultural historians before her, Desan believed that the family was a political entity. However, she argued that this was a place ripe for progress, where patriarchy was challenged. Even during a period of oppression for some women, including nuns and members of political clubs, laws on divorce and inheritance made family members more equal. Critically, inheritance laws continued in some form after the revolution. These laws permitted opportunities for changes in gender relations on which women actively capitalized. In this way, women engaged in the revolution by asserting their rights; they advanced measurably toward gender equality as they did so. In the family, both men and women "test[ed] out the daily meaning of equality."[17]

This argument modified the exclusion thesis. By "defin[ing] politics broadly," Desan argued that women participated in the revolution by "intertwining . . . personal and public matters."[18] Because the family was the "crucial matrix" that "linked each individual to the new nation-state," domestic relationships had an effect on the construction of the revolutionary state and society.[19] The division between public and private life has less analytical utility here. Because of the overlap between domestic and political life, women participated in revolutionary politics when they revised their relationships with their husbands, fathers, and brothers. This participation was not subversive but part of the celebrated project of refashioning French society. Jennifer Heuer's study of family law in the early nineteenth century confirmed Desan's argument by indicating that there was no comprehensive program of subordinating women to men in marriage.[20]

A trend in scholarship has been to turn to the detail of lived experience of specific families. Denise Davidson, Sian Reynolds, and others—I humbly add myself to this list—have exploited the few extant first-person accounts among revolutionaries that detail not only how they thought about, reacted to, and acted on the revolution but also much subtler changes that are visible by close, detailed, and prolonged looks into private life.[21] By examining families from the obscure to the famous, these scholars show how individuals and individual families, confronted with multifaceted problems created by the revolution, acted, sometimes surprisingly, in pursuit of advancement, self-preservation, or seemingly foolhardy ambition. Although accounts of individuals leads to a diverse historical record (indeed, that is the point), some general conclusions emerge from these varied portraits. Perhaps the most important conclusions for the purposes of this chapter are that these—mostly middle-class—women's main concerns were not women's issues but their family's survival and advancement. In the process, however, it was necessary and even enjoyable for them to become well informed on politics, opinionated, and slightly activist. These biographical studies bear witness to intimate relationships that evolved because of the revolution. They show the importance emotions (love, piety, fear, etc.) as explanations for behavior in conjunction with the more traditional interpretations of cause and effect: material concerns and ideology. The history of emotions bears significantly on these histories of private life.[22]

I provide details by focusing on my analysis of Rosalie Jullien, the wife and mother of political elites. Jullien's husband was a member of the convention; her son traveled for the Committee of Public Safety during the Terror. Jullien lived in Paris throughout the revolution and documented her experiences through letters, mostly to her son. She was extremely inquisitive, well informed, and thoughtful about current events. Like her husband, she became a Jacobin partisan. Her political activity seems not to have expanded far beyond the veil of privacy, however. Although she proudly went into public spaces to witness protests or legislative sessions, she did not participate in demonstrations, nor did she join political clubs. However, her personal connections gave her significant access to political discourse. She socialized regularly with the members of the Committee of Public Safety and counseled her son through private letters. I suggested that there was little practical division between political and private life for her, even though she stayed mostly within the limits of traditional female roles. In addition, to the extent that she developed an idea of femininity that was significantly autonomous and politically necessary, she experienced a revolution for her personal gender identity.[23]

The combination of studies like Desan's, which contains a large sample of petitioners in family courts, and biographical studies that detail individuals' daily experiences in the family can lead students to consider:

6. It is possible to define politics broadly, by including activities that took place within the private sphere. Indeed, changes in the way men and women interacted in private relationships might be the most significant arena for women's gains during the revolution.

These gains included better access to divorce and inheritance and increased parity in intimate relationships.

At this point, we must recognize that historians disagree about how we should think of the limits of women's revolutionary experience. Early histories asserted that women as a group, and femininity as an idea, either did not evolve during the revolution or evolved negatively. More recent histories claim that at the level of lived experience, women participated in the revolution, were sometimes accepted as important actors, and succeeded in reshaping family life to promote greater gender equality.

In this debate, the paradigm of public versus private looms large. For the former camp (arguing exclusion), it is an essential divide that shapes discourses of female oppression. For the latter, the division is unproductive because of the mutually influential relationship of public and private. Cultural historians find overwhelming evidence of both men and women discussing the moral necessity, decreed by nature, of women's enclosure in domestic space. Social historians see that in the practice of everyday life, this ideology of division was less influential than laws that promoted greater equality within the family and the work being done by average men and women to put that equality into practice.

The exclusion thesis is compelling because there is strong support for it in speeches, editorials, and laws. It also seems to explain how the ideology of domesticity, which was powerful in the nineteenth century, began at the end of the eighteenth. However, the revolutionary period was long, its phases diverse, and its actors multiple. Although there were prohibitions placed on women, a combination of laws and women's practices, especially in the domestic sphere, indicate that opportunities for greater equality existed, and women glimpsed and exploited them. The gender history of the revolution is nuanced, and its moral cannot be contained to a simple lesson of winners and losers. To best enter this debate into our teaching:

7. We should question how and why gender relations were the topic of political debate. We should seek to understand what factors led to poor critical thinking, in which cultural bias interfered with faithful logic and prevented universal rights from reaching women, and what factors led to better critical thinking, in which women

achieved some liberty in relation to their brothers and husbands. As we interpret the story of women and the revolution, we should think about the process of writing history. How does investigating women's subordination lead to a new approach to discussing the revolution? What contemporary point of view might be supported by history that instead celebrates women's achievements?

Teaching Opportunities

According to the Foundation for Critical Thinking, critical thinkers are "deep thinkers" who possess "intellectual humility" and nurture a "reasonable, rational, multi-logical worldview."[24] Students who think critically ask good questions, research responsibly, and behave ethically when presented with reasonable conclusions that do not advance their self-interest. Those equipped with excellent reason will build more a compassionate, productive, peaceful, and rational society. The Foundation for Critical Thinking argues that our world is "charged with fear and insecurity," which leads people "unthinkingly [to follow] leaders who tendentiously divide the world into good versus evil."[25] A similar assessment could be made of the French revolutionary period. To think critically about that historical event will prepare students to think critically about today's polarized debates.

Critical thinking is also the process of examining our reasoning ability. While thinking deeply about complicated problems, critical thinkers assess their thought process with the goal of becoming increasingly reasonable and rational. Similarly, the French revolutionaries—many of them lawyers, philosophers, and intellectuals—sought to improve their society through close examination of the reasoning process. Sometimes they were successful at becoming more rational, fair, and modern. Sometimes they were not able to overcome their self-interests or revise a theory that was objectively flawed because instinct led them to cling to it. By studying the thought process of revolutionaries, students will be able to apply similar tests to their own ability to reason. Students who assess their logic, assumptions, cultural bias, and competing arguments will likely reach more reasonable and fair conclusions and constantly improve their ability to think with nuance and sensitivity.

Productive and rational thought on this topic is particularly important today. In spite of my students' confidence that women are now unfettered by past inequalities, old discourses reemerge with remarkable resilience. Arguments seeking to limit women's freedoms today are descendants of a very old belief system in which fully autonomous women are symbolic of a world upside down. Critically examining the ongoing history of women's rights can serve as a model for interpreting inequality in many other contexts. In this final section, I list events in women's history that can be added to the chronology of the revolution during lectures and classwork and suggest critical thinking exercises at several points. They are intended to supplement the most common events and figures that already exist in textbooks and provide the starting point for locating fuller versions of texts to reproduce for students.[26]

Questioning Chronology

Fall 1790: Women, including Etta Palm d'Aelders, Théroigne Méricourt, and Pauline Léon, are full members and officers of the Société fraternelle des patriotes de l'un et l'autre sexe.

What does the title of this club suggest to you about the relationship between gender and patriotism for these members?

March 20, 1790: A decree orders nuns to be interrogated to verify that they were not forced to join the convent. Louis-Marie Prudhomme writes, "Citizens, citizenesses whom we have just freed, it is time to make yourself available to the nation and, through your caring, offer it the tribute of your utility."[27]

Why does Prudhomme consider nuns not to be "useful" or "free"?

July 1790: Condorcet publishes "Sur l'admission des femmes au droit de la cité" in July 1790 in the *Journal de la Société de 1789*. He argues that women have equal virtues of citizenship and capacity to reason, reiterating claims he made in 1787 in *Lettres d'un Bourgeois de New Haven à un citoyen de Virginie*, that no true republic has existed

How does Condorcet's thinking fundamentally differ from others who argue that inequality of the sexes was rooted in nature?

because none had extended citizenship to women.[28]

March 6, 1791: Pauline Léon demands women's right to arms from the National Assembly, saying, "Patriotic women come before you to claim the right which any individual has to defend his life and liberty. . . . Your predecessors deposited the Constitution as much in our hands as in yours. Oh, how to save it, if we have no arms to defend it from the attacks of its enemies?"[29]

On what does rationale does Léon base her request? How does she represent women in relation to the state?

1791 and 1793 constitutions: A foreign man who marries a French woman can easily become a French citizen.[30]

April 1791: As nuns are attacked for harboring refractory priests, riots ensue.

How does the fact that men procure their national affiliation through their wives affect women's relationship to the French nation? What assumptions about women are implicit in this decision? What assumptions about the place of France in the world are implicit in this decision?

April 1791: Estates not covered by a will must be divided evenly among all children.[31]

What positive effects did inheritance laws have for women?

April 1, 1792: Etta Palm d'Aelders asks the Legislative Assembly for equal rights to education and divorce, arguing, "Women have shared the dangers of the Revolution; why shouldn't they participate in its advantages? Men are free at last, and women are the slaves of a thousand prejudices."[32]

How did the revolutionaries think critically about gender equality? How does Etta Palm reason that women have a claim to these rights?

August 4, 1792: Monks and nuns are ordered to leave their convents; *August*

10, 1792: teaching convents are closed down. The abbess of the Benedictines of Montargis resisted surrendering her convent and said, "You can say, sirs, to those who sent you, that our feeble arms bend, no doubt, under the chains of oppression; but our consciences, stronger than death, only obey God alone . . . Ferocious souls, you drink our blood."[33]

How do you respond to the nuns' position? How do they represent themselves as women? As citizens?

September 20, 1792: Divorce is made legal and accessible to men and women equally, based on mutual consent, incompatibility, insanity, criminal punishment, cruelty, immorality, abandonment, long absence, or emigration. As many as 100,000 people divorced by 1803, and women were more likely to initiate. Divorce attorney François Belloc said, "Now more than ever, marriages should be the union of hearts."[34]

How do you suppose family courts dealt with associated issues of property division and child custody? How might this law have an impact on the relationship between people who stayed married?

1793: There are approximately sixty women's clubs in the provinces called Amies de la Constitution. They are often encouraged by male leaders, seen as useful in time of war, and considered appropriate for women because of their charity work. Some anxiety persists relating to women being too political in these clubs.[35]

What types of fears about women's organizations exist and why? When are revolutionaries able to overcome those concerns and when not?

1793: The government shuts down hospitals operated by nuns.[36]

February 25 and 26, 1793: There are large-scale and well-coordinated

How can we define citizenship to include the way disenfranchised people expressed their political will? How do we enter that

protests by sans-culotte women over the grain crisis.

March 1793: Laws strip émigrés of citizenship and say that émigrés can be either sex. Women cannot claim the defense that they had no choice but to follow their husbands.

April 29, 1793: Rosalie Jullien, a middle-class Parisian, wrote to her son, an assistant war commissioner, "I dare say, there are French women who, though not yet Spartans or Romans, are capable of achieving Republican virtues with less effort than men."[37]

1793–1794: All forms of inheritance are divided evenly among male and female descendants.

May 31–June 2, 1793: The Girondins are purged, assisted by the Society of Revolutionary Republican Women, whose members "stood guard at the doors of the Convention" and "pursu[ed] those who fled."[38]

June 1793: Illegitimate offspring are included among inheritors.

July 13, 1793: Charlotte Corday assassinates Marat. At trial, she was ordered to plead insanity and was executed July 17.

September 1793: The Society of Revolutionary Republican Women clashes with other women with different

participation into the master narrative of citizenship and democracy?

What is the significance of this assumed independence for women and their and responsibility to choose their country over their husbands?

What might Jullien's reason be? How and why might women, without leadership roles in the public sphere, be able to achieve Republican virtue in her eyes?

In what practical ways do these inheritance laws change the way society is organized? How might men and women feel about these changes?

Compare, as Nina Gelbart does, Jean-Jacques Hauer's Le Meurtre de Marat, *which features Corday as the active agent in Marat's death with David's* Marat à son dernier soupir, *in which she does not appear at all.*[39]

political goals, leading to the market women's petition on *October 30* for the society to be abolished. All women's clubs are declared illegal. Deputy Jean-Baptiste Amar says women should not be involved in government or political associations because "they will be obliged to sacrifice to [political associations] more important cares to which nature calls them. The private functions to which women are destined by nature itself follow from the general order of society . . . Each sex is called to a type of occupation that is appropriate to it."[40]

Where did revolutionaries' critical thinking about gender equality fail? Contrast this thinking with that of Condorcet.

November 3, 1793: Olympe de Gouges is executed. *La feuille du salut public* writes, "Olympe de Gouges, born with an exalted imagination, mistook her delirium for an inspiration of nature. She wanted to be a man of state. She took up the projects of the perfidious people who want to divide France. It seems the law has punished this conspirator for having forgotten the virtues that belong to her sex."[41]

Why might the author be inspired to publish an attack on Gouges as a gender transgressor rather than as a Girondin?

February 4, 1794: Slavery is abolished in French colonies. Deputy Camboulas says, "Since 1789 the aristocracy of birth and the aristocracy of religion have been destroyed; but the aristocracy of the skin still remains. That too is now at its last gasp, and equality has now been consecrated."[42]

How could this logic have extended to an "aristocracy of gender"? How can we examine democracy today to avoid excluding groups from rights that are declared universal?

February 27, 1794: Rosalie Jullien writes to her son, traveling agent for the Committee of Public Safety, "My dear son, be virtuous in the name of a mother's love. Work as hard as you are strong, be as zealous as you are capable, and know, without being prideful, that your existence brings prosperity to the Republic and happiness to your tender parents."[43]

How does Jullien blend public and private life through her relationship with her son?

June 1794: Women in Saint Vincent react to a de-Christianization assembly by exposing their backsides to the representative.[44]

1796: In a famous case, Hoppé-Lange, a girl, is born out of wedlock to a German man and French woman. Both parents want custody. The court decides to put her into a state-run institution where both have visiting rights.[45]

How and why has patriarchal authority within this family been abrogated?

March 1803: Access to divorce is restricted based on parental consent, length of marriage, and other factors.[46]

Conclusion

I suggest an approach to teaching the French Revolution that integrates women's experiences into the timeline of revolutionary events. This method promises to resolve the three problems mentioned at the outset. It will expose the nuances of women's history of this period—as both gains and losses become apparent, sometimes simultaneously—at many turning points. It will also impart to students the fact that both men's and women's experiences of political events are relevant, not only because all people have a claim to history but because the dialectic of gender equality and discord is a significant engine of historical change. Consequently, students will strengthen their critical thinking ability because they will be required to reject tidy narratives in favor of complicated stories without clear morals. In a society that is yet more complex than that of eighteenth-century France, the ability to parse contradictory outcomes and seek to resolve inconsistencies within an ideology is extremely valuable.

NOTES

1. I thank Nicole LaBouff for her attentive reading and helpful conversations.

2. For good overviews of women's experiences in other major revolutions, see Carol Berkin, *Revolutionary Mothers: Women in the Struggle for America's Independence* (New York: Vintage, 2006); Rosemarie Zagarri, *Revolutionary Backlash: Women and Politics in the Early American Republic* (Philadelphia: University of Pennsylvania Press, 2008); Philippe R. Girard, "Rebelles with a Cause: Women in the Haitian Revolution," *Gender and History* 21, no. 1 (2009): 60–85; Catherine Davies, Claire Brewster, and Hilary Owen, eds., *South American Independence: Gender, Politics, Text* (Liverpool: Liverpool University Press, 2006).

3. For this reason and others, Candice Proctor concludes that women's position after 1793 "was in many respects actually worse than it had been in the days prior to 1789." Candice Proctor, *Women, Equality, and the French Revolution* (New York: Greenwood Press, 1990), 171.

4. Ibid., 55.

5. Geneviève Fraisse, *Reason's Muse: Sexual Difference and the Birth of Democracy*, trans. Jane Marie Todd (Chicago: University of Chicago Press, 1994), 77.

6. Ibid., 134.

7. Lynn Hunt, *The Family Romance of the French Revolution* (Berkeley: University of California Press, 1992), 123.

8. Joan Landes, *Women and the Public Sphere in the Age of the French Revolution* (Ithaca, NY: Cornell University Press, 1988), 95.

9. Joan W. Scott, *Only Paradoxes to Offer: French Feminists and the Rights of Man* (Cambridge, MA: Harvard University Press, 1996).

10. Mita Choudhury, *Convents and Nuns in Eighteenth-Century French Politics and Culture* (Ithaca, NY: Cornell University Press, 2004), 180.

11. Olwen Hufton, *Women and the Limits of Citizenship in the French Revolution* (Toronto: University of Toronto Press, 1992), 154.

12. Suzanne Desan, "Constitutional Amazons," in *Re-creating Authority in Revolutionary France*, ed. Bryant T. Ragan Jr. and Elizabeth A. Williams (New Brunswick, NJ: Rutgers University Press, 1992).

13. Dominique Godineau, *The Women of Paris and Their French Revolution*, trans. Katherine Streip (Berkeley: University of California Press, 1988), 137.

14. Ibid., 137–38.

15. Ibid., 53–72.

16. Ibid., 90.

17. Suzanne Desan, *The Family on Trial in Revolutionary France* (Berkeley: University of California Press, 2004), 311.

18. Ibid., 12.

19. Ibid., 7.

20. Jennifer Ngaire Heuer, *The Family and the Nation: Gender and Citizenship in Revolutionary France, 1789–1830* (Ithaca, NY: Cornell University Press, 2005).

21. Sian Reynolds, *Marriage and Revolution: Monsieur and Madame Roland* (Oxford: Oxford University Press, 2012); Denise Davidson, "'Happy' Marriages in Early Nineteenth-Century France," *Journal of Family History* 37, no. 1 (January 2012): 23–35; Lindsay A. H. Parker, "Family and Feminism in the French Revolution: The Case of Rosalie Ducrollay Jullien," *Journal of Women's History* 24, no. 3 (Fall 2012): 39–61.

22. William Reddy, *The Navigation of Feeling: A Framework for the History of Emotions* (Cambridge: Cambridge University Press, 2001); Marisa Linton, *Choosing Terror: Virtue, Friendship and Authenticity in the French Revolution* (Oxford: Oxford University Press, 2013); Lindsay A. H. Parker, "Veiled Emotions: Rosalie Jullien and the Politics of Feeling in the French Revolution," *Journal of Historical Biography* (Spring 2013): 208–30.

23. Lindsay A. H. Parker, *Writing the Revolution: A French Woman's History in Letters* (New York: Oxford University Press, 2013).

24. Richard Paul and Linda Elder, *Critical Thinking Competency Standards* (Tomales, CA: Foundation for Critical Thinking Press, 2007), 5.

25. Ibid., 10.

26. Where not otherwise cited, many of the following topics can be found in Darline Gay Levy, Harriet Branson Applewhite, and Mary Durham Johnson, *Women in Revolutionary Paris: 1789–1795* (Urbana: University of Illinois Press, 1979).

27. Quoted in Choudhury, *Convents and Nuns*, 163.

28. Proctor, *Women, Equality, and the French Revolution*, 111–13.

29. Quoted in Levy et al., *Women in Revolutionary Paris*, 72.

30. Heuer, *The Family and the Nation*, 48, 67.

31. Desan, *Family on Trial*, 141.

32. Quoted in Levy et al., *Women in Revolutionary Paris*, 123.

33. Quoted in Choudhury, *Convents and Nuns*, 176.

34. Desan, *Family on Trial*, 98–99.

35. Desan, "Constitutional Amazons."

36. Choudhury, *Convents and Nuns*, 176.

37. Quoted in Parker, *Writing the Revolution*, 102.

38. Levy et al., *Women in Revolutionary Paris*, 145.

39. Nina Rattner Gelbart, "The Blonding of Charlotte Corday," *Eighteenth-Century Studies* 38, no. 1 (Fall 2004): 201–21.

40. Ibid., 215.
41. Scott, *Only Paradoxes to Offer*, 52.
42. Quoted in C. L. R. James, *The Black Jacobins: Toussaint L'Ouverture and the San Domingo Revolution*, 2nd ed. (New York: Vintage Books), 139–40.
43. Quoted in Parker, *Writing the Revolution*, 106.
44. Hufton, *Women and the Limits of Citizenship*, 118.
45. Heuer, *The Family and the Nation*, 86.
46. Desan, *Family on Trial*, 137.

KEY RESOURCES

Desan, Suzanne. *The Family on Trial in Revolutionary France*. Berkeley: University of California Press, 2004.

Fraisse, Geneviève. *Reason's Muse: Sexual Difference and the Birth of Democracy*. Translated by Jane Marie Todd. Chicago: University of Chicago Press, 1994.

Hufton, Olwen. *Women and the Limits of Citizenship in the French Revolution*. Toronto: University of Toronto Press, 1992.

Levy, Darline Gay, Harriet Branson Applewhite, and Mary Durham Johnson. *Women in Revolutionary Paris: 1789–1795*. Urbana: University of Illinois Press, 1979.

Mezler, Sara E., and Leslie W. Rabine, eds. *Rebel Daughters: Women and the French Revolution*. New York: Oxford University Press, 1992.

Understanding and Teaching the Boston Stamp Act Riots, 1765

COLIN NICOLSON

The 250th anniversary of the Stamp Act riots in North America has now passed. Bostonians have largely forgotten the twelve days in August 1765 that changed the world of colonial Americans. Instead, it is the Tea Party of December 16, 1773, that is more frequently memorialized, a historical turning point in its own right, when Boston strongly defied imperial authority. This "Epocha" in history, as John Adams then called the "destruction" of the tea, has been canonized as a defining moment in the progress of the colonial protest movement, when opposition gave way to outright resistance and criminality. That night, thousands of Bostonians lined the waterfront to watch in silence as organized cells of radicals destroyed property worth £9,000 on a scale never previously seen in peacetime. Even then the Stamp Act riots would have seemed no less pivotal in marking Bostonians' transition from passivity to active protest and the beginning of their own path to freedom. The riots of 1765 were a major factor in persuading the British government to repeal the act that had imposed direct parliamentary taxation on the Americans; the destruction of the tea set Boston and Britain on a course of confrontation that would be resolved only by force of arms. Inviting students to contemplate Boston's twelve forgotten days—rather than the overexposed Tea Party—is I think a useful exercise in bringing them closer to the eighteenth-century world. The earlier riots are less known and less toxified by current politics, which make them excellent candidates for freshening up course coverage and for deepening understanding of the purpose and form of revolutionary riots.

Introducing Riots

"Has anyone ever taken part in a riot?"

With this question, I open a seminar on the Boston Stamp Act riots of 1765 in my advanced class on the American Revolution. It usually elicits silence. Momentarily perplexed by my impudence, perhaps, the silent respondents soon counter with questions of their own. "Why would anyone ever incriminate themselves?" "Have *you* ever rioted?" I remain silent.

The power of silence: neither I nor they intend to confound each other as we quietly ponder the circumstances in which we might take to the streets and consider on which side of the barricades we might be found. The class room is not a confessional, I enjoin. Condemnation of violence may be instinctive for leaders of political democracies, but not for their scholars, of whom I demand only understanding of the nature of crowd action, violent or otherwise. We do not need to agree or disagree about the utility and morality of violence, but we should strive to understand why people riot and demonstrate and make sense of such activities across a wide spectrum of behavior driven by antagonisms of ideology, class, race, identity, and power. Personal experience is not a prerequisite for making sense of crowd action any more than it is for historicizing social movements. Yet historical sociology cannot convey the emotional intensity wrought from participation or close observation, where, with clouded judgment, perceptions of the other become dangerously distorted by individual acts of violence. On which side would I find you in 1765?, I ask. "The Bostonians'!"

Has anyone ever participated in a demonstration? My third question prompts a rush of examples from the class, recalling situations mundane and extraordinary. Sharing personal crowd experiences—from protest marches to sporting events—helps inculcate awareness of the many forms and dynamics of crowds. Crowd *action*, I propose, we might define with Eric Hobsbawm's celebrated phrase as "collective bargaining by riot." There follows a brief discussion of the taxonomy and typology of riots in colonial America and eighteenth-century Britain: so-called anti-impressment riots, food riots, land riots, machine riots, militia riots, and race riots (for which undertake keyword searches). Linkages with overtly nonviolent aspects of crowd behavior are easily made, encompassing demonstrations, mass assemblies, and community punishments such as "rough music" or tarring and feathering. A brief collective consideration of such episodes should lead discussants to the conclusion that crowd action was extralegal in the estimation of participants and observers, but strictly riotous only in the eyes of the law and power elites who felt threatened by it. Framed in terms of theorists, this is prompting the class to move beyond Hobsbawm's focus on violence and toward E. P. Thompson's thesis that largely peaceable crowds were the arbiters of a moral economy in early modern societies.[1]

Comparisons with episodic rebellions ought to be made at this point, and the purposeful and broader political agendas of social movements historicized by Charles Tilly might be usefully explored with reference to the American civil rights movement and antiwar movements. Crowds are not the unthinking, unwashed destructive multitudes of artistic depiction and rudimentary sociopsychology, we agree.[2] But time and place is everything, we continue. "They call it the law— apartheid, internment, conscription, partition and silence." I quote American folk émigré Jack Warshaw on the state-sponsored violence of the twentieth century. "In Boston, Chicago, Saigon, Santiago, Cape Town and Belfast. And the places that never made headlines, the list never ends."[3] Baghdad, Beijing, Paris, Ferguson, Baltimore: scenes of protest during the students' own lifetimes are more readily called to mind.

From this litany of protest narratives, I offer an exordium of crowds in action. First, the National Advisory Commission on Civil Disorders (aka Kerner Report) of 1968: my now-baffled class of apprentice historians is relieved to learn that this groundbreaking investigation of US urban riots was rooted in historiography as well as sociology and politics.[4] It seemed to the commissioners that crowds had but a fleeting presence in US history as it was then written; as everyone then assumed, the revolutionary processes of the American Revolution paled in comparison to the later upheavals in France, Russia, and China. The Kerner Commission thus provided much of the impetus for crowd studies in early US history that discovered the potency of nonelite agency and simmering class antagonisms. Crowd action in itself is not revolutionary, although it might lend its agency to deeply transformative political and social processes.[5] Back in the 1960s, I opine, American liberals believed that history mattered for its own sake as much for its utility in contextualizing modern problems, not least the deadly riots that paralyzed Detroit and other major cities in 1967. But destructive episodes from modern times, conveniently archived on YouTube, bear little resemblance to events in Boston in the long hot summer of 1765, my students good-naturedly object. But it was in the 1960s and 1970s, I retort, when historians and sociologists finally learned how crowds functioned. Liberal academics are crowds' best friends, I plead, and students are often the lifeblood of protest movements.

Rioters have had few friends among the artistic community, until the twentieth century, I point out. Artists are unreliable guides to crowd history (cue slide presentation—works mentioned are listed in the short bibliography). Where Hogarth's *Gin Lane* (1751) repels the viewer with detail of social putrefaction, Delacroix's *Liberty Leading the* [French] *People* (1830) inspires the downtrodden to arms, and in Lucas's *Gordon Riots, 1780* (1879) the crowd bravely awaits annihilation by terrifying military prowess. Drummond's little-known depiction (1855) of the Porteous Riots in Edinburgh of 1736, however, entices the viewer into the lives of bystanders caught in a human morass, while mobs in the distance lynch the captain of the city guard. Captain John Porteous's crime against the community was to order his soldiers to fire on a crowd protesting the execution of smugglers; respited by the British government in London, the Edinburgh mob, thousands strong, exacted its own form of vengeance (effortlessly dramatized in Sir Walter Scott's *The Heart of Midlothian* [1818]).

For Crown officers in Massachusetts responsible for pursuing rioters before the American Revolution, the Porteous Riot was the most notorious instance of crowd action, partly on account of Porteous's grisly fate but also because of the government's botched attempt to establish corporate liability and punish (by means of a hefty fine) the city of Edinburgh for failing to preserve law and order. A similar fate might have befallen Bostonians, following the Massacre of March 5, 1770, when British soldiers commanded by Capt. Thomas Preston killed five rioters in a scene inaccurately but gloriously propagandized by Paul Revere. "Fire," we can imagine Preston shouting above the din, whereupon the bloody victims of British tyranny fall dead. Famous for only one thing in history—something he did not do—Preston was defended by patriot lawyer John Adams and acquitted of murder (as were the soldiers, though two were found guilty of manslaughter). Yet throughout the trials, acting Governor Thomas Hutchinson feared that, in his words, the mob would "Porteous" Preston—if, fully expecting a guilty verdict, Preston's sentence was ever respited or Preston pardoned. No matter that observers (artistic or otherwise) have cast crowds as ugly instruments of iconoclasm or that historical sociology elaborates processes over actors, Drummond's painting, Preston's trial, Hutchinson's tribulations, and Adams's integrity demand we devote attention to the real-life dramas of victims and participants. Asking students to imagine how they might react in a real-life situation is only a starting point for understanding historical predicaments and vice versa of course.

That is easier said than done, at least for the Boston Stamp Act riots. There were no trials, no soldiers, no deaths, no punishments, no contemporary visual representations; commemorations were short-lived and memorials few and far between, as Alfred Young revealed. What follows aims to help students' understanding of crowd action during the American Revolutionary era by means of microhistory (the necessary documents are appended at the end). My objectives are to help students make sense of two major instances of crowd action and gauge their impact on the imperial crisis of 1765–1775. In terms of learning outcomes, I hope the class will be better able to appreciate the dynamics of crowd behavior and political protest and consider their places in the process of revolution. The lesson plan that follows is intended to take up around two to three hours of class time, and in my current module (an in-depth exploration of the American Revolution), it makes up the fifth in a series of ten weekly seminar topics that deal with the revolution's origins up to 1776. By the time the class comes to examine the Stamp Act riots in detail, they have already taken on board some insights into (a) theories and concepts of revolution, (b) the historiography of the revolution, (c) an overview of some of the key features of the American colonies' eighteenth-century relationship with Great Britain, and (d) the postwar conditions and legislative changes that precipitated the Stamp Act crisis in 1764–1766. Much of this content reflects and incorporates my own research interests, and I make available some of the work I have undertaken on a multivolume documentary edition, the *Bernard Papers*, through our virtual learning environment (VLE). No group of students, anywhere in the world, I stress to my Stirling crowd, has had the privilege of viewing the transcripts of manuscripts and editorial commentaries they will be considering.

Lesson Plan

Before attending to the riots that accompanied the introduction of the Stamp Act, the students need to understand the growing rift in imperial relations and the grounds on which colonists framed their opposition to direct parliamentary taxation in 1764 to 1766 (see chronology and primary sources provided at the end of this chapter). One effective way of bringing this to light is to assign individual or paired short readings (typically book chapters or articles) that address important themes: British colonial policy making, American responses, and the conduct of royal officials responsible for implementing the Stamp Act in Massachusetts.[6] Following an introductory presentation on continuity and discontinuity in British colonial policy (distributed in advance via the VLE), discussion addresses three main questions.

1. Why have historians assigned such importance to the Stamp Act crisis of 1764–1766?
2. To what extent did the Revenue Act of 1764 and the Stamp Act of 1765 signal a major change in British colonial policy?
3. Why did arguments over political authority and power figure so prominently in debates about the Stamp Act?

Thereafter, the class forms three groups to consider what some major documents reveal about the nature of the disputes over taxation and authority: the resolutions of the Virginia House of Burgesses of June 1765, the Declarations of the Stamp Act Congress of October 1765, and the American Declaratory Act of March 1766. The groups report back to the class in a plenary session, and my role is principally to connect their reports to the central historiographical themes of the module—which boil down to the notion of the American Revolution as:

i.   a transformative social process (as fleshed out in the work of Gordon Wood)
ii. a disjunction in institutional power (see Jack Greene)
iii. an ideological contest (Bernard Bailyn)
iv   the locus for aspirant radicalism and marginalized nonelites (Gary Nash)

The class on the Stamp Act riots is structured along similar lines and allows us to get more at the first and fourth of these interpretive models:

those often described as "neo-Progressive," to link them to earlier eras of scholarship that insisted on the deep social reach and revolutionary significance of American independence. Having begun with the personal and conceptual engagement with rioting and protests discussed already, two or more students offer a presentation (around twenty minutes) summarizing the crowd action of the imperial crisis—drawing principally on Pauline Maier's pioneering article and Edward Countryman's judicious reassessment of her and others' work (work published after the 1960s had run their course). The third component (about twenty minutes) uses a series of slides with marked-up images of a detailed contemporary map of Boston to trace the progress through the streets of the first riot of Wednesday, August 14.[7] Starting at the great elm at the junction of Orange and Essex Streets, where that morning Stamp Distributor Andrew Oliver had been hung in effigy, I lead the audience on a virtual tour to the residence of Governor Francis Bernard, then to the Town House in King Street (the present-day Old State House very near the Boston Massacre site), and then to Oliver's Dock on the waterfront, where the mob pulled down a small building where they believed the stamped papers were being kept. That night the mob trashed the garden of Oliver's home, vandalized the exterior and interior of the building, and finished off proceedings with a bonfire on nearby Fort Hill. I do much the same thing when plotting the course of the rioters on Monday, August 26, which culminated in the destruction of the house of the lieutenant governor and chief justice, Thomas Hutchinson, located in Garden Court Street (marked with a wall plaque). I use Google Earth to convey the claustrophobia of the famously crooked streets of Boston's North End, where Hutchinson's fine mansion sat, surrounded by the houses and tenements of Boston's middling and lower sorts. Students who have indulged in the game Assassin's Creed III (which allows exploration mode in Boston) already know what I mean.[8]

The remainder of the week's class time on this topic is devoted to group work—fittingly, given the subject matter. Students undertake preparatory reading on the riots in Boston and elsewhere. Generally I try to make sure that groups cover topics they might have missed previously, but on this occasion I also need to avoid repetition from the previous seminar while ensuring that assignments are tailored to the group work. So the students who had some grounding in the predicament of Crown officials and British policy get to read about the Sons of Liberty (via historians Pauline Maier, Dirk Hoerder, and Ben Carp), and those who looked earlier at political radicalism now get to see things through the eyes of protestors and law enforcers (via Dirk Hoerder, Gary Nash, and Colin Nicolson). When we put these pieces back together, it becomes possible to look collectively at key documentation and think about the methods and motivations of rioters and to reach judgments over when and where deeper social conflict was apparent. The key aspect to making this approach successful is to ensure, as with any good history, that all perspectives are brought into play: the government sources on one hand (the letters of Thomas Hutchinson or Francis Bernard, or the governor's proclamations), and the antigovernment sources (often expressed via the *Boston Gazette*) on the other.

A Word on the Documentary Sources and Teaching with Them

Governor Bernard's letter provides the fullest surviving account of the second Stamp Act riot. It is not based on personal observation—the governor had retreated to Castle William shortly after the first riot—but on information provided by his deputy, Thomas Hutchinson, and others whom he consulted over four or five days.[9] Hutchinson's fullest report is in the letter to province agent Richard Jackson, extracted below, but he wrote of his sufferings in numerous letters to friends in America and England. The *Boston-Gazette, and Country Journal* was the leading antigovernment newspaper in Massachusetts, but it had to compete with four other weeklies for a share of a local circulation market of around 1,500. The printers, Benjamin Edes and John Gill, were staunch supporters of the colonial cause, and their newspaper was the mouthpiece of local Whigs, including Samuel Adams. Edes was also a member of the Loyal Nine (as the Boston Sons of Liberty were first known). The *Gazette* reported the first riot in detail, but not the second, preferring to fill columns with the governor's proclamations, the resolves of the town meeting, and the proceedings of the governor and council.[10] A useful cross section of these sources is proposed in Table 2, and some of the juiciest excerpts can be found in "Extra Teaching Materials 2: Excerpts from the Sources" at the end of this chapter.

Many students and indeed some teachers will find that when dealing with these kinds of sources, some occasional steering is necessary to move analysis forward, clarify phrases, or decipher eighteenth-century print type and handwriting, so it is important to be on hand to help.

Table 2. Primary Sources on Boston Stamp Act

Primary Source	Origin
Account of the destruction of the home of Thomas Hutchinson (Hutchinson to Richard Jackson, August 30, 1765)	Tyler and Dubrulle, *Correspondence of Thomas Hutchinson*, 291–94
List of goods stolen from Thomas Hutchinson's house on August 26, 1765	Tyler and Dubrulle, *Correspondence of Thomas Hutchinson*, 318–35
Gov. Francis Bernard, letters on the Stamp Act riots (Bernard to the Board of Trade, Castle William, August 15 and 16, 1765; Bernard to the earl of Halifax [secretary of state for the Southern Department], Castle William, August 31, 1765)	Nicolson, *Papers of Francis Bernard*, 2:301–7, 337–45 at http://www.bernardpapers.com
Proclamations on the Stamp Act riots, given by the governor on August 15 and 28, 1765	Nicolson, *Papers of Francis Bernard*, 2:334–36 at http://www.bernardpapers.com, and *Boston-Gazette*, September 2, 1765, at http://www.masshist.org/dorr
Reports on the Stamp Act Riots in the *Boston-Gazette*, August 19 and 26, September 2, and September 9, 1765	http://www.masshist.org/dorr

Part of the thrill and experience of engaging with such firsthand sources also lies in the challenge of reading through others' eyes, so encouraging patience and acknowledging interpretative possibilities is also vital. Let's address some of the important contextual features, and the cast of characters, that will help teachers to illuminate any claims.

Who were the rioters? Governor Bernard later estimated that the group engaged in "demolishing" Hutchinson's house comprised "between 30 or 40 of the lowest of the people." Ebenezer MacIntosh, the recognized leader of the Boston mobs, was arrested on August 27 along with six other rioters. He was released within hours, and no rioter ever stood trial for offenses committed, the government failing to entice informers despite the promise of rewards in the governors' proclamations.

MacIntosh's influence was marked during 1765 and 1766, but local Whigs came to see him as a liability.

Who were the organizers? The riots were probably organized by the Loyal Nine, a group of local businessmen and craftsmen who largely succeeded in directing the activities of mob leaders. Bernard reported that "50 Gentlemen Actors" in disguise joined the mob during the first riot while the "heads of the mob . . . are some of the principal Men." The first riot was celebrated by the Sons of Liberty for the duration of the revolution at local political events and commemorative dinners. But the second riot raised the specter of social conflict for them as well as the governor and the British. A central issue of concern for the local Whigs in the aftermath of the riots was how to exert influence and control over crowds. On the whole, they managed to do that for the entire imperial crisis and to use crowd action to mobilize popular support at key moments.

Who were the victims? The wrecking of Hutchinson's house is generally taken to be indicative of class-based resentment of Hutchinson's wealth and status, as much as popular dislike of his plural officeholding. As such, it provides one of the few instances, clearly visible, of class antagonism during the Stamp Act crisis. Oliver, Hutchinson, Hallowell, and Story were compensated for their losses by the province legislature, the Massachusetts General Court, before the British government and Parliament insisted that all colonies make restitution to victims of riots. However, the Massachusetts Indemnity Act also promised the province rioters immunity from prosecution; although it was approved by the governor, it was subsequently disallowed by the British Privy Council.

Who were the observers? What may appear tame to us may have been shocking to our forebears. In awe of the lawlessness exhibited during the second riot, the town formed an armed volunteer guard to protect the Customhouse (which then held in storage £6,000 collected in duties) and patrol the streets. Fearing reprisals from the mob, the volunteers threatened not to turn out unless MacIntosh was immediately released, which he was. This is an excellent illustration of how local politicians and street leaders were able to impose "conditions" on the enforcement of imperial law.[11]

Who were the law enforcers? Bernard had no effective means of dispersing crowds. There was nothing resembling a modern police force; however, magistrates could assemble a *posse comitatus* of local people, the governors could summon the militia, and the governor and council could request military assistance from British troops. The local magistrates refused to intervene on either occasion; the militia also refused to turn out, and indeed, several of the men reputedly joined the processions. The nearest body of British troops was at New York, and although Bernard considered requesting their assistance in the aftermath of the riots, he wisely desisted lest he provoke more extensive violence and endanger the customhouse. From the governor's perspective, the king's law was effectively unenforceable. When the act took effect on November 1, the governor refused to direct officials to proceed without using stamped papers, and so the law courts and customhouses closed their doors for several months until it was evident that Parliament was going to repeal the Stamp Act. The Stamp Act was never enforced in Massachusetts or any other continental colony except Georgia.

What were the British reactions? It is highly likely, though not certain, that the British government first learned of the Boston Stamp Act riots when they received Bernard's account of the second riot, on October 5. His report on the first riot arrived in London two days later. This meant that the British were unable to appreciate how the protests escalated and were probably blinded to the comparative mildness of the first riot by the dazzling drama of Bernard's second letter. Within days the letters were considered by the Board of Trade (the government's main advisory body on colonial affairs), the secretary of state for the Southern Department (in charge of colonial affairs), and the Privy Council (the king's advisory council). Unable to devise a considered response, the British were in danger of overreacting and seriously considered sending Regulars to quell the revolt some believed had taken place. It was not until October 22 that the Rockingham administration (which had replaced Grenville's ministry the previous July) resolved against taking military action. In the meantime, governors were left to sort out the mess on their own and implement the Stamp Act as best they might. Not until the following February did the administration give a clear signal of its intent to repeal the act, which Parliament did on March 18.

Conclusion

Comparisons are everything if this lesson plan is to be effective. Comparisons with modern riots are useful to get the discussion going, drawing on students' knowledge of current affairs and contemporary history. Comparisons between the Boston Stamp Act riots and early modern riots need to be made by the teacher, preferably at the end of the class in a plenary session when the students have studied Boston and can reiterate their reading of eighteenth-century crowd action. The Stamp Act disturbances in other colonies provide a convenient body of material for direct comparison, notably the riots in New York, which exhibited violence on a larger and more threatening scale than in Boston (for which see Nash). Comparisons with riots of the American Revolutionary era can probably be undertaken in curriculum: in this module, the class engages with the disturbances in Boston (the Massacre, the Tea Party) and Massachusetts (the dismantling of royal government in 1774 and the rural rising against taxation in 1787, known as Shays' Rebellion), the North Carolina Regulators, and the land riots in New York. Aligning and comparing some of these popular uprisings serves many ends. It is a useful way of enriching students' sense of the historical contingency, the diverse makeup, and varied objectives of crowds in the Age of Revolutions. It allows students to engage with and try to capture in their minds the clash between institutional authority and popular energy on which so many revolutions fed. And it makes students think about their own citizenship, sense of place, and feeling of connection to revolutionary pasts and presents.

Extra Teaching Materials I: Select Chronology of the Introduction of the Stamp Act

March 9, 1764. Stamp duties for America proposed in the budget speech of George Grenville (1712–1770), First Lord of the Treasury and Chancellor of the Exchequer, August 1763 to July 10, 1765.

March 10, 1764. Stamp tax bill postponed for one year.

August 11, 1764. Secretary of state, the earl of Halifax, informs colonial governors of the planned stamp duties and requests information on government instruments and documents that could be taxed.

February 13, 1765. First reading of the stamp duties bill in the House of Commons. Petitions from the colonies are soon presented.

February 27, 1765. Third and final reading in the House of Commons.

March 8, 1765. Bill approved by the House of Lords.

March 22 1765. The Stamp Act receives royal assent and is enacted as
   Duties in the American Colonies Act 1765, 5 Geo 3, c. 12.
November 1, 1765. Stamp Act takes effect in North America.
August to November 1765. Stamp Act riots.
March 18, 1766. Stamp Act repealed by Parliament. Passage of the
   American Declaratory Act.

Extra Teaching Materials 2:
Excerpts from the Sources

On Methods and Motivation of Rioters

From the *Boston-Gazette*, August 19, 1765,
on the riot of 14 and 15 Aug.

[After the disturbances of 14 Aug.] . . . the Evening following they again
assembled, erected a Number of Stages with Tar Barrels, &c. in the
Form of a Pyramid, in the Centre of which was a Flagg Staff, and a
Union Flag hoisted; whereupon 'tis said the St—p M—r sent them a
Letter with the aforementioned Resolution of Non-acceptance [of his
commission], and Assurance of Endeavors to serve the Province, &c.
Upon which they thought proper to demolish the Bonfire and retire——
but did not disperse till they went down to his H—r the L—t G—r's,
with whom they said they wanted to have a Talk; but not finding him at
Home, they concluded the Business of the Night by loud Acclamations
in every Quarter of the Town, on account of the Resignation of the
Stamp Master.

From the letter of Hutchinson to Jackson
August 30, 1765, on the riot of August 26

In the evening whilst I was at supper and my children round me
somebody ran in and said the mob were coming. I directed my children
to fly to a secure place and shut up my house as I had done before in-
tending not to quit it but my eldest daughter repented her leaving me
and hastened back and protested she would not quit the house unless I
did. I could not stand against this and withdrew with her to a neighbour-
ing house where I had been but a few minutes before the hellish crew
fell upon my house with the rage of devils and in a moment with axes
split down the doors and entered by some being in the great entry heard

them cry damn him he is upstairs we'll have him. Some ran immediately as high as the top of the house others filled the rooms below and cellars and others remained without the house to be employed there.

From the letter of Bernard to Halifax, August 13, 1765, on the riot of August 26

After the Demolition of Mr Oliver's house was found so practicable & easy, that the Government was obliged to look on, without being able to take Any one step to prevent it; & the principal people of the Town publickly avowed & justified the Act; The Mob, both great & small, became highly elated, & all kinds of ill humours were set on float. Evry thing that for years past had been the cause of any popular discontent was revived; & private resentments against persons in office worked themselves in & endeavoured to execute themselves under the mask of the public cause. Among others the Affair of the Attack upon the Admiralty & Custom house above 4 years ago[12] . . . brought up again & became as fresh as if it had been a Business of yesterday.

On Social Conflict

From the letter of Bernard to Halifax, August 31, 1765, on the riot of August 26

On Monday Aug 26 there was some small rumour that Mischief would be done at night; but it was in general disregarded. Towards Evning some boys began to light a bonfire before the Town house, which is an usual signal for a Mob: before it was quite dark a great Company of People gathered together crying liberty & property, which is the usual Notice of their intention to plunder & pull down an House. They first went to Mr Paxton's House (who is Marshall of the Court of Admiralty & Surveyor of the Port); & finding before it the owner of the House (Mr Paxton being only a Tenant) He assured them that Mr Paxton had quitted the house with his best effects; that the house was his; that he had never injured them; & finally invited them to go to the Tavern & drink a barrel of punch: the offer was accepted & so that House was saved. As soon as they had drinked the punch, they went to the house of Mr Story, Registrar deputed of the Admiralty, broke into it & tore it all to pieces; & took out all the books & papers among which were all the records of the Court of Admiralty & carried them to the bonfire &

there burnt them. They also lookt about for him with an intention to kill him. From thence they went to Mr Hallowell's, Comptroller of the Customs, broke into his house & destroyed & carried off evry thing of Value, with about 30 pounds sterling in cash. This House was lately built by himself & fitted & furnished with great elegance.[13] But the grand Mischief of all was to come.

The Lieut Governor had been apprized that there was an evil Spirit gone forth against him: but being conscious that he had not in the least deserved to be made a party in regard to the stamp Act or the Custom-house, he rested in full Security that the Mob would not attack him; & he sat Supper with his family, when he received advice that the Mob were coming to him. He immediately sent away his children & determined to stay in the house himself: but happily, his eldest Daughter[14] returned & declared She would not stir from the house unless he went with her; by which means She got him Away, which was undoubtedly the Occasion of saving his Life. For as soon as The Mob had got into the house with a most irresistible fury they immediately lookt about for him to murder him; & even made a diligent enquiry whither he was gone. They went to work with a rage scarce to be exemplified by the most Savage people. Evry thing moveable was destroyed in the most minute manner, except such things of Value as were worth carrying off, among which was near 1000 pounds sterling in Specie, besides a great quantity of family plate &c. But the Loss to be most lamented is, that there was in one room kept for that purpose a large & Valuable Collection of Manuscripts & Original papers which he had been gathering all his lifetime, & to which All persons, who had been in possession of Valuable papers of a public kind, had been contributing as to a public Museum. As these related to the history & policy of the Country from the time of its settlement to the present & was the only collection of its kind, the loss to the publick is great & irretrievable, as it is to himself the Loss of the papers of a family, which had made a figure in this province for 130 years. As for the house, which from its structure & inside-finishing seemed to be from a design of Inigo Jones[15] or his Successor; It appears that they were a long while resolved to level it to the ground: they worked for 3 hours at the Cupola before they could get it down; & they uncovered part of the roof: but I suppose that the thickness of the Walls which were of Very fine brickwork adorned with Ionick Pelasters workt into the Wall, prevented, their completing their purpose; tho' they

Worked at it till day light. The next day the Streets were found scattered with money, plate Gold rings &c which had been drop't in carrying off. The whole Loss in this house only is reckoned at 3,000 pounds sterling....

It was now becoming a War of plunder, of general levelling & taking away the distinction of rich & poor: so that those Gentlemen who had promoted & approved the cruel treatment of Mr Oliver, became now as fearful for themselves as the most loyal person in the Town could be: they found, as I told some of them, that they had raised the Devil & could not lay him again.

From the letter of Hutchinson to Jackson, August 30, 1765, on the riot of August 26

The encouragers of the first mob never intended matters should go this length and the people in general express the utmost detestation of this unparalleled outrage and I wish they could be convinced what infinite hazard there is of the most terrible consequences from such daemons when they are let loose in a government where there is not constant authority at hand sufficient to suppress them.

Resolves of Boston town meeting of August 27, printed in *Boston-Gazette*, September 2, 1765

The Town having an utter Detestation of the extraordinary and violent Proceedings of a Number of Persons unknown, against the same of the Inhabitants of the same the last Night VOTED UNANIMOUSLY That the Selectmen and Magistrates of the Town be desired to use their utmost Endeavours, agreeable to Law, to suppress the like Disorders for the future, and that the Freeholders and other Inhabitants will do every Thing in their Power to assist them therein.

NOTES

1. Eric J. Hobsbawm, "The Machine Breakers," *Past & Present* 1 (1952): 57–70 (esp. 59); E. P. Thompson, "The Moral Economy of the English Crowd in the Eighteenth Century," *Past & Present* 50 (1971): 76–136.

2. On crowd psychology, instructors can use examples that are familiar and topical for their students. I have used Steve Reicher and Cliff Scott, *Mad Mobs and Englishmen? Myths and Realities of the 2011 Riots* (London: Constable and Robinson, 2011). In 2011 and 2012, I showed my American Revolution class

images of the mass protests against the raising of university tuition fees at Conservative Party headquarters and outside the Houses of Parliament on November 10, 2010, which involved petty arson and vandalism (akin to the events in Boston on August 14, 1765), and images of the more serious instances of life-threatening arson in Croydon and rioting throughout London between August 6 and 11, 2011, which drew widespread condemnation (as did the destruction of Thomas Hutchinson's house on August 26, 1765). The casual comparison between these episodes was only for effect, to illustrate how evaluations of crowd action are contingent on perceptions of rioters' motivations.

3. Jack Warshaw, "If They Come in the Morning," 1977, https://www.youtube.com/watch?v=fdP95uYzgeM.

4. An accessible summary of the Kerner Commission Report is available online at http://historymatters.gmu.edu/d/6545/.

5. United States and National Advisory Commission on Civil Disorders, *Report of the National Advisory Commission on Civil Disorders* (Washington: US Government Printing Office, 1968), https://www.ncjrs.gov/pdffiles1/Digitization/8073NCJRS.pdf.

6. Suggestions can be found in the key sources for fine readings on British colonial policy making (Peter D. G. Thomas, *British Politics and the Stamp Act Crisis: The First Phase of the American Revolution, 1763-1767*; John L. Bullion, "British Ministers and American Resistance to the Stamp Act, October–December, 1765"), American responses (Edmund Sears Morgan and Helen M. Morgan, *The Stamp Act Crisis: Prologue to Revolution*; Pauline Maier, *From Resistance to Revolution: Colonial Radicals and the Development of American Opposition to Britain, 1765-1776*; Benjamin L. Carp, *Rebels Rising: Cities and the American Revolution*), and royal officials (Bernard Bailyn, *The Ordeal of Thomas Hutchinson*; Colin Nicolson, *The "Infamas Govener": Francis Bernard and the Origins of the American Revolution*).

7. Map is available at http://maps.bpl.org/id/10343.

8. For relevant hyperlinks, see http://fineartamerica.com/featured/1-thomas-hutchinson-granger.html and http://dl.tufts.edu/imageviewer/tufts:TBS.VW0001.000692#page/1/mode/1up.

9. The digital editions of the *Bernard Papers* are being made available as open access online resources. Volumes 4 and 5 in 2015 are currently available at http://www.colonialsociety.org/publications.html#online; volume 2, from which the governor's letter has been extracted, will appear in digital form in due course; until then I make the material available via the project website at http://www.bernardpapers.com.

10. The *Boston Gazette* can be freely accessed at the Harbottle Dorr Collection, hosted by the Massachusetts Historical Society, though not the issue for September 9, 1765.

11. For a broader discussion of the "conditions" of law, see John Philip

Reid, *In a Defiant Stance: The Conditions of Law in Massachusetts Bay, the Irish Comparison, and the Coming of the American Revolution* (University Park: Pennsylvania State University Press, 1977).

12. In 1761, the Boston merchants failed to overturn the legality of the writs of assistance, general search warrants used by customs officers. Thomas Hutchinson had been chief justice for barely six months when he heard the case before the Massachusetts Superior Court.

13. The mob that invested customs officer Benjamin Hallowell's house may have been a detachment from the mob that had attacked Story's office. Both were probably being directed, since they came together for the assault on Hutchinson's house. Hallowell's house and contents were vandalized and looted.

14. Sally Hutchinson (1744–1780).

15. Inigo Jones (1573–1652), the influential English architect.

KEY SOURCES

Anderson, George P. "Ebenezer Mackintosh: Stamp Act Rioter and Patriot." *Publications of the Colonial Society of Massachusetts* 26 (1927): 15–64.

Bailyn, Bernard. *The Ideological Origins of the American Revolution*. Cambridge, MA: Harvard University Press, 1967.

———. *The Ordeal of Thomas Hutchinson*. Cambridge, MA: Belknap Press of Harvard University Press, 1974.

Bullion, John L. "British Ministers and American Resistance to the Stamp Act, October–December, 1765." *William and Mary Quarterly* 49 (1992): 89–107.

Carp, Benjamin L. *Rebels Rising: Cities and the American Revolution*. Oxford: Oxford University Press, 2007.

Countryman, Edward. "The Problem of the Early American Crowd." *Journal of American Studies* 7 (1973): 77–90.

Greene, Jack P., ed. *The Reinterpretation of the American Revolution c. 1763–1789*. New York: Harper & Row, 1968.

———. *Peripheries and Center: Constitutional Development in the Extended Polities of the British Empire and the United States, 1607–1788*. New York: Norton, 1986.

Hobsbawm, Eric J. "The Machine Breakers." *Past & Present* 1 (1952): 57–70.

Hoerder, Dirk. *Crowd Action in Revolutionary Massachusetts, 1765–1780*. London: Academic Press, 1977.

Maier, Pauline. "Popular Uprisings and Civil Authority in Eighteenth-Century America." *William and Mary Quarterly* 27 (1970): 3–35.

———. *From Resistance to Revolution: Colonial Radicals and the Development of American Opposition to Britain, 1765–1776*. London: Routledge, 1973.

Massachusetts Historical Society. *The Annotated Newspapers of Harbottle Dorr Jr.* http://www.masshist.org/dorr/ (accessed May 14, 2015).

Morgan, Edmund Sears, and Helen M. Morgan. *The Stamp Act Crisis: Prologue to Revolution.* New York: Collier Books, 1963.

Nash, Gary B. *The Urban Crucible: Social Change, Political Consciousness, and the Origins of the American Revolution.* Cambridge, MA: Harvard University Press, 1979.

———. *The Unknown American Revolution: The Unruly Birth of Democracy and the Struggle to Create America.* New York: Viking, 2005.

Nicolson, Colin. *The "Infamas Govener": Francis Bernard and the Origins of the American Revolution.* Boston: Northeastern University Press, 2001.

———, ed. *The Papers of Francis Bernard, Governor of Colonial Massachusetts, 1760–69,* 6 vols. Boston: Colonial Society of Massachusetts; distributed by the University of Virginia Press, 2007–.

Thomas, Peter D. G. *British Politics and the Stamp Act Crisis: The First Phase of the American Revolution, 1763–1767.* Oxford: Oxford University Press, 1975.

Tilly, Charles. *The Politics of Collective Violence.* Cambridge: Cambridge University Press, 2003.

———. *Social Movements, 1768–2004.* Boulder, CO: Paradigm Publishers, 2004.

Tyler, John W., and Elizabeth Dubrulle, eds. *The Correspondence of Thomas Hutchinson,* 3 vols. Boston: Colonial Society of Massachusetts; distributed by the University of Virginia Press, 2014–.

Wood, Gordon S. *The Radicalism of the American Revolution.* New York: Vintage, 1991.

Young, Alfred F. *The Shoemaker and the Tea Party: Memory and the American Revolution.* Boston: Beacon Press, 1999.

Modernity Confronted

Experiencing the Age of Revolutions
with Toussaint Louverture

CHRISTOPHER HODSON

The Haitian Revolution is back. Silenced, sidelined, and shunted toward the wings during the nineteenth and twentieth centuries, it has swaggered onto center stage in the twenty-first. If scholarship on the late eighteenth century was a high school, the Haitian Revolution would now be one of the popular kids. Sprawling across the lunchroom, its entourage would include those who liked Haiti before it was cool (among them David Geggus, Carolyn Fick, Yves Benot, and of course C. L. R. James); those who might otherwise have stuck to tradition, wearing the respective and respectable letter jackets of the American or French revolutions, but who find themselves drawn to the edgy, boundary-crossing possibilities embodied in the Caribbean (say, Laurent Dubois, Jeremy Popkin, Ashli White, and the like); and those prepossessed enough to recognize that the themes they like most—racial identity, slave law, gender, or creolization—are made all the more lively in Haiti's presence (John Garrigus, Malick Ghachem, Doris Garraway, and many more). Unlike the cliques at your school, this "in crowd" only gets more inclusive. From Latin Americanists to Africanists, from early modernists to last week-ists, from theory hounds to archive rats, the Haitian Revolution continues to attract researchers whose work resonates throughout—and beyond—the discipline of history.

Gone, then, are the days when R. R. Palmer's two-volume, thousand-page *Age of the Democratic Revolution* could lavish chapter-length attention on the Batavian and Cisalpine republics while including only two spare references to events in the French Caribbean.[1] Indeed, the past twenty years or so have seen Haiti play a key role in prying loose the death-grip once held by the American and French revolutions on no less a subject than the transition to modernity. For much of the twentieth century, scholars tended to trace the modern political world back to a birthplace somewhere between Benjamin Franklin's Philadelphia and Robespierre's Paris. Along this transatlantic axis, they explained, ambitious men of thought tore out the old regime's crumbling foundations, building in their place state institutions and public cultures rooted in Enlightenment ideas of liberty, reason, and capitalism.[2]

Both the eighteenth-century characters in this story and the historians who later wrote it down hemmed, hawed, or stared guiltily at their feet when the topic of slavery came up, unable to map its persistence onto the modern landscape of freedoms and rights emerging around them. Now, however, the Haitian Revolution has driven the brutal realities of Caribbean economics and the rebellious actions of African slaves into the heart of modernity so forcefully that the concept itself has fractured. What was once a coherent narrative about "how we got to now" is no more; in its place is a diverse group of trajectories shaped in no small part by Haiti's gravitational pull.[3]

To sum up: far more people are now writing about the Haitian Revolution than ever before, a shift that has moved the French Caribbean from the periphery of scholarship to its very core. But if you've been in a classroom lately, working with clever, relatively well-prepared, mostly sensible students like those who attend my university, you'll know that they know very little about Haiti. They've seen images, mostly in the context-free context of the Internet, and mostly of the January 2010 earthquake that struck near Port-au-Prince, killing as many as 150,000 Haitians. In the pages of *Newsweek*, President Barack Obama distilled as well as anyone what the world had witnessed: "heartbreaking images of devastation" that added up to "a horrific scene of shattered lives in a poor nation that has already suffered so much."[4] From Obama down, the earthquake tends to look like just one more page in a flipbook of Haitian catastrophes, blending together with fleeting visions of hurricanes, dictatorships, mudslides, invasions, and famines to form an unbroken narrative of national victimhood. Where historians see in Haiti an origin point for the rich, multifaceted, and (yes) tragic modern world, their students see a land that has nothing to do with modernity, if they see it at all.[5]

How do we leaven popular pity for Haiti's present (which too often dehumanizes Haitians and declaws their history) with scholarly wonder at its revolutionary past? How do we best connect the Haitian Revolution to the wide-ranging processes it helped kick-start—emancipation, the hardening of racial lines, decolonization, the transformation of nineteenth-century capitalism, and the emergence of political modernity? There are many ways to address these issues, and employing any one of them is certainly better than not addressing the issues at all. But faced with a topic that looms ever larger, we might be well served in the classroom by thinking small. Indeed, I suggest some of the benefits of a tight focus on the only figure from the Haitian Revolution students are likely to know: Toussaint Louverture.

True enough, there are some good arguments against scholarly Toussaint-centrism. The market for "great man" history is saturated, especially in the United States, where readers' seemingly boundless, often politically charged enthusiasm for the Founding Fathers continues to hamstring conversations about the late eighteenth century in the classroom and beyond. As T. H. Breen reminds us, "the insurgents who most often go missing from modern narratives of revolution are ordinary people."[6] In a more specifically Haitian vein, Carolyn Fick warns that "by seeing the embodiment of the Saint Domingue [Haitian] revolution in the figure of Toussaint Louverture," and by lumping him in with other old regime destroyers and modern state-builders of the late eighteenth century, we risk losing sight of the ex-slaves whose drive for personal independence, rooted in the soil of the plantation and the culture of Africa, made what happened in Haiti so distinctive—often by opposing Toussaint's plans.[7]

Whether in my survey of US history or in my upper-division courses on the Age of Revolutions, I've found that Toussaint remains indispensable. The trick, I think, is to approach him less as a biographical subject and take instead what we might call a microhistorical tack. That is, rather than assessing his (admittedly profound) impact on the world, I try to use certain moments in his well-documented life—a life that links Saint-Domingue's old regime to the Haitian Revolution, and whose echoes resonated in the nineteenth and twentieth centuries—to illuminate the unfamiliar contours of that world, and to suggest how *it* made an impact on *him*. Forays into these richly textured moments strike me as the best way to engage students in the heavy lifting of evidence that complicates their old views. With any luck, a brief introduction to Toussaint-in-the-flesh can set them on the road to what pedagogy scholars describe as a "radical restructuring" of knowledge on the relationship between revolution and modernity.[8]

What follows, then, are two conversations I like to have with my students after we've covered the revolution's outlines in class or via a brief reading assignment.[9] Toussaint figures in each of these discussions, but I try to make sure he does not become the sole focus. Instead, with microhistory in mind, I want students to try and see what Toussaint saw, examining the landscapes he walked and the relationships he fostered in search of the strange contradictions of an emerging modern age.

They usually come away surprised.

Toussaint's Home:
Saint-Domingue before the Revolution

Familiar only with the nation-state of Haiti, students often have a hard time grasping the nature of the French colony that preceded it. Absent the history of overseas imperialism and planter expansionism that gave rise to prerevolutionary Saint-Domingue, events of the late eighteenth century usually come off as products of universal impulses rather than particular conditions. All of which is to say that a firm grasp on Saint-Domingue matters a great deal.

Abandoned by the Spanish early in the seventeenth century, the northwest coasts of the island of Hispaniola were occupied in the 1640s and 1650s by French castoffs from Saint-Christophe, Guadeloupe, and Martinique. Sundry ne'er-do-wells became *flibustiers* (pirates), *boucaniers* (purveyors of smoked meat harvested from turtles and wild pigs), or *habitants* (farmers of tobacco, cacao, or ginger). By the end of the century, Saint-Domingue boasted a proper royal administration and a handful of sugarcane and indigo plantations. To Jean-Baptiste Labat, a Dominican friar who visited the island in 1701, the colony was already warped by unchecked capitalism: "I could name a number of men who came out as indentured servants . . . but who are now such great lords that they cannot walk but must always ride in their carriage and six horses."[10]

Eighteenth-century statistics (caution: use sparingly!) tell a story of demographic growth and economic vibrancy based increasingly on slave labor. As late as 1690, a roughly equal number of whites and enslaved Africans lived in Saint-Domingue (about 4,000 each). Between 1700 and 1713, as the number of plantations in the colony jumped from 18 to 138, the number of slaves skyrocketed to 25,000 while the white population ticked up modestly to 5,000. This unbalanced pattern would hold. The enslaved population reached 200,000 around 1760 and neared 500,000 in 1790; Saint-Domingue still counted fewer than 20,000 whites as late as 1771, topping out at just under 30,000 in 1790.[11] Wedged uncomfortably between white planters and their slaves were the *gens de couleur*, or free people of mixed-race ancestry. From 500 in 1700, their numbers swelled to 20,000 in the late 1780s.[12] Although faced with real, systematic racial prejudice beginning in the 1760s, the gens de couleur, many of whom owned plantations and slaves, remained integral to Saint-Domingue's surging economy.[13]

By the 1770s, the colony was dominant within the Caribbean and beyond, producing 40 percent of the world's sugar and 60 percent of its coffee, while seizing healthy shares of the Atlantic markets for indigo and cotton.[14] Saint-Domingue's trade enriched coastal towns on both sides of the French Atlantic. Cap-Français (now Cap-Haïtien on Haiti's northern shore), went from a primitive village, populated in Labat's day by "naked savages" barely recognizable as Europeans, to a sophisticated city of 15,000 by the 1780s. In France, colonial trade flowed up rivers, raising the fortunes of ports like Bordeaux and Nantes, as well as their agricultural hinterlands, even as more traditional sectors of the French economy stagnated.[15]

Saint-Domingue's profits, however, could be traced back to a regime of blood and terror. Jean-Baptiste Dubuc knew that regime well. It made him rich—so rich, according to the philosophe Denis Diderot, that he once calmly continued a game of whist even after receiving a mid-hand letter informing him that a hurricane had caused 60,000 *livres* in damages to his plantations. But slavery made him anxious. He was, Dubuc wrote in 1787, "a free planter on enslaved soil," a man "condemned to live violently" in an endless war against the source of his own wealth.[16] In effect, planters like Dubuc ran the dangerous, soul-crushing engine room of modernity, bankrolling Europeans' musings on human emancipation and the supremacy of reason by incinerating the bodies of slaves.[17]

What did modernity mean to a Saint-Dominguan slave? Toussaint's prerevolutionary life offers some insights. He was almost certainly not, as his son Isaac later claimed, the grandson of a West African warrior-king named Gaou Guinou; instead, his parents, Hippolyte and Pauline, were ordinary West Africans swept up in the early waves of Saint-Domingue's expansion. Toussaint was born to them in 1743 on the plantation of the Bréda family in the town of Haut-du-Cap, nestled between the boundless cane fields of the elevated "Northern Plain" and the bustling docks of Cap-Français. As plantations went, *chez* Bréda was no juggernaut. While "pleasant in terms of air and water," wrote a family employee, "it ends up costing more than it produces." The trouble may have been leeched soil, but most blamed Haut-du-Cap's location at the confluence of agrarian and commercial worlds. "All sorts of traffic" went on there, leaving the Brédas' slaves and plantation "spoiled by the neighborhood."[18]

Toussaint, then, grew up steeped in the rigid hierarchies and seasonal rhythms of the plantation as well as the fluid relations and haphazard exchanges of Cap-Français. His upbringing in Haut-du-Cap made for a remarkable, if not fully representative, journey into adulthood. Take, for instance, these wonderful fragments, culled from recent research on Toussaint's early days:[19]

- During the late 1750s, Toussaint probably received a basic education from Haut-du-Cap's Jesuits, who until their expulsion from Saint-Domingue in 1763 operated a hospital not far from the Bréda plantation and offered instruction to both free and enslaved blacks.
- In 1761 (we think), he married Cécile, the sister of the Bréda family's enslaved coachman, whose job Toussaint then took. Remarkably, Cécile was a free woman; also remarkably, the ceremony took place in a church, perhaps thanks to Toussaint's Jesuit connections.
- Toussaint gained his freedom sometime before 1776. He may have been rewarded for helping the Bréda family and their overseer, Antoine-François Bayon de Libertat, recover after a previous overseer's heavy-handedness drove numerous slaves to run away and, quite possibly, poison animals on the Haut-du-Cap plantation.[20]
- During the late 1770s, Toussaint leased a coffee plantation and thirteen slaves from his son-in-law, Philippe Jasmin Désir (one of

them may well have been Jean-Jacques Dessalines, the first ruler of independent Haiti). He also purchased two slaves, Jean-Baptiste and Pélagie, and later manumitted them.

- Toussaint's first marriage dissolved sometime in the 1780s. For reasons that remain a mystery, Cécile likely left him for a mixed-race builder named Pierre-Guillaume Provoyeur. Toussaint then began living with Suzanne Simon-Baptiste, an enslaved washer-woman. As per the 1685 slave code that regulated such matters in the French Empire, the couple's three sons (Placide, Isaac, and Saint-Jean) were born into slavery.

When I really want to push my students, I ask them to resist the biographical impulse and look for insights in this remarkable material that have nothing to do with Toussaint himself. These conversations usually begin slowly, with their sense that Toussaint and his friends in Haut-du-Cap "got away with" a lot of stuff. From hearing the Jesuits' catechism to marrying free women to temporarily running away (a tradition known as *petit marronage*) to, of course, obtaining freedom and leasing other slaves, the Africans of Haut-du-Cap appeared to possess greater negotiating power than most tend to expect. Beyond the Bréda plantation, there was plenty more to get away with.[21]

To the dismay of masters in Marmelade, a parish to the south and west of Cap-Français, slaves in the 1780s took a shine to the bizarre practice of mesmerism, a recent import from health-obsessed and quackery-soaked France. They gathered illegally in groups of several hundred for magnetic healing sessions that "surprised" and "frightened" plantation overseers.[22] Throughout the Northern Plain, others haunted an underworld of Afro-Caribbean practices, from dances to vodou rituals to shadowy political structures, most of which they carried on "in spite of . . . all of the precautions the masters take."[23] In the rugged mountains of the Southern Province, a former slave named Dompête, allegedly a poisoner and sorcerer linked to the Kongolese Petro cult, led a band of maroons that terrorized locals for years.[24] Like France's ancien régime, Saint-Domingue's slave society appeared unitary only from a long way off. Up close, it was a confused patchwork of institutions, peoples, and sources of power.

At the seams of that patchwork, much was up for grabs. Masters' authority over their slaves, for example, was challenged in the 1780s by Crown officials fearful that widespread torture might lead to uprisings.

Although inadmissible as evidence, the depositions of fourteen slaves from Plaisance led to the prosecution of their owner, Nicolas Lejeune, who described the affair as "a triumph for my negroes."[25] Like slavery, the nature of race was hardly settled. Since the 1760s, whites had tried to shore up Saint-Domingue's racial hierarchy through strategic lumping and splitting. Colonists lumped free mixed-race people in with slaves by applying what would later be known as a "one drop" rule, trying to ensure that the gens de couleur would become as "detestable" as Africans to whites; at the same time, they tried to short-circuit alliances between the mixed-race and African populations by funneling the gens de couleur toward service in the *maréchaussée*, the police force responsible for pursuing runaway slaves. A few even envisioned breeding a caste of "mulatto" soldiers to defend Saint-Domingue against enemies foreign and domestic.[26] Of course, mixed-race leaders such as Julien Raimond argued that wealthy gens de couleur ought to be considered "new whites" and that rights ought to be linked to status, not race.[27]

These debates shaped Toussaint's life. His two marriages, his manumission, his acquisition of land and slaves, and his fraught relations with gens de couleur all took place as Saint-Dominguans groped for solutions to problems created by the intertwined histories of planter colonialism, slave labor, and Atlantic commerce. My students often reach the conclusion that from Haut-du-Cap (a "seam" if ever there was one), Toussaint could see both sides of modernity's Janus face. Ruthless and severe, the first surveilled the plantations, ensuring the sacrifice of African bodies to the profit-making process; the second reflected the colony's jumble of institutions as well as the oceanic exchanges that drove its economy, both of which were saturated with the possibility of liberation. But, students admit, for slaves elsewhere—say, on the Laborde estate near Les Cayes, where for minor infractions overseers chained slaves to a sixty-pound stone and made them "work as usual"—the view must have been different and room to maneuver harder to come by.[28]

The upshot of all this is that there was no one way of seeing what was going on in Saint-Domingue for slaves—or mixed-race people, or poor whites, or planters, or Caribbean-born blacks, or recent arrivals from Africa. When the crisis of the French Revolution struck Saint-Domingue in 1789, the racial unity we often take for granted simply wasn't in force. Like the term *bourgeoisie* in France, Caribbean categories like "slave" and "black" were contested, and encompassed a great many people with very little in common.[29] Toussaint, I think, helps students see as much. Indeed, rather than painting all of Saint-Domingue with the broad brush of his own image, Toussaint's peculiarity brings into relief the diversity of experience created by the Caribbean's multifaceted confrontation with modernity. This perspective, I hope, prepares them for the disorientation they are almost sure to feel as we strike out for the revolutionary 1790s.

Toussaint's Kings:
Monarchy and Rebellion in Saint-Domingue

To help introduce that disorientation, I sometimes walk students through a pamphlet I found one day in the Archives Nationales in Paris. Published in Cap-Français, it recounts a party thrown on August 20, 1785, at the Charrier estate, a few hundred yards from the Bréda plantation in Haut-du-Cap. Set high up on a hill, the Charriers' house had been chosen to host a glitzy celebration of the birth of Louis-Charles, duc de Normandie, the third child of Louis XVI and Marie Antoinette. Although the party was quite an event, the pamphlet describing it seems not to have made an impact. As far as I can tell, the only surviving copy, which I stumbled across by accident, lies buried in the personal papers of a long-forgotten Saint-Domingue official. It has never been translated into English, which means that students must make do with my own reconstruction of goings-on at the Charrier estate. No free rides, of course: I make clear that the price of admission is some hard-nosed microhistorical thinking about kingship in a slave society.

The party began when planters, royal officials, and military elites from Cap-Français descended from their carriages and brushed past a crowd of commoners and slaves gathered near the Charriers' outer gate—given the spectacle, Toussaint may well have walked over to have a look. Inside, guests saw a great fountain, on which had been placed a portrait of the infant duc de Normandie and inscriptions from Virgil's *Aeneid*. Banners arched across the Charriers' reflecting pool, which ended at the stairway to the great manor. Climbing the stairs and entering the interior courtyard, guests encountered a "colossal statue" of Louis XVI and an *arc de triomphe* covered with royal symbols ranging from a dolphin (or *dauphin*, in honor of Louis XVI's oldest son) to the duc de Normandie's initials sculpted in bas-relief. After hobnobbing among the monuments, partygoers moved to a "festival room" for dinner, where they gathered near a large, four-columned structure made entirely of sugar. Inside the garland-draped pavilion was a sugar cradle with a sugar baby in it—a Bourbon homage made from the essential stuff of Saint-Domingue's economy.

During the meal, singers performed a much-edited number from Beaumarchais's opera *The Marriage of Figaro*, which had played in Cap-Français earlier that year, weeks after its Parisian debut. This song selection might have caused real trouble. *The Marriage of Figaro* offered a blistering assault on noble status that seemed to earn Beaumarchais the ire of every bewigged aristocrat in France, including Louis XVI himself. So revolutionary were the play's sentiments that, attempting to outwit the wit, the king had the aging author confined to Saint-Lazare, Paris's chief prison for delinquent boys.[30] As performed at the party in Haut-du-Cap, however, Beaumarchais's music was revolutionary only in that it encouraged listeners to turn their gazes toward the king's glorious person:

> Become ever-numerous,
> August race of Bourbons,
> Gods! To make fertile their blessed branch
> Is to augment your gifts.
> Your precious image
> In Louis shines before our eyes . . .

> Long live that August Queen,
> Who, by her fecundity,
> Lays the sure foundation
> Of our felicity.
> Upon this faraway beach
> We worship her charms,
> Like all good Frenchmen.

The guests blearily retraced their steps out of the plantation after dawn, as the ordinary folk of Haut-du-Cap trudged off to church or work.[31]

Par for the ancien régime course, my students usually say. Eight years later, however, everything had changed. Early in 1793, to mark a visit from representatives of France's new republican government, the last Charrier to live on the plantation ceremoniously pulled down the statue of Louis XVI that had anchored the 1785 party's decor.[32] Then known as Citizen Capet, the king had been executed in January; Marie Antoinette followed him to the guillotine in October. The duc de Normandie lived not at Versailles but in the Temple, a medieval fortress-turned-prison on the Seine's right bank. Two years later, when the boy was ten, he died there in rags. Taken together, all of this usually strikes my students as a proper trajectory for revolution in the modernizing French Atlantic. Kings and the hierarchies that sustain them collapse; popular rule and the leveling ideologies that promote it rise. As in Paris, so in Cap-Français.

At this point, the fine scholarship of John Thornton, perhaps paired with a primary document or two (the searing 1793 correspondence included in David Geggus's masterful new reader or the letters of the Afro-Caribbean insurgent Bramante Lazzary found in Laurent Dubois and John Garrigus's still-outstanding collection) hits my class like the proverbial ton of bricks. For they reveal that even as the Charriers stripped their estate of kings, Toussaint was fighting for one.[33]

"We know very well there is no more king, since you Republican traitors have had his throat cut on an unworthy scaffold," he seethed to a French official in the summer of 1793, declaring that "it is among us that the true rights of man and justice Reign!"[34] The "us" in Toussaint's statement referred to a coalition of black military leaders and armed ex-slaves then fighting in Saint-Domingue on behalf of the Spanish king Charles IV, Louis XVI's cousin. These included Jean-François and Georges Biassou, two of the earliest leaders to emerge from the massive slave revolt that struck the plantations of the Northern Plain on August 22, 1791.

They made no bones about their royalism. Biassou claimed to have wept daily since learning of Louis XVI's death, lamenting his inability to go to Paris and crush the "evildoers who call themselves *philosophes*," but who were in fact mere "cannibals." "Since the beginning of the world we have obeyed the will of a king," the pair wrote when approached by French emissaries: "We have lost the king of France but we are dear to him of Spain. . . . We therefore cannot recognize you until you have enthroned a king."[35] The depth of their attachment to monarchy was confirmed by Macaya, a Congolese lieutenant who described himself as "the subject of three kings: of the King of Congo, master of all the blacks; of the King of France who represents my father; of the King of

Spain who represents my mother," all of whom were descendants of the Magi who followed the star to Christ's birthplace in Bethlehem.[36] Less flowery, Toussaint was hardly less rigid. As for his rebel band, he told the French, "they wanted a king, and that they would not lay down their arms until he was recognized."[37]

My students get twitchy here. A royalist Toussaint, derided as a "General of the Armies of his Most Catholic Majesty" by French critics and a man who by most accounts professed true belief in Spanish promises of "protection and liberty for all those who would fight for the cause of kings," does not jive well with expectations.[38] Students tend to be more comfortable with Toussaint's actions after the spring of 1794, when he declared allegiance to the French Republic and helped seal the fate of slavery in Saint-Domingue.

This "volte-face" happened when it did for good reason. In June 1793, open conflict erupted in Cap-Français between Légér-Félicité Sonthonax, one of three "civil commissioners" sent to Saint-Domingue by the revolutionary government in France, and François-Thomas Galbaud, a general tapped as the colony's governor. With both men claiming to represent the French republic, urban warfare broke out, pitting Sonthonax and his allies among the gens de couleur against Galbaud and his backers among the city's soldiers, sailors, and wealthy whites. Fearful of losing the day, Sonthonax saw little choice but to issue an emancipation proclamation, initially freeing only slaves from Cap-Français who fought on his side. But there was no putting this particular genie back in the bottle; within weeks, Sonthonax had officially freed all of Saint-Domingue's slaves.[39] In February 1794, the National Convention in Paris, by now fearful of the rapacious British as well as the Spanish, confirmed the end of slavery in France's tropical colonies and the transformation of planter property into armed citizens. The news likely spurred Toussaint to switch allegiances, although as Geggus has suggested, ambition had something to do with it as well.[40]

In the end, of course, the forces of republicanism and emancipation end up joined, just as my students usually expect. But for a long time and for all races, kings were self-evidently the guarantors of freedom in Saint-Domingue. The French colony was no isolated case. As Brendan McConville and Eric Nelson have pointed out, the same phenomenon held true in British North America during the 1760s and 1770s. Whites turned to neo-absolutism in reaction to perceived parliamentary abuses, seeking redress from the British king; once the fighting started, thousands of slaves fled American republicanism, flocking to safety behind George III's standards.[41]

For the Charriers and many of their guests at the party in 1785, monarchism of a certain stripe lit the way to liberty of a certain stripe. In theory, Louis XVI was the planters' best hope in their fight against French merchants who, from Nantes and Bordeaux, advocated for mercantilist constraints on Saint-Dominguan trade with foreign competitors. Whether conceived along traditional lines or as a form of "enlightened despotism," a sort of liberating royalism suffused Saint-Domingue's prerevolutionary politics.[42] True enough, the slave-holding elite despised royal meddling in their domestic affairs. But fearful of radical antislavery thinking and stung by the condescension of wealthy, privileged would-be peers in France, Saint-Dominguan elites—like other politically vulnerable people—saw the king as a beacon. Indeed, the Charriers' pro-Bourbon party resembles nothing so much as celebrations held by French Jews at the birth of Louis XVI's children.[43]

As for freemen like Toussaint and Saint-Domingue's slaves, the calculus was pretty simple. Not unlike French peasants who leaned kingward because Louis XVI checked the local noblemen who were their natural enemies, slaves looked to kings because kings gestured, ever so slightly, at checking the planters who owned them—royal officials, after all, were the only people to whom a slave could appeal in cases of torture, mutilation, or malnourishment. Transplanted to Saint-Domingue via the slave trade, the cultures of West Africa also produced rich traditions of kingship on the plantation, driving what observers described as hybridized Afro-European royal ceremonies "to which Creole customs have added several variants."[44] Once the 1791 slave revolt was in motion, the world of kings gave men like Toussaint a world of opportunities. To the extent that fighting for the king of Spain allowed him to "stand up for" the emancipation of Saint-Domingue's slaves, to meet the demands of his Catholic faith, and to advance his own interests, Toussaint did so.[45] Only when the tide turned, diminishing Spanish prospects and unexpectedly thrusting the French republic into the role of liberator, did Toussaint move.

Perhaps Toussaint was simply an opportunist, placing him in good company among revolutionaries. I try to focus on what his participation in the colony's wide-ranging culture of royalism can tell students about the Haitian Revolution writ large. A dash of Alexis de Tocqueville often helps. In *The Old Régime and the French Revolution*, Tocqueville famously argued that although the revolutionaries spoke the language of radical change, they in fact accomplished the goals of the Bourbon kings, dismantling the corporate political order that had always blocked the French state from acting directly on its subjects. As Tocqueville's French Revolution emerged from the long history of state-building, Toussaint's Haitian Revolution bubbled up out of Saint-Domingue's long, multi-faceted relationship to monarchy in France and Africa. Whatever unity the rebels enjoyed was not a function of republicanism, racial solidarity, or even a shared commitment to emancipation—Jean-François and Biassou, for instance, owned and sold slaves long after 1791.[46] Instead, the uprising was held together by kings.

Conclusion:
Modern Lives

Whatever students might think about Haiti in the twenty-first century, Toussaint's Saint-Domingue was a profoundly modern place in many respects. No less than its planters, slaves there lived "modern lives," as C. L. R. James put it nearly eighty years ago.[47] Subjected to rationalized, profit-maximizing labor discipline, thousands upon thousands of transplanted Africans produced the staples that drove an increasingly global capitalist system. But in places like Haut-du-Cap, proximity to that system afforded some Africans different angles of vision, different social networks, and different economic opportunities. Too often assumed to lie at the heart of the 1791 uprising, racial consciousness was in reality forged in the crucible of revolution, as men as dissimilar as Georges Biassou, Toussaint Louverture, and Légér-Félicité Sonthonax scrambled to reorient themselves to a new and dangerous reality. Ironically, what turned out to be the most socially radical of all the revolutions—one that made rulers of ex-slaves and refugees of ex-planters—began with a defense of traditional monarchical principles.

These conversations can leave students in a bit of a muddle. Straight and well-lit, the traditional pathway from old regime to revolution to modernity remains in sight, but here they sit, mired in the particulars of intersecting African and French royalisms and the contradictory forces that shaped slave life in Haut-du-Cap. I've come to enjoy placing my students in this position and not out of mean-spiritedness. For one thing, their confusion gives them a glimpse into the mind-set of those actually caught in the snare of the revolution in Saint-Domingue—whether Frenchmen like Sonthonax, freedmen like Toussaint, or rebellious slaves like Jean-François and Georges Biassou, they all scrambled for footholds as the ground shook beneath their feet. Like these actors from the past, students have little choice but to press forward with "thoughtful and effortful processing" if they are to make any sense at all of these complex events.[48]

In the end, students' slog through the evidence often leads them to an appreciation not only of the multiple routes to modernity but of the process by which members of the revolutionary generation actually hacked those routes into the unknown. They did not simply abandon old instruments for new, nor did they cling to techniques tested in one environment but ill-suited for another. Rather, adjusting to changing conditions as best they could, they assembled their own particular toolkit out of the materials at hand locally—including, in the case of Saint-Domingue, notions of kingship and racial fluidity born, along with Toussaint Louverture, at the confluence of African and European worlds. From a teaching perspective, the larger point is that there is a real payoff for investing time and effort in microhistories in the classroom. In so doing, we help our students come to appreciate how quickly revolutionary expectations evolved and changed with the course of events, and they carry these insights into their understandings of the impact of political and geological quakes today.

Perhaps my persistence in presenting the overlapping worlds of Toussaint the slave, Toussaint the would-be coffee planter, Toussaint the hard-driving royalist, and Toussaint the republican convert may simply be reflections of my own hunger for the rich details of social and political life during this remarkable moment, in this remarkable place. Then again, the devil is in the details. In this case, the devil reveals the drudgery and terror that grew alongside freedom and rights at the dawn of the modern age, as well as the seemingly backward-looking political culture that inspired the most forward-looking of revolutions.

NOTES

1. An omission duly noted by David Armitage in his 2014 foreword to a new edition of Palmer's classic work, originally published in 1959 and 1964. See David Armitage, "Foreword," in R. R. Palmer, *The Age of the Democratic*

Revolution: A Political History of Europe and America, 1760–1800 (Princeton, NJ: Princeton University Press, 2014), xx.

2. See, for instance, the aggressive arguments for a Spinoza- and Eurocentric, fundamentally secular modernity in Jonathan Israel, *Radical Enlightenment: Philosophy and the Making of Modernity* (New York: Oxford University Press, 2001), and his subsequent works. For a bracing global history of modernity, see C. A. Bayly, *The Birth of the Modern World, 1780–1914* (Oxford: Blackwell, 2004); see also "AHR Roundtable: Historians and the Question of Modernity," *American Historical Review* 116, no. 3 (2011): 631–751; Elizabeth Mancke, "Modernity," in *The Princeton Companion to Atlantic History*, ed. Joseph C. Miller (Princeton, NJ: Princeton University Press, 2014), 340–44.

3. See Sibylle Fischer's bracing discussion in *Modernity Disavowed: Haiti and the Cultures of Slavery in the Age of Revolution* (Durham, NC: Duke University Press, 2004), 7–24, as well as her shorter "Unthinkable History? The Haitian Revolution, Historiography, and Modernity on the Periphery," in *A Companion to African-American Studies*, ed. Lewis R. Gordon and Jane Anna Gordon (New York: Blackwell, 2006), 360–76. For a broader discussion of a multifaceted, global transition to modernity, see Sanjay Subrahmanyam, "Connected Histories: Notes towards a Reconfiguration of Early Modern Eurasia," *Modern Asian Studies* 31, no. 3 (July 1997): 735–62.

4. Barack Obama, "Why Haiti Matters," *Newsweek*, January 14, 2010.

5. For two somewhat divergent takes on the postrevolutionary history of Haiti, see Laurent Dubois, *Haiti: The Aftershocks of History* (New York: Metropolitan Books, 2012); Philippe Girard, *Haiti: The Tumultuous History—From Pearl of the Caribbean to Broken Nation* (New York: Palgrave Macmillan, 2010).

6. T. H. Breen, *American Insurgents, American Patriots: The Revolution of the People* (New York: Hill and Wang, 2010), 25.

7. Carolyn Fick, *The Making of Haiti: The Saint Domingue Revolution from Below* (Knoxville: University of Tennessee Press, 1990), 250.

8. Janice A. Dole and Gale M. Sinatra, "Reconceptualizing Change in the Cognitive Construction of Knowledge," *Educational Psychologist* 33, no. 2/3 (1998): 110, 117. My thanks to Jeffrey Nokes for this reference.

9. I have used Laurent Dubois and John Garrigus's still outstanding "Introduction: Revolution, Emancipation, Independence," in *Slave Revolution in the Caribbean, 1789–1804: A Brief History with Documents*, ed. Dubois and Garrigus (New York: Bedford/St. Martin's, 2006), 7–45. I also highly recommend Jeremy Popkin, *A Concise History of the Haitian Revolution* (West Sussex, UK: Wiley Blackwell, 2012). As a supplement to these sorts of readings, I have also made use of a twelve-minute YouTube video, produced by the Khan Academy and hosted by John Green (author of *The Fault in Our Stars*), called "Haitian Revolutions: Crash Course History #30."

10. Cited in John Garrigus, *Before Haiti: Race and Citizenship in French*

Saint-Domingue (New York: Palgrave Macmillan, 2006), 29. Although there is no straightforward, one-volume history of prerevolutionary Saint-Domingue in English, Garrigus's excellent work on the political culture of race is indispensable for understanding the colony's eighteenth-century development. See also Philip Boucher, *France and the American Tropics to 1700: Tropics of Discontent?* (Baltimore, MD: Johns Hopkins University Press, 2008); James Pritchard, *In Search of Empire: The French in the Americas, 1670–1730* (New York: Cambridge University Press, 2004); on literary reflections on and cultural life in Saint-Domingue, see Doris Garraway, *The Libertine Colony: Creolization in the Early French Caribbean* (Durham, NC: Duke University Press, 2005); Madeline Dobie, *Trading Places: Colonization and Slavery in Eighteenth-Century French Culture* (Ithaca, NY: Cornell University Press, 2010); *Colonialism and Science: Saint-Domingue in the Old Regime* (Baltimore, MD: Johns Hopkins University Press, 1992); on the legal culture of prerevolutionary Saint-Domingue, see Malick Ghachem, *The Old Regime and the Haitian Revolution* (New York: Cambridge University Press, 2012).

11. Dubois, *Avengers of the New World*, 19; Frédéric Régent, *La France et ses esclaves: De la colonisation aux abolitions (1620–1848)* (Paris: Grasset, 2007), 336–37.

12. Grasset, *La France et ses esclaves*, 336–37.

13. On this crucial population, see especially Garrigus, *Before Haiti*, and Dominique Rogers, "On the Road to Citizenship: The Complex Route to Integration of the Free People of Color in the Two Capitals of Saint-Domingue," in *The Worlds of the Haitian Revolution*, ed. David Geggus and Norman Fiering (Bloomington: Indiana University Press, 2009), 65–78.

14. Herbert Klein, *The Atlantic Slave Trade* (New York: Cambridge University Press, 1999), 33.

15. Jean-Baptiste Labat, *Nouveau voyage aux Isles de l'Amérique* (La Haye, 1724), vol. II. On the impact of colonial trade on the French economy, see, for instance, James B. Collins, *The State in Early Modern France* (New York: Cambridge University Press, 2009), 242–43.

16. Jean Tarrade, *Le commerce colonial de la France a la fin de l'Ancien Régime: L'évolution du régime de "l'Exclusif" de 1763 a 1789* (Paris: Presses Universitaires de la France, 1972), 1:207, 2:701.

17. For a wide-ranging argument about modernity and the subaltern, see Patrick Wolfe, "Structure and Event: Settler Colonialism, Time, and the Question of Genocide," in *Empire, Colony, Genocide: Conquest, Occupation, and Subaltern Resistance in World History*, ed. A. Dirk Moses (New York: Berghahn, 2010), 110.

18. Jacques de Cauna, *Toussaint Louverture: Le grand precurseur* (Bordeaux: Editions du Sud Ouest, 2012), 58.

19. The latest word on Toussaint's prerevolutionary life comes via the meticulous research found in Philippe Girard and Jean-Louis Donnadieu,

"Toussaint before Louverture: New Archival Findings on the Early Life of Toussaint Louverture," *William and Mary Quarterly* 70, no. 1 (January 2013): 41–78.

20. On this point, see Madison Smartt Bell, *Toussaint Louverture: A Biography* (New York: Vintage, 2008), 67–69.

21. It is worth pointing out that on the basis of runaway slave reports in Saint-Domingue's official newspapers, only about 1 in 200 slaves ran away annually between 1770 and 1790. See Jason Daniels, "Marronage in Saint-Domingue: Approaching the Revolution, 1770–1791" (M.A. thesis, University of Florida, 2008), 52–53.

22. Karol Weaver, *Medical Revolutionaries: The Enslaved Healers of Eighteenth-Century Saint-Domingue* (Urbana: University of Illinois Press, 2006), 104.

23. On the African cultural underworld of Saint-Domingue, see Fick, *The Making of Haiti*, 41.

24. See Garrigus, *Before Haiti*, 201.

25. Ghachem, *The Old Regime and the Haitian Revolution*, 167–210, quote on 189.

26. See Garrigus, *Before Haiti*, 109–40, 195–226; on breeding, see William Max Nelson, "Making Men: Enlightenment Ideas of Racial Engineering," *American Historical Review* 115, no. 5 (December 2010): 1364–94.

27. See Garrigus, "Opportunist or Patriot? Julien Raimond (1744–1801) and the Haitian Revolution," *Slavery and Abolition* 28, no. 1 (April 2007): 5.

28. Bernard Foubert, "Le marronage sur les habitations Laborde a Saint-Domingue dans la seconde moitié du XVIIIe siècle," *Annales de Bretagne et des pays de l'Ouest* 95, no. 3 (1998): 300.

29. On bourgeoisie, see of course Sarah Maza, *The Myth of the French Bourgeoisie: An Essay on the Social Imaginary, 1750–1850* (Cambridge, MA: Harvard University Press, 2003).

30. Simon Schama, *Citizens: A Chronicle of the French Revolution* (New York: Vintage, 1989), 144.

31. *Fête bourgeoise et patriotique, donnée par les Citoyens du Cap-Français, Isle Saint-Domingue, à l'occasion de la naissance de Monseigneur le duc de Normandie* (Cap-Français, 1785), 1–7.

32. Sensibly, he did not destroy it. Instead, he hid it under the staircase, just in case counterrevolution came calling. See Elizabeth Colwill, "'Fêtes de l'hymen, fêtes de la liberté': Marriage, Manhood, and Emancipation in Revolutionary Saint-Domingue," in Geggus and Fiering, *The World of the Haitian Revolution*, 128, 148.

33. John Thornton, "'I Am the Subject of the King of Congo': African Political Ideology and the Haitian Revolution," *Journal of World History* 4, no. 2 (1993): 181–214; "Toussaint the Royalist," in David Geggus, ed. and trans., *The Haitian Revolution: A Documentary History* (Indianapolis: Hackett, 2015), 122–23;

"Insurgent Responses to Emancipation," in Dubois and Garrigus, *Slave Revolution in the Caribbean*, 125–28.

34. Cited in Smartt-Bell, *Toussaint Louverture*, 86.

35. See Jane Landers, *Atlantic Creoles in the Age of Revolution* (Cambridge, MA: Harvard University Press, 2003), 68–69.

36. See Thornton, "'I Am the Subject of the King of Congo,'" 181.

37. Smartt-Bell, *Toussaint Louverture*, 85.

38. Cited in Dubois, *Avengers of the New World*, 176, 179.

39. The best account of this episode is Jeremy Popkin, *You Are All Free: The Haitian Revolution and the Abolition of Slavery* (New York: Cambridge University Press, 2010).

40. See "The 'Volte-Face' of Toussaint Louverture," in David Geggus, *Haitian Revolutionary Studies* (Bloomington: Indiana University Press, 2002), 119–36.

41. See Brendan McConville, *The King's Three Faces: The Rise and Fall of Royal America, 1688–1776* (Chapel Hill: University of North Carolina Press, 2006); Eric Nelson, *The Royalist Revolution: Monarchy and the American Founding* (Cambridge, MA: Harvard University Press, 2014).

42. Cited in Gene Ogle, "The Trans-Atlantic King and Imperial Public Spheres: Everyday Politics in Pre-Revolutionary Saint-Domingue," in Geggus and Fiering, *The World of the Haitian Revolution*, 79.

43. See Ronald Schechter, *Obstinate Hebrews: Representations of Jews in France, 1715–1815* (Berkeley: University of California Press, 2003), 141–43.

44. Moreau de Saint-Méry, cited in Ogle, "The Trans-Atlantic King," 90.

45. Geggus, "The 'Volte-Face' of Toussaint Louverture," 127.

46. Ibid., 125.

47. See C. L. R. James, *The Black Jacobins* (New York: Dial Press, 1938), 392.

48. Dole and Sinatra, "Reconceptualizing Change," 117.

KEY RESOURCES

Primary Sources and Websites

Dubois, Laurent, and John Garrigus, eds. *Slave Revolution in the Caribbean, 1789–1804: A Brief History with Documents*. New York: Bedford/St. Martin's, 2006.

Geggus, David, ed. and trans. *The Haitian Revolution: A Documentary History*. Indianapolis: Hackett, 2014.

The Louverture Project, http://www.thelouvertureproject.org.

Marronnage in Saint-Domingue (Haïti): History, Memory, Technology, http://www.marronnage.info/en/.

Secondary Sources

Dubois, Laurent. *Avengers of the New World: The Story of the Haitian Revolution*. Cambridge, MA: Harvard University Press, 2004.

Garrigus, John. *Before Haiti: Race and Citizenship in French Saint-Domingue*. New York: Palgrave Macmillan, 2006.

Geggus, David. "The 'Volte-Face' of Toussaint Louverture." In *Haitian Revolutionary Studies*, by David Geggus, 119–36. Bloomington: Indiana University Press, 2002.

Geggus, David, and Norman Fiering, eds. *The Worlds of the Haitian Revolution*. Bloomington: Indiana University Press, 2009.

Girard, Philippe, and Jean-Louis Donnadieu. "Toussaint before Louverture: New Archival Findings on the Early Life of Toussaint Louverture." *William and Mary Quarterly* 70, no. 1 (January 2013): 41–78.

Popkin, Jeremy. *A Concise History of the Haitian Revolution*. West Sussex, UK: Wiley Blackwell, 2012.

———. *You Are All Free: The Haitian Revolution and the Abolition of Slavery*. New York: Cambridge University Press, 2010.

Smartt Bell, Madison. *Toussaint Louverture: A Biography*. New York: Vintage, 2008.

Taber, Robert. "Navigating Haiti's History: Saint-Domingue and the Haitian Revolution." *History Compass* 13, no. 5 (2015): 235–50.

An Age in Microcosm

The United States of Belgium

JANE JUDGE

Belgium is often a neglected country, certainly in most Anglo-American classrooms. Not until the world wars does the little state tucked between the Netherlands and France usually get a mention. Those who follow the World Cup or are connoisseurs of beer, mussels, chocolate, lace, or fries (chips) may know a bit more, but in general many pay little attention to the history of the home of NATO, the European Union governing bodies, and Stella Artois. Yet Belgium has a rich past, particularly during the Age of Revolutions. At the end of the eighteenth century, the people who lived in what is today Belgium engaged in their own revolution. It was not a product of the French upheavals just to the south, nor was it a copycat of the American Revolution. This chapter illustrates a way of putting the bigger revolutions of the eighteenth century into more focused perspective by drawing on a national history that most students (and many teachers) will likely have never encountered, one that hopefully inspires them to think more about connections and comparisons. In the classroom, therefore, Belgium offers opportunities for the study of a different model of revolution, in that it had strong traditionalist currents, as well as variants on themes which are more familiar, such as internal conflict and international intervention. Moreover, by dint of being a *Belgian* Revolution, it allows students to immerse themselves in a part of Europe that is often overlooked in even more specialized courses, asking them to engage with people and places that will give nuance and texture to their understanding of both this period and the Atlantic world.

One thing that inspired the revolutionaries of the Belgian Revolution was the palpable sense at the end of the eighteenth century that this was a revolutionary age. Throughout the upheaval of the end of the 1780s, the Belgians certainly knew they were participating in a broader movement. As the introduction to this volume suggests, people of the late eighteenth and early nineteenth centuries were aware that they were "living through a remarkable political, cultural, and indeed social transformation." Though the Belgians may not have been aiming to transform their society or culture, and some of them were fighting against political innovation, as we will see, they certainly knew they were living through a remarkable age. One lawyer for the provincial council in Brussels opened an address to the general Assembly of Estates on May 23, 1787, by asking his colleagues:

> Will sad experience force us to repeat every day that the eighteenth century is the century of revolutions? Never have enlightened people better felt the dignity of man & the price of civil liberty; never have Princes better known that despotism offends the peoples, that their happiness depends absolutely on that of their subjects; & yet we see almost everywhere a continuous struggle between the throne built by force, & liberty sustained by the voice of nature & the authority of the laws?[1]

The men who participated in the Belgian Revolution knew well that they were part of a much larger story. As such, it is entirely appropriate to use their revolution to investigate some of that story's motifs. Belgium provides an opportunity for teachers to ask their students where this revolution stood in relationship to the other, more well-known revolutions of this epoch.

The Age of Revolutions, as this volume illustrates well, encompasses varying themes that teachers can explore and highlight for their students. As a microcosm of the era, the Belgian revolution is at once a foil and a parallel for the momentous American and French revolutions. Its key players and moments offer examples of many central concepts: sovereignty, governance, and representation, and how these work within a society navigating the new Enlightenment emphasis on individual and natural rights; anticlericalism and the relationship between Church and State; international contexts beyond the revolutionaries' control; the difficulties in creating a uniform movement and combatting factions as well as counterrevolution; and national identity formation and how a people come to define themselves. Each of these shows up in the Belgian story. Sometimes, the events in the Belgian revolution serve to vindicate the fears of other revolutionaries, putting back into perspective the precarious nature of eighteenth-century politics and the risks involved in revolting against one's monarch. To examine these issues and think about how to implement them in a classroom, first we need to have a basic knowledge of the events of the revolution. Then I will examine a bit more closely the process of linking the story to some of the broader themes I have just mentioned.

The Belgian Revolution

At the end of the eighteenth century, the modern state of Belgium was home to ten independent provinces that belonged to the Austrian Habsburg Empire and a separate Prince-Bishopric of Liège. That bishopric will not concern us in this chapter, and so I leave it and its politics to one side. Collectively, the provinces were referred to as the Southern Low Countries, the Southern Netherlands, or the Austrian Netherlands, and increasingly the Belgian provinces. The provinces, among them Brabant, with Brussels as its capital, and Flanders (not to be confused with the general Dutch-speaking part of Belgium that is today called Flanders) belonged to the Austrians by way of the treaties that had ended the War of Spanish Succession (1701–1714). Before that, the Southern Low Countries had been Spanish, held by the branch of Habsburgs who were monarchs of Spain and, importantly, New Spain in the Americas. With the signing of the Treaties of Utrecht (1713) and Rastatt (1714), the major European powers agreed to transfer the Spanish Low Countries to the cadet Habsburg branch in Vienna, consolidating a balance of power by making Spain less powerful on the European continent and keeping the narrow strip of land out of the hands of the French. That the French should never own modern-day Belgium was important to the British (who would not want to see their old foe control the wealth of the highly urbanized Belgian territories and who also had strategic reasons for wanting the small strip of land directly across from Britain out of the hands of any great power) and the Dutch (who liked the buffer zone created by an imperial power owning land between them and Paris).

When the provinces were transferred to their rule, the Austrians largely left them alone. The treaties the new monarchs had signed stipulated that the provinces be considered a unit, inseparable, and that their old "constitutions" be respected. Though not like modern constitutions created by a special convention elected for that purpose, the constitutions the Southern Netherlandish provinces possessed were contracts between sovereign and subjects. For most of the provinces, they were a group of treaties and agreements cobbled together over the years under various sovereigns. These were not unlike the various charters that described the relationship many of the American colonies had to the Crown and dictated how they were governed. In the Southern Netherlands, the most important political province, Brabant, home to Brussels, had negotiated a more codified constitution, called the Joyeuse Entrée in French and the Blijde Inkomst in Dutch.

The provincial contracts regulated everything from how inhabitants were put on trial—many had stipulations that natives of the province had to be tried there by their peers—to the practicalities of governing. Within each province, there were various administrative bodies, among them a legal council and an Assembly of Estates, which represented the three "orders" of nobility, clergy, and the rest. "The rest" of society usually referred to representatives of several privileged towns or guilds. Importantly, though they had the same name and roughly the same makeup as the French Estates, in the Belgian provinces the First and Second were not more powerful than the Third when it came to voting in the assembly. Moreover, the Estates held real power as they voted the emperor his taxes, sending significant sums of money to Vienna twice a year. For all the provinces, the sovereign swore to uphold these various constitutions on his or her coronation day, as he or she was crowned separate ruler for each territory. Thus, when he came to power in 1780, Austrian Emperor Joseph II was crowned duke of Brabant and count of Flanders. By highlighting these facts and contrasting them to the French Estates, teachers can help their students see just how complex and diverse the ancien régime could be. It was different from place to place depending on regional history. For teachers of both US and European history, these Belgian examples can also help students flesh out the nature of the various charters that defined colonial governments and held vast empires together.

Joseph II is often touted as an example of an "enlightened monarch," and he did have a robust reform agenda based on what he saw as the major tenets of Enlightenment philosophies. Above all, he believed in the primacy of the state, which needed strong leadership and an efficient bureaucracy unfettered by pomp and circumstance or arcane practices. After he was crowned emperor, Joseph began enacting reforms throughout his empire to streamline government. He reformed tax laws, reorganized local governments, and took measures to bring the Church under secular control. Many of these measures were meant to better the lives of the emerging bourgeois middle class and to consolidate the empire's fiscal, military, and bureaucratic system to compete in a changing Europe. At first, Joseph concentrated on the monarchy's central holdings (mostly in modern-day Austria, the Czech Republic, and Slovakia), but by the mid-1780s he turned his eyes to his Low Country holdings. In 1783 Joseph ordered a general seminary created at the University of Leuven, founded in 1425, to replace the various diocesan seminaries at which bishops oversaw the education of priests. Alongside other ecclesiastical reforms, Joseph suppressed numerous convents and monasteries that housed contemplative orders because he felt these did not fit into his efficient state where everyone served a productive purpose. Although there was protest from priests, monks, abbots, and bishops, in general Joseph's ecclesiastical reforms were simply ignored, and there was little protest from the provincial political apparatus. Then, on January 1, 1787, Joseph announced a complete reorganization of the provincial administrations. He wanted the ten provinces abolished in favor of nine imperial circles headed by officials chosen in Vienna. With this move, he offended the group of people in the provinces best equipped to fight back; the Estates and provincial councils had many lawyers on their payrolls, and indeed counted many among their members, who now protested the emperor's moves on legal grounds. At this juncture, Belgium provides an interesting, manageable example for teachers of a wider pattern: how attempts at reform strike against interests and provoke resistance, which is at first legal and usually nonviolent.

For the next two years, the provincial Estates and Councils, as well as some corporate bodies, like the Brussels guilds, sent official grievances to the imperial governors in the provinces, as well as Chancellor Kaunitz and Emperor Joseph in Vienna. Conservative protestors did not want independence but a return to the status quo in which they would retain their age-old privileges. Joseph and the provincial Estates went back and forth, with his representatives in the provinces offering concessions only to have the emperor dismiss them and insist his reforms be implemented. The Estates used the leverage they had in voting the annual taxes against the emperor and refused to send the money several times between 1787 and 1789. This led to increasingly harsh measures on Joseph's part, and eventually blood was shed as imperial troops fired on rowdy crowds in the capital. Leaders of the resistance, rallying around a lawyer for the Estates named Henri Van der Noot, fled into exile in 1788. In June 1789, the emperor frustratedly declared that he was no longer beholden to the provincial constitutions and he sent word to the Estates that their contracts were henceforth annulled.

This sparked protest among an entirely new group of Belgians: bourgeois lawyers and professionals who agreed with some of Joseph's reforms, as they allowed them access to previously privileged positions, but could not agree with his heavy-handed tactics. Over the summer of 1789, a group of men organized around Brussels lawyers Jan Frans Vonck and Jan Baptiste Verlooy formed a secret society known as Pro Aris et Focis, usually translated "For Hearth and Home." For teachers who have time to dive into a bit more intellectual history, or who want to tie themes back to classical history, this society and its use of Roman imagery with Latin language can offer a nice comparison point with invocations of ancient Rome in the French and American revolutions; for example, pamphlets of the American Revolution, like the Cato letters, that used classical imagery to legitimate their cause. Together, the members of Pro Aris et Focis stockpiled weapons and fomented revolt among the rural and urban populations across the provinces, believing that a grassroots army could defeat imperial troops and achieve independence. Not nearly as radical as French Jacobins but more democratic than the conservatives led by Henri Van der Noot who were now in exile, leaders of Pro Aris et Focis envisioned Belgium as a new yet still conservative republic, with only minor changes to the old constitutions to broaden the franchise (to only a larger percentage of propertied white men) and do away with some of the most arcane privileges left over from the medieval era. The two tendencies—the one conservative, the other more radical—allow teachers to ask their students to reflect on the very nature of the term *revolution*: need a movement be "progressive" to be defined as "revolutionary"? In what ways does internal conflict within a revolution reflect social or cultural differences?

By September 1789, the patriots, as they called themselves, had gathered a sizable force of farmers, peasants, artisans, and others outside the Dutch town of Breda, just over the border from the Austrian provinces. It was there that the conservatives had congregated as Van der

Noot attempted to find a new sovereign for the provinces (he preferred a relative of the Dutch Stadhouder). He met with little success as the British, Dutch, and Prussians were all hesitant to become embroiled in an intra-imperial conflict. Though Van der Noot, Vonck, and their colleagues did not see eye to eye, they recognized the importance of strength in unity and combined their efforts to rid the provinces of imperial forces. The more democratic revolutionaries eventually convinced the conservatives that independence was a realistic aim, and Van der Noot stopped trying to find the provinces a new sovereign. On October 24, 1789, chosen because it was the feast day of Archangel Raphael, the Belgian patriot army marched into the provinces. With the help of the population primed by Pro Aris et Focis's efforts, they defeated imperial troops and in November successfully took the Flemish capital Ghent. A triumphant parade led by Van der Noot and other conservatives marched through Brussels on December 18, and some hailed the victorious leader as the "Belgian Washington."[2]

At this point in the story, teachers can use the Belgian Revolution to highlight a very important element of revolutionary history: the messy slide into revolution. At the beginning of these revolutionary stories, whether they are American, French, or Belgian, protestors were not dreaming of independence, of completely overthrowing their governments and starting anew. Yet this is what happened. Hindsight allows us to perceive domino-style effects across many of these events, but it is important to stress to students that the players in these stories did not know their outcomes. Henri Van der Noot did not know that his legal protests against measures to reform the provinces would become an armed revolt; the delegates to the Estates General at Versailles in 1789 did not think of dethroning and beheading Louis XVI; the Regulators who protested tax measures in North Carolina in the 1760s did not think they were contributing to a movement that would eventually see them leave the British Empire, to take three examples. Importantly, none of these people would even have wanted the outcomes they contributed to when they began their protests. Each of these three revolutions (and many of the others discussed in this volume) began with protests against innovation, usually by elites hoping to maintain whatever power they possessed. Other factors pushed protestors to become rebels and then revolutionaries—the intransigence of governments, mob mentality, the rise of other groups with more radical agendas. Teachers can go in any of several directions with this, whether it be direct comparisons to the French and/or American revolutions or broader discussions of historical events and their progression.

In the Belgian revolutionary story, the conservatives wasted no time creating a government after they seized political power at the end of 1789. By January 7, members of the Estates General were being sworn in as members of the new Congress, a hastily constructed government for the new United States of Belgium. Echoing the Americans in more than name, the Belgian revolutionaries mimicked and in some places directly copied the US Articles of Confederation when they wrote their constitution behind closed doors in Brussels in the early days of January 1790.[3] The democratic revolutionaries were shut out of this new government because the conservatives wanted no political innovations whatsoever. Their goal was a simple return to the status quo before Joseph's reforms. A vigorous debate ensued in the public sphere, and pamphlet writers offered all kinds of opinions on the best path for the new independent United States of Belgium. In the end, fighting between democrats and the conservatives in power (which resulted in most of the democrats fleeing into exile) weakened the Congress and the army. On the international stage, the situation turned against the Belgians. In 1790, after the provincial Estates declared independence and members of the Estates General drafted a constitution for the United States of Belgium, Britain and the United Provinces (Netherlands) began to express more and more concern at the situation. Along with Prussia, with whom the maritime powers had formed the Triple Alliance, they worked diplomatic channels to ensure the Belgian provinces remained stable and, if possible, were returned to imperial rule. Especially with the French situation ratcheting up—the members of the Third Estate had declared themselves the National Assembly and Parisians stormed the Bastille in July 1789—they wanted the narrow band of highly urbanized Belgian provinces to remain under control and out of French hands and influence. Joseph succumbed to ill health on February 20, 1790, leaving open the possibility for negotiation with his heir, his brother Leopold. Crowned Leopold II, the new emperor had a reputation for upholding local constitutions and compromising. At an international conference held in Reichenbach in July 1790, representatives for the Triple Alliance powers met with those for the Austrian Empire. There, Leopold agreed to end to his brother's war with Turkey and defuse what was becoming a tense situation between the Austrian Empire and Prussia. He also negotiated to regain the Belgian territories, which the

Triple Alliance would support as long as the emperor guaranteed to uphold their constitutions and avoid further unrest. Agents for Britain and the United Provinces informed the Belgians of the decision after the fact, telling them that the provinces would be restored to Austrian rule with a return to the status quo.

In Brussels, the Congress was not happy with this. At every turn, it rebuffed diplomatic entreaties and insisted the United States of Belgium would remain an independent country. Congress and the Estates General refused any compromise. In the end, inaction led to their downfall. After Reichenbach, Leopold issued a declaration asking the Belgians to return willingly and peacefully to his empire by November 23; in return, all participants in the revolution would be granted amnesty. The date came and went before Congress made any definitive replies to diplomatic agents at The Hague, and on December 3, 1790, Austrians again controlled Brussels. By mid-December 1790, the United States of Belgium was no more and the Austrians once more presided over the Southern Netherlands.

Sovereignty, Governance, and Representation

When he swore to uphold the Southern Netherlands' constitutions, Joseph II was pledging to uphold the principles therein, most of them centered on medieval and Renaissance notions of privilege. Enlightenment ideas had taken hold in the provinces as they had elsewhere in the European world, and there was general political consensus that contractual government meant that either side—ruler or subjects— could terminate the relationship if the stipulations were not upheld. The termination of a contractual sovereign relationship did not equate to complete independence of the kind Britain's North American mainland colonies fought for in the American Revolution. It was closer to the idea that a community could willfully transfer itself to a new sovereign, if there was ample evidence its own was abusive or inadequate. The Dutch had justified their revolt in these terms when they wrote the Act of Abjuration (the Plakkaat van Verlatinghe) in 1581, officially severing their ties to Philip II of Spain and installing the duke of Anjou as their new sovereign. When Henri Van der Noot and the conservative Belgian revolutionaries sought to find a new sovereign once they were exiled in 1788, they were tapping into this older sense of governmental change. The contract that bound the sovereign to his subjects was predicated on older notions of privilege bound up in medieval relationships wherein a corporate body—like a guild or representative estates—pooled their capital to gain favor from their ruler. The course of the Belgian Revolution illustrates well the clash between the older concepts that informed the sixteenth-century Dutch revolt and the newer Enlightenment philosophies of individuality and changing perceptions of representation embodied in the American Revolution. Teachers who focus on such Enlightenment philosophies could ask students to identify (or point out the lack of) some of these principles in the declarations of independence, both American and Belgian, which are discussed later in this section and included in the appendix to this chapter.

Ultimately, the biggest catalyst for the change between the Dutch Act of Abjuration and the Belgian assertion of independence within Europe as a new state was the American Revolution. Things had changed in the course of the eighteenth century, and the American Revolution's example had put newer ideas of governance and sovereignty into practice, which then filtered back to Europe and were used by other revolutionaries. The American rebels and revolutionaries saw the reforms implemented by Parliament and George III as unfair because their notions of representation had changed—they no longer accepted the idea that members of Parliament theoretically represented the entire British nation. We all know the American Declaration of Independence was important. It is one of the major cornerstones of teaching the founding of the modern United States. The Belgian Revolution highlights this importance, but in a way that may be new to students. We usually think of the second paragraph of Thomas Jefferson's declaration as its most important part. That is where we find the assertion of "certain inalienable rights," using John Locke's ideas about natural rights. However, the Belgian Revolution helps put the Declaration of Independence back into its own context. The individual rights portion of the declaration has become its most prominent feature, but when it was written emphasis fell harder on the political and diplomatic element. In 1776, it was primarily "an assertion of statehood," as historian David Armitage points out in his global study of the document.[4] His book is indispensable for anyone who wants more information on the global influence on the original document and the declaration's subsequent effect on the world.

For the Belgians, the American Declaration of Independence offered a successful example for how to claim a place on the world stage.

Between October 24, 1789, when Van der Noot penned the revolutionary Manifeste du Peuple Brabançon as the manifesto for patriot troops marching toward imperial soldiers, and July 1790, each of the Belgian provinces' Estates issued *manifestes* that publically justified their break with Joseph II. Just like the American Declaration of Independence, each provincial government enumerated a long list of grievances against the sovereign and then unequivocally announced their independence. The American declaration asserted that the United States would be a sovereign nation, deserving of the same respect as any other power. Though it did not make the colonies independent—military victory would have to force the British government to concede—the declaration did ensure that once independence was a reality, there would be no ambiguity about the United States's status. Even without using the entire document, which is a somewhat rambling thirty pages long, giving students the Flemish document's language alongside the American declaration should show them the extent to which the American Revolution was a model for others. What we must always stress in considering these questions of inspiration, though, is what these revolutions do not definitively show: cause and effect. It would be easy to say that the Americans, who created a domino effect that the French eventually radically changed, started the Age of Revolutions. But history is rarely that simple. Examples and "inspiration" (to borrow Marsh and Rapport's term) are much more appropriate ways to frame the relationships between these revolutions. The Declaration of Independence and the Belgian manifestos show just that—there was direct imitation without causation between revolutions and revolutionaries. Using the two documents side by side should also help students feel more comfortable with the unfamiliar Belgian texts, as they can go back to the well-known American declaration when necessary. What is more, looking at the American declaration through a Belgian lens, while showing the inspirational relationship among revolutionaries, may also help students see the famous document with fresh eyes.

The pensionary for Flanders' Estates, Jean Ferdinand Rohaert, directly copied the language (and even punctuation) of Thomas Jefferson's document. He began: "Since it has pleased the Divine Providence, through a combination of circumstances in all respects extraordinary, to return us to our natural Rights of Liberty & Independence, breaking the ties that bound us to a Prince of a House whose domination was always fatal to the interests of Flanders; we owe our contemporaries &

our descendants a faithful account of the causes & events that led to & achieved this happy revolution."[5] He closed: "In consequence, inherent to our preceding resolutions & declarations, & calling on the supreme Judge of the universe, who knows the justice of our cause, we publish & declare solemnly, in the name of the People, that this Province IS & has the right TO BE a *free* & *independent state*; that it is released from all obedience to the Emperor Joseph II, Count of Flanders, & the House of Austria."[6]

Though not completely word for word, the substance of these two quotes is almost exactly that of the American declaration's first and last paragraphs. Significantly, none of the Belgian declarations included any reference to individual rights, showing us that what was really important for them was the blueprint for becoming a new state. This also reinforces the newness of Enlightenment emphasis on individual liberty and happiness. The Belgian documents were still more focused on collective well-being and so the absence of any mention of individual rights can show students that the Lockean ideas Jefferson referenced were not as universal as they are today—a single switch did not flip to change societies overnight. Even though the Belgians had read the American declaration and used it as an example for their own purposes, this did not mean they agreed with every principle in it or had the same goals as the American revolutionaries.

Indeed, focusing on the elements of the American and French revolutions the Belgians did not imitate further illustrates how revolutions were models for each other when convenient and when society was ready for change, not as a series of progressions that improved with each scenario. The Belgian declarations of independence did not include Jefferson's language about individual natural rights, yet one of the more famous documents to come out of the French upheaval was the Declaration of the Rights of Man and the Citizen, proclaimed by the National Assembly in August 1789. Although the Belgian revolutionaries were well aware of developments in France, and the democratic faction proved sympathetic to some of them, they never issued any such declarations, nor did they implement any political innovations that might have hinted at support for such ideas. The conservative members of the United States of Belgium's Congress never entertained ideas of expanding the franchise or opening up some of the privileges of bygone centuries to the growing bourgeoisie. While there was one pamphlet published calling for the liberation of Belgian women and opportunities for women to participate in the political sphere, no moves were made by anyone in government to emancipate the "softer sex." Those in power attacked the democratic revolutionaries who did suggest opening the guilds, expanding the franchise, or changing the government administration to more strongly reflect Enlightenment notions, often forcing them to flee to France for their own safety. The Belgian revolution sharply illustrates the difficulties that could arise from the changing ideas of governance, representation, and how society functions at the end of the eighteenth century.

Reform, Church, and the State

Joseph II began his program of reforms in the Belgian provinces with measures against abuses and inefficiency of the Church. He closed convents and monasteries that housed contemplative orders and tried to streamline the seminary system by creating a general seminary at the University of Leuven. The seminary project, which would have also greatly diminished the power of the Belgian bishops, was never fully realized because of the disruption of the revolution, but Joseph's attempt became a rallying cry during the years of political protest. His administrative reforms were also meant to open bureaucracy to men with merit rather than privilege and simplify the government to reduce red tape and improve the economy. The Estates of Brabant, the province in which Leuven was located, specifically accused Joseph of interfering in Belgian institutions. Moreover the revolutionaries were able to mobilize the populace by invoking their anger that the emperor had made members of the clergy suffer. Indeed, parish priests and bishops were effective at garnering broader public support. All of the political grievances sent to Vienna made a point to defend the Church and demand that Joseph's ecclesiastical and administrative reforms be halted and reversed. The fierce Catholicism of the Belgians can serve two broad purposes when teaching the Age of Revolutions.

First, and perhaps most obviously, Belgian love for their clergy contradicts the extreme anticlericalism that often characterizes parts of the French Revolution. When emphasizing the very real backlash against the excesses of the French Church, it can help to put them into context by highlighting how the opposite was true in the Belgian provinces. Belgian priests tended to be local young men, known to their parishioners since their youth. Many of the religious orders (though some were quite disproportionately wealthy) genuinely served very real needs of the community. Pointing out these differences between the Belgian and French ecclesiastical situations can help especially when explaining the counterrevolution and the peasant backlash in the Vendée between 1793 and 1796 and other pockets of loyalism to the French monarchy. Not everyone in Western Europe felt wronged by the Church at the end of the eighteenth century. It can also show just how bad the situation was in France. If neighboring countries did not suffer abuses by their bishops and clergy, all the more reason to see the radicalism of the French Revolution as perhaps more understandable. Moreover, for the Belgians, a strong love of their religion—not anticlericalism or a fear of Catholic hierarchy—fed the fervor of the revolution. For the French, religion became a wedge as clergy were divided as "juring" or "non-juring," judged by whether they had sworn an oath to uphold the Civil Constitution (later those who had sworn the oath were marginalized as Napoleon reinstated Catholicism as the state religion).

Second, with regard to the American Revolution, Joseph II's measures serve as a way to recharacterize our understanding of the reforms monarchs began implementing in the second half of the eighteenth century. The Belgians did not want their Church interfered with by their sovereign, but his reforms were not outrageous. Similarly, the colonists in Britain's North American colonies saw Parliament's new taxes as unfair because they bypassed the colonial assemblies, but the tax rates were not disproportionate or wholly unjustifiable. We can ask ourselves and our students to think about whether resisting innovation and reform can be seen as "bad behavior" on the part of the soon-to-be revolutionaries. The reforms implemented from London and Vienna were meant to strengthen the state overall and make the British and Austrian empires, respectively, able to successfully weather future conflicts without going bankrupt.

"Successful" Revolution

What makes a revolution "successful"? Does it need to end in the creation of a new state or the writing of a new constitution? Do revolutionaries need to leave a lasting model for others, like the American Declaration of Independence or the French Declaration of the Rights of Man? At what point do "rebels" become "revolutionaries"? All good questions, and ones we can ask students to consider. Historians, too, struggle to find definitive answers. Ultimately, the question is one of chronology. We can take wider views and can see long-term success or failure of a revolution most clearly in its later impact. We can concentrate on specific events and proclaim certain episodes within a wider revolution successful or futile. Or we can even take a specific theme and determine a revolution's relationship to it. Was the American Revolution a success for women or Native Americans, for example? Was the French Revolution unsuccessful in changing the lives of peasants in all areas of France? Did the Belgians engage in a successful revolution overall or is their contribution to the Age of Revolutions just a failed footnote?

Where we choose to end our study of a revolution can dramatically change its measure of success. The Belgian Revolution can be seen as a success or a failure, and perhaps more easily since students do not have any preconceived notions of it. It is incredibly difficult to think of the American Revolution as anything but successful knowing what we know in hindsight, just as it is difficult to stress the weakness of the inchoate United States. Just as with state strength in a complex international community in the eighteenth century, using the Belgian revolution can effectively help students consider the possibilities.

It may not surprise students, or anyone reading the story, that the United States of Belgium were too weak to withstand international pressures. We are accustomed to thinking of Belgium as a small country at the mercy of the actions of its more powerful neighbors. But what the episode here illustrates is just how difficult the international situation was to navigate in the eighteenth century. At the heart of it, the Belgians could have done everything "right" and still have been thwarted by the international situation. Had Thomas Jefferson been born in Brussels and James Madison been from Ghent, all their intelligence and eloquence would not have been able to undo the fact that the British, Dutch, and Prussians wanted to keep the provinces from radicalizing like the French. The Marquis de Lafayette could have led the patriot army, but that would not have made it stronger against Leopold II's army or negated the vast difference in manpower. Moreover, being diplomatically isolated made it impossible to overcome these problems. The American Revolution was allowed to flourish the way it did in part because of geography. France and the United Provinces openly supported the American Revolution only after it was obvious the colonists could militarily prevail. Though the Belgian patriot army routed imperial troops, the United Provinces refused to openly interfere in imperial business because Austrian troops could easily be redirected to invade the Netherlands. Using the Belgian Revolution to point these things out can bring home for students how anomalous (or how lucky!) the American revolutionaries were and how precarious international relations could be.

Most would call the rebellion against the Habsburg Empire a failure: it did not result in a lasting independent state, and it did not produce any great example for history. Yet if we change perspective a little, the short-lived United States of Belgium could be counted as a success—no one ever thought the patriot army would be able to win a single fight against imperial troops, let alone chase them from the majority of the provinces long enough to set up a new state. More convincing is a *longue durée* lens: the 1830 revolution that produced the modern-day state of Belgium owed much to the eighteenth-century rebellion. The revolutionaries around Henri Van der Noot and Jan Frans Vonck first fostered a sense of Belgian-ness within the population, gave the leaders in 1830 examples of what to do and what not to do, and provided a usable, recent past nineteenth-century nationalists could tap to galvanize the population. So the Belgian Revolution of 1787–1790 can be seen as a middle ground between the "stable" success of the American Revolution and the more tumultuous outcome of the French. Using the United States of Belgium and the Belgian revolution more generally offers a teacher a useful springboard in the classroom from which to interrogate some of the key themes of the Age of Revolutions. Certainly it helps question how we think about revolutionary success and failure.

Appendix:
The Declaration of Independence and
The Manifeste of the Province of Flanders

Note the different ways "rights" and "privileges" are discussed in the two documents. Students can be encouraged to find parallels themselves or guided to see that the Belgians tie the "natural rights of man" to official government privileges and charters, rather than individual pursuit of happiness that the Americans raise. Both preambles invoke history—the history of human events and the specific history of their countries—as justification for the independence the documents are declaring. The documents are written to an international audience and state they want (and need) to justify their cause and their call for independence to the rest of the world. What does this tell us about international relations and the legality of revolution? These men were concerned about appearing to act within the respected norms of how subjects can interact with their governments and sovereigns.

The American Declaration of Independence begins:

When in the Course of human events, it becomes necessary for one people to dissolve the political bands which have connected them with another, and to assume among the powers of the earth, the separate and equal station to which the Laws of Nature and of Nature's God entitle them, a decent respect to the opinions of mankind requires that they should declare the causes which impel them to the separation.[7]

We hold these truths to be self-evident, that all men are created equal, that they are endowed by their Creator with certain unalienable Rights, that among these are Life, Liberty and the pursuit of Happiness.— That to secure these rights, Governments are instituted among Men, deriving their just powers from the consent of the governed,—That whenever any Form of Government becomes destructive of these ends, it is the Right of the People to alter or to abolish it, and to institute new Government, laying its foundation on such principles and organizing its powers in such form, as to them shall seem most likely to effect their Safety and Happiness. Prudence, indeed, will dictate that Governments long established should not be changed for light and transient causes; and accordingly all experience hath shewn, that mankind are more disposed to suffer, while evils are sufferable, than to right themselves by abolishing the forms to which they are accustomed. But when a long train of abuses and usurpations, pursuing invariably the same Object evinces a design to reduce them under absolute Despotism, it is their right, it is their duty, to throw off such Government, and to provide new Guards for their future security.—Such has been the patient sufferance of these Colonies; and such is now the necessity which constrains them to alter their former Systems of Government. The history of the present King of Great Britain is a history of repeated injuries and usurpations, all having in direct object the establishment of an absolute Tyranny over these States. To prove this, let Facts be submitted to a candid world.

At this point, the declaration lists King George III's various transgressions, almost in a bullet point format. Once the list is finished, it continues:

In every stage of these Oppressions We have Petitioned for Redress in the most humble terms: Our repeated Petitions have been answered only by repeated injury. A Prince whose character is thus marked by every act which may define a Tyrant, is unfit to be the ruler of a free people.

Nor have We been wanting in attentions to our Brittish brethren. We have warned them from time to time of attempts by their legislature to extend an unwarrantable jurisdiction over us. We have reminded them of the circumstances of our emigration and settlement here. We have appealed to their native justice and magnanimity, and we have conjured them by the ties of our common kindred to disavow these usurpations, which, would inevitably interrupt our connections and correspondence. They too have been deaf to the voice of justice and of consanguinity. We must, therefore, acquiesce in the necessity, which denounces our Separation, and hold them, as we hold the rest of mankind, Enemies in War, in Peace Friends.

We, therefore, the Representatives of the united States of America, in General Congress, Assembled, appealing to the Supreme Judge of the world for the rectitude of our intentions, do, in the Name, and by Authority of the good People of these Colonies, solemnly publish and declare, That these United Colonies ARE, and of Right ought TO BE *Free and Independent States*; that they are Absolved from all Allegiance to the British Crown, and that all political connection between them and the State of Great Britain, is and ought to be totally dissolved; and that as Free and Independent States, they have full Power to levy War, conclude Peace, contract Alliances, establish Commerce, and to do all other Acts and Things which Independent States may of right do. And for the support of this Declaration, with a firm reliance on the protection of divine Providence, we mutually pledge to each other our Lives, our Fortunes and our sacred Honor.

The Flemish Manifeste begins:

Since it has pleased the Divine Providence, through a combination of circumstances in all respects extraordinary, to return us to our natural Rights of Liberty & Independence, breaking the ties that bound us to a Prince of a House whose domination was always fatal to the interests of Flanders; we owe our contemporaries & our descendants a faithful account of the causes & events that led to & achieved this happy revolution.[8]

Flanders, by advantage of her position & by the products of her soil combined with an industry born of her inhabitants, has enjoyed a prosperity uninterrupted, so long as she has the happiness to counts among her inhabitants the Sovereign Princes of the Country. The old Counts of Flanders & subsequently the Princes of the House of Bourgogne born, educated, placed in the midst of their subjects, imbued with the same principles & motivated by the same national spirit, they respected their Rights, their Privileges, their Charters, if one can call the hopes of the People, who, fundamentally, are but the natural Rights of man & Citizen, as such. They [the princes] recognized in this way the tie that attached them to the Nation, tie inviolable that consisted in the inaugural pact consecrated by a solemn oath sworn throughout the august Act of the inauguration. If there were some difference of opinion, the presence of the Sovereign, in these places, soon lent ease to resolve it by way of compromise, & thus warned of dangerous consequences. At the hand of a Government so gentle and just, Flanders gradually reached the highest degree of grandeur. The Cities of Ghent & Bruges were rivaled in splendor and riches by no other City whatsoever; Flanders, in its entirety, seemed to have the one and only City [in the world], & Philip of Bourgogne's Court, his Countship, was without doubt the most brilliant of Europe.

. . . Flanders & Belgium were already at that time the center of arts and sciences, while Austria, who today pretends to have given us enlightenment, was still plunged entirely in barbarity.

At this point, the manifesto goes into great detail about the history of the province and, in rather convoluted prose, lays out the various abuses the Estates of Flanders feel Joseph II committed against them and the other provinces. The imperial court system would also no longer hold jurisdiction. Then, the document continues:

In consequence, inherent to our preceding resolutions & declarations, & calling on the supreme Judge of the universe, who knows the justice of our cause, we publish & declare solemnly, in the name of the People, that this Province IS & has the right TO BE a *free & independent state*; that it is released from all obedience to the Emperor Joseph II, Count of Flanders, & the House of Austria. We declare furthermore that every one, regardless of order, whether civilian or military, absolved & released from all obedience & fidelity to the so-called Emperor. We declare additionally any & all Officers, Justices, & vassals, of whatever state or condition they can be, free and absolved of all engagements & services respectfully due & sworn to the said Emperor in his capacity as Count of Flanders.

The Flemish declaration then includes various practicalities the Estates intend to employ in establishing independence: the emperor's coats of arms would all be erased and money would no longer be coined to Vienna's specifications, for example. Finally, the document ends on an official note:

> We order that these stipulations be printed, published & affixed [publicly] in the Province of Flanders in the usual places, & wherever need will be, so that no person could profess ignorance.
>
> So we give as a Mandate to those of our Council of Flanders, which We hereby declare erected by this document as Sovereign Council of Justice, & all who belong to it, to observe & to enforce the strict observation of the entirety of the contents of this document; to the effect of which we sign this through our Counselor-Pensionary, & have here affixed the seal. Done in our Assembly, 4 January 1790. Signed, J. F. Rohaert.

NOTES

1. Charles Lambert d'Outrepont, *Considerations of the Constitution of the Duchies of Brabant and Limbourg*, May 23, 1787, held at the University of Leuven, Belgium. Unfortunately, a lot of the primary source material for this revolution is still confined to the archives. This particular quotation comes from a speech given to the Assembly of the Brabantine Estates in Brussels that was later published as a pamphlet by its author, Charles d'Outrepont.

2. Janet Polasky, *Revolution in Brussels, 1787–1793* (Brussels: Palais des Académies, 1985), 133. Dr. Polasky's book, which is the definitive English-language volume on the Revolution, can be difficult to find outside university libraries; however, she has an excellent article that outlines her main arguments, which is more widely available online: "Traditionalists, Democrats, and Jacobins in Revolutionary Brussels," *Journal of Modern History* 56, no. 2 (June 1984): 227–62. Additionally, for those interested in aspects of gender in the Belgian Revolution, a good place to start is her article, also available through online databases, "Women in Revolutionary Belgium: From Stone Throwers to Hearth Tenders," *History Workshop* 21 (Spring 1986): 87–104. For aspects on nationalism and how the Belgian Revolution of 1787–90 shaped Belgian nationalism going forward,

see her chapter "Liberal Nationalism and Modern Regional Identity: Revolutionary Belgium, 1786–1830," in *Liberty and the Search for Identity: Liberal Nationalisms and the Legacy of Empires*, edited by Iván Zoltán Dénes, 75–90 (Budapest: Central European University Press, 2006). It is available online through GoogleBooks.

3. Excerpts of these two texts are available in the appendix at the end of this chapter so they can be compared.

4. David Armitage, *The Declaration of Independence: A Global History* (Cambridge, MA: Harvard University Press, 2007), 18.

5. J. F. Rohaert, *Manifeste de la Province de Flandre*, January 4, 1790. Held at the University of Leuven, Belgium. The appendix at the end of this chapter provides a longer, side-by-side comparison of this document and the American Declaration of Independence.

6. Ibid., 175. See the appendix at the end of this chapter for more in-depth textual comparison.

7. Text taken from the US National Archives, "Charters of Freedom" web portal: http://www.archives.gov/exhibits/charters/declaration_transcript.html.

8. Taken from a copy kept at the University of Leuven, Belgium. Translation mine.

KEY RESOURCES

Armitage, David. *The Declaration of Independence: A Global History*. Cambridge, MA: Harvard University Press, 2007.

Beales, Derek. *Joseph II. Volume II: Against the World, 1780–1790*. Cambridge: Cambridge University Press, 2009.

———. *Prosperity and Plunder: European Catholic Monasteries in the Age of Revolution, 1650–1815*. Cambridge: Cambridge University Press, 2003.

Maier, Pauline. *American Scripture: Making the Declaration of Independence*. New York: Knopf, 1997.

Polasky, Janet. *Revolution in Brussels, 1787–1793*. Brussels: Palais des Académies, 1985.

Teaching the Terror and Its Lessons

DAVID ANDRESS

One of the most significant lessons that can come from teaching the Terror is that history very often finds itself in a losing race against myth. The very phrase "the Terror" is itself a mythic creation—if later politicians had little doubt that it had ended decisively on 9 thermidor II (July 27, 1794), they could only frame that ending through processes of scapegoating that rewrote the immediate past extremely creatively and took some time to settle down to a dominant accepted understanding.[1]

Outside of the narrow confines of revolutionary historiography, the word *terror* imposes problems of understanding for contemporary students. A starting point for classroom engagement can be the exploration of what the word means to them. Insofar as they have encountered it outside history books, it is likely to be as a grimly catch-all term for forms of violence that are portrayed as lacking any political logic beyond the expression of deep-seated hatreds and as an incomprehensible, reprehensible "other" to Western civilization.[2] If they have met the idea of terror within history books, it might well be as an expression of Stalinist policy in the 1930s, leaving a series of impressions—about the overweening power of a police state, about programmatic ideological dictation, and about the long-term, professionalized, committed partisanship of the "revolutionary" and "terrorist"—quite at odds with the situation of the 1790s.

Both these forms may need to be unpacked for students, if they are going to grasp that whatever France in the 1790s was like, it was not like Russia in the 1930s, Northern Ireland in the 1980s, or Syria in the 2010s.[3] In what follows, I offer a series of suggestions for reframing the unique historical circumstances of the French Revolution in ways that encourage reflection on the emergence of something that we call "the Terror," without losing sight of the slippery nature of that label.

When Was "the Terror"?

When the Terror had begun depended—and still depends—on a complex calculus of whom one wishes to blame. Some historians see it as a phantom potential hovering over the events of 1789, a portent of doom embedded in decisions of a whole political class.[4] Others connect it to ideas of the influx of popular agitation and consequent violence to the heart of politics, notably with the fall of the monarchy on August 10, 1792, and the subsequent September Massacres.[5] It has often been suggested that terror was formally placed "on the order of the day" a year later, after an invasion of the National Convention by petitioning crowds on September 5, 1793—but that now appears to be a misreading of the record.[6] If we examine how politicians at the time used the word *terror* itself, we find that even into 1794 there was no agreement on whether it was a virtue or a dangerous flaw. The more one looks, the harder it is, in fact, to say that the Terror was anything more than the vague period we have agreed to label as such, for no reason except convenience and precedent.[7]

Even if we don't really know when it began or how it ended, our general culture has a very strong idea of what happened. Again, this is an opportunity to explore with students their perceptions of a period immortalized in many works of fiction and other cultural productions. Whether students are more attuned to Charles Dickens's *Tale of Two Cities* and Baroness Orczy's *Scarlet Pimpernel*, or to the recent video game Assassin's Creed Unity, some of the same tropes will likely reappear: the Terror filled the streets of Paris with blood, tumbrels trundled aristocrats to the guillotine on a daily basis, the social world was turned upside down as grimy *sans-culottes* lorded it over anyone with money or education, the cold hand of the state and its spies reached out into every home, and a ruthless leveling campaign of ideological purity clamped down on all dissent. The makers of Assassin's Creed even commissioned a special artistic trailer that rehearsed many of these clichés in gruesomely loving detail: marked by YouTube as containing "content inappropriate for children," this could be a good starting point for discussing how the image of revolutionary blood lust persists.[8]

Why all these events occurred is often less clear in such popular accounts, but often seems to come back to an idea that "liberty, equality, fraternity" was a direct programmatic statement about the destruction of all social distinction, pursued without hesitation or ambiguity through a state apparatus fully captured by committed partisans of that program. From a historical point of view, this is not just rubbish but pernicious rubbish. Any attempt to teach on this period nonetheless confronts the challenge of unpacking it and often confronts the fact that historians have helped plant many of the seeds of such problematic views.

The dominance of the "classic" Marxist interpretation from the early twentieth century to the 1970s relied extensively on implicit and explicit claims about the coherence and significance of the views behind the deeds of radical leaders and groups to frame the questionable achievements of the period as a staging post on the road to wider social liberation.[9] "Revisionists" of the schools led by François Furet and Keith Michael Baker in the 1980s and 1990s also emphasized coherence and consistency, but for the opposite purpose of indicting the revolutionaries' road to bloody tyranny.[10] Such are the political stakes of this debate that it still continues, with Sophie Wahnich defending the state's imposition of terror as preferable to less controlled alternatives and Eric Hazan making a bold narrative claim for the continued validity of the "classic" view of popular radical rectitude.[11]

In sum, there are many very good reasons for beginning to "teach the Terror" by emphasizing that the word itself is a fundamentally misleading term, packed with presuppositions that offer nothing to help us understand what actually happened through 1793 and 1794 in France. What we might instead try to do is think through some of the processes and situations that came to a head in those years as they might have appeared to the actual actors of history caught up in them.

Understanding the Perils of Political Leadership

One place to begin is with the instability at the very pinnacle of political leadership that marked the period. Students who may have met "terror" through study of later generations of revolutionaries can be led to contemplate that unlike Stalin, who was an active Bolshevik for over a decade before the Russian Revolution and spent another decade working his way to power after it, French revolutionaries lived and acted in a context of stunningly rapid change.

Maximilien Robespierre famously sat on the Committee of Public Safety (CPS) for exactly a year before his fall.[12] Before he joined, he had essentially no experience of administration or government, having made his reputation as a spokesman for popular aspiration and something not far short of a prophet of doom with regard to the nefarious intentions of others. In autumn 1792, the so-called Girondins, who had been the closest things he had to allies, damned him as an aspiring dictator, but it was those Girondins who had actually moved closest to real power and continued to drive events forward. They split the National Convention down the middle over the fate of the king in January 1793 and in the late spring seemed to be making a brutal power play against Parisian radical leaders, incarcerating several and putting the fiercest of them, Jean-Paul Marat, on trial for his life. By the first days of June 1793, those Parisian radicals had bullied the convention into ejecting the Girondin leaders, and by the time Robespierre joined the CPS, Marat was dead at the hands of a Girondin-sympathizing assassin, and their leadership, on the run, had turned a growing crisis of regional political loyalty into a sputtering civil war that spanned Normandy, Bordeaux, and the cities of the Rhône Valley.

Two months later, by the end of September, the CPS had been obliged to give in to popular Parisian demands for economic regulation (going against their deeply held free-market convictions) and to admit two more radical spokesmen, bringing their number to twelve. Robespierre had just given a speech in which he lambasted the convention for their lack of confidence in the committee, but with the southern port city of Toulon fallen into rebel hands and a massive royal and Catholic army rampaging in the northwest, the situation was one of deepest crisis. A further two months of stop-at-nothing political and military mobilization saw the smashing of almost all the serious rebellions as winter loomed, but France was still fighting foreign enemies on every frontier as well, and savage disputes about the conduct of internal and external wars were once again starting to gouge at the political class.

Rumors of wide-ranging plots combining self-enrichment and counterrevolutionary intent flared through the winter, as did a painful dispute over curbing some radicals' enthusiasm for militant atheism— a "de-Christianization" that threatened a decisive alienation of the rural majority. The early spring of 1794 saw merciless moves to quell internal opposition, identified (more or less hollowly and cynically) as masked counterrevolution. The Parisian radical leadership outside the convention, caught up in their own self-righteous demands to purge "compromisers," were condemned as plotters and guillotined in March. In early April, the CPS smashed opposing calls for relaxation of policy by executing, among others, one of its own members, Marie-Jean Hérault de Séchelles, the larger-than-life revolutionary hero, Georges-Jacques Danton, and Robespierre's own childhood friend, Camille Desmoulins.

Within another two months, the CPS's control over national policy had begun to splinter, even as the war effort produced a wave of victories and a flood of new legislation promised a remolding of society and culture on austerely republican lines. Here we find a source for much of the imagery of what "the Terror" was working to achieve—in theory. But at this point it had only weeks to run. More ruthless commitment to the execution of counterrevolutionaries was accompanied by growing alarm on many sides of the convention (including among men who had decisively bloodied their hands in repression) that anyone might be next to fall under suspicion. Robespierre himself, the supposed "dictator," was only intermittently present, having been ill for weeks early in the year and preferring the Jacobin Club as a venue for ideological speeches. When the CPS met to explore new policies, discussions seemed (at least in the memoirs of those present) to have an edge of manic hysteria and mutual menace to them.

By mid-July, as the revolutionary month of thermidor began, Robespierre and a handful of his political allies and administrative appointees were almost completely isolated, although they had yet to realize it. On 8 thermidor, Robespierre made a speech that is a monument to political delusion, announcing that counterrevolutionary corruption riddled the convention and the CPS and calling for all the guilty to be purged. The result, the next day, was a remarkably unviolent "coup," driven by the determination of the bulk of the convention that repression was reaching altogether too close to home. Robespierre and his allies could mount only token resistance and died under the guillotine on 10 thermidor, thoroughly unmourned by large crowds and ripe for subsequent ruthless scapegoating.[13]

Working through such a narrative account is useful particularly in countering the "Stalinist" image of terror as a stable formation, and might for example be explored by mapping it against students' own previous twelve months, contemplating how they met any challenges of change and how such a drumbeat of confrontations might have felt. Of course at another level for students an account of this type can be simply mind-boggling: figures flit onto the historical stage, change their names twice, Brissotins-Girondins-Federalists, Indulgents-*citras*-Dantonists, then have their heads chopped off in short order. What, one might well ask, was that all actually about?

There might be a temptation at this point to turn to the kind of metaphor used famously by Crane Brinton, and think of the Terror as a feverish paroxysm in the body politic, its very rapidity marking it as a product of disorder-as-disease.[14] Yet notwithstanding the casual dehumanization involved in such an image, its deeper implication is that the violence of 1793–1794 is emergent from something alien to wider social processes—an infection from some unidentified outside (which of course a certain kind of historian has always been happy to identify, whether the Freemasons denounced by Abbé Barruel in his bestselling 1797 *Memoirs Illustrating the History of Jacobinism*, or the more generic power-hungry intellectuals that stalk the pages of Schama's *Citizens*). Revolution-as-disease is little more than a metaphoric restatement of the idea of revolution-as-conspiracy. We cannot dispute that politics ran at a fever pitch in 1793–1794, or that they were convulsed repeatedly by old and new conflicts, but we do need to bring our explanations for those situations down to actual facts and not merely grope for superficially plausible analogies. Nevertheless, it can be helpful to reflect on what kinds of image and analogy can illuminate the revolutionary process, once grounded in more factual accounts.

A Tale of Two Metaphors

Many of the most important "facts" in understanding the Terror concern the perceptions of those living through the events of the 1780s and 1790s. Understanding how people experienced what was going on around them is essential to framing an understanding of why they acted as they did. Putting aside the counterrevolutionary perceptions of the revolution as variously a wickedly disloyal rebellion, a satanic attack on religion, or simply a hideous parade of criminal opportunism, there remain two significantly different perceptions of the revolutionary process at work in politics running right through from 1789 to 9 thermidor and beyond—standing not in direct opposition but at an awkward and conflictual tangent. If we can tease these out and present them as more or less solid images in the classroom, students can use them to appreciate what lay behind the frantic political action.

The first was a more elitist view, ironically a more optimistic one in general terms; the second, more popular, more radical, more fearful. The first view was that the revolution was a series of achievements that could soon be brought to a successful and stable conclusion. The second was that the achievements of the revolution of 1789 were epochal but insecure and threatened. The first we might liken to the image of a broad and stable staircase of political progress: different groups among the political class, from the Monarchiens and Fayettists of 1789 to the Feuillants of 1791 and the Girondins of 1792, had different views about which step the revolution was on and which step it should be stopped on, but all at their various points agreed that ascent to the right step had been achieved and was a foundation for turning political attention to such things as rebuilding the nation's diplomatic standing, promoting international trade, or stimulating the growth of national industry.[15] Here in particular, students could be encouraged to review the different attempts to stop the revolution under different leaderships, identifying what constituted a "proper" state of affairs for each.

The second view positioned the full realization of the benefits of 1789 at the top of a steep and slippery slope, one the French had not yet managed to fully ascend because, alternately weighing them down and actively clawing at their heels, the aristocrats of the counterrevolution were fighting to make that goal unattainable, and indeed to drag the nation so far back that the hope of equal liberty and rights faded from sight. For the holders of such views—a group embracing much of the more popular press, many of the Jacobin clubs, and in particular the more vociferous radicals of the Parisian public sphere (and of course Robespierre and his perpetual prophecies of doom)—there could be no safe place to rest. The revolution could not be finished yet, all its best hopes remained unfulfilled, and every day brought more evidence of the work going on to break it down.[16] The nature of that evidence— from major events like the flight to Varennes to the kind of persistent suspicion that dogged the Girondins—can again be explored in the classroom.

The difficulty for those who espoused the more optimistic view of revolutionary achievement was twofold. First it required them to stand in opposition to those who mostly loudly proclaimed their revolutionary credentials and deny that the threats they complained of were real;

second, as time marched on, more and more plausible evidence accumulated to brand such optimists as, in fact, traitors. The political narrative of the French Revolution was saturated with treachery and its consequences. In this sense in particular, reflecting on the events we call the Terror is completely inseparable from a grasp of how the preceding years had been experienced, digested, and understood as a certain kind of lived reality.

The Facts of the Rumor(s)

The revolution, simply and factually, in terms of its acknowledgment as a process of forceful change, began with an aristocratic court plot to unseat the popular minister Necker and replace him with a cabal of hardliners who would curtail the pretensions of the National Assembly.[17] In the resultant uprising, the governor of the Bastille might have kept his head on July 14, 1789, if the view of the crowd had not been that most of the casualties they had suffered came through a treacherous invitation to enter the fortress to receive a deadly cannonade.[18] Two weeks later, when Jacques-Pierre Brissot launched his newspaper, the *French Patriot*, the first item it chose to report indicated how central conspiratorial claims were to be to revolutionary journalism. It cited a National Assembly deputy's claim that an aristocratic judge from Besançon had blown up a party of patriots. Brissot denounced the "atrocious action" and reported that

> This infamous aristocrat had drawn a great number of Citizens to his château for a festival. After the meal, the guests were led into a wood. A mine had been laid under the ground. Servants in on the plot with their master lit the fuse. The explosion took place; several people were killed and buried under the piles of earth and stones; others were grievously injured. The monster who had imagined this infernal manoeuvre was already in flight, and no one knows where he has taken refuge.[19]

Although there had indeed been an explosion at a local chateau, everything else about this narrative was essentially the elaboration of horrified rumor and fearful, suspicious speculation as fact. Yet this alarm, like the contemporary "Great Fear," built on a hard core of real betrayal, real counterrevolutionary plotting and violence. Conspiracy theories did not come from an eccentric fringe of self-generating extremism.

This was the dominant pattern of the revolutionary public sphere: rampant alarmism that in hindsight verged on pure paranoia, yet always enough indisputable hard evidence and real treachery to justify, particularly in radical eyes, the most fulminating alarm. When Parisian crowds forced the royal family to move to Paris from Versailles in October 1789, their concerns about an aristocratic "famine plot" to starve the city were a repetition of well-established cultural beliefs, but the royalist sentiments expressed by newly arrived troops that had triggered the popular action were an attested reality.[20] When revolutionary authorities decided to launch an elaborate judicial investigation, seeking their own destabilizing scapegoats for this affair, they added more fuel to the idea of continuing, widespread, nefarious plotting.[21] In a political climate where not only did a growing number of emigrated aristocrats proclaim their enmity but up to a quarter of the National Assembly formed a recalcitrant opposition, denouncing all moves away from the old regime, and where by the end of 1790 up to half the clergy were manifesting stark unwillingness to accept the end of their corporate privileges, the notion of the revolution as a secure achievement simply made no sense to those most invested in its ultimate success.[22]

The course of revolutionary events continued to throw up examples of what appeared necessarily to be staggering treachery. When the king attempted his flight to Varennes in June 1791, denouncing the revolution and all its works in a written testament, he escaped from under the noses of a Parisian National Guard militia whose commander, General Lafayette, had repeatedly proclaimed the integrity of royal security. The cover story of "kidnapping" that the assembly's leadership concocted (to mask the reality that they were in fact recapturing a fugitive king) made a mockery of those pronouncements, and when National Guards shot down dozens of protestors the following month, the notion that the revolution was being led by men who were essentially counterrevolutionaries was sealed with blood in the minds of many.[23] The split in the Jacobin Club that left a "Feuillant" leadership to drive through a royal reinstatement while "Brissotins" paraded their republican suspicions, lined up the political class for further declamations about treachery. These duly followed as Brissotins in the new Legislative Assembly spent the autumn and winter of 1791–1792 campaigning for a war to cleanse the frontiers of enemies and belaboring a secret "Austrian Committee" allegedly concealed within the royal government.

When the war demanded by the Brissotins came and was not the short, victorious campaign they had promised, more astonishing treachery followed. By the summer of 1792, with a foothold in government, the Brissotins were trying to preserve the monarchy: fending off the forces of republican radicalism they had helped conjure and seeming to seek power hand in hand with counterrevolution. General Lafayette, meanwhile, plotted a military coup against Parisian radical power and Jacobin influence; after the monarchy's final fall in August, he tried again to march his troops on the capital before fleeing to sanctuary behind enemy lines. Over the course of the next year, in what to historians are a series of monumental tactical blunders, the Brissotins, now more usually labeled Girondins, painted themselves in radical eyes as vile traitors— turning savagely, as noted, on Robespierre and other radicals, resisting furiously the efforts to judge the king, and associating themselves with a new military and political leader, General Dumouriez, who in April 1793 carried out a virtual copy of Lafayette's betrayal of the previous summer.

All of this high-level political turncoating, deceit, and treachery happened in a context of daily anxiety, and a month-by-month emergent calendar of new evidence of counterrevolutionary, aristocratic, and clerical betrayals. The massive War in the Vendée that began in early 1793 to radical eyes was merely the final outcome of a process of well-attested plotting that went back to at least 1790, with firm evidence of émigré agency behind sectarian violence across the south and open defiance of revolutionary laws by the priesthood and their "misled" flocks. Misled or led astray (égaré) was the default term to describe ordinary people who resisted the revolution—because there was always someone ready and willing to lead them astray. If such people were a little too poor and marginal, they became brigands—allegedly professional criminals widely asserted to be in the pay of the aristocrats, roaming bands of whom had been the pretext for the Great Fear, even if none were ever found. There were reportedly 30,000 such brigands in Paris from the beginning of 1791 onward, living in the abandoned townhouses of émigrés and awaiting the signal for pillage and massacre.[24]

Paris was of course the immediate context for all the high political maneuvers of the period, and it was particularly struck by the desperate consequences of the perpetual collision of rumor and reality. Those who stood for basic law and order, as the National Guard largely tried to do, swayed back and forth between suppressing "incendiary" speech and being taken in by its alarms—joining en masse the October Days march on Versailles, struggling to suppress rumors of royal deceit at the celebratory Fête de la Fédération of July 1790, and by 1791 embroiled in some truly labyrinthine clashes, epitomized by the events of February 28 that year. On that day the guard had been called out in a city-wide general alarm to stop hundreds of radicals from the Faubourg Saint-Antoine destroying refurbishment works at the chateau of Vincennes (under development as a new prison but with rumors of its looming role as a Bastille for persecuted patriots and of a secret escape tunnel from the royal apartments at the Tuileries); marching there, General Lafayette reportedly was shot at by unknown assailants. Meanwhile in the city, a nobleman wearing the insignia of a Knight of Saint Louis had been arrested near the Tuileries carrying a concealed dagger; rumor flashed around the city that it was an assassination attempt on the king; several hundred young nobles appeared at the palace, many armed, all later purported to be carrying special *cartes d'entrée* signed by a royal official. New rumors flowed of a coup attempt, a popular crowd gathered in a stand-off with the men immediately dubbed "Knights of the Dagger"; the National Guard marched back from Vincennes and finally restored order—disarming the Knights and in the process cementing the view that they had been there to do mischief.[25]

Unusual in its complexity and bizarre concatenations, this day was far from unique—less than a week earlier, the Tuileries had been surrounded with anxious and aggressive crowds after the king's aunts departed on a "pilgrimage" to Rome, and in April the royal family was physically prevented from leaving the city by a crowd, persuaded that a planned trip to Saint-Cloud was a pretext for flight. The Varennes episode, of course, proved such fears justified in hindsight, and the role of the National Guard only weeks later in launching a "police riot" against radicals (who they had been told were in fact brigands) continued cementing destabilizing uncertainties, speculations, and assertions at the heart of political processes.

Living with Uncertainty

What starts to emerge from this narrative framework is that the lived experience of revolutionary France was horrible. Where one common perception of events might be as a kaleidoscope of incomprehensible change, students should also be encouraged to think about what appeared to be constant in the lives of people in these years and how difficult that must have been to live with. While people repeatedly told themselves that they had escaped by the skin of their teeth—by something little short of a miracle—from a thousand years of aristocratic tyranny, they also obsessed about the fear of falling back into it while wrestling with a fundamentally disrupted daily reality.

None of the story above has taken notice of the other problems the French lived with: the steady inflation of too-easily-forged paper money and the literal disappearance of reliable coinage; the essential breakdown of long-understood frameworks of economic organization for work and credit; the straightforward unemployment of hundreds of thousands who had serviced, especially in the cities, a luxury economy that nobody was spending in; the sight of shuttered shops and mansions; the constant nagging dread that the enemy was both outside and inside, lurking in every unknown face, every odd piece of behavior, every piece of news blown out of proportion and plastered across the public sphere by billposters, hawkers, and inveterate gossips.[26] Such contexts could be compared with modern social media to reflect on how powerfully rumor can take hold, how perceptions (of celebrities, politicians, situations) can crystallize around apparently revelatory moments—even if unproven (or proven false)—and how the circulation of information is driven as much by what people want to believe as by what they need to know.

Within this context, the continual, demonstrable worsening of the position of the revolution, particularly in the wartime context from April 1792, comes into focus as a nightmarish situation of impending doom: a circle of enemies closing ever tighter around the patriotic French. Acts of aggression or repression that might be used to portray the "evils" of the Terror—the September Massacres, the Revolutionary Tribunal, the Law of Suspects—can be seen as reactive and contextually framed. When the actual detail of such topics is further exposed—that hundreds of prisoners were "judged" and liberated in those "massacres," that the Revolutionary Tribunal continued to record acquittals throughout its operations, that the vast majority of those targeted as suspects survived the period unharmed—then the stage begins to be set for considering what of the Terror is a history that can be understood as being like many other periods of crisis and what is continuing myth.[27]

This is not to propose that classroom activity should seek to justify any of the elements that made up the Terror, merely that there is no need to demonize them. To go into a detailed examination of any dimension of this period is to reveal both the desperate actions of people driven to extremities and the many deep flaws of those thrust into unexpected prominence. No amount of nuanced understanding can make the figure of the radical emissary Claude Javogues into any less of a thug, but as Colin Lucas showed many years ago, we can understand the perilous circumstances in which his thuggishness seemed essential and proved effective.[28] The more that historians have laid out about the social and cultural origins of the War in the Vendée rebellion, the easier it has become—beyond any partisanship over their larger goals—to see the western peasantry as a group actively afflicted by the choices made by urban revolutionary leaderships and fighting for the survival (as they saw it) of their communities.[29] We might also note that even historians who clearly profess sympathy for the assumed wider goals of the sans-culottes have increasingly had to acknowledge the brutality, misogyny, and self-seeking machinations of their self-appointed leaders.[30] Peasants and sans-culottes alike contributed to making the Vendée a war of massacres from beginning to end.

Around, beyond, and beneath all of this is also one of the largest but often elided facts about the Terror: it worked. All of its key measures were enacted in a situation of escalating war emergency, and they achieved their essential aims. The embattled (and in its own mind, besieged) Republic of mid-1793 had by the end of that year shattered rebel armies that numbered over 100,000 in the west, retaken three of the nation's largest cities, and driven out the rebels and their foreign allies who had seized the entire Mediterranean fleet and its base in the southeast. By spring 1794, not only had price controls, rationing, and requisitions succeeded in keeping the population fed through a winter when disruptions might otherwise have brought famine, but tens of thousands had been marshaled to build a massive new armaments industry and hundreds of thousands enrolled and drilled into whole new armies.[31] By summer 1794, as the "Robespierrists" passed beneath the blade of justice, French armies were poised for an era of military victory and expansionism that would last into the new century. For many at the time of the revolution's centenary, this was enough in itself to excuse everything else that had been done—but one does not need to accept such a chauvinistic perspective to recognize that this enormous practical mobilization adds another dimension to the helter-skelter picture of Jacobin politics.[32] Confronting students with the notion of practical success, of ends justifying means, perhaps in the context of more recent wars and other uses of state violence, is a further way to destabilize easy assumptions about the exceptionality and "otherness" of these events.

Conclusion

Of course, to teach the Terror in sufficient depth to bring these contextual realities and conundrums to the fore is an increasing challenge in itself. With rising attention to the "globality" of the French Revolution, issues other than the precise circumstances of these events have come crowding into the field. To give race and sex the fair share of attention that once only had to be split between class and ideology shrinks the scope for any detail about anything—not to mention that to teach the globalized, racialized consequences of 1789 at all clearly also means making space for some further powerfully ambiguous, complex, and context-dependent intersections of identity, freedom, and power.[33]

But if the French Revolution and the Terror within it are to be taught as history, then this conundrum of confronting simple narratives and emblematic images with the complexity of lived experience needs to be addressed. To do otherwise is not to do history as that discipline should be done, with solidity, credibility, and empirical plausibility, but to go back to history without its standing as a discipline: simply picking a congenial story and jumping forward through it to the desired moral.

NOTES

1. See the classic text by Bronislaw Baczko, *Ending the Terror: The French Revolution after Robespierre* (Cambridge: Cambridge University Press, 1994). More recent brief guides have been provided by Laura Mason, "The Thermidorian Reaction," in *A Companion to the French Revolution*, ed. Peter McPhee (Oxford: Wiley-Blackwell, 2013), 313–27, and "Thermidor and the Myth of Rupture," in *The Oxford Handbook of the French Revolution*, ed. David Andress (Oxford: Oxford University Press, 2015), 521–37.

2. An extensive online definition of *terrorism*, based on academic debate and amenable to classroom discussion, can be found at http://www.terrorism analysts.com/pt/index.php/pot/article/view/schmid-terrorism-definition /html (accessed June 8, 2015).

3. Arno J. Mayer, *The Furies: Violence and Terror in the French and Russian Revolutions* (Princeton, NJ: Princeton University Press, 2000), is a strong attempt

to make comparisons about revolutionary terror, but avoids extension into the Stalinist period and thus often discusses the cruelties of civil war within revolution.

4. This is the whole drift of Simon Schama, *Citizens: A Chronicle of the French Revolution* (New York: Viking Penguin, 1989), and it is also addressed at an intellectual level in Keith Michael Baker, *Inventing the French Revolution* (Cambridge: Cambridge University Press, 1990).

5. Explicitly claimed by J. F. Bosher, *The French Revolution: A New Interpretation* (London: Weidenfeld & Nicolson, 1989), 178.

6. Discussed by Jean-Clément Martin, *Violence et Révolution: Essai sur la naissance d'un mythe national* (Paris: Seuil, 2006), 186–93.

7. A perspective discussed at more length in David Andress, *The Terror: Civil War in the French Revolution* (London: Little, Brown, 2004), and concisely in David Andress, "The Course of the Terror, 1793–94," in McPhee, *A Companion*, 293–309.

8. "Assassin's Creed Unity Presents: Rob Zombie's French Revolution," https://www.youtube.com/watch?v=TEjcVvxjZIc (accessed July 31, 2014).

9. A perspective most programmatically worked out in Albert Soboul, *The French Revolution 1787–1799: From the Storming of the Bastille to Napoleon*, trans. Alan Forrest and Colin Jones (New York: Vintage, 1975).

10. François Furet, *Interpreting the French Revolution*, trans. Elborg Forster (Cambridge: Cambridge University Press, 1981); Baker, *Inventing the French Revolution*.

11. Sophie Wahnich, *In Defence of the Terror: Liberty or Death in the French Revolution* (London: Verso, 2012); Eric Hazan, *A People's History of the French Revolution* (London: Verso, 2014).

12. For two thorough, recent, and contrasting accounts of how Robespierre got to this position, and how he then worked his way through his final year, see Ruth Scurr, *Fatal Purity: Robespierre and the French Revolution* (London: Chatto & Windus, 2006); Peter McPhee, *Robespierre: A Revolutionary Life* (New Haven, CT: Yale University Press, 2012).

13. For a close examination of the traumatic experiences of the core revolutionary leadership through the Terror, see Marisa Linton, *Choosing Terror: Virtue, Friendship and Authenticity in the French Revolution* (Oxford: Oxford University Press, 2013).

14. Crane Brinton, *The Anatomy of Revolution* (New York: Vintage, 1938).

15. For a discussion of how the National Assembly tried to "close" the revolution on such terms, see Michael P. Fitzsimmons, *The Remaking of France: The National Assembly and the Constitution of 1791* (Cambridge: Cambridge University Press, 1994).

16. On this, see various contributions to the *Oxford Handbook of the French Revolution*, notably David Andress, "Politics and Insurrection: The Sans-culottes,

the 'Popular Movement' and the People," 401–17; D. M. G. Sutherland, "Urban Violence in 1789," 272–89; and Charles Walton, "Clubs, Parties, Factions," 362–81.

17. Micah Alpaugh, "A Personal Revolution: National Assembly Deputies and the Politics of 1789," in Andress, *Oxford Handbook*, 180–98.

18. Peter McPhee, "A Social Revolution? Rethinking Popular Insurrection in 1789," in Andress, *Oxford Handbook*, 164–79.

19. *Patriote François*, no. 1, p. 2.

20. David Garrioch, "The Everyday Lives of Parisian Women and the October Days of 1789," *Social History* 24, no. 3 (1999): 231–49.

21. Barry M. Shapiro, *Revolutionary Justice in Paris, 1789–1790* (Cambridge: Cambridge University Press, 1993).

22. Edward J. Woell, "The Origins and Outcomes of Religious Schism, 1790–99," in McPhee, *A Companion*, 145–60.

23. Timothy Tackett, *When the King Took Flight* (Cambridge, MA: Harvard University Press, 2003); David Andress, *Massacre at the Champ de Mars: Popular Dissent and Political Culture in the French Revolution* (Woodbridge: Boydell Press, 2000).

24. See Andress, *The Terror*, chaps. 1, 2.

25. See Andress, *Massacre at the Champ de Mars*, 85–87.

26. Two essential recent works on the breakdown of economic trust and stable functioning are Rebecca L. Spang, *Stuff and Money in the French Revolution* (Cambridge, MA: Harvard University Press, 2015), and Michael P. Fitzsimmons, *From Artisan to Worker: Guilds, the French State, and the Organization of Labor, 1776–1821* (Cambridge: Cambridge University Press, 2010).

27. See Andress, *The Terror*, chap. 3, and "Course of the Terror," esp. 300–301, 305.

28. Colin Lucas, *The Structure of the Terror: The Example of Javogues and the Loire* (Oxford: Oxford University Press, 1973).

29. Jean-Clément Martin, "The Vendée, *Chouannerie* and the State, 1791–99," in McPhee, *A Companion*, 246–59. See also Claude Petitfrère, "The Origins of the Civil War in the Vendée," *French History* 2, no. 2 (1988): 187–207.

30. Morris Slavin, *The Hébertistes to the Guillotine: Anatomy of a "Conspiracy" in Revolutionary France* (Baton Rouge: Louisiana State University Press, 1994).

31. Jean-Pierre Gross, *Fair Shares for All: Jacobin Egalitarianism in Practice* (Cambridge: Cambridge University Press, 1997), discusses the work of building a war economy in areas without large-scale violence and civil disturbance.

32. See Andress, *The Terror*, 371–72.

33. McPhee, *A Companion*, and Andress, *Oxford Handbook*, take complementary approaches to these issues, discussed in the latter's foreword, v–vii. See also Suzanne Desan, Lynn Hunt, and William Max Nelson, eds., *The French Revolution in Global Perspective* (Ithaca, NY: Cornell University Press, 2013);

David Armitage and Sanjay Subrahmanyan, eds., *The Age of Revolutions in Global Context, c. 1760–1840* (Basingstoke: Palgrave, 2010).

KEY RESOURCES

Andress, David. *The Terror: Civil War in the French Revolution*. London: Little, Brown, 2005. Published in the United States as *The Terror: The Merciless War for Freedom in Revolutionary France*. New York: Farrar, Straus & Giroux, 2005.

———, ed. *The Oxford Handbook of the French Revolution*. Oxford: Oxford University Press, 2015.

Armitage, David, and Sanjay Subrahmanyan, eds. *The Age of Revolutions in Global Context, c. 1760–1840*. Basingstoke: Palgrave, 2010.

Desan, Suzanne, Lynn Hunt, and William Max Nelson, eds. *The French Revolution in Global Perspective*. Ithaca, NY: Cornell University Press, 2013.

Linton, Marisa. *Choosing Terror: Virtue, Friendship and Authenticity in the French Revolution*. Oxford: Oxford University Press, 2013.

McPhee, Peter, ed. *A Companion to the French Revolution*. Oxford: Wiley-Blackwell, 2013.

Tackett, Timothy. *The Coming of the Terror in the French Revolution*. Cambridge, MA.: Belknap Press of Harvard University Press, 2015.

Independence and
Revolution
in Latin America

MARCELA ECHEVERRI

In 2009 began a wave of bicentennial celebrations of Latin American Independence. Since final independence did not come until the 1820s (dates vary, see map), the celebrations will continue until 2025. In this commemoratory spirit, the history of Latin American independence has been tremendously revitalized, becoming one of the themes that has received most attention by scholars in Latin America, Spain, and to a lesser extent the United States in the past couple of decades. Although academic thinking and writing about these regional processes has transformed profoundly, there seems to be a lag in the impact that new interpretations have had in curricula and popular understandings of the process.

Approaches to the topic in the classroom can aim at clearly presenting Latin American independence during the Age of Revolutions by using up-to-date materials and analysis. In this essay I break down the main contrasts between earlier and current interpretations (popular as well as academic), exploring four essential questions implicit to any conceptual and narrative synthesis of the theme. "What?" is an inquiry into the types of transformations that took place as a result of the independence wars; "when?" allows us to think about periodization; "why?" speaks to the issue of causality of the imperial breakdown; and "who?" is a question that helps address the subjects of the independence story. There is not a single or correct order in which to deal with these questions, and there will be significant overlap among them, but by raising these questions in the classroom, teachers can enable students to unpack the complexities of the struggles for Latin American independence.

One of the first challenges for teachers and students is to absorb both old and new interpretations. Like the historiography of nationalism in Napoleonic Europe explored by Alan Forrest in this volume, nationalist perspectives on the Latin American revolutions still carry considerable weight. In broad terms, in fact, there are two schools that dominated the historiography until the 1990s. Nationalist tropes have been at the heart of the region's history since the nineteenth century, framing the story of the early nineteenth-century independence wars within the boundaries of each nation. The wars were famously led by men such as Miguel Hidalgo in Mexico, Simón Bolívar in the northern part of South America, and José de San Martín in the Southern Cone. The nationalist narratives put these military figures in the forefront and are deeply teleological in the sense that they assume the inevitability of the anticolonial struggles and the existence of national identities predating the emergence of the nation-states. The materialist or Marxist approaches of the mid-twentieth century wrote revised versions of these nationalist stories, condemning the Creoles (Spanish Americans) for having failed to produce any real changes to Latin American societies. These new histories were especially critical of the republican states these Creole leaders created, questioning the revolutionary character of the independence wars.[1]

Though there are significant debates among historians working to revise these interpretations, the core of the current approach to the period simultaneously challenges the nationalist and the Marxist tropes by framing the Latin American independence processes in the Atlantic Age of Revolutions. As we will see, historians have undone the nationalist trope by placing the Latin American independence wars in the Atlantic context and highlighting regional and imperial processes that do not assume the preexistence of nations. With the Atlantic focus, and acknowledging their connection to the revolutionary processes of the eighteenth and nineteenth centuries, historians also have redefined the Latin American independence processes as "revolutions." Teachers can therefore use the Atlantic interpretation to show students an example of how old orthodoxies can be tested by new perspectives and contexts.

The most relevant Atlantic connection that historians in the current paradigm began to explore is the interimperial conflict that resulted from the Napoleonic wars. In 1807 Napoleon's armies invaded the Iberian Peninsula with revolutionary results for both the Portuguese and Spanish empires. The Portuguese court relocated to Rio de Janeiro, while the Spanish monarch Fernando VII was abducted by Napoleon and replaced by his brother Joseph Napoleon I. The radical changes in government and politics unleashed by the French invasion were accompanied by reactions at the micro or local levels everywhere in the Iberian territories, reactions that expanded or transformed the political landscape. This means that the revolutions in the Iberian world were not simply a top-down process. Revolution entailed the redefinition of sovereignty as much as changes in political symbols and practices at the imperial and local level, and in both monarchies/empires resulted in the independence of the American territories by the 1820s. These broad processes—the transformation of imperial sovereignty and subjecthood and the emergence of independent states with their own legal and political redefinition of identities—had meaningful consequences for peoples across social lines and were in fact negotiated in day-to-day practices. In this respect, the current historiography challenges the continuity principle implicit in the Marxist narratives that presumed that independence was a superficial and ideological process with no real sociopolitical consequences.

Indeed, the current studies of the period emphasize the political nature of revolution, and this bold redefinition counters the Marxist portrayals of the independence wars, which denounced their failure as social revolutions. The new cultural history has productively transformed our understanding of categories such as "political" and "social," and from today's point of view it is as possible as it is necessary to explore the self-understanding that multiple social groups had of the historical changes under way. This means that we define the independence processes in Latin America as revolutionary given the extraordinary changes produced during the first two decades of the nineteenth century (both at the political and social levels) as they were experienced by the multiplicity of actors that participated in and shaped them. From this perspective, the focus is less on the Creole elites, and larger sectors of the population, including indigenous peoples and people of African origin and descent, have become core actors in the new narratives of independence and revolution in Latin America.

What?

The work of historian R. R. Palmer, published in the mid-twentieth century, was foundational to the Age of Revolutions historiographic paradigm.[2] Palmer specifically wrote about an age of *democratic* revolutions, a period in the late eighteenth century when two "pure" and original historical processes in the United States and France produced exemplary political revolutions. Like Palmer, other historians writing in the twentieth century used a definition of revolution molded on the eighteenth-century American and French revolutions. As a result of the particular way revolution was defined (largely pinned to white male democratization and North Atlantic modernization), and periodized (1760–1800), the independence processes of Latin America were written off from the Age of Revolutions narrative.

As Lester Langley writes in his chapter in this volume, shifting the focus from the earlier studies of the revolutions that privileged Anglo or French processes to looking at the hemispheric dynamics during the Age of Revolutions is a strategic turn for enriching our understanding of the period. Moreover, as Langley says, the other two revolutions in the Americas—Haiti and Latin America—are transatlantic in origin and deeply linked to the European revolutions during the late eighteenth and early nineteenth centuries. Overcoming the conceptual and chronological limits of the narrow Palmerian paradigm, we see the relevance of the French Caribbean and the Iberian Americas for a deeper understanding of the revolutionary age. This development provides excellent opportunities for students to grapple with the multidirectional, multicultural nature of the Atlantic world and with the rich varieties of aims and impulses at work in the revolutions across this space.

Much of the scholarship on the Haitian Revolution in the past fifty years has criticized Palmer's definition by chronological criteria of the Age of Revolutions and the exclusions that it implied. With its inescapable focus on issues of slavery and race, such research has further challenged the substantial understanding of the Age of Revolutions as a period characterized by the seamless rise of democracy. Studies about the Haitian Revolution revealed the varied stakes in the emergence of a new type of sovereignty, popular sovereignty, in anticolonial and nationalist processes across the hemisphere. Far from being complete or finished emancipatory processes, revolutions were also not limited to the North Atlantic setting.

In the same vein, in the past two decades historians have also revised the Iberian world's exclusion from the Age of Revolutions. The temporal distance between the eighteenth-century revolutions and those that took place in the nineteenth century obviously means that there are particularities in the Iberian experience, and these particularities point teachers and students to the multiplicity of experiences in the era.

To understand such multiplicity, it is relevant to remember that what sets the Iberian empires apart from the British and French empires is that they had withstood the crisis of colonialism unleashed in the mid-eighteenth century in North America and the Caribbean. Thus adaptation or reform was the most salient characteristic of the Spanish and Portuguese empires during the eighteenth century, until 1807. After the Napoleonic invasion, in the Portuguese and Spanish empires expediency led to experimentation based on older principles, practices, and categories.

For instance, as historian Kirsten Schultz has shown, across the Portuguese empire people perceived the Braganza family's relocation to Rio de Janeiro as a "revolution in favor of preserving the empire and the monarchy."[3] And preserve it they did. But the changes that followed the inversion of the metropole/colony relation between Portugal and Brazil were not only revolutionary in their degree of innovation, they also had irreversible consequences for Portugal's and Brazil's histories. In 1822 Brazil broke away from Portugal without an independence war, as a result of diplomatic negotiations, and formed an empire. In spite of this major difference from all other anticolonial processes in the Americas—the transition to independence without a war and the foundation of an independent Brazilian empire—we should include the Portuguese monarchy in the repertoire of revolutionary events and processes in the period. The history of the Portuguese Atlantic as a whole and the Brazilian empire in particular are important reminders for teachers and students that linear narratives (about anticolonialism as a necessary character of revolution, or revolution as leading exclusively to republican states) are deceiving when it comes to the Atlantic world in the nineteenth century.

Studying and understanding the Iberian revolutions encourages students to trace transatlantic lines of causation. Just as the Haitian Revolution was linked to the French Revolution, so the Iberian revolutions were also related to the long-term French revolutionary process. Napoleon Bonaparte and his expansionary project triggered a series of radical events in the Iberian empires. These significant connections suggest that it is not possible to argue that the Iberian empires were following the "path" of the earlier revolutions. It is neither useful nor necessary to speak in those terms, because there are important particularities of the nineteenth-century revolutions that need to be taken into account to explain process and change during the period. These upheavals therefore allow students to explore revolutions that diverge from the American or French models. They provide an excellent point of comparison.

The long-standing assumption about the derivative nature of Iberian modernity is fully questioned by acknowledging the plurality of revolutionary histories and its offspring, liberalism. Moreover, incorporating Latin America into the Age of Revolutions and understanding its place in such an Atlantic set of events does not mean ignoring crucial differences in the development of Hispanic liberalism.[4] For instance, a crucial particularity of the first Hispanic liberalism was that it was monarchical.

During the crisis of the Spanish monarchy and in the context of the Napoleonic invasion, a liberal, revolutionary government leading the resistance against France produced a constitution for the empire in 1812. The Cádiz charter created an imperial nation that recognized the authority of the monarch. The Cádiz Constitution also expanded citizenship to indigenous people while simultaneously maintaining many of their privileges. In my work, by focusing on royalism (or monarchism) during the independence wars, I have shown how the reconstruction of local histories in regions that continued to be tied to the Spanish constitutional monarchy enriches our understanding of the impact of liberalism and its practice among nonelites. Indigenous people became central to the defense of the Spanish Crown in regions where the Cádiz Constitution was implemented and adapted the premises of the liberal transformations. Thus, the particularity of these early liberal/constitutional experiments can be appreciated by looking specifically at the ways in which indigenous people (or, in other cases, Afro-Latin Americans) interpreted liberalism to suit their interests.[5]

When?

A map of the dates of the independence declarations across Latin America shows many different dates. Yet by fixing independence in time, these do not indicate the extent to which independence is a contentious theme in Latin America. The dates rather make it seem like independence is an immovable fact. But like in the United States or other postcolonial countries, the story of the emergence of any and all nations in Latin America embodies the challenges, promises, and silences of the region's political history. The Latin American revolutions therefore provide a rich opportunity for teachers to discuss the interpretive problems of periodization and how the chronological choices that are made can alter perspectives on the struggles for independence.

A noteworthy event that illustrates the contentiousness of periodizing Latin American independence is the Túpac Amaru rebellion of the early 1780s in the viceroyalty of Peru. Indigenous people from the highlands of Peru and Upper Peru (today Bolivia), along with *mestizos* and Creoles in rural and urban areas mobilized in the largest and longest uprising to take place in the Spanish Empire before the independence wars. This massive event shook the foundations of Spanish power in the Andes and has been the object of significant historiographical attention. In spite of the anticolonial tones of the movement, however, it has been excluded from the narrative of Peruvian independence and from the narrative of the Age of Revolutions more broadly.[6] In a stark contrast with the narratives about indigenous rebellion in Peru in 1780s, when historians speak about "independence" proper they tend to identify the process with the decolonization of Spanish and Portuguese America resulting from the anticolonial movement led by European-descended people.

As I mentioned, in the past two decades or so historians have revised the assumption that the Age of Revolutions was exclusively linked to European peoples, ideas, and institutions and have expanded the revolutionary period to include the Haitian Revolution. The debate that this revision prompted exposed the assumptions behind Haiti's exclusion, such as the silencing of Africans' political imagination. It also pointed to the centrality of slavery and race for the Age of Revolutions, revealing the period's limits and contradictions.

Perhaps Haiti's inclusion has been facilitated by its connections to France's own revolution. Indeed, as Laurent Dubois's work has shown, Enlightenment ideas played a central role in and were produced by the Haitian revolutionary dynamics.[7] In contrast, the ideas underlying the Túpac Amaru rebellion, which were in their own measure quite radical, are seen as foreign to the Age of Revolutions because of their Andean substance.[8] To some historians this exclusion is evidence of the

Eurocentric bias of the historiography: it overlooks the rebellion's significance as an Atlantic event and even ignores the fact that it actually falls squarely within the (most conservative) eighteenth-century timeframe.[9] The rebellion provides teachers with an example of the multiracial dimension of the Age of Revolutions.

Unearthing the links of Latin American independence to the Hispanic revolutionary process unleashed by the Napoleonic invasion foregrounds other equally relevant aspects of periodization. Whereas earlier interpretations of the process that produced national histories narrowly focused on the military juncture of the independence wars (1810–1820s), today historians are more concerned with understanding the connections between the monarchical crisis and the rise of liberal government in the Spanish Empire. This has led to reconsidering the specific nature of the early nineteenth-century transformations from a political perspective and to an interest in the contingencies of the earlier phase of the conflict (1808 to 1815) adding to our understanding of the better known latter years when independence was finally achieved (the 1820s).

These first years of what has generally been called the independence wars were actually much less about an open military confrontation than they were about the adaptation of all peoples and jurisdictions in Spanish America to the crisis of monarchical rule after the abduction of Fernando VII. In other words, the first independence experiments in most Spanish American cities or municipalities were not preordained. The focus in contemporary history—as it can be in the classroom—is on the path toward such declarations of independence; the most interesting aspects of such a process comes into relief when we put these early years in the context of imperial crisis and the interimperial conflicts. It was, after all, the juncture for the rise of constitutional government in the Hispanic world, which framed all Spanish American experiments for local rule.

Why?

Why great historical events occur, of course, is one of the central questions that teachers will always ask their students. Here again, the Latin American revolutions offer ample opportunity for teachers to use this question to introduce students to historical debate. For the nationalist and Marxist narratives the roots of the Spanish

American independence movements were in the late colonial years, during the period of Bourbon rule. The Bourbon dynasty came to power in Spain in 1700 and, after outlasting the crisis in succession for the Spanish throne, the eighteenth was a century of reform. Based on the narratives written in the nineteenth century by the Creole pro-independence leaders, historians described the Bourbon period as one that had laid down the bases for the crisis of Spain's rule in the Americas. Historians thought the reforms were deeply destabilizing to the fabric of colonial society; especially in the upper echelons of society, among the Creoles, they cemented a local identity that was key for the growth of nationalist and independence movements in the nineteenth century.

That the reforms were crucial in destabilizing aspects of Spanish rule is not in question. During the eighteenth century, multiple sectors of society manifested discontent, as was the case of the Túpac Amaru rebellion in Peru. The reforms were not exclusively disruptive processes, and it is possible to simultaneously view their limits in actually transforming government and society in Spanish America as much as to map out important ways sectors of Spanish American society actively engaged the reformist thrust. For example, two viceroyalties that were created during the eighteenth century, New Granada and Rio de la Plata, turned into nations after the independence wars. In other words, the reforms shaped long-lasting jurisdictions in Spanish America.

Thus a problem with the narrative that sees Bourbon rule as a radical break is that it produces a teleology of independence—it makes independence seem inevitable since the eighteenth century. In other words, that account seeks for the nationalist spirit or identity in the eighteenth century to give ideological and social body to the anticolonial process that took place in the early decades of the nineteenth century. It is, from the perspective of theories of nationalism, a romantic view of nation-state building, arguing that nations emerge on the basis of a social and cultural ground that precedes them. In this respect, therefore, nationalist interpretations provide students with perspectives that are familiar to historians of revolution and nation-building in many parts of the world. Students can be asked why these views have proved to be so compelling and enduring.

The process of nation formation looks very different from a constructivist perspective that does not assume the preexistence of a national spirit or identity. As we saw in the previous section, there are a variety of dates that could potentially mark the beginning of the independence wars across Latin America because the period was, in fact, all but a simple, linear process.

This constructivist approach also understands nation formation as a trial. In this view the conflicts, contradictions, and overlaps in visions implicit to the independence process are absolutely relevant and very interesting. To fully appreciate the transformations that took place in these years, the challenge in understanding this period is to avoid presupposing the results of independence. We should make the effort to position ourselves not looking back from now into the turn of the nineteenth century but looking forward from the 1800s. What were people's choices and expectations for stability and change? Jeremy Adelman has written about the years from 1808 up to the 1820s, when the Iberian world entered a process of redefinition of imperial sovereignty, the same time when national identities began to take shape at the imperial level and across Latin America. Adelman finely shows that what is crucial is to see it as an open-ended process.[10]

Given that in the nationalist histories Creole independence heroes fought to overcome Spanish colonialism, the narratives produced in the nineteenth century strongly rejected Spain. Now a crucial shift in our historiographic perspective challenges the traditional interpretation that portrayed independence as a struggle between Spanish America and Spain. It grapples with the connection between the Spanish American experiments with local rule and the liberal experiments in the Iberian Peninsula and embraces the complexity or "gray areas" that were characteristic of the conflict. For instance, the factions that emerged and evolved between insurgents and royalists were not simply grounded in national (or proto-national), ethnic, or racial identities. Recognizing such views may encourage students to think beyond a simple struggle between "progress" and "reaction" or even "good" and "bad" sides.

Especially in the two years between 1808 and 1810, people in Spanish America were concerned about the interimperial conflict with France, which represented serious risks of falling under the control of the French, who had ambitions to take over Spain's American territories. During these early years, Spanish Americans of all classes declared their loyalty to the abducted king, Fernando VII. Officially, even the *juntas* that were created in all cities across the Indies proclaimed to be seeking to protect the territory from the French. Over time, these experiments with local rule did evolve toward claims for independence, particularly after conflicts arose with the Spanish Junta Suprema, which claimed to be ruling in the name of the monarch. However, it is fundamental to take into account the unevenness of this process and recognize the bottom line that independence was not necessarily desired at the outset. People in Spanish America were willing to negotiate their position within the new imperial nation that emerged during these years.

The contingencies that are revealed from this perspective make clear that we must focus on fundamentally local and specific processes and practices that explain the turn toward independence. Structural interpretations are less accurate because they are based on broad generalizations and the assumption of necessity that overlooks historical dynamics of negotiation today considered crucial for the revolutionary political process.

Who?

We finally turn to the question about who the subjects of this history are, and here teachers can take their students far beyond the usual heroes to look at the rich texture of cultures and peoples of the populations of the Latin American world. Textbook histories have always been centered on men such as Bolívar, Hidalgo, San Martín, and other "independence heroes." These are the visible military leaders who led the independence campaigns and later became statesmen. Histories with such a thin cast of characters implicitly assume that the popular classes were disengaged from the revolutionary processes and ideas that underlay them. That story is being rewritten today by historians exploring the indigenous and African participation in the independence process. Going beyond the narrative that construes Latin American nations as exclusively grounded on European influences, these studies offer evidence of rich popular participation in shaping the politics of nation building.

Much of the work that has been produced in recent years has recovered the participation of the lower classes in the independence wars. Peter Blanchard's work for Spanish South America is exemplary in that respect and an excellent place to engage students with the current research on this important theme. Blanchard's remarkable research proves the significance of enslaved and free people of African descent for the military process of independence. From Venezuela to Rio de la Plata (present-day Argentina and Uruguay), the contending armies of insurgents and royalists drew on the enslaved population. This had significant effects on the political process across the region as well.

In this regard, the wars of independence in Latin America neatly illustrate the critical connections between anticolonialism and antislavery that were evident in the Haitian Revolution and the tensions that slavery and race relations represented in the process of republican state formation, such as those that characterized the United States. Overall, the mobilization of people of African descent during the wars brought these themes into the heart of the discursive and legal priorities of the period.

Indigenous people were central to the military and political dynamics during the independence wars, as the work of scholars such as Peter Guardino (for Mexico) and Maria Luisa Soux (for Bolivia) illustrates.[11] The nationalist and Marxist views shared a long-standing belief that indigenous people were not articulated ideologically with the larger nineteenth-century processes of revolution and modernization. Current research has undone that perception by uncovering evidence of the participation of indigenous people in the legal and political battles that accompanied the military struggle for independence.

An excellent example of the relevance of the Indian populations in South America for the political process under way since the beginning of the monarchical crisis was the expedition led by Juan José Castelli going from Buenos Aires to Potosí. Castelli circulated a speech on February 13, 1810, in Spanish, Quechua, Aymara, and Guarani languages, intended to reach and mobilize Indian communities in favor of the Buenos Aires project and against the viceroy of Peru Fernando de Abascal. Later in Cádiz legislators took measures to expand citizenship to indigenous peoples. Incorporating these and other similar processes into the history of the period has important consequences, because it suggests that indigenous people were political players, they were openly considered as such, and they were informed about the opportunities to negotiate in the changing circumstances according to their interests.[12]

The case of the viceroyalty of New Granada has received attention in the work of scholars like Marixa Lasso (whose research is on the Caribbean city of Cartagena), Steinar Saether (in a study about the Caribbean city of Santa Marta), and myself (I have written about the southwestern region of Popayán).[13] All three cases point to the engagement of nonelites in the politics of citizenship during this period. These studies also provide interesting elements for rethinking the political history of Latin America in the independence wars from diverse social perspectives.

Lasso rewrites Cartagena independence history by proving that the participation of the lower classes was crucial and that given the racial composition of the lower class, made up by a majority of *pardos* or free blacks, racial equality became central to the independence cause and the rhetoric that accompanied it. Lasso also frames the local political process between 1810 and 1815 in the context of the promulgation of the Constitution of Cádiz. This illustrates why and how the Cartagena elites and their pardo allies were maneuvering within a wider imperial process of the emergence of liberalism and citizenship in the Spanish world.

On the other hand, Saether and I have looked at the legal and political strategies of Indians and people of African descent in the two royalist strongholds in New Granada: Santa Marta and Popayán. In these regions indigenous peoples and free and enslaved people of African descent were crucial to the military defense of Spanish rule. This was not simply a case of clientelism or false consciousness; these people negotiated with royalist elites as much as with the discourse of royalism—which was, moreover, changing rapidly during these years—and Sather and I have uncovered the multiplicity of positions that indigenous people and people of African descent took to defend their interests during this period. Students can be asked to engage with the influence of royalism with profit, exploring how it fits within revolutionary struggles and perhaps making comparisons with other places where such loyalties played an important role, like Haiti.

As my work and Saether's has shown, viewing royalism historically demonstrates that it was first of all dynamic and that it varied in its interpretation across class lines. In other words, royalism in this period was not simply the opposite of the insurgency, as it is portrayed in the dichotomist view of the process as a confrontation between modernity and tradition or between forward-looking and backward politics. Royalism was also the product of dynamic negotiation, it was not antagonistic with liberalism, and there were significant commonalities between the language, symbols, and processes underlying both the royalist and the insurgent camps. These are elements that have come to the surface in scholarship on the revolutionary age elsewhere, notably the Haitian Revolution (as discussed in the chapters by Julia Gaffield and Chris

Hodson in this volume), which likewise stress the complexity of the links between race and politics and the dynamism in political alliances across class lines. In this regard, the Latin American independence processes are crucial cases for exploring and understanding the dynamics whereby discourses and institutions in the hemisphere were negotiated in the emergence of democratic politics.[14]

Conclusion

Precisely because it is problematic to generalize regarding the political process unleashed in the nineteenth century across Latin America (that is, Brazil and Spanish America), the region's inclusion in the Age of Revolutions period and paradigm opens up the possibilities for a broader understanding of revolution in the eighteenth- and nineteenth-century Atlantic world. Inextricably linked to the previous American, French, and Haitian revolutions, the Latin American revolutions were embedded in the particular social and legal Iberian realities. For this reason alone, the Latin American struggles provide rich material for teaching revolutions. Moreover, to understand and measure the political changes across Latin America following 1808, it is crucial to keep in mind that empire is a category that deserves to be at the center of the analysis. Rather than begin with assumptions about national identity (the end results), students can be encouraged to consider that both in the Spanish American and Brazilian/Portuguese cases, imperial reconstitution was foundational to the revolutionary processes on both sides of the Atlantic, so a useful starting point for students is the crisis of monarchical rule.

When seen not as an exception but as illustrative of nineteenth-century political transformations, the Portuguese/Brazilian case suggests that revolution does not have to be necessarily defined as anti-monarchical or to imply military mobilization. It provides an invitation to rethink the revolutionary age through the lens of empire and its reinvention in the eighteenth- and nineteenth-century Atlantic world.[15]

How should we understand citizenship in this context? This is another question that will immerse students into the historical context. To begin with, it is important to recall that in the Spanish empire, for example, the category of vassal—through which people engaged both the Crown and their local communities—was the foundation for the emergence of citizenship in the Spanish world. We are also talking about political revolutions in which sovereignty was redefined not only as a result of political debates or ideas but, most important, through the massive engagement of the population with legal and military processes under way. Citizenship was born out of such engagements.

To a large extent, because of the links between the social group that the "heroes" of independence represented (the Spanish descendants or whites) and the foundational narrative of nation building (that is, the creation of a national myth based on Eurocentric values), historians of independence tended to assume that the lower classes, most of which were people of indigenous and African descent, had been marginal to the independence process. Yet this picture is being radically revised.

Of course, it is important to discuss the nuances that need to be accounted for in any treatment of this particular theme. The nationalist and Marxist interpretations had referred to the lower classes but in a starkly different way, assuming that these social groups that were culturally marginal from European influences were ignorant and incapable of understanding the enlightened principles of the independence period. What students can be encouraged to see today is that such an elitist discourse is far from reality, because from a political perspective neither Indians nor people of African descent (free or enslaved) were outside of the networks of news or in practice irrelevant to the rearrangement of power relations at the base of the independence wars.

NOTES

1. See, for example, Heraclio Bonilla and Karen Spalding, *La independencia en el Perú* (Lima: Instituto de Estudios Peruanos, 1981); John Lynch, *The Spanish American Revolutions, 1808–1826* (1973; New York: Norton, 1986).

2. R. R. Palmer, *The Age of Democratic Revolution: A Political History of Europe and America, 1760–1800*, 2 vols. (Princeton, NJ: Princeton University Press, 1959–64).

3. This decision was consistent with some debates in the Portuguese empire during the eighteenth century exploring means to take better advantage of the Brazilian territory. See Kirsten Schultz, *Tropical Versailles: Empire, Monarchy, and the Portuguese Royal Court in Rio de Janeiro, 1808–1821* (New York: Routledge, 2001), chapter 1.

4. Gabriel Paquette, "Introduction: Liberalism in the Early Nineteenth-century Iberian World," *History of European Ideas* 41, no. 2 (2015): 153–65.

5. José María Portillo, *Crisis atlántica: Autonomía e independencia en la crisis de la monarquía hispana* (Madrid: Marcial Pons, 2006); Marcela Echeverri,

"Race, Citizenship, and the Cádiz Constitution in Popayán (New Granada)," in *The Cádiz Constitution of 1812 and Its Impact in the Atlantic World*, ed. Scott Eastman and Natalia Sobrevilla Perea (Tuscaloosa: University of Alabama Press, 2015).

6. See Sergio Serulnikov, *Revolution in the Andes: The Age of Túpac Amaru* (Durham, NC: Duke University Press, 2013); Charles Walker, *The Tupac Amaru Rebellion* (Cambridge, MA: Harvard University Press, 2014).

7. Laurent Dubois, "An Enslaved Enlightenment: Rethinking the Intellectual History of the French Atlantic," *Social History* 31 no. 1 (2006): 1–14.

8. The Andean insurgents aspired to self-government and the subversion of the ethnic logic of colonial rule, which justified the domination of indigenous people.

9. Sinclair Thomson, "Sovereignty Disavowed: The Tupac Amaru Revolution in the Atlantic World," paper presented at the Future of History conference, University of Pittsburgh, May 2014; Serulnikov, *Revolution in the Andes*; Walker, *The Tupac Amaru Rebellion*.

10. Jeremy Adelman, "Iberian Passages: Continuity and Change in the South Atlantic," in *The Age of Revolutions in Global Context, c. 1760–1840*, ed. David Armitage and Sanjay Subrahmanyam (New York: Palgrave Macmillan, 2010), 70.

11. Peter Guardino, *Peasants, Politics, and the Formation of Mexico's National State: Guerrero, 1800–1857* (Stanford, CA: Stanford University Press, 1996); Maria Luisa Soux, *El complejo proceso hacia la independencia de Charcas (1808–1826): Guerra, ciudadanía, conflictos locales y participación indígena en Oruro* (La Paz: Instituto Francés de Estudios Andinos, 2010).

12. Soux, *El complejo proceso hacia la independencia de Charcas*, 126. Following the publication of the Cádiz Constitution in 1812, the Cortes emitted a proclamation in Quechua that was sent to Peru to make it circulate among indigenous people in 1813.

13. Marixa Lasso, *Myths of Harmony: Race and Republicanism during the Age of Revolution, Colombia 1795–1831* (Pittsburgh: University of Pittsburgh Press, 2007); Marcela Echeverri, "Popular Royalists, Empire, and Politics in Southwestern New Granada, 1809–1819," *Hispanic American Historical Review* 91, no. 2 (2011): 237–69; Steinar Saether, "Independence and the Redefinition of Indianness around Santa Marta, Colombia, 1750–1850," *Journal of Latin American Studies* 37 (2005): 55–80.

14. Hilda Sábato, "On Political Citizenship in Nineteenth Century Latin America," *History Cooperative* 106, no. 4 (2001): 1290–315; James Sanders, *The Vanguard of Modernity: Creating Modernity, Nation, and Democracy in Nineteenth-Century Latin America* (Durham, NC: Duke University Press, 2014). On loyalism in the French and American revolutions, see Maya Jasanoff, "The Other Side of Revolution: Loyalists in the British Empire," *William and Mary Quarterly* 65, no. 2 (2008): 205–32.

15. Gabriel Paquette, *Imperial Portugal in the Age of Atlantic Revolutions: The Luso-Brazilian World, c. 1770–1850* (Cambridge: Cambridge University Press, 2013).

KEY RESOURCES

Primary Sources

Chambers, Sarah, and John Charles Chasteen, eds. *Latin American Independence: An Anthology of Sources.* Indianapolis: Hackett, 2010.

Peabody, Sue, and Keila Grinberg. *Slavery, Freedom and the Law in the Atlantic World* Boston: Bedford/St. Martins, 2007.

Secondary Sources

Adelman, Jeremy. "Iberian Passages: Continuity and Change in the South Atlantic." In *The Age of Revolutions in Global Context, c. 1760–1840,* edited by David Armitage and Sanjay Subrahmanyam, 59–82. New York: Palgrave Macmillan, 2010.

Andrews, George Reid. *Afro-Latin America, 1800–2000.* Oxford: Oxford University Press, 2004.

Blanchard, Peter. "Slave Soldiers of Spanish South America: From Independence to Abolition." In *Arming Slaves: From Classical Times to the Modern Age,* edited by Christopher Leslie Brown and Philip Morgan, 255–73. New Haven, CT: Yale University Press, 2006.

Caplan, Karen. "The Legal Revolution in Town Politics: Oaxaca and Yucatán, 1812–1825." *Hispanic American Historical Review* 83, no. 2 (2003): 255–93.

Dubois, Laurent. "An Enslaved Enlightenment: Rethinking the Intellectual History of the French Atlantic." *Social History* 31, no. 1 (2006): 1–14.

Echeverri, Marcela. *Indian and Slave Royalists in the Age of Revolution: Reform, Revolution, and Royalism in the Northern Andes, 1780–1825.* Cambridge: Cambridge University Press, 2016.

———. "Popular Royalists, Empire, and Politics in Southwestern New Granada, 1809–1819." *Hispanic American Historical Review* 91, no. 2 (2011): 237–69.

Geggus, David. "Slavery, War, and Revolution in the Greater Caribbean." In *A Turbulent Time: The French Revolution and the Greater Caribbean,* edited by David B. Gaspar and David P. Geggus, 1–50. Bloomington: Indiana University Press, 2009.

Landers, Jane. *Atlantic Creoles in the Age of Revolutions.* Cambridge, MA: Harvard University Press, 2011.

Larson, Brooke. *Trials of Nation Making: Liberalism, Race, and Ethnicity in the Andes, 1810–1910.* Cambridge: Cambridge University Press, 2004.

Lasso, Marixa. "Revisiting Independence Day: Afro-Colombian Politics and Creole Patriot Narratives, Cartagena, 1809–1815." In *After Spanish Rule:*

Postcolonial Predicaments of the Americas, edited by Mark Thurner and Andrés Guerrero, 223–47. Durham, NC: Duke University Press, 2003.

Paquette, Gabriel. *Imperial Portugal in the Age of Atlantic Revolutions: The Luso-Brazilian World, c. 1770–1850*. Cambridge: Cambridge University Press, 2013.

Racine, Karen. *Francisco de Miranda: A Transatlantic Life in the Age of Revolution*. Wilmington, DE: Scholarly Resources, 2003.

Sábato, Hilda. "On Political Citizenship in Nineteenth Century Latin America." *History Cooperative* 106, no. 4 (2001): 1290–315.

Saether, Steinar. "Independence and the Redefinition of Indianness around Santa Marta, Colombia, 1750–1850." *Journal of Latin American Studies* 37 (2005): 55–80.

Sanders, James. *The Vanguard of Modernity: Creating Modernity, Nation, and Democracy in Nineteenth-Century Latin America*. Durham, NC: Duke University Press, 2014.

Schmidt-Nowara, Christopher. *Slavery, Freedom, and Abolition in Latin America and the Atlantic World*. Albuquerque: University of New Mexico Press, 2011.

Schultz, Kirsten. *Tropical Versailles: Empire, Monarchy, and the Portuguese Royal Court in Rio de Janeiro, 1808–1821*. New York: Routledge, 2001.

Serulnikov, Sergio. *Revolution in the Andes: The Age of Túpac Amaru*. Durham, NC: Duke University Press, 2013.

The Dutch Revolution(s)

ANNIE JOURDAN

Teaching the Dutch Revolutions
(Suggestions for Teachers)

Each point treated in the following discussion of the Patriot and the Batavian revolutions can be discussed and compared with the great revolutions—French and American, for example. They are living proof of the specificity of each revolution and their particular priorities according to their past and present circumstances. Teachers can find in the Dutch revolutions important examples of how reform selectively elided into revolution and fertile ground for exploring the dilemmas that revolutionaries and their opponents faced in negotiating internal and external changes.

The Dutch experiences offer a rich source of comparison for students interested in seeking and discussing nuances among different models of revolutionary upheaval and constitution making. The debate about how a nation of separate provinces might be constructed resonates strongly when held up against the United States of America, for instance, and this can lead to productive discussions about the balances of central and federal power (and the geopolitical and cultural distinctions that influenced them) in either polity. Held up against the ferment of revolutionary France, the Dutch exiles' experiences and the various constitutional drafting processes can bring students to a deeper appreciation of how lawmaking and nation building did not take place in intellectual or geographic isolation but were shaped by the pressures and circumstances of the time. By going beyond the old staples of the American and French revolutions, students can better discern what those events heralded and their limitations and specificities.

The likely unfamiliarity of the Dutch Revolution to international students arguably offers them a more open historical environment—one in which they can address themes or questions with confidence and imagination and one whose questions remain important to politically engaged citizens in the twenty-first century. For example, how do we create stability in times of war and upheaval, or abide by models of human rights in the face of violence? How much more or less democratic is our own relationship with our societies and politics? What are the eighteenth-century revolutions missing in our modern eyes? Above all, teachers can use the material to help explain that models of revolutions differ, and none is a simple copy, since all depend on national histories and legacies.

Teaching the Dutch Revolution is not easy. To be accurate, the historian has to go back to the 1780s, when what has been recently called the "Patriot revolution" took place. This revolution broke out as a consequence of the Dutch naval defeat against the British during the Fourth Anglo-Dutch War (1780–1784) that coincided with and was provoked by the American Revolution. During the following years, most of the Dutch provinces implemented political reforms to throw off the yoke of the stadholder, William V, prince of Orange, who monopolized political power and appointed his own candidates to official functions, such as in the States Generals. William V did worse. For years, he had neglected the national navy for the benefit of the land army, and by doing so, he weakened Dutch trade and supremacy on sea in favor of Britain. The naval defeat of 1781 was proof of his treason, at least in the Patriots' eyes. Six years long, with a climax in 1784–1787, the Patriot revolution experienced burghers' militias, provincial or municipal constitutions—called "regulations" in Dutch—and a very active patriotic press. But in the fall 1787, Prussia invaded the United Provinces and put the stadholder back in power. Some 25,000 patriots took the road to exile. Four thousand found refuge in France; the others set out for the Austrian Netherlands or the German states. Eight years later, they came back home with the French army. An alliance treaty was signed between France and Holland in May 1795, which sanctioned Dutch independence and alliance with revolutionary France. It was the dawn of a new era: that of the Batavian revolution, which enforced a republic bearing the same name (1798–1806).

Another problem arises when one has to choose which approach is the best to study revolutions. One can analyze their political, economic, social, religious, or cultural ideas, or one can concentrate on the means and the ends of their protagonists or on the consequences for the country and for the world. But one can also examine the practices; the discourses, true or rhetorical; the contexts and contingency. Some historians and teachers favor a top-down perspective; others prefer a bottom-up one. The same is true when it concerns local or peripheral points of view or a central one—from the center or a metropolis. Historians and teachers may choose to favor legal and juridical aspects or military and police ones. Finally, there are some who prefer biographical elements and find it interesting to focus on great actors, their relations, and emotions. Recently a new approach—one worth testing in the classroom—has tried to shed new light on exchanges and interactions between peoples in revolution: the American Revolution, the Republic of Geneva, the United Provinces, and the Belgian (or Brabant) Revolution explored in Judge's chapter in this volume. However, it is virtually impossible to teach, depict, and analyze a revolution in all these aspects, because a real revolution dramatically disrupts the whole of society.

When a small country is concerned, things get even more complicated. Strangely enough, historians and many teachers do not take revolutions in small nations seriously. How could a Lilliputian republic such as Geneva or Holland have influence over great European countries or over the Western world? French philosopher Georges Gusdorf called this kind of revolution "a storm in a teacup."[1] Fortunately, US historians Robert Palmer and Wayne Te Brake disagreed with this contention and devoted great attention to the Dutch revolutions of the 1780s and of the 1790s. They believed that little is as representative as big. The more so, since eighteenth-century peoples were used to traveling and exchanging ideas and plans. This is an important feature of these revolutions: the people's skills in communicating with their immediate precursors and their contributions to the events that followed. Key figures of the French Revolution, for instance, spent a lot of time with foreign patriots who were exiled in Paris long before the fall of the Bastille. They talked about reforms to implement in France or in their home countries. Lafayette, for instance, had an engraved copy of the American Declaration of Independence displayed in the entry hall of his house. Beside it was an empty frame, "waiting for the declaration of the Rights of France."[2] Consequently, he was concocting his own draft some months before July 1789 and he discussed it with Jefferson—who sent Lafayette's draft to James Madison. In spring 1788, another great French patriot and one of the most impressive revolutionary speakers, Mirabeau had already published a modern bill of rights in his book *To the Batavians on the Stadholderate*, while in his *Analyses des Papiers Anglais* he gave a translation of some articles of a declaration written in 1785 by the militias of Leiden. Discussions between French, American, Dutch, and Swiss patriots were frequent and thus inspired the Parisian elites who became preeminent after 1789. This is not to say that the French dreamed of a revolution, but they certainly dreamed of reforms.

On the European continent, the United Provinces were also very peculiar. This country had already carried out a revolution in the sixteenth century. To be sure, historians have long called this revolution "the Revolt." The issue of this war against Spain (1566–1581) had been the independence of the seven northern provinces of the Netherlands and the formation of a republican federation (Treaty of Utrecht from 1579). In a book chapter, Dutch historian Marjolein 't Hart called it "a national revolution,"[3] because in this dangerous context, a strong coalition had unified provinces and nobility against the Spanish. Worth noting is that this Dutch revolt was not a religious war. It had brought about new political principles and the creation of a federal state based on representation, liberty, virtue, and republicanism. On the European continent, Holland or the United Provinces were an exception because of their freedom of thought and their representative regime. Admittedly, the new republic was not so democratic as some Swiss cantons, but in the beginning, Dutch elites who were members of the burgher militias had the right to elect their representatives and regents. Consequently, like Switzerland, the Republic of the United Provinces prided itself on being a free and tolerant nation. It indeed became a place of refuge for Spanish Jews and French Protestants during the sixteenth and the seventeenth centuries. It remained a model for North America, at least until 1787, when the new Republic of the United States rejected a political system that would be harmful to the strengthening of the central government which the Federalists tried to enforce. Students and teachers can find it a useful exercise to compare these political systems.

During the eighteenth century, the prince of Orange had succeeded in gaining the right to hereditary rule for his dynasty. From 1747 on, when the French army invaded some Dutch provinces, the stadholder increased his power. Instead of elections, there were more and more personal appointments. Burgher militias decreased. An army of hired soldiers replaced them. But there was more. Dutch regents and merchants turned out to have other interests than the prince, who favored the land army for fear of France, whereas the commercial elites wanted the Dutch navy to be protected against British supremacy on the seas. This quarrel divided the federation, too: land provinces did not see why they should have to pay for the navy, while the sea provinces showed no interest in keeping a land army. After the Fourth Anglo-Dutch War, which resulted in a shameful defeat, disturbances broke out and pointed clearly to the prince's guilt. William V would have neglected the Dutch navy because he was a friend of Britain. This was also the interpretation of the patriots' leader, Johan Derk van der Capellen tot den Pol, who wrote a pamphlet in 1781 called "To the People of the Netherlands," where he affirmed that the stadholder had betrayed the fatherland and violated popular sovereignty and the natural rights of man.[4] He recalled that "All men are born free," before concluding that "God had created them to pursue Happiness." Here can clearly be heard the American motto. It is not so strange when one is aware that Van der Capellen knew John Adams, who was in Holland at that time to secure funding for the American war effort. Consequently, the Dutch patriot must also have known the bill of rights of Massachusetts, where Adams came from. He certainly was familiar with the Declaration of Independence, which had been published in the *Gazette de Leyde* as early as August 1776.

The Patriot Revolution
(1781–1787)

Unjustly ignored or unknown by most international historians, the Patriot revolution is nevertheless a real political revolution, with citizens' militias and new representatives who were elected to replace the regents appointed by William V. But to be elected, they had to be members of a militia. They also had to be Dutch and Protestant. At that time, and despite the American example, which was well known by the elite, most of the towns that claimed to be sovereign did not envision proclaiming a bill of human rights. Only three of them did. The Deventer's bill of 1786—a town in the east of the country where Van der Capellen was living—looks more American than all other drafts produced in the country. It was not fortuitous because, as mentioned, Van der Capellen had good contacts with John Adams, US ambassador in the United Provinces. Furthermore, he had translated several dissidents' writings published in Britain, and he was well informed about what was going on in the United States of America.

Here again, the comparison between the American and Dutch cases can prove particularly stimulating for students. The Patriot revolution appears to be timid, when compared with the American precedent: above all where universal rights of man and representative democracy are concerned. It is true that like in America town meetings and militias were created, but nobody thought of suppressing corporations and privileges of the dominating church, or even those of towns and provinces. Conversely, towns and provinces prided themselves on restoring their power, which the stadholder had destroyed. Nobody talked of reforming the legal and criminal system or making it more equitable and humane. People were still tortured in prison, corporal punishment still existed, and inequality between rich and poor continued. But some provinces imagined creating a committee of citizens who would control public finance and expenditure and check officials' behavior, a kind of censors as antiquity had known. Nonetheless, the Patriot revolution turned out to be a "burgher" one, directed and organized by the elite— judicial, commercial, and financial. What they were claiming was an actual representation—not a virtual one. The same claim can be heard at the beginning of the American Revolution, with its credo "No taxation without representation." Never was the Utrecht Treaty of 1579 attacked. Quite the contrary: the patriots demanded that it be restored in its original form. It is why Étienne Clavière, a Genevan refugee in France, who became minister of French Finances during the Girondins' ministry, condemned the Patriot revolution as too elitist to succeed. He concluded that the Dutch patriots could not win because they did not call the people into action. That is not to say that the Patriot revolution brought nothing. Over four years, political discussions and writings were arguing about what a real representation had to be and what a popular government by representation really meant. By doing so, a number of patriots discovered new principles and envisaged putting them into practice. As Hannah Arendt contended, reform talks may lead to the unexpected.[5]

The Dutch Patriots and the French Revolution

Over the following years, the exiled Dutch patriots experimented with the 1789 revolution. Not only did they participate in French discussions and popular clubs, they tried time and again to export the revolution to their own country, with the help of the French. This ambition motivated their revolutionary and constitutional drafts. It explains why most of them resembled the French ones. Two months after the first French constitution was proclaimed in September 1791, an influential patriot and professor of law, Johan Valckenaer, published a draft grounded on national unity—an innovation in a Dutch draft— and on a constitutional monarchy, an inconceivable idea for Holland. Dutch reactions from home are illustrative as far as the second point is concerned. They rejected that idea. But about unity, the reactions were less negative. Nicolas van Staphorst, an influential banker and patriot still in the Netherlands, did not disapprove of this great change. Indeed, he argued that the 1579 constitution had to be completely destroyed and replaced by a new republican regime. In November 1791, some Dutch patriots were seriously thinking of a united country based on human rights and a broad franchise. Yet the drafts did not propose to modify the status of the reformed Church or grant civil rights to the Jewish nation—as the French assembly did in September 1791. All these plans suggest that beside some kinship with France, there were also fundamental differences; students can immerse themselves in these to explore the nuances in the Age of Revolutions.

Over the ensuing years, Dutch drafts were still inspired by the French ones. When the Bourbon monarchy was abolished, Valckenaer and his friends no longer spoke of a constitutional monarchy but of a united and centralized republic. Provinces would be abolished and replaced by departments. But this Dutch republic had to be nationalized, that is, adapted to the Dutch nation: a colonial empire and a commercial country. Therefore, the new draft had articles about the colonies and the navy, and it was highly concerned with the prosperity and the commerce of the republic. This November 1792 draft indeed was more a plan of government, including positive laws and civil rights, than an exposition of universal principles. The patriots intended to abolish all corporations and companies and dismiss foreign hired troops, before starting anew. This was innovative in the Dutch context.

A new draft from February 1793, published one week after Condorcet's draft had been debated in the French convention, betrayed a further shift in the patriots' political thought: it proclaimed the "eternal principles of human rights," equality of religions, and a popular government by representation with a one-house legislature. This draft seemed to be more consonant with French conceptions. Innovative was the very fact that the executive would have the right to examine the laws before promulgating them. Not only is this draft further evidence that the Dutch nurtured their own views, it also shows how opportunistic the patriots were or had to be in the hope France would help them revolutionize their country. To be sure, the Dutch desired both a Dutch constitution and a text that would please the French government. This was an uneasy task to fulfill and makes it difficult for a historian to discover their true aims.

Be that as it may, their stay in France did teach some influential patriots (who were later elected in the first Dutch National Assembly) many things. In this sense only, the French Revolution was a "high school in revolution." First, it taught them that revolutions often devoured their own children and that some achievements had to be avoided if the Dutch wanted to be spared certain French tragedies. Second, they absorbed the idea that national unity was necessary to strengthen state power and stimulate national prosperity. Another new insight inspired by the French Revolution and deriving from national unity was that a deputy had to represent the whole people and not corporate interests. That in turn condemned the corporate bodies in the long run, while national unity entailed the end of provincial sovereignty. The Dutch experience of the French Revolution helps students grasp the complexities and challenges in connecting "universal" ideals with local circumstances and traditions.

The Batavian Revolution

In winter 1794–1795, General Pichegru won decisive victories in the north of France. In the meantime, the counterrevolutionary coalition was falling apart. Prussia and Austria worried about their setbacks and chose to protect their own territories instead of fighting for unthankful allies—such as the Dutch, who were complaining about their brutality. The closer the French army got, the more the Dutch

"Vive les deux Républiques Unies," an allegorical decoration for the Alliance celebration (June 19, 1795), planned for the Beurs Straat in Amsterdam. (detail of print from A. Verkerk [1795]; author's private collection)

inhabitants took sides against the allies. British acts of violence and destruction above all led them to join the patriots' party.[6] Thanks to the French success, this party increased and was able to help the Batavian-French army. In December 1794, Pichegru was asked by Paris to go on and eventually invade Holland. The weather was favorable, too. Rivers were frozen. All over the country, the people were singing the Marseillaise or the Carmagnole. In a few weeks, the campaign was over. On January 17, the French were in Utrecht. On January 18, the stadholder fled to Britain with his family. On January 19, General Kraaijenhoff, a patriot in charge of military affairs, arrived in Amsterdam and convinced the commandant to resign immediately. Two days after the French invasion, the Batavian Revolution seemed complete. When Pichegru entered Amsterdam on January 20, the township had been regenerated. A liberty tree was decorating the Dam place and the inhabitants were wearing a tricolor cockade. The other provinces followed the impulse. The commissioners or representatives of the French Republic who were on the spot were presented with a fait accompli and decided to proclaim the independence of the Dutch republic and their accession to the reign of liberty. This means that the Dutch patriots had done their job and won their challenge. They were not a vanquished people but were France's revolutionary partners. What followed provides students with an excellent case study of the spiky relationships between France and the "sister republics" and a fascinating example of constitutional disputes during the process of revolutionary state-building, an example that students aware of the more familiar example of constitution-making in the United States will find very instructive.

The news was well received in Paris, but the French Republic demanded a high price, since the emancipation of the Dutch from the Orangist yoke took many sacrifices and cost a lot of money. National independence depended on their willingness to compensate these sacrifices. Four months of discussions were necessary before a compromise was reached and an alliance treaty signed—on May 16, 1795. Each party had made concessions: the French would get 100 million guilders, some territories in the south (such as Venlo, Maastricht, and the Dutch Flanders), and would share the haven of Flushing. That was all the Dutch consented to sacrifice, but it was enough to make the French happy. Sieyès, one of the representatives who had fixed and signed the treaty, was delighted and contented that with the Dutch Republic as ally, France had gained "a great and superb naval and commercial future."[7]

But the alliance was both defensive and offensive. That meant that the Batavians—as they called themselves—had to support France against Britain in a war that was still unsettled.

Once the treaty was signed, the United Provinces were free to choose the government they wished. The only condition imposed by France was that it had to be a republic without stadholder and no federation as in the United States. The sister republic started the organization of elections to convene a national assembly—a convention—which would write a constitution. But as soon as the elections were organized, problems arose. Four to five provinces refused to participate and required a restoration of their old provincial government. Riots broke out in Friesland, where the provincial assembly refused to lose its prerogatives. In Overijssel, Gelderland, Zeeland, and Groningen, similar opposition protested against a nationalization of the revolution. Dutch provinces invoked their provincial sovereignty. Thanks to popular societies that longed for unity and thanks to the French troops who wanted the country to be peaceful, the provinces progressively joined the national assembly in The Hague. The provincial problem already made a great difference with France, where national unity had been a priority of the Bourbons. Even if imperfect, French centralization and unity were no longer revolutionary issues. They were an old tradition, which the United Provinces ignored. For a great number of Dutch inhabitants, there was only one system thinkable: federalism.

That explains why uprisings and disturbances went on and on. The French representative in The Hague, François Noël, was very surprised. He had been told that the Dutch people were phlegmatic and calm, but between the end of 1795 and spring 1796, he was witnessing intense conflicts and dissensions. Even in Amsterdam, quarrels opposed highly politicized popular societies and district meetings and the rather moderate municipality. On January 19, the people had been told, "You are Free! You are Equal!," but these promises had been broken, since elections were strictly limited to wealthy people. Consequently, in Amsterdam, Leeuwarden, Utrecht, Rotterdam, or Delft, the people claimed its sovereignty in a few clear-cut words: "The representatives . . . are only the executors of our will, since we have not given up our sovereignty. We the People, are sovereign, because we are the active and working part of the nation, and peace and wealth are depending on us."[8]

The power vacuum between January 1795 and March 1796 aggravated the situation, even more so since several towns limited the franchise to men aged over twenty-five who earned more than 300 guilders a year. That meant that in Amsterdam, for instance, 55.1 percent of the inhabitants had no right to vote and choose their magistrates. Moreover, there was a food shortage that inspired rioting. During summer and fall 1795, uprisings and disturbances were sharpened by rumors about a counterrevolution the Orangist party was preparing at the German frontiers, near Osnabruck. This threat provoked a kind of panic, which in turn caused tumultuous disorders in several provinces. Last but not least, there were radical journals and libels calling for revenge and asking for a despoilment of the Orangist regents to compensate the refugees who were back home and had lost everything in 1787.

Meanwhile, the legislature had convened in The Hague. On March 1, 1796, 90 deputies out of 126 were able to sit in the stadholder's ballroom, which had been transformed into a house of representatives. The latecomers followed over the next days. The representatives' mission was to write a constitution for the whole country. On January 30, 1795, the province of Holland had already proclaimed its own bill of rights. Other provinces had drawn up their own on this example. They all proclaimed equality as the first principle from which derived liberty, security, property and resistance to oppression. Among the fundamental principles was the freedom of press and expression. Finally, the end of society would be the peaceful enjoyment of the natural rights of man. To conclude, this bill mentioned the limits brought on these rights by living in society. Thanks to these bills, the National Assembly had a base to start its work. But hardly had the assembly started its work than the gulf between unitarists and federalists became obvious. While the opposition to the nationalization of the revolution had been vanquished in the provinces, it had moved into the benches of the house of representatives. This explains why, during two years, a merciless struggle broke out about the constitutional principles. One party fought for unity and indivisibility in the republic, and the other one for a political order that would leave their financial and political autonomy to the provinces. Finally, a constitutional draft including more than 900 articles was ready in spring 1797. Because it was marked by *juste milieu* measures, it displeased everyone. Disagreement rose about the unification of taxes and the suppression of the old quota system.[9] The richest province of Holland was the first to wish for a united system of taxation and relied on amalgamation to get rid of its debts. This indebtedness was due to its expenses for the protection of the union, but land provinces contested this interpretation and lamented that they, too, had made colossal expenses during continental wars. Be that as it may, on August 8, 1797, the Dutch people rejected the constitutional draft, 109,000 against 28,000 votes, because it was not democratic and not unitarist enough or, on the contrary, because it was too democratic and not moderate enough. The campaign against the draft was a success for the radicals. In Amsterdam, for instance, primary assemblies were convinced by the radicals' arguments that the constitution was too elitist and too federalist. In August 1797 this long-lasting work was simply reduced to nothing. A new assembly had to start from scratch. The "mother" republic was highly displeased about this still provisional situation. It needed a strong ally with a government able to reorganize the Dutch navy and pay the compensation stipulated in the 1795 treaty. However, it was not easy to transform a confederation in a united nation.

In September new elections took place for the second National Assembly. More radicals were nominated, but by no means did they make up a decisive majority. Soon after they convened, quarrels about provincial prerogatives and unity started up again. Radicals published petitions and manifestos on their principles and asked the Dutch people to renounce the regulation imposed at the beginning of 1796 by the former States General, which had not anticipated absolute unity and amalgamation of provincial debts. The Dutch radicals also tried to win over the French government and force the removal of François Noël. They found him too moderate and wanted a French representative who would be more open to their plans. They succeeded—by bribing some French politicians. At the end of December, Charles Delacroix, former minister of Foreign Affairs, was sent to The Hague. His task was to speed up the constitution's completion. When he arrived in Holland on January 2, 1798, Delacroix had to discover which party was the most consonant with French views. However, his secretary, Brahïn Ducange, an adventurer and fortune hunter, encouraged him to join the radicals— who had bribed him, too. Delacroix was seduced by their arguments and principles. Meanwhile, the Batavian assembly feared that a coup was coming. Its federalist members were afraid and decided to speed up. But on January 19, 1798, three days before the actual coup, the representatives were still fighting about the degree of national unity that would be acceptable.

Delacroix came to Holland with a draft made up by his French colleagues, especially Pierre Daunou, who became the legislator of the Roman Republic. Daunou had corrected and modified the 1797 Dutch draft. But once in Holland, Delacroix was impressed by another draft made by the radicals: the so-called Manifesto of the 43. Although he disliked its radicalism, he also discovered in it some "excellent articles." This manifesto became the base for the "Agreed Constitutional Points," which in turn were used to supply the constitution with its fundamental principles. Delacroix and above all Ducange controlled each article written by the Dutch radicals, particularly William Ockerse. Daunou's draft was not taken into account, because "it was not submitted to us until after our own plan was very far advanced" (so they said). They recalled that in contrast with the French, the Dutch people had more need "of the spur than the bridle." On January 21, forty-nine representatives had accepted the "Constitutional Points." The following day, with the support of Delacroix and Joubert, the French general of the Batavian-French troops and his colleague, Herman Daendels, the radicals executed their coup. No blood was shed.

Some twenty representatives were arrested and taken into custody. The National Assembly was purged with the benevolent support of Delacroix. That meant the hard job could be completed and that the sister republic would soon get rid of its interim government. Indeed, the Constitution of 1798 was completed on March 17, and the plebiscite organized for April 23. Meanwhile, primary assemblies had been purged and the constitution was accepted by a great majority of the Dutch people. Delacroix was delighted and believed that with a stable government the Batavian Republic would help France defeat "perfidious Albion." But not all the Batavian representatives were so enthusiastic. Several disapproved of the brutality and illegality of the coup. Twenty-three among them resigned their functions. Furthermore, there was discontent among the Dutch people because of the purges. Popular societies and clubs had been overzealous: future diplomat Rutger-Jan Schimmelpenninck, for instance, had been excluded from the poll. But with the radical government in the saddle, the popular voice could be heard again. In Amsterdam, Lucas Butot, an extreme radical, asked for equality of property and a better distribution of wealth. Elsewhere, popular patriots invaded their township and claimed the jobs carried off by the enemies of the revolution: Orangists, federalists, and all those who refused to take the oath implemented by the constitution. The situation was explosive in towns where there were thousands of these kinds of jobs. In Amsterdam alone, 3,000 were available: they had to be given to true patriots or to former refugees. Enemies of the people would have to be put in custody. From this episode, students can draw examples of the problematic relationship between France and its sister republics and of internal conflict between revolutionaries—radical and moderate—that is such a common component of the revolutionary process.

What else can students take from the first democratic constitution of the new Batavian Republic? It offers a radical point of comparison for other constitutions in the Atlantic world. Like the 1797 constitution, this new version had a preamble with a bill including fundamental rights (eight articles) and political and civil principles (no fewer than sixty-four articles). First, one article mentions that the social compact does not suppress the natural rights of man, as long as they do not encroach on others' rights. This precision had been suppressed in France under the 1795 constitution. The primary assemblies gained more power than before and were asked to establish a list of candidates, among whom the electors were to choose. Moreover, they received the right to ask for amendments. The elective system was still indirect, but the fact that the people had the right to draw up their own list provided a "direct" popular influence that Ockerse had absolutely required. In the primary assemblies all men over twenty who paid a tax on coffee and tea would be allowed to vote. More important still, the people had the right to control their government, while the representatives were responsible to the people. Finally, it was explicitly said that each power and each authority were always temporary. The declaration also paid attention to social rights and to the right of the people to work, to be educated, and to receive relief. Orphans would get a proper education. Public health would become a government priority. Furthermore, it promised to be thrifty with public finances, to enforce a uniform codification, and create cultural institutions promoting public education and general enlightenment. It insisted not only on the rights and duties of man but also on the government's obligations—far more than France or the United States did.

To be sure, the 1798 constitution could have been more democratic if the French government had not intervened. By order of the French Directory, Daunou and Delacroix reminded the Dutch that popular societies had to be closed and replaced by constitutional circles—which would only be convened at election time. The judicial power had to be less powerful, the executive power should work with ministers and not with committees, and the legislative body would be divided. Apart from national unity and nationalized finances, which were also Dutch radicals' aims, this was all that France wanted to impose on the sister republic. Daunou did not even protest against social rights and poor relief. He did not complain about the fact that the Dutch had rejected juries and the justices of the peace. It seems that in France, too, these two institutions no longer enjoyed official favor. The measures imposed on the Dutch radicals speak volumes about the priorities of the French Directory: first, the fear of popular influence and the distrust of the judiciary; second, the need to return power into wealthy hands, or at least enlightened spirit; and third, the need to strengthen the executive. Strikingly enough, Daunou also appreciated some Dutch institutions, like the division of electoral districts and the drawing of lots to settle the voting. He introduced them in the constitution he drafted for the Roman Republic—also in 1798.

The 1798 constitution functioned until September 1801, even though the radicals were eliminated. In June 1798, indeed, a coalition of ministers, moderate representatives, and generals complained about the arbitrary measures taken by the January government. Everywhere in the country, new municipal administrations had been nominated. But the new administrators were not always literate. Most of them knew nothing about legislation, judicial laws, and banking affairs. Their real obsession was the punishment of the 1787 regents, who had betrayed the Patriot revolution. To meet this general expectation, the representative body decided on March 30, 1798, to arrest these regents or their heirs and seize their fortunes, so that they would be able to pay compensation to the refugees and help their "poor fatherland." This decree was precisely what the popular patriots asked for since the beginning of the Batavian revolution. But the wealthy disagreed and shouted "anarchy." Isaac Gogel, minister of Finances, did not agree either. He feared that Dutch capitalists would emigrate with their money and shares or investments. He also recalled that in 1794 the stadholder had found no money when he needed it to pay the Dutch army and resist the French. To be sure that the Netherlands remained independent, Gogel knew that popular measures would not suffice. He had to win over the wealthy, the ones who really might have helped the little republic survive. Another problem alienated the Dutch against the radical government. Like the

French Republic in 1795, the new government wanted two thirds of the previous representatives to continue in office, so that there would be some continuity in government. Only one third would be elected. A majority of Dutch disapproved this measure and protested. On the other side of the frontier, the French government was dissatisfied, too. It criticized the radicals for not obeying the French and favoring their own country at the expense of the alliance. General Joubert, particularly, was humiliated by the radical government, which tried to supplant him and did not respect the agreement that he alone was in command of the Dutch-French army. Another quarrel concerned the French privateers, who were arrested by the Dutch navy and whose goods were confiscated. Furthermore, a slanderous campaign launched by moderates focused on the radicalism of the new government and on the popular patriots, who they alleged would have introduced arbitrary decrees. Since 1795, the French government condemned popular activism as anarchic and arbitrary, and it no longer tolerated disorder, even in the sister republics. All these motives of discontent explain why, on June 12, 1798, a new coup removed the radicals from power—with the tacit agreement of Paris. They, too, were taken into custody. Legality and morality became the new motto. But the democratic constitution was maintained.

A great difference with France is that here political enemies were not executed, simply excluded from the public scene and put in prison—another point of comparison that students can explore with profit: why should the Dutch case have been different from that of France?[10] After the June 1798 coup, some political radicals among the people were not always treated with great humanity. Some of them were arrested, branded, and flogged in the public space. Corporal punishment was still not abolished by the constitution, even though torture had been. The Dutch government did not abolish slavery, either. Before they were in power, the radicals thought it had to be abolished. But once in power, they hesitated and renounced the introduction of a novelty that could bring further damage to their colonies and thus to national prosperity. The French example in Saint-Domingue was dissuasive. The Dutch did not emancipate women, either. Although some women were enthusiastic patriots, they did not get political rights and did not become fully fledged citizens.

The people disapproved of the June coup. They feared that popular government would no longer be tolerated. In several Dutch towns, revolts and protests blew up during July and August 1798. In September

1798, a great popular revolt terrorized Amsterdam. Three hundred patriots—most of them workers and mechanics—complained that the moderate government would oppress them and that the revolution's enemies were taking their jobs, although the constitution forbade them from official responsibilities. Furthermore, by being reintegrated, these enemies would have every opportunity to betray the revolution. Amsterdam was once again in danger during these tumultuous days. But the French army was there to stop popular insurrections. The Amsterdam municipality called on it to help, and two days later, the popular action was crushed. The leaders were arrested and put on trial. This was the last important popular revolt in the Batavian Republic. Thereafter there were still rumors of conspiracy. The government was afraid that the so-called anarchists were planning a new revolution, as for instance when the French general Guillaume Brune and representative Joseph Fouché came to the Netherlands in 1799. Neither gentlemen tried to change the Dutch government and replace it with radicals, as they did in Italy. Their task was to inspect Dutch defenses against Russo-British invasion and collect some funding. Meanwhile the Dutch people had returned home and concentrated on their private lives. For them, the revolution was over. For the elites, there was a respite until 1805–1806, when the Dutch Republic was transformed into an autocratic republic by Napoleon and then into a monarchy with Louis Bonaparte as king.

Historians have forgotten or were not interested by this fantastic episode, when everything seemed possible; when each man and woman became equal to others; when everyone could speak and write about politics and give his opinion; when women, men, and youth were asked to think for themselves and elect their representatives or write petitions; when the people were permitted to go to popular societies, to write partisan papers, and to influence and control their political leaders. This state of grace became synonymous with anarchy for some, and for others a bone of disorder. That is the lot of actual democracy. Students today can do well to ponder the conflicts and debates that arose in the Dutch struggle to secure its foundations.

Conclusion

The final failure of the Batavian Republic certainly does not mean that there were no actual revolution(s) in the Netherlands or that their outcomes were fruitless.[11] The Batavian revolution succeeded in implementing a primary education that would become an inspiration

Cornelis Bakker, Dutch Liberty showing to a Dutch citizen the chair of sovereignty. (Detail from Carel F. Bendorp, "Allegorie op de Conventie," print, 1795, after Cornelis Bakker; author's private collection)

to its neighbors, including France. It also succeeded in enforcing national unity: an extremely important achievement for a two-centuries-old federal republic such as the United Provinces. The full abolition of corporate bodies took longer and was only definitive between 1808 and 1818. Meanwhile justice had been reformed and was public. There was no longer secret investigation, and no longer torture or inequality in punishment. The 1798 constitution was at times forgotten and at times revived as the first democratic political draft ever made by and for the Dutch people. At the end of these tumultuous years, Dutch republicanism had once and for all disintegrated and was replaced by monarchic constitutionalism. Constitutionalism and representation are the obvious winners of all these contests and not just in the Netherlands. It means above all that government would no longer be arbitrary but limited by law and that taxation had to be voted by elected representatives. As in other European countries that experienced a revolution in the eighteenth century, political rights for all disappeared but civil rights remained. Property was protected by law; merit and talents replaced privileges and corporate society; no one would be arbitrarily arrested, and the police had to tell the people the charge against them. Much more was done for popular education and national prestige, as could be seen in museums, archives, and libraries. In the Batavian Republic, poor relief did not disappear, either. But the right to be enlightened and politically active vanished. The "populace" needed to read and write and behave as virtuous citizens, but that was all. Politics had to be maintained in the hands of the elites. Popular societies and assemblies were forbidden and eventually disappeared. Actual equality was no longer on the agenda, nor was progressive or proportional taxation. Democratic elections were replaced by exclusive vote. Meanwhile the police, the gendarmerie, and the tribunals were strong enough to uphold public order. They, too, were an unexpected revolutionary creation.

The conclusion, however, must be that the eighteenth-century revolutions did not reach their ultimate goal. Students can ponder the balance of achievements and limitations. The whole episode is not only progressive but also reactive: one step forward, one step backward. At the end of these revolutions, at least in Europe, there were no longer bills of rights, nor social rights such as the right to work or to be protected and educated, nor popular participation.[12] Take a look at our today's ultra-liberal and global world and try to find some comparisons with this period. It will not be so difficult to discover that despite the revolutionary dreams about a free and equitable society, the world has not dramatically changed. Since the 1970s, in my opinion, it has regressed. Now, too, it goes one step forward, one step backward.

NOTES

1. Geoges Gusdorf, *Les Révolutions de France et d'Amérique: La violence et la sagesse* (Paris: Libr. académique Perrin, 1988), 105–33, quote on 110.

2. William Howard Adams, *The Paris Years of Thomas Jefferson* (New Haven, CT: Yale University Press, 1997), 95–96.

3. Marjolein 't Hart, "The Dutch Revolt, 1566–81: A National Revolution?," in *Revolutions and the Revolutionary Tradition in the West, 1560–1991*, ed. David Parker (London: Routledge, 2000), 15–33.

4. A translation of this document into English can be found at http://members.casema.nl/wilschut/ahvvne.htm (accessed September 10, 2015).

5. Hannah Arendt, *On Revolution* (Harmondsworth: Penguin, 1973), 43–45.

6. On the war and the Dutch antipathy for the Britons, see the *Annual Register for the Year 1795* (London, 1800), 42–50.

7. *Le Moniteur*, XXIV, 516; 535–38 and 618–19.

8. D. Kraakman, "De volkssciëteiten in de Bataafse Republiek," *Skript* 2 (1980): 16–26; 22.

9. The old quota system differently taxed the seven Dutch provinces. Holland paid 62 percent while Zeeland paid 3.8 percent. See also Marjolein 't Hart, Joost Jonker, and Jan Luiten van Zanden, *The Financial History of the Netherlands* (Cambridge: Cambridge University Press, 1995).

10. During the period 1793–1794, political enemies were executed in France as traitors or conspirators ("the Terror"), as discussed in the chapter by David Andress. Executions were still on the agenda during the following period (1795), but now against the radicals.

11. About the success of a failed patriot revolution, see Wayne Te Brake, *Regents and Rebels: The Revolutionary World of an Eighteenth-Century Dutch City* (Cambridge, MA: Blackwell, 1989).

12. Poor relief was maintained in the Netherlands, since it was a century-old Dutch institution.

KEY RESOURCES

Secondary Sources

de Gou, Leonard. *De Staatsregeling van 1798. Bronnen voor de totstandkoming*, 3 vols. The Hague: Bureau der Rijkscommissie voor Vaderlandse Geschiedenis, 1988.

———. *Het Ontwerp van constitutie van 1797*, 3 vols. The Hague: M. Nijhoff, 1984.

Jourdan, Annie. *La Révolution batave entre la France et l'Amérique*. Rennes: Presses Universitaires de Rennes, 2008.

———. "The Netherlands in the Constellation of the Eighteenth-Century Western Revolutions." *European Review of History* 18, no. 2 (2011): 199–225.

Oddens, Joris, Marc Rutjes, and Erik Jacobs, eds. *The Political Culture of the Sister Republics 1794–1806*. Amsterdam: Amsterdam University Press, 2015.

Palmer, Robert R. "Much in Little: The Dutch Revolution of 1795." *Journal of Modern History* 26 (1954): 15–35.

Schama, Simon. *Patriots and Liberators: Revolution in the Netherlands, 1780–1813*. New York: Knopf, 1977.

Te Brake, Wayne. "How Much in How Little? Dutch Revolution in Comparative Perspective." *Tijdschrift voor Sociale Geschiedenis* 4 (1990): 349–63.

———. *Regents and Rebels: The Revolutionary World of an Eighteenth-Century Dutch City*. Cambridge, MA: Blackwell, 1989.

Online Resources

On the Batavian Republic: http://www.parlement.com.

On the Batavian constitution: http://www.republicanisme.nl (follow link to "Nederland" then to "staatsregeling 1798").

On the parliamentary discussions: http://www.dagverhaal.nl.

For important documents in Dutch, French, and English (online with an English index): http://resources.huygens.knaw.nl/gedenkstukken/index_html_en (H. T. Colenbrander, *Gedenkstukken der Algemeene Geschiedenis van Nederland* [1795–1840]).

For understanding the European context during the revolutions, it is worth consulting *The Annual Register* (created by Edmund Burke, a conservative) and *The New Annual Register* (by Andrew Kippis, a dissident), both available through GoogleBooks.

Understanding Nationalism

Napoleon's Sword Arm and Achilles Heel

ALAN FORREST

Few historians would question the importance of nationalism as one of the defining ideologies of the early nineteenth century, in Europe and across the globe. It lay at the heart of a cultural renaissance in many parts of the European mainland, inspiring poets and pamphleteers in equal measure and allowing the people of Europe to dream of a shared heritage and an often imagined identity. The experience of Napoleonic Europe offers ways of breathing life into understandings of nationalism in the classroom. At the outset, students can be confronted with its slipperiness by explaining that "the nation" did not even have to have a concrete existence: it could be an ideal, the conscious creation of intellectuals to fill a vacuum caused by the decline of religion and other forms of transnational community, or what Benedict Anderson has called an imagined community.[1] Each country had a different narrative. Austria, for instance, tied its past to its transnational role in the Holy Roman Empire; in England, much was made of the history of parliamentary institutions. In northern Germany, where there was little by way of a shared political tradition to draw on, the intellectual nation was constructed in terms of cultural heritage, largely hinging on a common language, which had been, as Heinrich Herder imagined it, an important vector for a common corpus of ideas.[2] But if such concepts were widespread in intellectual circles, the stuff of salon conversations and student meetings, they were too amorphous to be easily transferred into popular politics, and until late in the eighteenth century they remained largely confined to an educated public sphere.

With the Age of Revolutions, however, that changed. Revolutions spoke a language of nationalism, too, whether it was the colonists in North America who pitted themselves against the British monarchy, the new states of Central and Latin America shaking themselves loose from metropolitan Spain, or the Jacobin leaders in France, who persuaded themselves that only the French could fully understand the ideals of their revolution. In the political context of the Age of Revolutions, nationalist discourse achieved a new relevance and a new potency. Teachers can encourage students to explore the complexities of nationalism in this era by using the lens of Napoleon's career, first because he appealed to national pride in France and second because as his armies marched across Europe, he, his soldiers, and his officials encountered a variegated and conflicting range of national sentiments, political loyalties, and local attachments. The subject allows students not only to engage with a pivotal era in European history but also to think critically about the very problematic nature of nationalism in the Age of Revolutions.

Napoleon is a figure who readily fires up discussions—as a military commander, as the legatee of the French Revolution—and he was fully aware of the power of nationalism and the potential that a growing French national sentiment placed at his disposal. For men of his generation (he was born in 1769) it could hardly be otherwise. His boyhood in Ajaccio had awakened him to the power of collective identity and the levels of enthusiasm they could attract. As a young man he had been seduced, like his father, to lend support to the cause of Corsican nationalism under the colorful and often charismatic leadership of Pasquale Paoli.[3] As a young army officer during the early 1790s, he watched as the universal goals of the early revolution and the offer of liberty it held out to all mankind, rapidly gave way to a new nationalist discourse that could seriously contend that only the French could be good revolutionaries. He served that revolution loyally, even at the height of the Terror, making friends with Jacobin deputies and putting down the counter-revolutionary insurrection in Toulon that had threatened to hand the dockyard and the French Mediterranean fleet to the enemy. In the last weeks of the convention he suppressed an insurrection in Paris by turning his fire on the crowd. He then led revolutionary armies into Italy and on to the territories of neighboring states, bringing the revolutionary message of liberty and fraternity, but often accompanying it with the more mundane realities of theft and pillage, death, and material destruction. The revolution was no longer in danger—indeed, the last fighting on French soil dated back to 1793 in Perpignan—and Bonaparte's mission was aggressive: to annex foreign lands and drive the Austrians out of Italy.

Relations with local people were often tense and hostile. French armies traveled light and lived off the lands they passed through, and disagreements were unavoidable. Ideals played little part. With the passage of time, the youthful enthusiasm of the soldiers gave way to a more battle-hardened realism as they trudged across Europe in a succession of campaigns. They were more concerned with survival and military success, their morale and motivation closer to those of conventional armies and their loyalties increasingly focused on their comrades, their regiment, and the army itself. The armies Napoleon led to Jena or Russia were conscript armies drawn from across most of occupied Europe. They were no longer the revolutionaries of 1792, the "nation in arms" of the first years of the French Revolution. In the words of Jean-Clément Martin, the transition was clear for all to see, in France and in the countries France invaded. "Begun as a way of uniting the enemies of despotism," he writes, "the war declared by revolutionary France rapidly ceased to be a revolutionary crusade and became instead a way for France to control, conquer and pillage its neighbours."[4] War had become a mechanism for invading foreign lands to acquire extra resources and establish the natural frontiers that had been a French foreign policy goal since the time of Louis XIV. The revolution was first and foremost French.

As a revolutionary general, Napoleon had appealed to national pride and French values to exploit their patriotism. In the early years of the war, he leaned on the rhetorical images of the revolution, identifying himself with the Republic by seizing on its patriotic vocabulary: words like *liberty*, the *fatherland*, or *the French people*. In his addresses to his troops—sources that can be used to good effect in the classroom, precisely because they are problematic in many ways—he urged them on to further efforts, further sacrifices, by appealing to their honor and patriotism, using his own highly military adaptation of revolutionary discourse. "Soldiers," he proclaimed to his army in a typically confident address, "there is not a man among you who does not wish to return to France by any other route than that of honor. We must only return beneath triumphal arches."[5] His tone betrayed a degree of paternalism toward his troops, an interest in his soldiers' welfare he retained in the years of the empire. The result was to create a bond between himself and his troops, which was enriched by seasons of victorious campaigning but was also sufficiently strong to survive the defeats of the final years. How the soldiers responded can be explored in their letters home, a rich if again problematic source (since such testimonies are often intended to reassure loved ones), examples of which can be found in many sourcebooks. The relationship was based, as Michael J. Hughes explained, as much on a shared concept of honor and of military masculinity as on any sense of patriotism, a powerful mixture of *gloire* and *patrie* which helps explain the powerful cult of the emperor that developed in his armies, even as revolutionary idealism was fading and they were being developed into a powerful instrument of expansion and exploitation.[6]

Napoleon could not be blind to the changes that were taking place around him; indeed, it is arguable that he was himself a major player in the process of change. In a few short months the revolution became more nationalistic and more intolerant of dissent. It was not just foreigners who found themselves excluded from France's vision of revolution—so were many Frenchmen. During the 1790s Napoleon had been able to observe the transformation in the revolution's discourse, the repeated redefinition of the republic, the regular outbursts of paranoia directed at those perceived as the regime's enemies, and the convention's repeated habit of purging its members in the pursuit of its goals.[7] Through a series of exclusions—whether of royalists, counterrevolutionaries, moderates, Girondins, federalists, anarchists, atheists, or supporters of Robespierre—men who had previously been praised as good revolutionaries and honorable Frenchmen were purged and guillotined in the revolution's name, and the revolutionary nation continually restricted and redefined itself, leaving it as an emasculated shadow of its former self, what Pierre Serna has called the "weathercock republic" (*la république des girouettes*). Now emerged those, often of little clear principle, who sought stability and moderation as a prime political goal and who would accept any compromise if it allowed them to hold on to power.[8] Students often wrestle constructively with the question of why the appeal to nationalism seemed an obvious tool in a country at war (often relating it to their own times). Even though France set up sister republics in the territories surrounding its frontiers—like the Batavian Republic in Holland or the Helvetic Republic in Switzerland—their purpose was always strategic as well as political. France might aim at creating a new republican model and encourage the spread of republican ideas in the territories it conquered: all these countries were given a constitution closely modeled on France's own Constitution of the Year III. But it was still a question of conquest. The original generosity of spirit that had dreamed of the liberation of mankind had long been subsumed into France's own national interest.[9]

Of course Napoleon was still serving as a revolutionary general in the Directorial years, leading French armies in the Italian and Egyptian campaigns, though he was careful to stay involved with the political leadership back in France and was well aware of the strength of public opinion. He knew that the political class in Paris was following his triumphs with an ill-concealed enthusiasm, the more intense for the lack of interest it showed for the political battles at home. In appealing to domestic opinion Napoleon was unashamed in milking both the incisiveness of his victories—which he did not hesitate to exaggerate if circumstances demanded—and the manner of his military leadership. With an astute awareness of the power of propaganda, he turned to the best journalists of the day (including men whose careers seemed to have ended with the overthrow of the Jacobins) to win over the French public, praising his soldiers for their sacrifice, painting vivid images of their triumphs, and comparing himself to Alexander the Great or Hannibal. Even as he curried favor with the public, building his reputation in the French capital in advance of the coup d'état at Brumaire, he was also inspiring his soldiers to fight for France and its people. It is clear that in Paris and on the slopes of the Alps, Napoleon understood the value and the potency of the nationalist message and was keen to exploit it. In so doing he showed his genius for self-promotion and his skill in using modern media for propaganda. But he also revealed the gulf that existed between the army and its government and the degree to which the military looked to comradeship and unit loyalty before any feelings of loyalty to the French state.[10]

If Napoleon benefited from nationalist sentiment in France itself and did not hesitate to appeal to it, did he underestimate its emotional appeal elsewhere in Europe and its ability to stimulate patriotic reactions in the states he invaded? Seeking answers to this question allows teachers to open up the jagged landscape of nationalism in the Age of Revolutions. It is certainly true that in intellectual circles this was the period when cultural nationalism was beginning to become a significant movement across Europe, one that left a deep mark on writers, artists, philologists, and others in the last years of the eighteenth century and the early decades of the nineteenth. Cultural societies sprang up in many parts of Europe: among them, John Hutchinson lists the Russian Academy in 1783, the Royal Bohemian Society of Sciences in 1794, and the Magyar National Museum in 1807.[11] In some instances these cultural forces did spread into politics in the wake of Napoleon's invasion. In Prussia Ernst Moritz Arndt famously urged his fellow countrymen to unite in driving out the invader, and there were cultural festivals in many German states after the victory over the emperor at Leipzig in 1813. Does this really mean that the men from different parts of Germany who followed their princes and generals into battle against Napoleon did so out of a shared sense of national identity? The varieties of European experiences offer a good way of encouraging students to grapple with the nuances. Their political leaders' speeches may have encouraged a patriotic response, and the case would continue to be made, of course, throughout the nineteenth century, by a romantic generation for whom Leipzig became a moment to savor in the rise of German nationalism. But should we believe them? It is certainly true that many of the states that had previously supported Napoleon turned against him in the Sixth Coalition and fought alongside other Germans in defense of German soil. But that does not prove they did so out of a shared German identity, or indeed that they were fighting in the cause of a German nation. These constructs belong to the nineteenth century and to the era of national myth making, part of a Prussian and later German grand narrative.[12] Mainly they joined forces against the French in 1813 for more material reasons, because they saw it as being in their interests to do so. The leaders of the German states had no interest in turning popular loyalties away from their persons and their dynasties.

In France national sentiment had deeper roots. Of course it had enjoyed hundreds of years of a political existence based on a monarchy that had ruled since the Middle Ages in the Île-de-France and had extended and consolidated its territory progressively over the centuries; the most recent additions to the French state, Lorraine, Alsace, and Corsica, had been acquired in the seventeenth and eighteenth centuries, Corsica as recently as 1768. It was this long political history that the revolution had been so keen to obliterate. But a strong sense of French identity remained: besides their identification with a territory the majority of Frenchmen had a shared literature and culture and a shared adherence to the Catholic faith, albeit to a Catholicism with a distinctively

Gallican flavor and approach. During the revolution, thanks largely to the political influence of Rousseau, France had proclaimed a civic national ideal, a sense of humanist citizenship that united the nation in a common cause. That nation was declared to be "sovereign," taking the place of the monarch as the incarnation of the French people. Once again the idea of a specific French identity was accentuated, an identity that was lacking in many other parts of Europe. Although areas of the periphery (the west, parts of Brittany, Flanders, and the southeast) proved resistant to the ideas of the revolution, the majority of Frenchmen did not question the claim that they were a "one and indivisible" nation. But where they did—most especially in the Vendée—trouble continued to flare, even during the Hundred Days.[13]

Much of Europe, however, was not divided neatly into nation-states. Nationalism was still the affair of poets and intellectuals, dreamers and idealists. Politics dealt in states, the possessions of kings, princes, and electors, which had little to do with ethnic nationalism, and men served in the armies of their rulers, not their nations. They did so for money, out of a sense of duty, or because they sought a career as soldiers. Some may have shared the traditional motives of young men from time immemorial—a sense of adventure, a lack of career prospects, a family quarrel, or a desire to see the world all helped determine personal choices to join the army. Most served not out of conviction but because they were given no choice. It did not occur to the troops of Bavaria or Saxony or Hannover that they should be fighting in the cause of Germany. They were born and they died as political subjects of their prince, and their loyalty was to him and the state in which they lived at a time when modern Germany was divided into more than thirty different political units. Across history they had fought against other Germans as often as they had fought outside enemies. Throughout the Napoleonic years, in both the imperial army and the armies that fought against Napoleon, soldiers routinely lined up alongside men of many different nationalities, cultures, and languages. Soldiering had long been an international experience, a world of cultural transfer and exchange. Unlike the intellectuals who led the student movements of their respective states, the men in the ranks may have had little concept of being German. They almost certainly felt little obligation to any wider imagined community of the German nation, whatever nationalist preachers and academics might tell them.

If parts of Europe retained a highly regional focus, others had been coagulated into huge multinational empires that had been acquired by military conquest and dynastic succession and often had no common language, culture, or historical roots. What they did have was legitimacy, and by the time of the French Revolution, there was little to suggest that these were in decline. Thus the Romanovs ruled a huge Russian landmass that spread across Asia to the east and included peoples of vastly differing cultures, languages, and ethnicities. The Habsburg Empire controlled much of southern and eastern Europe from its court in Vienna, imposing its rule on the peoples of Bohemia, Hungary, Lombardy, and much of northern Italy; it was also the heart of the Holy Roman Empire, until 1806 (when Napoleon abolished it). In Prussia since Frederick the Great, the Hohenzollerns had set out to become a major imperial power in the northern part of German Central Europe. The partition of a national state, Poland, in 1795 between these three empires (Austria, Prussia, and Russia) seemed to indicate that the age of European land empires was not about to end.[14] After all, there were few nations that strictly corresponded to states in Europe: if Britain, France, Spain, and Portugal had not extended their boundaries to any major degree across the European landmass, this was because their focus lay elsewhere, and it had not prevented them from establishing huge and lucrative overseas empires; indeed, many of the wars in which they had engaged in the eighteenth century had had their roots in India or America as much as in Europe. In the Americas only the infant United States had freed itself from European control. In global terms, the eighteenth-century world still belonged to great dynastic empires, whether to the Ottoman Empire in Turkey or the Manchu Empire in China. Cultural nationalism did not make any significant impact there until the late nineteenth or early twentieth century.[15]

Arguably the most significant effect of the French Revolution was less to spread nationalism to other countries than to create another European land empire; it certainly produced—for all its warnings about the dangers of a "new Cromwell"—an emperor and a strong military leader in Napoleon.[16] By the time of the Directory and Consulate, the French seemed more concerned to impose stability and order than they were to spread revolutionary ideas, to collect taxes and revenue, to ensure that laws were enforced. Beyond France's borders the revolution acted like an old regime empire. It turned increasingly to military conquest and annexation, to colonizing Europe with French administrators and French laws, a process Michael Broers has aptly compared to the nineteenth-century European colonizations of Asia and Africa.[17]

Such comparisons across time and space are one way of sparking student discussion. A stimulating and revealing exercise is to ask the class to compare maps of Europe—in 1789 with 1810 or 1812—to discuss how the Napoleonic empire in Europe reshaped boundaries and political institutions. A further comparison with the continent after the Congress of Vienna in 1815 is also a way into the question of legitimacy: the attempts by post–Napoleonic European statesmen to recast Europe in a more conservative framework provide a useful foil to the changes wrought a few years earlier. Another way of stirring student discussion is to relate the Napoleonic project to modernity. In the countries they invaded and annexed, the French saw themselves as the harbingers of modernity and civilization, and they judged the peoples they encountered by the values they ascribed to themselves and treated them accordingly. Where local elites showed a willingness to participate in the imperial project, they were rewarded with offices and titles, entrusted to implement the French project. Where they showed a reluctance to play the role ascribed to them, their rank and status counted for nothing: they were contemptuously cast aside and their place taken by Frenchmen. In such cases the French cared little about local sensibilities, believing that Italy, the Netherlands, and the princedoms beyond the Rhine were all being modernized for their own good, especially for the good of their people. Poverty, illiteracy, and religious obscurantism were taken to signify backwardness, and opposition was identified with a reluctance to accept the values of the modern era. Modernity, in contrast, bestowed rights and created liberties; it also demanded obedience to the law and to the state, obedience that was imposed by local administrators and gendarmes. Taxes had to be paid, smuggling was repressed, and the state judged a country's loyalty more by its willingness to provide conscripts for the imperial army than by any other criterion.[18]

This represented a significant change to the relations between state and society, one that local people often found difficult to accept and that across Europe led to outbreaks of violence and communal resistance to the authorities. But such outbreaks did not necessarily have their roots in nationalism or in any political ideology. In some the reaction stemmed from religious fanaticism, in others from demands that threatened local people with impoverishment. But in many countries there were outbursts of resistance; it is enough to think of the memories attached to the Neapolitan revolution of 1799, those of French repression in the central cantons of Switzerland, or in the Peasants' War in Belgium.[19] French-style modernity came at a cost, and that cost would always pose a threat to men's loyalties.

We should not exaggerate the extent of resistance, and students can and should be invited to explore the more positive side of Napoleonic rule. In large swaths of Europe—and especially in northern countries and in regions close to France's frontiers—much of what the French promised could seem very attractive to some. In urban Europe, for example, and in areas with high degrees of literacy, the expansion of the empire created new bureaucratic structures that offered salaried posts for local people, and with them new opportunities for social advancement. Some of those annexed also benefited from the new religious freedoms that were decreed, with Protestants and especially Jews given civic privileges and an equality of status they had never previously enjoyed, including rights of political representation. These rights were duly carried into law. Wherever the French army went, the Napoleonic code went with it, promulgating what were often startling new rights for local people. Across Italy, for example, Napoleon brought sweeping changes that standardized the various branches of justice and administration, ended the last vestiges of feudalism, and sought to undermine the political and economic power of the Church.[20] In large parts of Central and Eastern Europe peasants were freed from serfdom and from the petty tyranny of local lords—freedoms without precedent in their history. Local people discovered for the first time what impartial justice and effective local government meant; or they found out that it was possible to envisage administration without corruption. There were benefits to be accrued from cooperating with the French emperor. Some were sufficiently won over by the new institutions the French imposed that they retained them long after the French had been expelled from their territory. In places from Brussels to Milan, it was possible for people to distinguish the effects of French occupation, some of which had brought unquestioned benefits, from the military invasion that had brought it about. Few people like being invaded or turn to thank the invader, whatever language is used to justify it. Had not Robespierre himself warned that soldiers coming in the name of liberty would always be seen as invaders, as men in arms to whom the population of the lands invaded would seldom feel gratitude? Besides, he knew that war would pose a threat to the revolution within France, too. In turbulent times, he warned, "army chiefs become the arbiters of the fate of their country," while abroad sweet-sounding promises of liberty, equality, and fraternity were as nothing compared with the sight of foreign soldiers armed with muskets and cannon.[21] Such considerations, of course, had earlier played important roles in influencing American mobilization and demobilization during the Revolutionary War, in which French arms played a seminal role.

By the end of the 1790s there was little attempt to sugar the pill with words of comfort. Napoleon's aim in annexation could not have been clearer: it was to serve France's and the emperor's interests in an expansionist war with the other European powers and provide him with the resources, human and material, his armies required. Political ideals and citizens' rights became a secondary consideration in an increasingly militarized polity where everything risked being subordinated to victory. To this end he needed access to resources: men, of course, whether to serve in the ranks of his armies or to service the troops, as tailors and cobblers, blacksmiths and bakers; horses, some for use by the cavalry or to haul artillery pieces on the battlefield, others to carry supplies on the long marches across Europe; and money, huge sums of it, to fund the war effort. With the passage of the years and the expansion of the war across the European landmass, Napoleon's needs became greater. France alone would have been quite unable to fund these wars, far less to provide the huge numbers of men and horses that were called for. Napoleon's tactics depended on speed and maneuverability; to this end he instructed his officers to live off the lands they passed through, buying food and fodder from local suppliers, forcing them to part with their stocks at gunpoint if need be. Belgium, the Rhineland, and the wide plains of northern Germany were the bread baskets on which his armies depended. Without them he could not have pursued his policy of war, and he increasingly saw them as resources to be plundered and exploited, forced allies in his campaigns, puppet states on which he could call to serve the interests of France and its empire. In the same way, the continental system was conceived as a means of turning Europe's economies to the service of France, an ill-concealed exercise in economic exploitation that neighboring countries understandably resented and frequently resisted.[22]

Exploitation took various forms in territories that were either annexed to France as departments of an expanded *hexagone*—by 1812 the original 83 departments of 1790 had expanded to 130—or reconfigured, first as sister republics and then after 1804 as vassal kingdoms of the empire, which were routinely rewarded with the allocation of a king or a prince drawn from among the emperor's considerable stock of relatives. As with France's own provinces, the annexed territories were judged by their tax revenues and especially by the numbers of conscripts they raised for the armies. Crops were requisitioned from unwilling farmers, horses counted and seized for state service. Huge sums were collected in taxes and what were described as voluntary contributions for the war effort. Those who tried to resist by hiding their crops or who resorted to smuggling across frontiers or along the coast faced the full rigor of the law. The rapaciousness of the French became infamous as Napoleon extended his demands to include paintings and other artistic treasures, to stock the Louvre in Paris—his new Musée Napoléon—and to fill his coffers. In Italy Classical sculptures were seized on his orders and brought to Paris; in Germany great paintings were taken from museums and palaces. It became increasingly difficult to distinguish between legitimate taxation and simple pillage, the alienation of other peoples' heritage to enrich France. In these circumstances the new vocabulary of patriotism and revolutionary zeal was hard to maintain, and the opposition they aroused was necessarily ambiguous.

This ambiguity is an opportunity for students to grasp one of the central problems of this era. Casting his eye around Europe at the various resistance movements that formed against the French occupation, Pierre Vilar asks the critical question. "When the defensive 'patriotism' of 1792 transformed into a spirit of conquest and annexation," he writes, how should we interpret this? "Was resistance, in Prussia and the Tyrol, Russia and Spain, undertaken in the name of the forces of tradition or rather for the principles of the French Revolution itself?"[23] They often resorted to the same language as the revolutionaries, claiming to speak for the people as a whole and battling the forces of imperialism and the military might of the invader. Vilar sees conflicting strands in the European reaction to Napoleon: on one hand it resonates with a seemingly libertarian discourse that championed economic freedoms;

on the other, it is backward-looking and nostalgic, longing for the restoration of past liberties and dreaming of a world that was lost.[24] Culture, language, folklore, and a sentimental loyalty to myths and historic institutions all played their part; they also spoke a language of liberty, steeped in the revolution of 1789. Which, if either, should we believe? One way of encouraging students to grapple with this question is to ask them to find and be ready to discuss one European example of the different and conflicting meanings of "freedom," "people," and "nation" in the years of the French Revolution and Napoleonic wars and balance them against the weight of more traditional loyalties. They will encounter interesting challenges in doing this.

The first problem for students and teachers is to find a way to discard the assembled baggage of nineteenth-century nationalism: the writers and publicists, following Napoleon's defeat, who sought to attribute it to a new spirit of romantic or cultural nationalism. Some of the conflicts that are contained within the envelope of the Napoleonic wars did take on the character of national struggles: Finland's war to gain independence from Sweden, for instance, or Poland's eagerness to embrace Napoleon's Grand Duchy of Warsaw, Haiti's struggle against France and the restoration of slavery, or the cluster of anticolonial wars that broke out in Central and South America after 1810. But these conflicts, as other chapters in this volume clearly demonstrate, were seldom attributable to nationalism alone. Resentment of France's imperial ambitions often blended with other aspirations: anticolonial or internal status struggles in the case of the Americas; in Europe, religious faith, dynastic calculation, and the residue of ideals sown by the French Revolution all played their part. In some countries—France among them—people rose against the ideals of 1789, rejecting individualism and civic freedom in defense of their traditional society, monarchy, or the Catholic Church. There was no law that said people always wanted to be free, at least where freedom came through annexation and loss of identity, and counterrevolution and the arrival of French noble émigrés played their part in anti-Napoleonic movements, too. Nor was the Napoleonic empire always viewed with distaste. In Lombardy and throughout much of northern Italy, for instance, the expulsion of the Austrians was widely welcomed, to the point where the leaders of the Risorgimento wrote in praise of Napoleon and the reforms he implemented.[25] In Poland, which Napoleon had rescued from partition through his championing of the Grand Duchy of Warsaw, the French emperor became a hero for the people.

It is in Germany, perhaps, that nationalist myths proved most enduring.[26] For Prussian nationalist writers like Ernst Moritz Arndt, the Napoleonic wars, and more specifically the Battle of Leipzig in 1813, reflected the flowering of German nationalism, the rising of the German people to repel the French invader. Writers and poets sang the praises of brave Germans who fought and died at Leipzig, supposedly in the cause of the German people, until the idea that it was a battle fought in the national cause became rooted in the national psyche and became one of the foundation myths of the German empire in 1870. Germans celebrated Leipzig as the major battle of the Napoleonic wars, a battle fought on German soil that had finally seen the various German states— with the notable exception of Saxony—lined up alongside one another in defense of German territory. The Prussian monarchy was quick to lavish praise and honors on those who had fought at Leipzig, and the victory was celebrated throughout the nineteenth century through festivals and military commemorations. To mark the fiftieth anniversary in 1863, a foundation stone was placed on the spot where Napoleon ordered his retreat, and the centenary in 1913 was marked by the inauguration of the Völkerschlachtdenkmal, a huge and (many would argue) heavily militaristic monument on the outskirts of the city. At first a symbol of Prussian military leadership within Germany, the Battle of Leipzig had become the unquestioned symbol of German nationhood.[27]

Germany was not alone, of course, in forging the struggle against Napoleon into one of the foundation myths of the new nation; the romantic spirit of the early nineteenth century ensured that across Europe, nations looked to their experience in war to define themselves and their qualities. Kings and emperors were as likely to use and burnish these myths as republics or revolutionary regimes. If Germans referred to their war as a War of Liberation, Russia had its Patriotic War, and much of South America basked in the triumph of the Spanish-American Wars against colonial Spain. Often the manner of making war was itself an important part in this myth making, especially in those cases where citizen-soldiers, irregular forces, partisans, or guerrilla fighters played a prominent part in the fighting. Spain was probably the most flagrant instance of this, as the guerrilla fighters who took to the hills to impede the French attack were often more akin to bandits than patriots, though it was as patriots that they would be remembered in the nineteenth century, immortalized in folk tales and Goya's depictions.[28] Other countries had heroes, too: from the *barbets* of the Pyrenees and the foothills of the Alps to the partisans of Tyrol or the *ordinantes* of Portugal, every country produced its patriots and its legends. If Russia remembered its Patriotic War for Borodino and the passage of the Berezina, it recalled the exploits of its irregular fighters, its peasant heroes who thwarted the French advance, with as much pride. For nineteenth-century romantics these were the real patriots—the ordinary people who had risen in arms to drive out the invader, those who had risked their lives for their country. In truth, though, nationalism may have played little part in stimulating their opposition to an army that threatened pillage and despoliation. Their actions were often inspired by the need to defend their homes, their cattle, and their property. The role of nationalism may quite simply have been overplayed as intellectuals and political leaders tried to capture the spirit of the age.

NOTES

1. Benedict Anderson, *Imagined Communities: Reflections on the Origins and Spread of Nationalism* (London: Verso, 1983).

2. John Breuilly, *Nationalism and the State* (Manchester: Manchester University Press, 1982), 337.

3. For a discussion of Napoleon's relationship with Corsica, see Michel Vergé-Franceschi, *Napoléon, une enfance corse* (Paris: Larousse, 2009).

4. Jean-Clément Martin, "The French Revolution and Its Historiographies," in *Transnational Challenges to National History Writing*, ed. Matthias Middell and Lluís Roura Aulinas (Basingstoke: Palgrave Macmillan, 2013), 343–76, 347.

5. Nada Tomiche, *Napoléon écrivain* (Paris: Librairie Armand Colin, 1952), 191–92.

6. Michael J. Hughes, *Forging Napoleon's Grande Armée: Motivation, Military Culture and Masculinity in the French Army, 1800–1808* (New York: New York University Press, 2012).

7. Mette Harder, "A Second Terror: The Purges of French Revolutionary Legislators after Thermidor," *French Historical Studies* 38 (2015): 33–60.

8. Pierre Serna, *La république des girouettes, 1789–1815 et au-delà: Une anomalie politique, la France de l'extrême centre* (Paris: Champ Vallon, 2005).

9. Pierre Serna, "Introduction: Le Directoire, miroir de quelle République?,"

in *Républiques soeurs: Le Directoire et la Révolution atlantique* (Rennes: Presses Universitaires de Rennes, 2009), 11–20.

10. Michael Rowe, "The French Revolution, Napoleon and Nationalism in Europe," in *The Oxford Handbook of the History of Nationalism* (Oxford: Oxford University Press, 2013), 133.

11. John Hutchinson, "Cultural Nationalism," in *The Oxford Handbook of the History of Nationalism*, ed. John Breuilly (Oxford: Oxford University Press, 2013), 77.

12. Patrick Bahners, "National Unification and Narrative Unity: The Case of Ranke's *German History*," in *Writing National Histories: Western Europe since 1800*, ed. Stefan Berger, Mark Donovan, and Kevin Passmore (London: Routledge, 1999), 57–68.

13. Aurélien Lignereux, *Chouans et Vendéens contre l'Empire. 1815: L'autre guerre des Cent Jours* (Paris: Vendemiaire, 2015).

14. John Breuilly, "Nationalism and National Unification in Nineteenth-century Europe," in *The Oxford Handbook of the History of Nationalism*, ed. John Breuilly (Oxford: Oxford University Press, 2013), 150.

15. For an excellent overview, see Christopher A. Bayly, *The Birth of the Modern World, 1780–1914: Global Connections and Comparisons* (Oxford: Wiley-Blackwell, 2003).

16. Alan Forrest, "Un anti-héros de la Révolution Française: Oliver Cromwell," in *Héros et héroïnes de la Révolution Française*, ed. Serge Bianchi (Paris: Éditions du Comité des travaux historiques et scientifiques, 2012), 17–31.

17. Michael Broers, "Cultural Imperialism in a European Context? Political Culture and Cultural Politics in Napoleonic Italy," *Past & Present* 170 (2001): 152–80.

18. Charles J. Esdaile, "Popular Resistance in Napoleonic Europe: Issues and Perspectives," in *Popular Resistance in the French Wars: Patriots, Partisans and Land Pirates*, ed. Charles J. Esdaile (Basingstoke: Palgrave Macmillan, 2005), 201–24.

19. Breuilly, "Nationalism and National Unification," 349.

20. Lucy Riall, *Risorgimento: The History of Italy from Napoleon to Nation State* (Basingstoke: Palgrave Macmillan, 2009), 8.

21. Peter McPhee, *Robespierre: A Revolutionary Life* (New Haven, CT: Yale University Press, 2012), 114.

22. Geoffrey Ellis, "The Continental System Revisited," in *Revisiting Napoleon's Continental System: Local, Regional and European Experiences*, ed. Katherine B. Aaslestad and Johan Joor (Basingstoke: Palgrave Macmillan, 2015), 25–39.

23. Pierre Vilar, "Les concepts de 'nation' et de patrie chez les Espagnols du temps de la Guerre d'indépendance," in *Nations, Nationalismes et Questions Nationales* (*Iberica*, nouvelle série 4, 1994), 76.

24. Ibid., 85–90.

25. Significantly, the first three rooms of the Museum of the Risorgimento in Milan are devoted to the Napoleonic period in Italy.

26. Michael Broers, *Europe under Napoleon, 1799–1815* (London: Hodder Arnold, 1996), 234–39.

27. Karen Hagemann, "Celebration, Contestation and Commemoration: The Battle of Leipzig in German Memories of the Anti-Napoleonic Wars," in *War, Demobilization and Memory: The Legacy of War in the Era of Atlantic Revolutions*, ed. Alan Forrest, Karen Hagemann, and Michael Rowe (Basingstoke: Palgrave Macmillan, 2016), 335–52.

28. Charles J. Esdaile, *Fighting Napoleon: Guerrillas, Bandits and Adventurers in Spain, 1808–1814* (New Haven, CT: Yale University Press, 2004).

KEY RESOURCES

Students looking for useful works on both Napoleon and nationalism are faced with an embarrassment of riches, and it is impossible to do more here than suggest a few useful openings. Biographies of Napoleon abound, even in English: among single-volume works I would particularly recommend those by Steven Englund (*Napoleon: A Political Life*, Cambridge, MA: Harvard University Press, 2005) and Luigi Mascilli Migliorini (*Napoléon*, Paris: Tempus Perrin, 2001), while his early career is especially well covered by Patrice Gueniffey, *Bonaparte, 1769–1802* (Cambridge, MA: Harvard University Press, 2015), and Michael Broers, *Napoleon: Soldier of Destiny, 1769–1805* (London: Faber and Faber, 2014). In both cases second volumes are eagerly awaited. Nationalism has been critically analyzed by both historians and political scientists. Older works include Hans Kohn, *The Idea of Nationalism: A Study in Its Origins and Background* (New Brunswick: Transaction Publishers, 1961), and Elie Kedourie, *Nationalism* (London: Hutchinson, 1966); a less theoretical approach is John Breuilly, *Nationalism and the State* (Manchester: Manchester University Press, 1982). For a more up-to-date set of analytical essays, see John Breuilly, ed., *The Oxford Handbook of the History of Nationalism* (Oxford: Oxford University Press, 2013).

My emphasis in this chapter has principally been on the Napoleonic wars and imperial expansion beyond France's boundaries. These subjects are well discussed in Stuart Woolf, *Napoleon's Integration of Europe* (London: Routledge, 1991); Michael Broers, *Europe under Napoleon* (rev. ed., London: I. B. Tauris, 2015); and various collections of essays, including Philip Dwyer, ed., *Napoleon and Europe* (Harlow: Longman, 2001); Philip Dwyer and Alan Forrest, eds., *Napoleon and His Empire: Europe, 1804–1814* (Basingstoke: Palgrave, 2007); Michael Broers, Agustin Guimera, and Peter Hicks, eds., *The Napoleonic Empire and the New European Political Culture* (Basingstoke: Palgrave, 2012); and, most recently, Ute Planert, ed., *Napoleon's Empire: European Politics in Global Perspective* (Basingstoke: Palgrave, 2016). The most comprehensive and up-to-date military history of the Napoleonic wars is Charles Esdaile, *Napoleon's Wars: An International History, 1803–1815* (London: Penguin, 2007), though there are many others; while David Bell asks fundamental questions about the nature of warfare in this period in *The First Total War: Napoleon's Europe and the Birth of Warfare as We Know It* (London: Bloomsbury, 2007). There is no shortage of well-written campaign histories. A few stand out, among them Martin Boycott-Brown, *The Road to Rivoli: Napoleon's First Campaign* (London: Cassell, 2001); Charles Esdaile, *The Peninsular War: A New History* (London, 2001); and Dominic Lieven, *Russia against Napoleon: the Battle for Europe, 1807 to 1814* (London: Allen Lane, 2010). Students interested in guerrilla warfare and people's war may also wish to consult Charles Esdaile, *Fighting Napoleon: Guerrillas, Bandits and Adventurers in Spain, 1808–1814* (New Haven, CT: Yale University Press, 2004), and Michael Broers, *Napoleon's Other War: Bandits, Rebels and Their Pursuers in the Age of Revolutions* (Oxford: Peter Lang, 2010). For a more general conspectus of the Age of Revolutions, see Roger Chickering and Stig Førster, eds., *War in an Age of Revolution, 1775–1815* (Cambridge: Cambridge University Press/German Historical Institute, 2010).

The Napoleonic wars left long shadows. On the memory of the wars across Europe, see Alan Forrest, Etienne François, and Karen Hagemann, eds., *War Memories: The Revolutionary and Napoleonic Wars in Modern European Culture* (Basingstoke: Palgrave, 2012); for a more detailed study of Prussia, see Karen Hagemann, *Revisiting Prussia's Wars against Napoleon: History, Culture and Memory* (Cambridge: Cambridge University Press, 2015).

Those wishing to consult a comprehensive encyclopedia on this subject should go to Gregory Fremont-Barnes, *The Encyclopedia of the French Revolutionary and Napoleonic Wars* (3 vols., Santa Barbara, CA: ABC-CLIO, 2006); and those looking for relevant material on the Internet should visit the website of the Fondation Napoléon in Paris, http://napoleon.org.

Revolutionary Environments

Nature, Climate, and Teaching Revolutions

SHARLA CHITTICK

When students analyze the Age of Revolutions, primary emphasis often falls on ideological, political, and socioeconomic factors. Without diminishing existing complexities, this chapter emphasizes the value of an environmental element in revolutionary studies. As with locating the start of the Enlightenment (discussed by Ambrogio Caiani in this volume), debates rage and definitions vary on locating a point at which humankind's impact on the planet became a dominant geologic epoch. Though the recognition and dating of an "Anthropocene" varies, there is growing evidence and stronger consensus that the global impact of human actions and societies accelerated dramatically with the take-off of industrialization from the late eighteenth century—and we are only now coming to terms with the stark implications. The Age of Revolutions, in other words, coincided with—and arguably contributed to—an intense deepening of our collective environmental footprint. This is a critical subject for the twenty-first century. Presented with contemporary examples, students should be able to recognize the influence of extreme weather events and prolonged droughts on revolutionary behavior today. This conversation provides the opportunity for reflection on how climate change and nature affected eighteenth- and nineteenth-century revolutions.

Environmental pressures are most evident in the Age of Revolutions in the way they compounded duress and contributed significantly to the physical and psychological sense of urgency and desperation fueling revolutionary action. Scholars must look hard for these pressures, not least because contemporaries often missed them, and it is a fairly new approach. Sherry Johnson's *Climate and Catastrophe in Cuba and the Atlantic World in the Age of Revolution* serves as a good illustration for students of how environmental factors can be evaluated within the context of colonial events in the Caribbean.[1] This methodology of exploiting multidisciplinary evidence provides educators with an opportunity to reach a new generation of students who are familiar with the role of forensic and scientific investigations in determining historical narratives. It is essential for students to acknowledge that the natural world always holds sway over human survival. While not entirely deterministic, environmental factors influence every facet of human existence, and the Age of Revolutions was no different. Environmental stressors and extreme climate anomalies, like today, were present at the onset of these revolutions. They were influential "in the course of human events," and they contributed to the outcomes. Exposing students to a process of historical inquiry that includes analysis of empirical evidence provides additional texture to existing narratives. It also brings a more holistic understanding of the physical environment into the fold of human experience. Once these concepts have been introduced, they become impossible to ignore for any historical period. The advantages are dual: first, the range of methods and data stretches students; second, the introduction of new variables and influences stretches their subject matter in productive ways.

Revolutions are shaped by internal and external forces. Initially, students in revolutionary studies may categorize competing systems of power in their simplest binary forms as "the new versus the old" or even "the good guys and the bad guys," dissecting causation according to ideological differences between perceived oppressors and oppressed. In doing so, they typically see revolts as the actions of a populace fed up with the circumstances imposed by their adversaries. This form of analysis is an exercise in empathy that often directs the learning experience toward understanding the interests of either set of revolutionary actors. The student becomes engrossed in a study of human behavior where the circumstances of conflict appear to be within the control of one side or the other, where frustrations with sociopolitical and economic conditions create a very literal tug-of-war, and where superior strategies and intelligence are deciding factors in the outcome of each revolution.

Educators can remind their students of a third actor—the environment—and ask the class, "What of the nonhuman pressures— the external forces of nature beyond the control of either player?"

"What of the daily trials posed by unforgiving weather or environmental obstacles, including the need for protection from the elements, threats to food security and human health, or access to resources like firewood necessary for survival?" Of course, we must remain wary of suggesting that environmental factors always determine the human experience; history is messy, and human behavior is too complex for such a simplification. But there is no arguing that natural resources are often at the heart of geopolitical conflicts, and no denying that repercussions of extreme weather and sudden environmental events have the ability to change, hinder, and sometimes paralyze human agency. Especially in the case of revolutions before mechanized transport, the forces of nature made conditions and decisions precarious in agitated towns, on the oceans, across battlefields, in camps, and throughout surrounding communities. They hindered the ability of commoners to acquire sustenance, crushed morale, and inadvertently affected each side unequally. They affected physical health, psychology, and energy levels, and they obstructed transportation and trade. This directly impacted the theater of war and the outcomes of revolutions (or counterrevolutions). Indeed, in some ways, we see nature's impact most clearly at the nexus between the most long-standing and the newest branches of historical interest: military history and environmental history. Consider the iconic moments in the American and French revolutions: George Washington on Christmas 1776 or suffering at Valley Forge; John Burgoyne trying to hack his way through the forested Hudson River valley in 1777; Napoleon and his grande armée's retreat from Russia in 1812.

Opening Exercise and Introduction to Environmental History

Introduce the subject matter by asking students to reflect on the role of nature in their own lives: how many times have their flights been grounded, events canceled, or activities hindered by the weather? They will most likely concede that the best-laid plans are easily thwarted by storms and extreme temperatures. Have them imagine the chore of procuring food or medicine on foot during a harsh winter or severe drought. Make them consider the challenges of recovering from an earthquake or volcanic eruption that has devastated their community. Ask them to contemplate their own capacity for decision making when hungry or sick, especially when there is little prospect for relief. Prompt them to consider the vast obstacles to a daily life void of modern technology, especially when nature may eliminate food by laying waste to agricultural and pastoral resources. Personalize these concepts and they will probably acknowledge that environmental factors have the capacity to impact human behavior. This means they can imagine the influence of nature on decisions made prior to and during the theater of war. Such exercises (adjusted for the level of the participants) create an open mind-set for students to better understand and accommodate the environmental history of the Age of Revolutions.

Second, provide students with the tools to determine past environmental conditions. Historians traditionally rely on written documents and periodically struggle with the lack thereof. To determine environmental influences in the past, we must use and then go beyond conventional textual primary sources. Fortunately, contemporary scholars can now address the periodic dearth of historical sources with findings gleaned from paleoclimatology. For this reason, investigation into environmental factors influencing historical narratives has gained popularity over the past three decades. Students should be introduced to one of the first historians to do this. Donald Worster encourages us to consider a three-tiered multidisciplinary methodology for acquiring a holistic understanding of the relationship between nature and human behavior.[2] He recommends examining (a) the organic and inorganic elements of nature as it affects humans, (b) the impact humans have on nature as they develop their societies and expand their economies, and (c) the influence nature has on the human psyche.[3]

Students should understand that for the environmental historian to explore all three paths, we construct a synthesis of the evidence from the humanities and natural sciences. We combine our knowledge from primary and secondary sources with the findings of economic, psychological, and sociological studies. We enhance our understanding of the past by consulting the science: soil geomorphology, which examines the chemistry of soils to determine past climates, vegetation, and land use; archaeology, which studies physical and material remains to determine past culture, diet, and human health; paleoclimatology, which analyzes ice core isotopes to determine past temperatures on a hemispheric level; and dendrochronology, which evaluates tree rings to determine annual changes in regional environments. For the Age of Revolutions, a synthesis of hybrid evidence indicates there were natural and anthropogenic (human-made) changes taking place in the eighteenth- and nineteenth-century environment, which created additional stressors for a populace engaged in conflict. These conditions influenced decisions on and off the battlefield. They affected the ability to fight, move about, and stay healthy. Environmental factors also affected the physical, emotional, and psychological states of those who rioted against existing systems of power. At times, they even transformed the balance of power itself.

It is worth reinforcing to students that because they are not scientists, they do not need to know precisely how the science works. Using a multidisciplinary methodology means relying on the expertise of those who do know how the science works, and recent discoveries from a growing body of paleoclimate proxy data are invaluable to environmental historians. Students must wrap their heads around the fact that there is a plethora of scientific evidence providing us with the history of Earth as a dynamic organic entity. Findings in ice core isotopes, lake and sea-floor sediments, pollen, tree rings, corals, alpine glaciers, and even cave formations provide us with an incredibly comprehensive picture of past temperatures and conditions around the world. Some students may prefer to know how the science works, and they will find several papers in the joint *Climate of the Past/The Crysophere* special issue that resulted from the IPICS: 2012 First Open Science Conference.[4] They may explore several regional climate reconstructions, including Cullen and colleagues' analysis of North Atlantic Oscillation from 1701 to 1979 and Mann and colleagues' "Global-Scale Temperature Patterns and Climate Forcing over the Past six Centuries,"[5] For most students, a much more manageable scientific description of the Earth's climate history constructed with this diverse set of proxy data is online by the National Climate Data Center at NOAA and the Earth's Observatory at NASA.[6]

Once students digest the major trends in climate history since the Ice Age, they will want to focus on multidisciplinary evidence pertaining to temperatures, weather anomalies, and natural events (particularly those affecting the Atlantic world). The following sections offer a set of case studies or samples to get students thinking and to break into the subject matter more concretely, but they are not intended to be prescriptive or definitive. As for where the Age of Revolutions falls in the greater historical narrative, students should know that over five centuries prior to the late eighteenth century, the North Atlantic experienced a cold snap referred to as "the Little Ice Age." Brian Fagan provides an excellent student-level narrative that integrates scientific findings with harrowing historical accounts of human struggles under environmental pressures due to this period of climate change.[7] Students should know that human populations were still growing substantially as the natural world was recovering from stunted growing seasons, loss of mammals and marine life, and a general decrease in resources. The string of revolutions that occurred between the 1770s and the 1840s were taking place during the final stages of a long transition to warmer temperatures. As a result, revolutions were subject to extreme weather anomalies not so different from what we are experiencing today. Between North America, France, the Caribbean, Mexico and Central/South America, environmental pressures included droughts tempered by sudden heavy rainfall, harsh winter storms, hurricanes, earthquakes, and even a volcanic eruption. The evidence will show that the timing and repercussions of these events unquestionably complicated wars for independence or regime change in ways of which we are only now becoming acutely aware.

The American Revolution

Of all the environmental factors influencing the American Revolution, students will find that the weather was undoubtedly the most significant. The problem with weather in a society without modern technology is that there were no means to provide warning and therefore little time or ability to prepare. Even worse, prolonged environmental pressure caused by adverse weather led to desperation. A course curriculum should include a sampling of meteorological data, dendrochronology studies, letters, farmers' records, and media circulations from the New England area. These provide a treasure trove of scientific and testimonial evidence demonstrating the difficult conditions of the late eighteenth century and their impact on the course of revolutionary events.[8]

Between 1770 and 1774, winter temperatures in North America and Europe dropped significantly due to a see-saw effect caused by a phenomenon students should come to understand: a negative North Atlantic Oscillation (NAO) pattern. This happens naturally when wind pushes warmer air west into the Arctic, thereby forcing Arctic air south. Evidence found in the Greenland ice core isotopes confirms the observations of a Danish missionary named Hans Egede Saabye, who reported

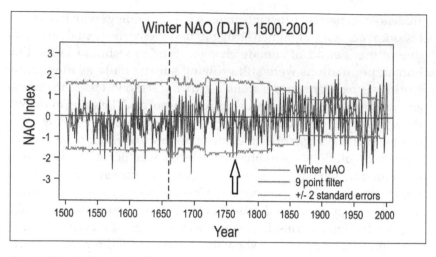

Chart of North Atlantic Oscillation reconstructions. (adapted from J. Luterbacher et al., "Extending North Atlantic Oscillation Reconstructions Back to 1500," *Atmospheric Science Letters of the Royal Meteorological Society* [2002]: 114–24)

extraordinary weather while living in Greenland between 1770 and 1778. The frigid temperatures resulting from this NAO effect were so severe that they caused the advancement of the Vernagtferner glacier in Tirol, Austria. Extreme cold was also responsible for some major challenges to resources in the American colonies. This concept of a warmer than usual summer followed by a colder than usual winter may resonate with students who have experienced it themselves. Over the past few years, Arctic temperatures have been the warmest on record, while parts of North America, Europe, and Russia have experienced abnormally cold winter storms and the dreaded polar vortex. Warming temperatures in the Arctic today may mean this see-saw effect of extreme weather could become a temporary norm over the next decade. On the eve of the American Revolution, as the conditions of the Little Ice Age were waning, the opposite was true. Extreme winter temperatures were becoming anomalous and such unexpected anomalies had very real effects on the agricultural and pastoral resources of the colonies.

Presenting students with the work of historian David Smith and climatologist William Baron provides a concise lesson in how multidisciplinary evidence is synthesized. They have analyzed more than 27,000 data points over three centuries in New England to determine air temperatures and record killing frosts (temperatures so low they put paid to all but the hardiest vegetation).[9] Their findings reveal that killing frosts were frequent and harvests ranged from below average to poor between the 1740s and 1776. This was attributed to cooler and unpredictable growing seasons that fluctuated in length between 80 to 170 days. A loss of Indian corn and wheat surplus below subsistence level meant that New England farmers struggled to provide their own sustenance, let alone to pay taxes still required of them by the British Crown. To exacerbate this economic pressure, there was a series of crop failures during the years just prior to the passage of the Stamp Act, and again on the eve of the Coercive Acts. Tree ring data combined with Thomas Jefferson's testimonial of the terrible drought followed by frost in 1774 "which destroyed almost everything" support Baron and Smith's conclusions: the severity and longevity of these conditions, especially between 1772 and 1775, would have significantly fueled colonists' desire to revolt against the Crown.

Students should consider the impact of environmental pressure on the psyche. Between 1776 and 1779, there were more than thirty food riots in New England. Traditional studies attribute protests to an underlying surge in politicization, which created a united front against British policies.[10] Failed crops meant duress on people and animals. There was a real scarcity of community resources, prompting a ripple effect tempered or amplified by political and economic grievances. Anger over hoarding merchants, escalating food prices, and British regulations meant public demonstrations went beyond proto-nationalism. Women initiated almost a third of all protests, indicating a threat to basic food staples like grains, sugar, salt, and tea. In 1776, women went so far as to enter the chambers of the Committee of Safety in Kingston, warning that their "husbands and sons shall fight no more" should food shortages not be addressed.[11] The fact that women were under duress, and not just demonstrating their newfound political identities (considered in a different context in Parker's chapter in this volume), is best illustrated by their threats to interfere with the war effort itself.[12]

Crop failures, of course, had a very real long-term impact on colonial communities, but students should also consider daily obstacles provided by the weather. During the summer of 1777, colonial forces suffered several military defeats. By September, the British had taken Philadelphia, ensuring their ability to stick out the cold winter months in comparative luxury, near food supplies and medicine, and in the comfort of brick homes with fireplaces. Because the British paid in gold and silver, rural farmers even traveled to the city to sell their food. In short, the British wanted for very little. The patriot forces, on the other hand, were in dire straits. Students will find the best testimony for this in George Washington's letters from Valley Forge (1777–1778), where we find winter weather conditions caused myriad problems. Writing to the Continental Congress, Washington even threatened that his soldiers were nearly "forced to starve, dissolve, or disperse in order to obtain subsistence."[13] The winter of 1777–1778 made for an extended period of stagnation and desperation. Soldiers struggled to obtain enough firewood to warm their cramped and unsanitary encampments, most of which had degenerated into cesspools of typhus, typhoid, dysentery, and pneumonia. Washington's letters emphasize his desperation for food, clothing, medical care, and supplies. He was frustrated with local farmers who hoarded their limited supplies or sold to the British. Believing the morale of his men would be their ultimate downfall, he was deeply concerned with poor mental health. More than 2,000 of the 12,000 soldiers died as they attempted to wait out the winter. What is generally considered the darkest episode in the American Revolution has typically been viewed uncritically as a triumph of American will against environmental pressure. Determination was undoubtedly important, but Washington and his troops demonstrated human agency by turning to environmental factors to fuel their striking comeback. They exploited an unusual early spawning of shad in the Schuylkill River, cut drying timber during the spring thaw, and added windows to their cabins using mud chippings to create better ventilation.[14] Students will recognize this famous turning point in US history as environmental history.

Presented with visual evidence, students will find that weather did not always serve the British. In a scene celebrated in M. A. Wageman's famous painting "Retreat from Long Island," it was only a year prior to that terrible winter that nature acted as a strategic ally to Washington, when his ill-equipped troops retreated behind a veil of dense fog at the Battle of Long Island (August 22, 1776) and managed to avoid a robust British army.[15] Other examples for consideration may include the failed attempt by the British to take Charleston when high winds and rain prevented them from entering the narrow channel at Sullivan Island. By the time the British finally attacked, the Americans had finished fortifying their fort and could protect the channel. A few weeks of bad weather provided opportunity for increasing their supply of cannon, ensuring British defeat. Prior to the terrible winter of 1777–1778, poor conditions also favored the Americans. At the Battle of the Clouds in Chester County, Pennsylvania, heavy storms and fog created physical and visual barriers protecting American troops from the British advance. In many ways, the proverbial tides changed during the years following that harsh winter at Valley Forge. In October 1781, Rear Admiral Thomas Graves documented the British flotilla's frustrating experience with heavy rain, wind, and sheets of hail, causing their ships to collide and run aground in the Bay of Yorktown. Days later, Lord Cornwallis was literally defeated by winds and squalls in the York River, leaving over 1,000 of his men stranded on the opposite shore. Students will find that time and again, evidence supports the direct influence of environmental factors in the theater of war—and Yorktown is a great case study to use (bringing together disease, weather, and a definitive military moment).

In addition to studying the weather during the American Revolution, students can consider how flooding destroyed colonial infrastructure and eliminated drinking water, how an animal plague caused meat prices to skyrocket and eliminated beasts of burden, and how disease served as an unpredictable biological weapon against both sides of the conflict. Smallpox was a continual threat to colonial forces, malaria literally plagued their British adversaries, and lack of a cure for scurvy under poor conditions was a problem for both sides.[16] The ability for disease to affect the course and outcome of revolutions will be better exemplified below, as the American Revolution was the first of many where tropical disease played a determinant role.[17] Students may also contemplate how intimate relationships with nature favored the revolutionary over the British. Last, students could explore personal perceptions linking environmental to political—most obviously, how the American landscape was romanticized and invoked for everything from the struggle for independence during the 1770s through to the Louisiana Purchase and the explorations of Lewis and Clark.[18]

The French Revolution

There is general consensus among historians that during the late eighteenth century the ancien régime in France was financially bankrupt, the country was embroiled in a quasi class war, and intellectuals were determined to transform culture and align political structure with Enlightenment ideals. Students should first be presented with scholarly research into environmental conditions in France on the eve of revolution.[19] It is widely accepted that major natural occurrences, compounded by population density, contributed to the course of revolutionary events. These scientific studies reveal long-term stressors in the form of extreme weather, crop failures, droughts, hailstorms, flooding, and livestock diseases. Economic and political documentation confirms high food prices due to disastrous harvests coinciding with heavy taxes and an inability of the state to provide relief or security during food riots. Historical documents such as testimonials, farmers' diaries, and correspondence highlight the influence of these severe conditions on the human psyche. Recent applied economic theory even confirms a strong connection between duress, the locations of revolts, and a timeline of political protest. Together, this combination of evidence provides students with a clear and obvious link between environmental factors and the French Revolution. What I like to leave until the end, for a "grand reveal," is that this poisoned bouquet of natural disasters was triggered by a volcanic eruption in Iceland.

The class will learn how on June 8, 1783, the Icelandic volcano Laki erupted with fury, emitting over 200 megatons of devastating atmospheric aerosols, including sulfur dioxide, hydrochloric acid, and ash. This ignited nine months of volcanic pollution, acid precipitation, and extreme weather throughout the Northern Hemisphere. Scientific evidence for this event was trapped in ice cores, tree rings, and soil sediments, the examination of which reveals the worst gas levels in over 1,000 years. Vividly captured in hundreds of historical records, the ruin was widespread. As "the haze" moved its way southeast, more than 23,000 people in Britain died from inhalation. In mainland Europe and much of Eurasia, extraordinary amounts of crops and livestock were destroyed. Due to the unfortunate timing of the eruption, which collided with negative NAO and El Niño conditions, the winter of 1783–1784 in North America was the worst on record until 2009–2010 (relevant for those exploring the social and economic chaos plaguing the Confederation period in the fledgling United States). The Inuit called it "the summer that did not come." As the dust spread around the globe, very little of the Northern Hemisphere was left unscathed. The monsoon season in India was affected, and the Japanese and Egyptians experienced their worst famines on record. The timing was obviously ominous for France. On the eve of the revolution, as the country simmered with anger toward their king, a Catholic priest made a failed attempt to chase the "dry fog" away with an exorcism.[20]

The eruption columns, which were visible for nearly three months, have been estimated by scientific model calculations to have been between ten and twelve kilometers high, and teachers can invite students to discuss the fallout in accessible charts such as that produced by Haraldur Sigurdsson.[21] As that volcanic pollution spread, what went up began to come down in the form of ash fall and acid rain. In France, there was damage to soil, vegetation, animals, and humans. The acid burned right through vegetation, poisoned the ground, and wounded everyone it touched. For months, there was a sulfurous stink and people reported asthma attacks, respiratory problems, headaches, and burning eyes. Vegetation withered and died. Staple crops like corn and wheat were scorched and blackened, as was the hay on which animals were dependent. This led to mass slaughtering as humans competed with animals for food. When the acid precipitation stopped, the climate began to change. Overnight frosts during the summer were followed by dry and hot days. The emissions created short-term greenhouse warming, trapping warm air and disrupting the atmospheric circulation pattern over Europe. This unfortunate combination made summer temperatures in 1783 the warmest on record until 1995, and the extremes did not stop there. The following winter was the coldest on record until 2010 when negative NAO and El Niño combined to cause extreme cold. To further complicate conditions, when snow and ice finally began to melt in May 1784, water levels became so high that flooding wiped out infrastructure throughout Europe. In France, homes and buildings were flooded, bridges and dykes destroyed. The River Seine saw a three meter rise above normal water levels near the de la Tournelle Bridge. With the radiative thermal balance of the atmosphere still reeling and the westerly jet stream still weak, Laki's presence was felt for another three years. Long-term devastation to natural ecosystems and habitat made living conditions in France tenuous. As people foraged for wood to heat their homes, the two frigid winters that followed no doubt compounded this stress.

Students will now be capable of determining how these years of environmental challenges influenced the French Revolution. Although Laki's destructive effects had waned somewhat by the French Revolution, they undoubtedly contributed to a medium-term fall in living standards among the French, especially the twenty-four million peasants who made up around three quarters of the population. Years of weather extremes had destabilized the marketplace, and a large contingent of vagrants traveled the country begging for resources. This was the situation by the summer of 1788, when tragedy struck once again. Students may examine a sampling of primary sources revealing annual cycles of drought followed by extreme weather like hailstorms and severe flooding destroying much of France's food supply, causing more crop failures and skyrocketing food prices. Harvests had been good the year before, but the government chose to export surplus to pay the national debt. The appetite for protest, riot, and ultimately revolution can only have been deepened by the combination of environmental stress and political disaffection. Students may view price lists estimating commoners spent as much as 88 percent of their income on bread. The string of events must have been déjà vu: drought, subsistence crisis, skyrocketing food prices, and a harsh winter with a deep freeze followed by a thaw with terrible floods. If students combine the historical evidence with scientific findings, they can understand how these disasters may have triggered or exacerbated protest.

For decades, historians have used testimonials to highlight the influence of hunger on rioters. Familiar with this phenomenon during the American Revolution, students can explore the empirical evidence proving a similar connection. Luterbacher and colleagues provide climate data using ice core isotopes and dendrochronology, providing exact temperatures and timelines for erratic growing seasons. Maria Waldinger created an economic model with a basic data set of annual/monthly temperatures, crop failures, and protest locations from 3,596 French cantons, a cross-section covering the total territory of continental France. Her findings demonstrate a direct correlation between adverse climate anomalies and food riots. The high temperatures and lack of rainfall in the late spring and summer of 1788 were responsible for drought and loss of grains, leading to steep increases in food prices and a loss of livestock by 1789. An extremely harsh winter followed, limiting timber supplies and threatening human health. That was followed by another severely hot summer in 1789. These environmental factors affected the rural/agricultural population more than the urban poor. Waldinger's model clearly plots the dates and locations of protests following severe climate anomalies and subsequent sharp decreases in resources. The findings are obvious: the timing, likeliness, and locations of protests by the rural poor correlate with environmental pressures.

Beyond the extreme weather and environmental impact following Laki, the catastrophic drought of 1788, and the difficult winter of 1789, students may consider the human impact on nature during the revolution. They will find that the French were not subject only to climate anomalies and their consequences. Much of the devastation to the countryside during the revolution was anthropogenic. State regulation and supervision of forests collapsed by 1789, just as winter exploitation of timber escalated among the masses. Between 1789 and 1792, many common lands were subject to illicit clearing. As extreme weather conditions exacerbated the need for fuel, food, and grazing land, acts of desperation were common. Initially, the Jacobins wished to increase the number of French landowners by dividing common lands between village community members, while conservative deputies believed divisions should be held by the landowning class. Revolutionary Jacobins eventually issued a decree on June 10, 1793, whereby common land could be restored and partitioned between the members of each village. Noelle Plack's study reveals a significant shift in agricultural practices during this restoration in the department of the Gard, province of Languedoc.[22] Villages that participated in the process of restoring and partitioning common lands were subject to socioeconomic changes taking place during the revolution: declines in the textile and pastoral industries. For this reason, many villagers responded by converting to viticulture, and the wine industry played a large part in restoring the French economy. Despite nearly ten years of environmental degradation, the rural population's understanding of local ecosystems allowed them to make the best of chaotic natural pressures and recuperate in a postrevolutionary environment.

Latin American Wars of Independence

Environmental factors played a significant role in the revolutions for independence in Latin America. Case studies from Mexico and Venezuela exemplify three of the most destructive forces of nature: drought, earthquake, and the mosquito. Although this is just a small sampling for students, it highlights that the Southern Hemisphere was home to its own variety of natural occurrences that deeply affected the course and prospects of popular revolutions and military confrontations.

A good start is to introduce students to Enrique Florescano, who has plotted maize prices between 1708 and 1810 demonstrating that a drought in Mexico (1808–1809) created an agricultural crisis resulting in steep food prices.[23] Susan Swan has analyzed correspondence from the Tulancalco region of north-central Mexico, determining that droughts in 1808 and 1811 caused further deterioration of environmental conditions affecting all aspects of daily life.[24] Periods of drought were complicated by changes in traditional patterns of rainfall. Rather than relieving the dry conditions, early rains often ruined crops due to soil erosion. This affected maize, turnip, and barley production. Even the normally drought-resistant agave (also referred to as maguey) was badly stunted. Mexicans relied on the agave plant's leaves for paper, and its fibers were commonly used for fabrics and rope. They fermented its sugary sap into *pulque*, which served as a staple drink. The loss of agricultural produce was not the only problem. These droughts meant poor grazing conditions and a lack of water and food for livestock, which adversely affected birth and mortality rates. Loss of animals (especially sheep) meant skyrocketing meat prices. As with the Americans and French, Mexicans in the Tulancalco region were dealing with food shortages, high prices, and a lack of livestock for transportation and by-products. The physical effects on humans were difficult enough, and the psychological toll was extreme. When resources were scarce, a cycle of social unrest, including hoarding and robbing, pitted the masses against landowners. To exacerbate frustrations, landowners attempted to collect taxes and fees when agricultural production was low. Florescano has argued that these extreme environmental pressures may have initiated the revolutionary movement. Swan concludes that the crisis of 1811 may have been the greatest and final instigator of revolution. Again, students should consider the impact on the psyche—a great, open subject for productive and imaginative discussion. Desperation caused by widespread hunger went beyond prompting simple food riots to fueling revolt. The atmosphere of fear may have even influenced the rhetoric of Catholic-priest-turned-revolutionary Miguel Hidalgo, who channeled the energy of the hungry masses to win independence from Spain in 1821.

Environmental factors in Venezuela on the eve of independence provide students with another excellent case study unrelated to climate. Following the deposition of King Ferdinand VII of Spain by Napoleon in 1808, political structures in the Spanish colonies began to crumble (discussed in more depth by Marcela Echeverri in this volume). Some elites ruled in their king's name and awaited his return to the throne, whereas others viewed destabilization as an opportunity to revolt. A grand effort on behalf of the revolutionaries Simón Bolívar and Francisco de Miranda resulted in Venezuela declaring its independence from Spain in July 1811, making it the first colony to do so. The victory was short-lived. On March 26, 1812, during the infancy of the First Republic, a catastrophic earthquake changed the course of the revolution. The anomalous droughts and winter deep freezes that hampered the course of the American Revolution and the three-year fallout of the Laki eruption that complicated the French Revolution were cascading events providing time for contemplation and human response. The earthquake of 1812 paralyzed an entire nation in a matter of minutes. Killing an estimated 30,000 people, it destroyed the infrastructure of cities like Caracas, Mérida, La Guaira, San Felipe, and Barquisimeto. This seismic event, and the subsequent aftershocks continued well into April, bringing buildings down, eliminating access to clean drinking water, disrupting the flow of food supplies, and creating a spiritual crisis. Students can get a visual sense of the rings of impact by looking at a useful reconstruction online.[25]

The trauma caused by loss of life and destruction to community resources was extraordinary, and inviting comparisons with recent disasters—tsunamis and hurricanes, for instance—can help students tease this out. Fear, grief, and hopelessness made the masses psychologically and emotionally vulnerable. Still loyal to the Spanish Crown, the upper echelon of the Catholic Church used the catastrophe for propaganda purposes, claiming the earthquake was divine punishment for revolution. They openly questioned the legitimacy of an independent Venezuela. As a result, the superstitious turned to prayers and rituals for forgiveness, mourning and repenting to the point of inhibiting any immediate recovery. The earthquake was considered an omen, a sign from God that the revolutionaries had sinned. Their support for "freedom of religion" was an obvious threat to the Catholic establishment. Embedded in the new constitution a year prior, this policy angered Church representatives who used the opportunity to demonize those responsible. Criticism of the revolutionary movement grew as Venezuelans debated whether God was literally destroying imperial power or inflicting punishment for society having abandoned the Spanish king. The psychic confusion was a detriment to cooperation, healthy healing, and material reconstruction. Like many of his contemporaries, Bolívar was keenly aware of the capacity for environmental factors to

Tito Salas, *El terremoto de 1812 con Simón Bolívar en Caracas.* (1929, mural, Casa Natal de Bolívar, Caracas; https://www.flickr.com/photos/ctam/5636530829/in/photostream/; photograph by Cristóbal Alvarado Minic under Creative Commons)

affect political and social ambitions. Yet his call to arms and declaration "If nature opposes us, we will struggle against her and force her to obey us," fell primarily on deaf ears.[26] It was obvious that any formidable patriot response would take time.

Students will find the earthquake also weighed heavily on the political climate. Whether perceived as bad luck or divine design, patriot cities were disproportionately devastated, while cities still under royal control were primarily spared. The agricultural industry was nearly paralyzed. Harvests below subsistence level stunted exports of coffee, cocoa, and sugar. The economy ground to a halt. Reports of starvation, homelessness, looting, and a general state of misery in the patriot-inhabited regions of Venezuela reached royalist ears. This provided leverage to an existing Spanish system of power with the ability to provide provisions to victims. In addition, many patriot garrisons were leveled in the quake and royal forces benefited from those deserters whose switching of sides was likely an act of self-preservation. The reality was clear—the revolutionary First Republic did not have the resources to care for a society overwhelmed by natural disaster. Survival trumped ideology and altered the path to independence. Five months after the earthquake, the First Republic crumbled to the ground. Revolutionary momentum had been leveled in one day. This earthquake and its aftermath illustrate how natural forces can further complicate the human struggle for independence, regardless of region. Had it not occurred, the "First Republic" might have just been "the Republic." But this was not the end of the story. By the next year, the Venezuelans' crisis of confidence waned and a new energy rose from the rubble. For nearly seven years, revolutionaries championed their own earthquake rhetoric: a fortified republic would be able to handle any natural disaster.

Venezuela provides an example of how natural disasters can affect the course of a revolution, but it is also a fascinating illustration of how the smallest of nature's creatures can solidify the outcome. The earthquake may have aided the Spanish Crown, but the mosquito served as a most powerful ally when Venezuela finally did achieve independence. Students should remember (or be reminded) that centuries before these revolutions, European imperial forces had unwittingly carried diseases with them to which they were immune.[27] This gave them their original advantage over indigenous peoples, who were ravaged by smallpox, influenza, and the bubonic and pneumonic plagues. During the Age of Revolutions, the advantage was reversed. Essentially, their empire struck back. European exploitation of a seemingly endless store of resources transformed the natural environment. They created sugar plantations and port cities to suit their own imperial interests, all of which put in motion a set of circumstances that eventually worked against them. During the seventeenth and eighteenth centuries, the largest group of migrants to Latin America were West and West-Central Africans forced into the mining, timber, sugarcane, and indigo economies. With them, again unwittingly, came diseases to which they also bore immunities: malaria, yellow fever, and dengue. The *Aedes* and *Anopheles* genuses of mosquitos carrying these devastating diseases were simply stowaways who made their home in new tropical environments, and the ecological transformation of the tropics made for extremely favorable conditions. New World inhabitants built up their immunities over several centuries of biological diffusion, and as imperial forces returned in the eighteenth century to protect their interests, the tables were turned.[28]

To flesh out the influence of disease in war, students should consider revolution orchestrated by ex-slaves in the Caribbean. It was in Haiti in

1802 where approximately 50,000 British and 40,000 French died, primarily from yellow fever. The Haitians knew they had "insect and viral allies." As Jean-Jacques Dessalines waged guerrilla warfare against imperial armies, he even proclaimed to his forces, "The French will not be able to remain long in San Domingo. They will do well at first, but soon they will fall ill and die like flies."[29] Epidemic diseases were having an obvious and direct impact on the geopolitics of the period, with an estimated 180,000 lost lives during revolutions in the West Indies. But the Spanish did not retreat from an obstacle such as differential immunities. In 1814, Spanish Commander Pablo Morillo and 14,000 soldiers sailed for Costa Firme on the coast of New Granada (now Colombia, Venezuela, Ecuador, and part of Panama) with their "unprepared immune systems." As long as they were fighting along the coast, the Spanish were victorious. By 1815, Bolívar had fled to Jamaica and then Haiti. To maintain control of New Granada, Morillo needed *los llanos*, the vast grassland of savannah—an ecosystem favoring the mosquito. By 1817, tempered by high temperatures, he had lost a third of his troops when he wrote, "The mere bite of a mosquito often deprives a man of his life."[30] Men returning to Spain brought back news of epidemiological challenges in New Granada. They also carried yellow fever and malaria back home. Fear caused the 20,000 new recruits authorized by Ferdinand VII to mutiny. By 1820, Morillo was negotiating with Bolívar, and by 1823, Venezuela was independent. McNeill estimates that nearly 17,000 European troops fought in Venezuela over six years, and that only 1,700 survived by 1821. Although many would have died in the conflict, there is no doubt that differential resistance and immunity contributed to Spanish defeat. Perhaps Bolívar learned in Haiti that he had allies of the insect variety waiting for him in Venezuela. This admittedly abbreviated narrative may provide students with enough evidence to ponder whether Venezuelans today should celebrate Bolívar or the mosquito as "El Libertador."

Reflection and Relevance

For each revolution, students attending to the environment will find common themes: natural disasters, climate anomalies, and subsequent environmental factors directly threaten the basic necessities for survival and influence human behavior. At times, they combine with exacerbating circumstances like political corruption, oppressive social and economic policies, or shifts in social norms and ideological beliefs, to revolutionary effect. Sometimes they are the final straw in a long line of stressors or irritants that plague both sides, but often they aid one side over the other. These exercises demonstrate for students that nature is simply an unpredictable and threatening third player in the theater of war—one that cannot be ignored. Therefore, it is an element that must be studied and integrated into the revolutionary context.

These short summaries and selected content are meant to invite students to rethink the place of nature in some of these sweeping political transformations. In the case of the American Revolution, the environment was an irritant and then a threat. It was an ally and an obstacle to overcome. Eventually, it was one of many strategic weapons used to win independence. In the case of the French Revolution, environmental pressures were a constant and heavy burden proven to push humans toward protest. In France, the level of desperation caused by a series of unfortunate natural events was widespread. That shared experience empowered an oppressed demographic and created a united front. Further research is necessary to determine impact in the whole of Mexico, but environmental factors had a very similar influence in the Tulancalco region of north-central Mexico. Meanwhile, in Venezuela, natural disaster served one side, while an insect inadvertently assisted the other. It is impossible to examine this particular struggle for independence completely without considering either factor.

In each example, environmental factors played a significant role in the causes, strategies, and outcomes of revolution. As a curriculum, this material provides students with a very clear objective when tasked with applying environmental history to revolutionary studies. They are meant to identify natural influences and determine impact. In the process, students should not simply ponder the physical damage or the way environmental pressures seem to have directed human agency. They can draw parallels: these are issues of the past with lessons for the future. In many respects, environmental history was born out of a moral responsibility. We attempt to identify how the natural world has changed, how it has affected humans, and how we have reacted to that pressure. More important, we do this so that we might provide some insight into what can be done now and in the future. The ideologies, politics, and economics of revolutions have evolved with advances in technology, democracy, and communication, but environmental factors still prevail. Exacerbated by the repercussions of anthropogenic climate change, they pose a formidable threat to existing systems of power, as well as the universal human psyche.[31] This may be the most obvious justification for incorporating environmental history more firmly within revolutionary studies.

All of this takes us back to Worster's third category for analysis: the impact of the natural world on the human psyche. Psychological and sociological studies show that environmental pressures exacerbate all other stressors because they stimulate fear.[32] Fear can distort and thwart "common sense" by cloaking rational thought and manipulating human impulses. Historically fear can be an engine for irrational and paranoid thoughts, which can lead to hysteria. This is precisely why studying the environment is so relevant. Environmental pressure intensifies stress by psychologically toying with the known, accentuating the unknown, and catapulting humans to action.[33] Acemoglu and Robinson have used economic models to determine how recessions trigger revolutions, particularly in twentieth-century Latin America.[34] Their hypothesis considers the way extreme economic duress can stunt the opportunity costs of the masses to contest power, a conclusion that is supported by these earlier revolutionary studies. When survival is threatened by nature and suffering is compounded by perceived oppression, feelings of helplessness are agitated by hunger or illness, and a "nothing to lose" mentality can lead to much more intense and urgent political and ideological engagement. On the eve of the French Revolution, a rumor circulated among the weary and starving rural poor: brigands were being sent by the aristocracy to destroy their next harvest to "starve the country people into submission."[35]

This curriculum starts by asking students to consider the impact of nature on contemporary events. Once they have been exposed to the case studies, I encourage you to return them to the present. Recently, the effects of climate change on human psychology have received much scholarly interest. In 2011, as part of an executive report from the American Psychological Association, Doherty and Clayton determined there are three different psychological impacts.[36] First, direct impact is experienced by those who are immediately traumatized by an environmental event. Like the floods following a frigid winter in France, there have been extreme contemporary floods in Pakistan and India, the Balkans, and the state of Colorado. These events directly affect those societies and cause immediate material needs like housing, food, and protection from future crisis. They also create direct psychological damage. Second, indirect impact affects those on the front lines of future climate catastrophes who fear unknowns. These include coastal societies who are threatened by sea level rise, agricultural communities threatened by temperature rise, and poor countries with less recourse. Finally, there are the chronic psychosocial effects to communities who experience slow stressors: droughts, heat waves, deep freezes, and escalating subsistence crises. Throughout history, these long-term stressors tear apart communities when natural tendencies toward self-preservation lead to competition and hoarding, weighing heaviest on the less fortunate.[37]

Exploring how the environment influenced the Age of Revolutions, then, provides a proper premise for stimulating greater awareness and preparedness in our own time. This is beginning to happen. The Stimson Center and the Center for Climate and Security prepared a report on *The Arab Spring and Climate Change: A Climate and Security Correlations Series*.[38] Johnstone and Mazo of the International Institute for Strategic Studies have investigated the effects of global warming on the Arab Spring, with particular focus on how drought may not have caused the revolution but brought it about much sooner.[39] Troy Sternberg of Oxford University has connected drought and subsequent subsistence crises in China to revolts in Egypt, while journalist Robert Worth found that the drought in Syria left more than 800,000 people without a livelihood. Studies of this kind are in their infancy, but they definitely support the idea that changes to the global order are being prompted by anthropogenic warming.[40]

We can and we should read back to identify what environmental pressures existed and determine how they compounded duress and contributed to the sense of urgency and desperation that fueled conflicts during the Age of Revolutions. In doing so, especially in the classroom, we elevate these processes and make them more visible—not only those in the past but also those in our own time and the future. Connecting environmental elements, anthropogenic and natural, to the complex fabric of revolutionary studies provides a more holistic understanding of challenges in the past and potential solutions for our future. What better justification could we need for studying environmental history?

NOTES

1. Sherry Johnson, *Climate and Catastrophe in Cuba and the Atlantic World in the Age of Revolution* (Chapel Hill: University of North Carolina Press, 2012).

2. Donald Worster, "Transformations of the Earth: Toward an Agroecological Perspective in History," *Journal of American History* 76, no. 4 (1990): 1088.

3. Donald Worster, "Appendix: Doing Environmental History," in *The Ends of the Earth: Perspectives on Modern Environmental History* (Cambridge: Cambridge University Press, 1988), 290–93.

4. C. Barbante, K. Kawamura, A. N. LeGrande, G. Winckler, J. Chappellaz, E. Wolff, M. Albert, R. Greve, E. Isaksson, and M. Van den Broek, eds., *Climate of the Past/The Cryosphere*, special issue from the International Partnerships in Ice Core Sciences (IPICS): 2012 First Open Science Conference in Giens, France. Retrieved from http://www.clim-past.net/special_issue55.html.

5. Heidi M. Cullen, Rosanne D. D'Arrigo, Edward R. Cook, and Michael E. Mann, "Multiproxy Reconstructions of the North Atlantic Oscillation," *Paleoceanography* 16, no. 1 (February 2001): 27–39; Michael E. Mann, Raymond S. Bradley and Malcolm K. Hughes, "Global-Scale Temperature Patterns and Climate Forcing over the Past Six Centuries," *Nature* 392 (April 1998): 23.

6. Holli Riebeek, "Paleoclimatology: Explaining the Evidence," http://earthobservatory.nasa.gov/Features/Paleoclimatology/paleoclimatology_intro.php. This is an explanation covering each process and how the evidence is interpreted. Also see NOAA Paleoclimatology Program, *Introduction to Paleoclimatology: Paleo Proxy Data*, https://www.ncdc.noaa.gov/paleo/proxies.html. This is a much shorter overview of how each form of data is used.

7. Brian Fagan, *The Little Ice Age: How Climate Made History 1300–1850* (New York: Basic Books, 2002).

8. See, for example, A. W. D'Amato and D. A. Orwig, "Stand and Landscape-Level Disturbance Dynamics in 848 Old-Growth Forests in Western Massachusetts," *Ecological Monographs* 78 (2008): 507–22.

9. William R. Baron and David Smith, "B846: Growing Season Parameter Reconstructions for New England Using Killing Frost Records, 1697–1947," *Maine Agricultural and Forest Experiment Station Bulletin* No. 11 (1996).

10. One of the most accessible is Barbara Clark Smith's article. Now dated but still something of a classic in addressing the "moral economy" of American revolutionary crowds, this may serve as a prelude to thinking about environmental contributions. Barbara Clark Smith, "Food Riots and the American Revolution," *William and Mary Quarterly* (1994): 3–30.

11. New York Convention Proceedings, August 1776, *American Archives*, 5th series, 1:1542–43.

12. See Thomas S. Wermuth, "'The women! In this place have risen in a

mob': Women Rioters and the American Revolution in the Hudson River Valley," *Hudson River Valley Review* 20, no. 1 (Summer 2003): 65–72.

13. George Washington Papers, 1741–1791, Manuscript Division, Library of Congress, http://memory.loc.gov/ammem/gwhtml/gwhome.html.

14. For an excellent account textured with ample primary accounts, see Russell Freedman, *Washington at Valley Forge* (New York: Holiday House, 2008).

15. This image can be found online at the National Archives and Records Administration's website, "Campaigns in the Northeast, 1776–77," number 30, http://www.archives.gov/research/military/american-revolution/pictures/.

16. Mary C. Gillet, "From Siege to Retreat, 1775 to May 1777," *The Army Medical Department, 1775–1818* (Washington, DC: US Government Printing Office, 1981), courtesy of the Office of Medical History: http://history.amedd .army.mil/booksdocs/rev/gillett1/ch3.html. See also Elizabeth Fenn, *Pox Americana: The Great Smallpox Epidemic of 1775–82* (New York: Hill and Wang, 2001).

17. For the impact of disease on military strategy in the American South, see Peter McCandless, "Revolutionary Fever: Disease and War in the Lower South, 1776–1783," *Transactions of the American Clinical and Climatological Association* 118 (2007): 225–49.

18. This could be an opportunity for some primary source analysis of Jefferson's *Notes on the State of Virginia*, Lewis and Clark's *Journals of Lewis and Clark*, or romantic landscape paintings like *The Oxbow* by Thomas Cole. A general source on this topic would be Simon Schama, *Landscape and Memory* (London: Harper Collins, 1995), 179–80.

19. Excerpts about environmental pressure may be found in Georges Lefebvre, *The Great Fear of 1789: Rural Panic in Revolutionary France* (New York: Vintage Books, 1973); J. Neumann, "Great Historical Events That Were Significantly Affected by the Weather: The Year Leading to the Revolution of 1789 in France," *Bulletin of the American Meteorological Society* 58 (1977): 163–67; Rudolf Brazdil, Gaston R. Demarée, Matthias Deutsch, E. Garnier, Andrea Kiss, Jürg Luterbacher, Neil Macdonald, Christian Rohr, Petr Dobrovolny, Petr Kolář, and Katerina Chromá, "European Floods during the Winter 1783/1784: Scenarios of an Extreme Event during the 'Little Ice Age,'" *Theoretical and Applied Climatology* 100 (June 2009): 163–89.

20. G. White, *The Natural History and Antiquities of Selborne* (London: Walter Scott, 1789).

21. H. Sigurdsson, "Volcanic Pollution and Climate: The 1783 Laki Eruption," *Eos, Transactions of the American Geophysical Union* 63, no. 32 (1982): 601–2. The graphic can be found at http://volcano.oregonstate.edu/laki-iceland-1783.

22. Noelle Plack, "Environmental Issues during the French Revolution:

Peasants, Politics and Village Common Land," *Australian Journal of French Studies* 47, no. 1 (2010): 290–303.

23. Enrique Florescano, *Precios del Maiz y Crisis Agricola en México: 1708–1810* (Mexico City: Ediciones Era, 1969).

24. Susan Swan, "Drought and Mexico's Struggle for Independence," *Environmental Review* 6, no. 1 (Spring 1982): 54–62.

25. José E. Choy, Christl Palme, Carlos Guada, María Morandi, and Stephanie Klarica, "Macroseismic Interpretation of the 1812 Earthquakes in Venezuela Using Intensity Uncertainties and a Priori Fault-Strike Information," *Bulletin of the Seismological Society of America* 100, no. 1 (2010): 241–55, electronic supplement at http://webdelprofesor.ula.ve/ciencias/carlosg/html/1812/BSSA-D-08-00345-esupp.html (see esp. figure 8).

26. Jose Domingo Diaz, *Recuerdos sobre la rebellion de Caracus* (Caracas: Academia Nacional de la Historia, 1961), 98–99.

27. For excellent coverage of environmental history during the colonial period, see Alfred W. Crosby, *The Columbian Exchange: Biological and Cultural Consequences of 1492* (Westport, CT: Greenwood, 1972), and *Ecological Imperialism: The Biological Expansion of Europe, 900–1900* (Cambridge: Cambridge University Press, 1986).

28. John McNeill, *Mosquito Empires: Ecology and War in the Greater Caribbean, 1620–1914* (Cambridge: Cambridge University Press, 2010).

29. As cited in C. L. R. James, *The Black Jacobins* (New York: Vintage Books, 1989), 314.

30. "Morillo al Ministro de la Guerra, 10 septiembre 1817," *Rodriguez Villa* No. 3 (1908): 442–43.

31. See, for example, Henk-Jan Brinkman and Cullen S. Hendrix, "Food Insecurity and Conflict," Occasional Paper no. 24, World Food Programme, 2011.

32. See, for example, S. Clayton, C. M. Manning, and C. Hodge, *Beyond Storms and Droughts: The Psychological Impacts of Climate Change* (Washington, DC: American Psychological Association and ecoAmerica, 2014).

33. See, for example, Louise A. Tilly, "Food Entitlement, Famine, and Conflict," *Journal of Interdisciplinary History* 14, no. 2 (Autumn 1983): 333–49.

34. Daron Acemoglu and James A. Robinson, "A Theory of Political Transitions," *American Economic Review* 91 (2001): 938–63.

35. John Merriman, *A History of Modern Europe: From the Renaissance to the Present* (New York: Norton, 2010), 447.

36. Thomas J. Doherty and Susan Clayton, "The Psychological Impacts of Global Climate Change," *American Psychologist* 66, no. 4 (May–June 2011): 265–76.

37. Doherty and Clayton have recommended intervention and education that might promote "emotional resiliency and empowerment" to offset destitution. This examination and professional protocol was further explored by the APA in *Beyond Storms and Droughts*, with conclusions meant to engage the public

and help communities strengthen their ability to respond. Because the more extreme effects have been felt primarily outside developed countries, however, there has not yet been urgency in those societies possessing the resources to do the most.

38. Caitlin E. Werrell and Francesco Femia, eds., *The Arab Spring and Climate Change: A Climate and Security Correlations Series* (Center for American Progress, Stimson Center, and Center for Climate and Security, 2013).

39. Sarah Johnstone and Jeffrey Mazo, "Global Warming and the Arab Spring," *Survival* 35 (2011): 11–17. An additional source on this topic would be Michael Werz and Max Hofman, "Climate Change, Migration, and Conflict, the Arab Spring and Climate Change," *Climate and Security Correlations Series* (February 2013).

40. Troy Sternberg, "Chinese Drought, Bread, and the Arab Spring," paper presented at the University of Nottingham and Royal United Services Institute joint workshop on "China's Engagement in Non-Traditional Security: Challenges and Opportunities for UK-China Military Co-operation on Environmental Security," June 3, 2014; Robert F. Worth, "Earth Is Parched Where Syrian Farms Thrived," *New York Times*, October 2010.

KEY RESOURCES

General Works

Brooke, John L. *Climate Change and the Course of Global History: A Rough Journey.* Cambridge: Cambridge University Press, 2014.

Corvol, A. *La Nature en révolution: 1750–1800.* Paris: L'Harmattan, 1993.

Crosby, Alfred W. *The Columbian Exchange: Biological and Cultural Consequences of 1492.* Westport, CT: Greenwood, 1972.

———. *Ecological Imperialism: The Biological Expansion of Europe, 900–1900.* Cambridge: Cambridge University Press, 1986.

Ladurie, E. Le Roy. *Time of Feast, Times of Famine: A History of Climate since the Year 1000.* London: Allen & Unwin, 1971.

Miller, Shawn William. *An Environmental History of Latin America.* Cambridge: Cambridge University Press, 2007.

Specific Revolutions

McNeill, John R. "Ecology, Epidemics and Empires: Environmental Change and the Geopolitics of Tropical America, 1600–1825." *Environment and History* 5, no. 2 (1999): 175–84.

McPhee, P. "The Misguided Greed of Peasants? Popular Attitudes to the Environment in the Revolution of 1789." *French Historical Studies* 24 (2001): 247–70.

Smith, Barbara Clark. "Food Rioters and the American Revolution." *William and Mary Quarterly*, 3rd series, 51, no. 1 (January 1994): 3–38.

Waldinger, Maria. "Drought and the French Revolution: The Effects of Adverse Weather Conditions on Peasant Revolts in 1789." Postdoc paper, London School of Economics, 2014.

Technical References

Brazdil, Rudolf, Gaston R. Demaree, Mathias Deutsch, Emmaneul Garnier, Andrea Kiss, Jurg Luterbacher, Neil Macdonald, Christian Rohr, Petr Dobrovolny, Petr Kolar, and Katerina Chroma. "European Floods during the Winter 1783/1784: Scenarios of an Extreme Event during the 'Little Ice Age.'" *Theoretical and Applied Climatology* 100 (June 2009): 163–89.

D'Arrigo, Richard Seager, Jason E. Smerdon, Allegra N. LeGrande, and Edward R. Cook. "The Anomalous Winter of 1783–1784: Was the Laki Eruption or an Analog of the 2009–2010 Winter to Blame?" *Geophysical Research Letters* 38, issue 5 (March 2011).

Fenn, Elizabeth A. "Biological Warfare in Eighteenth-Century North America: Beyond Jeffery Amherst." *Journal of American History* 86, no. 4 (March, 2000): 1552.

Gill, Harold B. "Colonial Germ Warfare." *Colonial Williamsburg Journal* (Spring 2004). http://www.history.org/foundation/journal/spring04/warfare.cfm (accessed November 30, 2014).

Grattan, J. P., and M. B. Brayshay. "An Amazing and Portentous Summer: Environmental and Social Responses in Britain to the 1783 Eruption of an Iceland Volcano." *Geographical Journal* 161, no. 2 (1995): 125–34.

Le Golft, L. "Lettre de Mademoiselle Lamasson Le Golft a M. l'Abbé Mongez." *Auteur du Journal de Physique* 24 (1783): 206–7.

Luterbacher, J., D. Dietrich, E. Xoplaki, M. Grosjean, and H. Wanner. "European Seasonal and Annual Temperature Variability, Trends, and Extremes since 1500." *Science* 303 (2004): 1499–503.

McCook, Stuart. "The Neo-Columbian Exchange: The Second Conquest of the Greater Caribbean, 1720–1930." *Latin American Research Review* (2011): 11–31.

———. "Nature, God, and Nation in Revolutionary Venezuela: The Holy Thursday Earthquake of 1812." In *Aftershocks: Earthquakes and Popular Politics in Latin America*, edited by Jürgen Buchenau and Lyman Johnson, 43–69. Albuquerque: University of New Mexico Press, 2009.

Neumann, J. "Great Historical Events That Were Significantly Affected by the Weather: The Year Leading to the Revolution of 1789 in France." *Bulletin of the American Meteorological Society* 58 (1977): 163–67.

Thordarson, Thorvaldur, and Stephen Self. "Atmospheric and Environmental Effects of the 1783–1784 Laki Eruption: A Review and Reassessment." *Journal of Geophysical Research* 108, no. 1 (2003): 4011.

The World Wide Web

Using the Internet to Teach Revolutions

STUART SALMON and BEN MARSH

The online chapter accompanying this volume offers a framework for understanding how the digital revolution of recent years can connect with teaching on the Age of Revolutions—particularly teaching with the use of primary sources.[1] The chapter is divided into two sections: the first section invites us to think about how the digital turn intersects with notions of revolution and offers a set of annotated links to useful resources and repositories with information on the Age of Revolutions. It concentrates on digital resources that are free at the point of access and emphasizes some of the strengths and possibilities inherent in sites dedicated to American, French, Haitian, and Latin American revolutions. The second section illustrates how directed engagement with selected primary sources from the Age of Revolutions—not always the most well-known works—can bring out important and sometimes unexpected insights. Drawing on four particular sources from across the Age of Revolutions, we suggest how larger themes such as individual rights, gender, loyalism, and national identity can be identified and compared—often a good exercise in introducing students to the larger context and significance of the subject matter.

NOTE

1. Online at http://goldbergseries.org (doi: 10.3368/bk.313043.chwww).

347

Contributors

David Andress is a professor of modern history in the School of Social, Historical and Literary Studies at the University of Portsmouth. His main interest in both research and teaching has been to explore the complex ways in which succeeding generations of historians have sought to co-opt or condemn the relationship between the French Revolution and European modernity. Among his major publications are *The Terror: Civil War in the French Revolution* (2005), *The French Revolution and the People* (2006), and *Massacre at the Champ de Mars: Popular Dissent and Political Culture* (2000). His teaching interests include refining study skills and historical methods, especially incorporating interdisciplinary and conceptual approaches; he is particularly interested in examining the ethical position of the historian as teacher and commentator. He has worked with high school teachers and students, on behalf of the Society for the Study of French History, to assemble online resources and podcasts on the Age of Revolutions.

James Jackson Ashton earned his PhD in 2015 from the department of history at Johns Hopkins University. His work links patriotism and nationalist ideologies to the culture and practice of music in nineteenth-century America, and he holds multiple degrees in history and music. He was postdoctoral fellow for the Twenty-First Century Cities Initiative at Johns Hopkins University and teaches in the Africana Studies Department at Johns Hopkins, as well as at the Peabody Institute of Johns Hopkins University and Loyola University Maryland. His previous career was in arts management, where he worked in development and program administration for a variety of not-for-profit arts organizations in the Cincinnati, Ohio, area.

Ambrogio Caiani is a lecturer in modern European history at Kent, having previously taught at the universities of Greenwich, York, and Oxford. His teaching focuses on eighteenth- and nineteenth-century Europe, and his main area of expertise is in the French Revolution and Napoleonic Europe, with a particular interest in how the ancien régime was invented and conceptualized during the nineteenth century. He is the author of *Louis XVI and the French Revolution, 1789–1792* (2012).

Mark C. Carnes is a professor of history at Barnard College, Columbia University, where he joined the faculty in 1982. He has pioneered the "Reacting to the Past" pedagogy, in which college students play elaborate games set in the past, their roles informed by classic texts. "Reacting to the Past" games, now used at over 350 colleges and universities, are published by W. W. Norton and the Reacting Consortium Press. Carnes analyzes the pedagogy in *Minds on Fire: How Role-Immersion Games Transform College* (2014). He was co-general editor of the twenty-four-volume *American National Biography*.

Sharla Chittick is a World History course mentor and lecturer in the History Department within the School of General Education at Western Governors University, an online university that serves more than 100,000 students. Besides her doctorate in comparative environmental history, she has over twenty years of teaching experience at North Idaho College, Stirling University, and Central Oregon Community College. She has received several teaching awards and designs curriculum for a range of theme-based world history courses with emphasis on the environment.

Marcela Echeverri is an assistant professor in the Department of History at Yale University. Her expertise lies in the political and social history of the Hispanic world, focusing on gender, nationalism, and state formation in Latin America. She is an interdisciplinary scholar with a background in anthropology and political theory and has taught and written extensively on a range of Latin American independence movements during her time at CUNY and Yale, some of which feature in her recent book, *Indian and Slave Royalists in the Age of Revolution: Reform, Revolution, and Royalism in the Northern Andes, 1780–1820* (2016).

Alan Forrest is Emeritus Professor of Modern History at the University of York, United Kingdom. He has published widely on modern French history, especially on the French Revolution and Empire and on the history of war. Authored books include *Napoleon's Men: The Soldiers of the Revolution and Empire* (2002), *Paris, the Provinces, and the French Revolution* (2004), *The Legacy of the French Revolutionary Wars: The Nation-in-Arms in French Republican Memory* (2009), *Napoleon* (2011), and most recently *Waterloo* (2015), a study of the battle and its place in public memory. He is the coauthor, with Jean-Paul Bertaud and Annie Jourdan, of *Napoléon, le monde et les Anglais: Guerre des mots et des images* (2004). He has coedited several works on the French

Revolutionary and Napoleonic period, including *Napoleon and His Empire* (2007, with Philip G. Dwyer), *War Memories: The Revolutionary and Napoleonic Wars in Modern European Culture* (2012, with Etienne François and Karen Hagemann), *The Routledge Companion to the French Revolution in World History* (2015, with Matthias Middell), and *War, Demobilisation and Memory: The Legacy of War in the Era of Atlantic Revolutions* (2016, with Karen Hagemann and Michael Rowe).

Julia Gaffield is currently an assistant professor in the Department of History at Georgia State University. Her work and teaching studies the early independence period in Haiti and seeks to understand the diverse relationships that state leaders in Haiti held with the international community. In April 2010 she received international media attention for her archival discovery of the only known extant government-issued copy of the Haitian Declaration of Independence. She is the author of *Haitian Connections in the Atlantic World: Recognition after Revolution* (2015).

Christopher Hodson is an associate professor in the Department of History at Brigham Young University, where he has taught extensively about the Age of Revolutions since 2007, before which he taught at Northwestern University and in Paris. He has published two books on the subject of the Atlantic and global reach of French events, among them *The Acadian Diaspora*, and is at work on *Discovering Empire: France and the Atlantic World from the Age of the Crusades to the Rise of Napoleon*. His outstanding teaching has been recognized with awards at Brigham Young (2008 and 2013) and Northwestern (2001), and he has convened survey courses on US and French history as well as more specific courses, such as "Eighteenth-Century Revolutions: America, France, and Haiti" and "Revolutionary America: Microhistory."

Annie Jourdan is a research fellow at the University of Amsterdam in the Department of European Studies, having previously acted as visiting professor at the University of Sussex (2007) and at Florida State University (2010). She is an expert on the political and cultural transfers of the Age of Revolutions, and her research interests are primarily in revolutionary and Napoleonic studies, as reflected in her major publications, including *La Révolution: Une exception française?* (2004), *La Révolution batave: Entre la France et l'Amérique (1795–1806)* (2008), *L'empire de Napoléon* (2000), *Napoléon, heros, imperator, mécène* (1998), *Les monuments de la Révolution* (1997), and *"A Tale of Three Patriots in a Revolutionary World"* in *Early American Studies*, as well as numerous articles in journals such as *French History, French Historical Studies, Annales historiques de la Révolution française*, and *La Révolution française*.

Jane Judge earned her PhD in history from the University of Edinburgh in June 2015. She wrote her doctoral thesis on the history of the United States of Belgium and its place within the wider Age of Revolutions, with the assistance of a fellowship at the Robert H. Smith International Center for Jefferson Studies. Since then, she has been a postdoctoral fellow of the Belgian American Educational Foundation and KU Leuven working with the early modern history group at the University in Belgium. She is transforming her doctoral thesis into a book to be published by Leuven University Press. While at Edinburgh, she taught American history at the undergraduate and graduate levels and coordinated the transatlantic American History Video Seminar with the University of Virginia. She has been involved in a number of public history projects and history tours and was a teaching assistant in Lille and Paris, France (2007–2009).

Lester D. Langley is a professor emeritus of history at the University of Georgia. His many books on Latin America and the Caribbean include *America and the Americas: The United States in the Western Hemisphere* (2010), *The Banana Wars: United States Intervention in the Caribbean, 1898–1934* (1983), and *The Americas in the Modern Age* (2003). He has a lifetime's experience of teaching the history of the Americas and comparative history, and he is the author of one of the preeminent textbooks used for teaching the subject: *The Americas in the Age of Revolution, 1750–1850* (1996). He is also a coeditor (with David M. K. Sheinin of Trent University) of the University of Georgia Press series The United States and the Americas.

Edward Larkin is a professor in the Department of English at the University of Delaware. After studying at Harvard University and then Stanford University, he published *Thomas Paine and the Literature of Revolution* (2005) and subsequently edited an edition of Paine's *Common Sense*. His new book, *The American School of Empire*, was published in late 2016.

Mark Ledbury is the Power Professor of Art History and Visual Culture at the University of Sydney. His publications include *Sedaine, Greuze and the Boundaries of Genre* (2000) and *James Northcote, History Painting, and the Fables* (2014). His research interests are in the history of European art, particularly French art, in the eighteenth and early nineteenth centuries, and he is specifically interested in the relationships between theater and visual art and in concepts of genre in Enlightenment philosophy and aesthetics. He has published extensively on the history of art, artists, and on interarts networks and relationships. In his current role as director of the Power Institute, he is involved in many projects oriented toward teaching and public engagement and understanding of visual art.

Ben Marsh is a senior lecturer in American history and the director of Public Engagement (Humanities) at the University of Kent, having previously taught at a number of institutions throughout the United Kingdom, including Stirling, Oxford, Brunel, and Cambridge. He has convened and taught a wide range of courses relating to the Age of Revolutions and published on the American Revolution, gender, Atlantic textile history, and loyalism, including the award-winning *Georgia's Frontier Women* (2007) and his forthcoming book on *Silk and the Atlantic World*.

Peter McPhee is a professor emeritus at the University of Melbourne, where he has published and taught extensively on the subject of the French Revolution and its larger context. He previously taught at La Trobe University and the Victoria University of Wellington, New Zealand. His publications include *Revolution and Environment in Southern France, 1780–1830* (1999), *A Social History of France 1789–1914* (2004), *Living the French Revolution 1789–1799* (2006), *Robespierre: A Revolutionary Life* (2012), and his most recent book *Liberty or Death. The French Revolution* (2016). The university's first provost in 2007–9, he was made a Member of the Order of Australia (AM) in 2012.

Colin Nicolson, a lecturer in history at the University of Stirling, is among the leading historians working on the imperial crisis and the American Revolution. He is the author of *The "Infamas Govener": Francis Bernard and the Origins of the American Revolution* (2001) and editor of *The Papers of Francis Bernard, Governor of Colonial Massachusetts, 1760–1769*, 6 vols. (2007–). He has worked extensively with archival collections in the United Kingdom and United States dealing with the American Revolution and is presently writing a book on John Adams and friendship.

Lindsay A. H. Parker is a lecturer in the History Department at San Diego State University. Her book, *Writing the Revolution: A French Woman's History in Letters* (2013), explores the history of family and private life during the French Revolution through close analysis of a revolutionary woman. Her research and teaching emphasize the subjects of women, gender, and personal narrative in early modern and modern Europe.

Mike Rapport is a reader in modern European history at the University of Glasgow, where he specializes in the history of France and of the eighteenth- and nineteenth-century European revolutions. He has taught and published extensively on the French Revolution and its global linkages, including *Nationality and Citizenship in Revolutionary France: The Treatment of Foreigners* (2000), *1848: Year of Revolution* (2009), and *The Napoleonic Wars: A Very Short*

Introduction (2013). Recently, he has worked on the eighteenth-century revolutions in urban context with *The Unruly City: Paris, London and New York in the Age of Revolution* (2017). He is currently writing a book on places and spaces in revolutionary Paris.

Stuart Salmon is a postdoctoral researcher at the University of Stirling and has taught courses on the Age of Revolutions across a number of institutions in Scotland, including Edinburgh, Glasgow, and Dundee. He completed his doctorate in 2010 on the Loyalist Regiments of the American Revolution and has taught advanced classes using multimedia on the American Revolution and Europe in the Age of Revolutions, and a course on computer approaches in history, which focused on databases and web resources.

Index

Adams, John, 3, 68, 146, 148, 157, 188, 284, 285

Adams, Samuel, 133–34

Adelman, Jeremy, 271

Africa, Africans, 9, 206, 208, 210, 211, 214–15, 216, 217, 268, 272–73, 274, 276

Age of Atlantic revolution, 5–7, 20–21, 26, 265

Age of Democratic revolution. *See* Age of Atlantic revolution

Age of Imperial revolution, 9–10

Age of Revolutions, 3, 4–10, 13–14, 23, 24, 25, 31, 44, 78, 92, 225

Agulhon, Maurice, 21

Alquier, Jean-Baptiste, 102

Americas, 37–51. *See also* Caribbean; Haiti; Latin America; North America; United States of America

Andall, Anne-Marie, 102

Anderson, Benedict, 45, 302

Angers, 19, 20

Appleby, Joyce, 30

Arab Spring, 4, 10, 11, 30, 341

Ardouin, Beaubrun, 84

Arendt, Hannah, 38, 285

Argentina, 50, 272

Armitage, David, 25, 83, 87, 89, 90, 233

Arndt, Ernst Moritz, 307, 315

art and visual culture: crowd action in, 188; in the French Revolution, 110–27; in teaching, 57–59, 110–11, 114–15, 123, 126–27

Assassin's Creed, 191, 246–47

Assembly of Estates (Belgium), 225, 227, 229

Atlantic world, 7, 79, 90, 92, 265. *See also* Age of Atlantic revolution

Austria, Austrians, 226, 228, 287, 302

Austrian Netherlands. *See* Belgium; Brabant; Flanders

Bailey, Colin, 122

Bailly, Jean-Sylvain, 101

Bailyn, Bernard, 21, 190

Baker, Keith Michael, 247

Barre, Chevalier de la, 60

Barruel, Abbé, 250

Bastille, fall of, 112–13

Batavian Republic, 281

Bayly, Christopher, 9, 25, 26

Beauharnais, Joséphine de, 57

Beccaria, Cesare, 69

Belgium, 84, 224–43. *See also* Brabant; declarations of independence, Brabant; declarations of independence, Flanders; Flanders

Bell, David A., 97

Benot, Yves, 204

Bernard, Francis, 191, 192, 193–95

Bernard Papers (Massachusetts Historical Society), 189

Biassou, Georges, 214, 217, 218

Billaud-Varenne, Jacques-Nicolas, 97

Billings, William, 132–35, 141

"Black Atlantic," 23

Blaine, James G., 50

355